Max Yergan

Max Yergan

Race Man, Internationalist,
Cold Warrior

David Henry Anthony III

NEW YORK UNIVERSITY PRESS
New York and London

NEW YORK UNIVERSITY PRESS
New York and London
www.nyupress.org

Library of Congress Cataloging-in-Publication Data
Anthony, David Henry, 1952–
Max Yergan : race man, internationalist, cold warrior / David Henry
Anthony III.
p.   cm.
Includes bibliographical references and index.
ISBN-13: 978-0-8147-0704-3 (cloth : alk. paper)
ISBN-10: 0-8147-0704-1 (cloth : alk. paper)
1. Yergan, Max, 1892–1975. 2. African Americans—Biography.
3. African American political activists—Biography. 4. African
American intellectuals—Biography. 5. African Americans—Politics
and government—20th century.   I. Title.
E185.97.Y47A58 2005
323'.092—dc22   2005018268

10 9 8 7 6 5 4 3 2 1

Contents

All illustrations appear as a group following p. 218.

Preface

This book is the culmination of a journey of three decades. It mirrors the odyssey of its subject and the larger migrations of millions of diasporic peoples, first and foremost those of African descent, or "Africans born in exile," as Kwame Nkrumah often described them. Because the author shares that designation, this cannot be an impartial undertaking. At its start, Max Yergan's biography seemed a straightforward story of one person's engagement with the ideas, fictions, dreams, and realities of his time(s); in its unfolding it has become far more, as it is also what Dr. Du Bois might have argued is in its own way part of the tale of a "race."

The very scope of this drama has dictated that it be related from multiple vantage points, on several distinct "screens," shifting sets and casts of characters at a dizzying pace. Because it is a story of dispersal, it could not easily be retraced by one researcher alone, and so my debts are many. As I suspected at its outset, and subsequently came to know all too well, it was also a saga that could not be written alone. I have been helped by scores of colleagues in large and small ways, during the long life of this complex and singularly challenging project. Many of those helpers are no longer with us, but they remain a vital part of the telling of this tale, and thus deserve mention.

The idea for this project took shape in conversations with Tom Wing Shick, my "big brother" at the University of Wisconsin–Madison. When we met in 1972, he took me under his wing and helped me explore our mutual interest in Pan-Africanism and allied trends showing the enduring connections between Africa and African-Americans. First as my supervisor when I worked as a project assistant helping him with a pathbreaking course on Pan-Africanism, and during and afterward as a mentor, guide, colleague, and friend, he helped prepare me for what lay ahead.

It is impossible to imagine how this work could have taken shape without the University of Wisconsin–Madison. My adviser, Steven Feierman, deserves special mention in this regard. By asking probing questions and responding to draft upon draft, he played a major role in transforming an inchoate idea into a master's essay, laying the groundwork for this book. Of equal importance were my M.A. committee members, Jan Vansina and William Allen Brown, each of whom shared more than an academic interest in this project, each having migrated far from home, thus imparting insights from a variety of viewpoints. Their guidance helped me through a particularly challenging period of my life, and their example gave me both the persistence and the technical skill to find and incorporate evidence of almost every kind. Moreover, I deeply appreciate their willingness to support research that flowed from and epitomized the broader subject of the pull that a diaspora can have upon people of African descent.

There were also those whose teaching deepened my appreciation of South Africa, such a vital part of this story. These included Daniel Kunene, Harold Scheub, Wandile Kuse, and, beyond the classroom, my erstwhile comrades in MACSA, the Madison Area Committee on Southern Africa. The work itself took me literally around the world—from the State Historical Society of Wisconsin and the Memorial Library of the University of Wisconsin to the former YMCA Bowne Historical Library in New York City, where Cheryl Gaines and John Randle helped me immeasurably, literally loaning me the keys to the kingdom on weekends. There I pored over manuscript collections from YMCA personnel posted at the far corners of the globe, from North America to Africa, Asia, and Latin America. At the Y I was also helped by Ruth Hartson, formerly of the International Division, and Leo G. Marsh of the Black and Nonwhite Ys, or BANWYS. After the YMCA files were relocated to the YMCA of the USA Archives in St. Paul, Minnesota, I received aid from Andrea Hinding, David Carmichael, and Dagmar Getz.

Correspondence between Yergan and ecumenical, humanitarian and philanthropic leaders led me to the Sterling, Beinecke, and Divinity School Libraries at Yale. In this connection I would like to thank Africana bibliographer Moore Crossey and the archival staffs of the Beinecke and Sterling libraries and Martha Lund Smalley and staff at the Divinity School Libraries, Yale University; former Yale graduate students Lewis Warren and Joseph "Kip" Kosek; and Yale anthropology professor Kamari Clarke.

I also thank the staff of the Schomburg Center for Research into

African-American Culture, especially the late Ernest Kaiser. At the Paul Robeson Archives, I was given considerable aid by Roberta Yancey "Bobbi" Dent and by Paul Robeson Jr., who shared personal recollections and granted access to the Robeson papers, as well as granting me permission to use photographs taken by his mother, Eslanda Cardozo Goode Robeson, during her 1936 tour of South Africa on which Paul Junior accompanied her.

Ms. Mary Yergan Hughes facilitated my access to an unpublished manuscript biography by Ruby Pagano, drawn from correspondence inaccessible to other researchers.

Patricia Haynes, record manager of Carnegie Corporation of New York, provided me with copies of correspondence concerning Max Yergan. The assistance of Karen L. Jefferson, Elinor Des Verney Sinnette, Esme Bhan, Ida Jones, and other archival assistants and staffers at Howard University's Manuscripts and Archives Division proved invaluable.

I also thank the following:

The late Richard Newman and Randall Burkett, formerly of Harvard and now at Emory University, who helped me acquire a Du Bois Institute Fellowship.

Susan McElrath, archivist, Mary McLeod Bethune Museum and Archives; Bernard R. Crystal, Rare Books and Manuscripts, Butler Library, Columbia University; and the Bailey Howe Library, University of Vermont in Burlington, for material on Ned Carter and the Institute of Pacific Relations.

Wilson N. Flemister, director, Division of Archives and Special Collections, Robert W. Woodruff Library, Atlanta University Center; Amy Hague, assistant curator, Sophia Smith Collection, and Archives, Smith College, for help with the Mary van Kleeck correspondence.

Erika Tysoe-Dülken of the Communication Department of the Library of the World Alliance of YMCAs in Geneva, Switzerland.

Matthew Gilmore, reference librarian, Washingtonia Division, D.C. Public Library.

David Wigdor and staff, Manuscript Division, Library of Congress.

Ann Allen Shockley and Fritz Malval, archivists, Fisk University, Nashville; Khalil Mahmud, archivist, Lincoln University, Pennsylvania.

Rockefeller Archive Center, North Tarrytown, New York, for access and a grant-in-aid to consult the RAC archives and the Russell Sage and Carnegie Foundation records.

The New York City Department of Records and Information Service, Municipal Archives and Research Center, for access to the papers of the late Mayor Fiorello La Guardia.

Regina Greenwell, archivist, Lyndon Baines Johnson Library, Austin, Texas.

Marilla B. Guptil, chief, Archival Processing and Preservation Unit, United Nations Organization; Nancy S. MacKechnie, curator, Rare Books and Manuscripts, Vassar College Library, Poughkeepsie.

Christine Ledger and Manuel Quintero, cosecretaries general, and M. François Burgy, archivist, World Student Christian Federation, World Council of Churches Library, Geneva, Switzerland.

The staff of the Houghton Library at Harvard University; the staff at the West Virginia State College Archives for material from the collection of President John W. Davis; Nancy Cricco and at New York University Archives.

In South Africa I owe thanks to Ms. A. C. M. Torlesse and Ms. Susan de Villiers, Cory librarians, Cory Library for Historical Research, Rhodes University Library, Grahamstown; Mrs. Hanna Botha, curator of manuscripts of the Stellenbosch University Library; the staff of the National Library of South Africa; the staff of the library of the University of Cape Town; the late Govan Mbeki; the late Walter Sisulu, Vusi Kaunda, Stan Fish, Christopher Saunders, Pam Allen, and visiting students Cara Moyer and Amber Willat.

In Tanzania, East Africa, I met a number of South Africans, some freedom fighters, some allies in struggle, who offered me cordial hospitality and shared vital information. These included the late I. B. Tabata, Jane Gool, N. "Chucha" Honono, Essie Bullock Honono, Archie Mafeje, and my own diasporic kinsman, Clyde Daniels-Halisi.

In Southern Africa itself, I was helped both by mail and later in person by an astounding array of persons during ten months in Lesotho and in shorter but no less meaningful sojourns in South Africa itself in 2000, 2001, and 2002, along with Robert R. Edgar, whose collegial camaraderie deserves special mention. In Lesotho I benefited from the kindness of Howard and Donice Jeter, Joan and Paseka Khabele, May and Bill McClain, Kwesi and Pumza Prah, Tefetso Mothibe, Motlatsi Tabane, David Ambrose of the National University of Lesotho, and the sage recollections of W. M. and Blanche T. Tsotsi, Fanana "Roch" Fobo, and J. M. Mohapeloa. Stephen Gill and the staff of the Morija

Museum and Archives, especially T. M. Leanya, helped find and translate documents from *Leselinyana*.

Generous and heartfelt assistance also came from the late Herbert L. Aptheker, Keletso Atkins, Villiers G. Bam, Jonathan Beecher, Arnold Beichman, Thomas A. Brady, Michael Brown, David Brundage, Paul Buhle, Carolyn and Edmund "Terry" Burke, Randall K. Burkett, William Cadbury, Alan Christy, Wilmoth D. Carter, Peter Coleman, Marvel Cooke, R. Hunt Davis Jr., Dave Dodson, Martin Bauml Duberman, Kathy Durcan, Penny von Eschen, Susan Rosenfeld Falb, Frederick V. Field, Jack Foner, John Hope Franklin, George S. Frederickson, Glenda Gilmore, John Haley, Charles P. Henry, Robert A. Hill, Adam Hochschild, William L. Holland, Sylvia Holmes, Dorothy Hunton, Joyce F. Kirk, Harvey Klehr, Phyllis Ntantala-Jordan, Robin D. G. Kelley, Saul Landau, Sid Lemelle, Earl Lewis, Marvin Liebman, Jack Maddex, Nana Mahomo, Pat Manning, Ntongela Masilela, Joe Matthews, Laura McShane, the late August Meier, Ed Mesnick, the late Donald G. S. M'Timkulu, Mark Naison, the late Richard Newman, Richard D. Ralston, Edwin S. Redkey, Don Rothman, Maxine Scates, the late Tom Wing Shick, Carol Smith, the late Louise Thompson Patterson, Adell Patton Jr., Daniel Pope, the late Morris Urman Schappes, Buchanan Sharp, Zoe Sodja, Tyler Stovall, David G. Sweet, the late Mary Ellen Sweet, Cheryl Van de Veer, Jan Vansina, the late James M. Washington and Howard Winant.

I also owe a special debt of gratitude for the following former University of California–Santa Cruz students: Christine Bering, Ken Brown, Amber Maisha Carter, Anthony D. Crawford, Africa Evangeline Davidson, Chris Duvall, Riyad Koya, Kristal Edwards, Andrew M. Generalao, Melita McNeil, Ryan Monihan, Hawa Macalou, Francisca Olaíz, Hyim Jacob Ross, Phoebe M. Schraer, Alainna Ceton Thomas, and Lightfoot Wilhite.

I do not know where to begin in thanking the staff of the McHenry Library of the University of California–Santa Cruz, among them Deb Murphy, Margaret Gordon, and Stan Stevens.

Special thanks go to Bob Edgar, for taking an unusual interest in this project from our first meeting when C. R. Daniels-Halisi introduced us in the mideighties, steadfastly supporting it in ways exemplifying the essence of collegiality. I cannot thank Bob enough.

I have been assisted in myriad ways by the institutions with which I have been affiliated during the life of this book. These include Coppin State College, the University of Oregon, the Center for African Studies of the University of Florida at Gainesville, the William Edward Burghardt Du Bois Institute of Harvard University, the University of California President's Fellowship Office, and the Department of History, the Faculty Senate, the Division of Humanities, and the Center for Cultural Studies of the University of California–Santa Cruz.

Sylvia G. Holmes helped me enormously as well, both from the vantage point of the steno pool of Oakes College and then as provost and CAO assistant during the years I served as provost of Oakes College, writing scores of letters, helping in transcriptions of interviews, making telephone calls, and otherwise making herself indispensable.

Most importantly, I wish to thank my family, first and foremost Allison Anitra Sampson-Anthony, for reading, reacting to, resisting, discussing, dissecting, divining, and deconstructing drafts and for putting up with a disruptive presence for longer than anyone should have had to. Next, peace and praise to my parents, Carolyn F. Metcalf Anthony and the late David Henry Anthony Jr., and to my late maternal grandmother, Ella Wilma Allen Metcalf, "Chickasaw Freedman," for sparking and nurturing a thirst for the field of historical reconstruction. I hope that what follows is worthy of what they each taught me. Finally, to Adey, Djibril, and Daoud for being.

Frequently Used Abbreviations

AAC	All African Convention
ABCFM	American Board of Commissioners for Foreign Missions
AFL	American Federation of Labor
AME	African Methodist Episcopal
AMEZ	African Methodist Episcopal Zion
ANC	African National Congress
BANWYS	Black and Nonwhite YMCAs
CAA	Council on African Affairs
CCF	Congress on Cultural Freedom
CCNY	City College of New York
CPSA	South African Communist Party
ICAA	International Committee on African Affairs
ICU	Industrial and Commercial Workers' Union
IIRI	International Industrial Relations Institute
IPR	Institute of Pacific Relations
KUTVU	University of the Toilers of the East Named for Stalin
NAACP	National Association for the Advancement of Colored People
NNC	National Negro Congress
SCA	Student Christian Association
SCM	Student Christian Movement
SNYC	Southern Negro Youth Congress
SVM	Student Volunteer Movement
WASU	West African Student Union
WSCF	World's Student Christian Federation

Introduction

In Search of Max Yergan

In the summer of 1916, a 24-year-old African-American man stood on a platform at Storer College in Harper's Ferry, West Virginia. The airy site held enormous significance for the entire assemblage, especially several Black YMCA secretaries, their White ecumenical and philanthropic benefactors, and the youth they were attempting to groom for future service. It was here that John Brown led his raid against the ruling class of slaveowners by laying siege to the federal arsenal in 1859. Fifty-seven years later, the gesture had not lost its luster for the sons of slaves comprising the vast majority of those gathered to pay solemn tribute to Brown, his allies, and the grandson of a bondsman, Max Yergan.

On the stage with the strikingly handsome young student secretary were a college president and a stage full of veteran YMCA organizers. Black and White, young and old, North and South, cleric and layperson —all were represented on that day. And each of these constituencies sensed something special in the young man with the piercing stare and the eloquent turn of phrase that made a lasting impression. It was one of many times when Max Yergan would accomplish this august feat. A man of words who used them to propel himself and others to faithful, principled action, this intrepid son of the South was now on his way to the far end of the earth. Soon he would become the first Black American to do YMCA work in India. In an era in which Black progress was often measured by pioneering endeavors, this YMCA secretary was about to make history in a time of war in a land held by the most widely ramified empire in the modern world. And all this from modest Raleigh, North Carolina.

Five years earlier Max Yergan had walked into the Shaw University YMCA and inquired about what they were doing. Before long this sophomore was fully engaged in the group's work. By the time he graduated in 1914 he was prepared to devote a substantial portion of his life to it. In a progression that led to workshops and a succession of local conferences and retreats, he quickly rose to prominence in the organization, becoming one of its national figures by the time the Storer ceremony was held. In an age in which foreign mission service held special appeal for an equally special type of person, Yergan made ready to share the gospel with the sons of Mother India. In the back of his mind was another voice, that of his late maternal grandfather Frederick, who left him the year after he started with the YMCA but whose words yet echoed in his consciousness exhorting him to become a missionary to what he had called "our people" in Africa. When the time came, therefore, he would try his best to find a way to realize grandfather Frederick's dream. This is the story of how that dream came about, what it led to, and why it matters to the modern world. Telling this tale also requires relating several other sagas, some of which, like his, are told here for the first time.

In 1916 very few African-Americans had been to India, though there were Indians who had been to America and were curious about and in some cases captivated by the American Negro. The stimuli for this concern were primarily color and caste, features sharpened by colonialism but recognizable as mechanisms of differentiation that facilitated the control of the powerful over the powerless. In deciding to enter India at this time, Yergan took a step into a world that even now is not clear for those who want to know what and whom he found at that time. Although known to write obsessively, typically every day, he left little that is accessible about this experience.

Apart from a few choice anecdotes that survived thanks to other hands, we know nothing about how his Indian sojourn struck him, and yet it had to have affected him deeply, for from there he did in fact get to serve Africa. These encounters and their impact upon this diasporic traveler reveal a hidden part of the history of people of African descent: the fact that some of them have stubbornly insisted upon getting back to Africa and making it a vital part of their lives in America.

Many who have looked into this phenomenon have focused on the Pan-African movement, and at an earlier stage this writer considered this movement a key to unraveling some of the mysteries of Max Yergan's life. However, Yergan would probably not have felt comfortable with the term, even though once bitten by the African bug he was never able to get it out of his system. Some people might analogize this to the literal bite of a bug that leaves one with a permanent living organism, a parasite that those who have spent time in Africa know only too well as a reality and not as a metaphor for what such a trip to the tropics can bring in its train. But however real these opportunistic organisms may be, they do have metaphoric parallels in the diaspora. Indeed, there was and is for many orphaned Africans exiled in the New World something biting them, tearing at their innards, leaving them febrile or insomniac or nauseous, as they wonder who they were before they were given their slave names and what villages their forebears emanated from.

So it was not so strange that Yergan sought to put things right as best he could under the harrowing circumstances, or at least to do some investigating so that his grandfather's soul might rest in peace.

In the course of devoting himself to this endeavor he founded scores of branch YMCAs, got to know the Imperial British East African Protectorate (Kenya), historic Tanganyika (Tanzania), South Africa, historic Basutoland (Lesotho), and Bechuanaland (Botswana), co-led an organization called the International Committee (later Council) on African Affairs, introduced a lively course on Negro History and Culture at New York's City College, became associate and then assistant to the national secretary, then second president of the National Negro Congress, an internationally known leader in ecumenical concerns, and a conspicuous member of an eccentric coterie of repentant ex-radicals. Each one of these public roles produced its own voluminous body of documents—scores, hundreds, and in some cases thousands of documents, including a critical mass of intelligence files from federal agencies over a period of more than two decades of close surveillance.

Facing this quantity of documentation has been a demanding and at times depressing chore. More challenging perhaps was the recognition that as public as Yergan was, he and his heirs have fiercely sought to protect their privacy, a difficult thing to accomplish when so much paper is strewn about in the public domain, especially when a protagonist is as adept at writing and publishing as Yergan was. Thus when the project started it seemed a simple matter to work out of the YMCA Bowne Historical Library, then housed in New York City in the shadow of a then still relatively new World Trade Center. This writer became such a regular fixture there in the summer of 1974 as he prepared a master's thesis on the subject that the staff simply gave him the key on Friday and let him have the run of the place over the weekend, asking only that he return it on Monday morning.

But then it became clear that there was other material in other archives from different eras in this person's post-YMCA life. Indeed, he seemed to live more than one life. By the 1930s, for example, he said and did things that seemed wholly out of character from those for which he became known in the teens and twenties, in this country, India, and Eastern and Southern Africa. It was as if, having moved on to something new, he was able to leave almost everything preceding it behind, as if putting on a new pair of clothes and discarding the old. This was how it must have seemed to some of his fellows, as if there were a disconnect between the now and the then—not once and not twice but thrice in his life. It happened again in the forties and fifties and sixties when even as a rapidly aging man in increasingly frail health he wrote and lectured and gave interviews and traveled like someone one-third his age, standing against the mainstream of society as he now looked backward to build what he thought should be a better, freer world. But the price of these changes proved exceedingly high.

He left behind friends, accumulated enemies, and ended his life in relative isolation. Anyone who looked closely at his trajectory would not wonder why it has not been retraced. He did his best to cover his tracks and in some respects for good reason. This version of that narrative has left out many of the details, concentrating primarily on what seems essential to help delineate the contours of a life that, while not always easy to fathom, was nevertheless endlessly fascinating. In the year that it has taken to transform this text it has been reduced to its present size from a weighty tome approaching nine hundred manuscript pages, then 712, now half of that. Much that has been excised has been painful to leave out, for Yergan's was a life that deserves more than superficial and facile judgments. Like the Africa he loved so well if not always wisely, nothing about it discloses itself easily or painlessly, and this author has himself paid a phenomenal price in order to try to tell it. What matters most is that you the reader permit yourself the luxury of suspending disbelief and withholding judgment until such time as you have tried to work your way to the bitter end. In a work that has preoccupied this author intermittently through much of his adult life, the investment is incalculable. It is hoped that this tale will help in understanding not only him but ourselves as well.

1

Beginnings
Boyhood, Baptists, Bangalore

At the dawning of the twentieth century, Dr. William Edward Burghardt Du Bois correctly anticipated that the supreme challenge of the century would be "the problem of the color line." From the vantage point of many Americans of African descent his words rang resonantly, fueling divergent ideas and actions, regional, national, and supranational in scope. For one, Max Yergan, the more relevant of these contending currents of opinion would be African Redemption, accommodationism, Pan-Negroism, Pan-Africanism, and the burgeoning movement for world socialism. A product of an era, indeed a millennium, of transformation, he stood as heir to these traditions, his life a mix of them.

In a beautiful but race-conscious Raleigh, North Carolina, in a handsome old house at 210 East Cabarrus Street, built by his grandfather Frederick Yeargan (also spelled Yeargin or Yergin), Mack Yergan was born on Tuesday, July 19, 1892, to Frederick's elder daughter, Lizzie. In time, "Mack" became "Max" and, late in life, the bearer would aver, somewhat grandiloquently, that his given appellation had originally been Maximilian, recalling a name used by several Holy Roman emperors, but little additional documentary evidence verifies this impressive-sounding assertion.[1] Max's mother (born June 1873) and her sister Eliza lived with their widower father, and both were mothers with a number of children by the century's turning (Lizzie had borne five by 1900), making Frederick a grandfather and patriarch of an extended family.

Fred Yeargan was a pillar of the Black community of Raleigh. A carpenter born in slavery in 1838, he actively supported the Baptist church, in which he wielded considerable influence, as well as occupying a seat on the Board of Trustees of Shaw Institute, later Shaw University, the subsequent alma mater of grandson Max. Well before his birth, then, young Mack was poised to inherit a significant portion of the nineteenth-century legacy of Christian-inspired education and the mission to "uplift" dark folk that proved personally and socially vital in the fin de siècle era.

Little has surfaced on Max Yergan's father. His name is absent from Yergan's birth certificate, and nothing yet proves that he cohabited with Lizzie Yeargan at the time their boy was born. Yergan may have deliberately avoided referring to him for personal reasons. We cannot be certain of his name, for the birth record lists "unknown" in the designated space, but the handwritten words "Ed Price," possibly added at a later date, replace a stricken initial entry. Anecdotal evidence hints that Max knew precisely who sired him, a man of mixed Native and Black heritage, and that little love was lost between them.[2]

As to the Yergans' social context, eight years before the grand drape descended upon the nineteenth century, upwardly mobile brown-skinned Raleighians had an oasis in a desert of doubt, denial, devastation, and degradation. Formal segregation still had not reached them as it had so many of their African-American relatives across the Southland. Near Shaw University, as Jonathan Daniels, White elite editor of the *Raleigh News and Observer*, reports, "all around our house Negroes and questionable white people came more and more to live."[3] Daniels suggests the tone of the neighborhood of Shaw:

> At least one of Booker T. Washington's sons went to college there. And next door to us lived Wesley Hoover, as dignified an Anglo-Saxon gentleman, for all the little Negro blood in him, as I ever saw. . . . But Wesley Hoover had made his money, a great deal for a Negro in Raleigh in those days, running a saloon. That was an occupation which we understood was a special service rendered in assistance to the Devil. Yet he was a good neighbor and man. The South was not entirely simple, even then. But from us and from the Hoovers and from Shaw, the neighborhood fell off precipitately.[4]

But the neighborliness that Daniels's narrative suggests obscures some of the harder-edged realities of Negro Raleigh. The *News and Observer* was in Jon Daniels's youth edited by his unrepentantly Negrophobic, segregationist father, Josephus, later a valued cabinet official in several presidential administrations. Its pages did not then announce the birth of Negro children but regularly served up lurid tales of bestial Black criminals getting their just deserts. One story about a lynched

Mississippi rapist was headlined "FOOD FOR VULTURES." An interracial clash "culminating in bloodshed—9 Negroes and 2 White men reported killed," topped by a vengeful bout of "whitecapping," was headlined "A Race War in Arkansas."[5] And "He Got His Dues: A Camden County Fiend Hanged and Riddled: A Negro Brute Who Makes a Horrible Assault Is Visited with Retribution" headlined the story of how one Joe Barco, accused of the murder of Mrs. Frank Sanderlin with a hoe following a sexual assault, was dragged from his jail cell by a mob of five to six hundred men, emasculated, mutilated, hanged, and riddled by what a reporter took to be a thousand bullets fired into his "suspended carcass."[6]

The genteel nostalgia of Daniels's reverie and the brutish reportage of the lynchings each speak eloquently about Raleigh. It was a place of civilized pretensions of every sort, yet tempered by a baser element of strict, retributive, racialistic comeuppance. This was rooted in a fierce fire-and-brimstone moralism, the kind that kept kids in Sunday school but also gave impetus to corporal and capital punishment, vigilantism, and the fearsome Ku Klux Klan. At the same time, the more positive benefits of religion were manifested by the Yankee Republican missionaries who traveled south from New England to uplift those benighted millions who had endured the base travails of bondage in the land of liberty. Max remembered one such bearer of the sacred word, Mary Phillips, a teacher at St. Ambrose Episcopal Parish School.[7] With his memories of a strict upbringing at the hands of a firm but nurturing mother and a benevolently despotic grandfather, Yergan testified to having matured in an orderly environment, tightly bound by an ethos of piety, duty, and respect, all practiced in a rigidly evangelical Christian framework that often touted "old-time religion."[8]

An aspect of that framework was orientation to Africa. Max later reminisced that his grandfather had told him, on his deathbed, that it was his fervent wish that one day one of his grandsons would go as a missionary to "our people in Africa."[9] This injunction would become Yergan's raison d'être, both symbolically and literally. And the elder man's desire was by no means unusual in African-American communities during the 1890s. This was a time of great interest in Africa, especially among literate people of African descent, and in the notion of a divinely inspired mandate for "African Redemption" (a concept connecting certain Black and sympathetic White Christians). It found expression in "Ethiopianist" churches and back-to-Africa movements in

predominantly Black localities throughout the far-flung African diaspora of the New World. Especially keen was the linkage between Africa
and Christian mission, a pathway created by generations of Black Protestants, principally Baptists, Presbyterians, and members of the African
Methodist Episcopal (AME) and African Methodist Episcopal Zionist
(AMEZ) churches. Yeargan, a Baptist, is said to have regularly discussed Africa with at least one of his closest friends and was associated
with a scholarly endeavor that held deep and abiding concern for his
natal continent's transformation, Baptist-run Shaw University.

In this regard, Yeargan was one of a select but not insignificant set of
African-derived, Christian-inspired seekers of racial salvation. In the
brutal post–Reconstruction era South, in order to endure in an epoch of
heightened racial repression, choices seemed stark: migration or pros-
tration. Those electing not to leave their localities often deemed it desirable to conciliate reactionary White "redeemers." Precisely these circumstances made possible the ascendance of Booker T. Washington, the
key Black figure from 1895 to 1915.

In a landmark speech on September 18, 1895, at the opening cere-
monies for Atlanta's Cotton States and International Exposition, Tuskegee Institute principal Washington lamented to a receptive, racially
mixed audience that through ignorance and inexperience the post-
Reconstruction African-American had begun focusing exclusively on the
top professions, neglecting industrialism and manual labor. He urged
these Black masses to "cast down your bucket where you are," i.e., to
acknowledge the existence of an "identity of interests" linking Black
and White southerners beyond race and to accept the inestimable value
of human effort as the engine of socioeconomic advance.

For Washington race advancement was forthcoming only through
hard work, dedication, and patience. In his early years, Max Yergan
subscribed to that belief. Implicit and frequently explicit was the principal's scorn for social protest as a vehicle through which to pursue
racial uplift. This scorn made Washington's policy of accommodating
Redemption seem to be a capitulation to the resurgence of White supremacy. In Atlanta Washington phrased his anti-protest stance in chas-
tening terms:

> The wisest of my race understand that the agitation of questions of
> social equality is the extremest folly, and that progress in the enjoyment
> of all the privileges that will come to us must be the result of severe and

constant struggle rather than of artificial forcing. No race that has anything to contribute to the markets of the world is long, in any degree,
ostracized. It is important and right that all privileges of the law be
ours, but it is vastly more important that we be prepared for the exercise of those privileges. The opportunity to earn a dollar in a factory
just now is worth infinitely more than the opportunity to spend a dollar
in an opera house.[10]

In the short run, Washington's nationally reported Atlanta address
appeared to promise all things to all audiences. Southern Whites tended
to treat it as acceptance that Blacks would no longer threaten their
reassumption of political and racial suzerainty. Well-heeled northern
Whites, including some socially minded robber-baron benefactors, re-
acted to accommodation as a rise in industrious Black self-reliance
meriting moral and material aid. Northern African-Americans saw accommodation as inspiring them to continue struggling. But to African-
Americans who remained in the South the Atlanta speech confirmed
that constant effort, forbearance, and initiative were the requirements
of the new age. Nowhere would this need become more apparent than
among those African-Americans striving to secure an education. Yet
there was another element evident in Washington's philosophy and in
the minds of each literate woman, man, and child of African descent
who confronted the challenges of the latter 1800s. This was the position
of Africa in the world and of their own conflicted connection as cultural
castaways.

Since their arrival on these shores, countless generations of Africa's
daughters and sons had grappled with the questions that their tragic
transportation across the Atlantic had presented them with, maybe
never as harshly as in the nineteenth century. Prior to 1808, the fate of
America's minions seemed more or less academic, as slavery's power
promised to persist forever. With a formal end to the legal Atlantic slave
trade, however, the issue of what role the Africans were to play in New
World society in general and in North America in particular returned to
frighten the framers of a Constitution countenancing slavery. Many of
these men, including the ostensibly most enlightened, from Washington
and Jefferson in the Revolutionary and early republican eras right down
to the "Great Emancipator" Lincoln, proved incapable of conceiving of
a United States where Blacks, ceasing to be chattel, could cohabit freely
alongside Caucasians.

Most presidential office holders and the rank and file who looked to them for leadership saw Africans as useful in slavery but outlandish and unassimilable in any other status in America. Their prescription was to return these misbegotten souls to the continent of their ancestors, through deportation. African repatriation was to be accomplished by the American Colonization Society (ACS), founded in 1816. In spite of growing evidence that this entity had been organized primarily to safeguard proslavery forces from myriad perceived threats posed by the free Negro group by repatriating them to Africa (thereby reducing the likelihood of their sparking slave rebellions, either actively or by example), wary free people of color and a few kindred White advocates sometimes genuinely saw emigration as a viable alternative to the restrictions leveled specifically against free Negroes across the nation. Reverend William Meade, an ACS agent, started a Raleigh branch of the nascent association in June 1819.[11] However, African-American ardor for African colonization waxed and waned, and though interest in Liberian emigration dropped off during the Civil War years, it reappeared to some degree in the aftermath of Reconstruction, in 1877. In that year a series of mass meetings was held in Durham, Concord, and Raleigh, for the purpose of garnering support for African colonization. The fact that only 318 African-Americans quit North Carolina for Liberia under ACS auspices in 1876 and 1894 suggests a lack of enthusiasm for the African alternative.[12]

Never entirely eliminated by the nineteenth century's close, African Redemption resurfaced for one group of Black Christians. Aged supporters of African Redemption such as Alexander Crummell, Edward Blyden, and even Martin Delany had looked to Africa as a potential refuge for embattled New World Negroes anxious to share the Bible's bounties and aid in Africa's ascent. By midcentury Ethiopianism and African Redemption had entered the lexicon of mission societies and had reached Christians of every color, including the Baptists who bankrolled Shaw University. Moreover, as foreign invaders more actively intervened in Africa and African lives, a dialogue began among people of African descent concerning the roots of crises then afflicting Africa's ancestral homelands. Imbued with the spirit of the times, some of the elect became persuaded that the responsibility for this situation lay not so much in the designs and activities of European imperialists as in the purported spiritual poverty of Africans themselves, in their allegedly unbridled ways. The antidote for this condition would be evangelization —to "uplift" a bedeviled, prostrate Africa, "benighted" and rent asunder by primitive superstition and heathen ignorance.[13]

Support for the idea of emigration to Africa in the final quarter of the nineteenth century was especially strong within the African Methodist Episcopal Church, shepherded by charismatic and uncompromising Bishop Henry McNeal Turner, who will be discussed in a later chapter.

Besides the AME congregants, the Negro Baptist Foreign Mission Board placed special emphasis upon Africa and should be seen as an independent force advocating at least temporary emigration with a fervor nearly identical to that motivating Turner and his AME disciples. Baptists galvanized other Black Christians into action, and one of them must have been Frederick Yeargan.

It is well known that the Black church played an important role in both accommodation and amelioration, and education did the same. Frederick Yeargan made a point of informing the enumerator who took the 1900 census that he and his daughters were literate. This would suggest the value he placed on reading and writing. For nineteenth century Americans literacy was often synonymous with schooling, even if one was self-educated, a fact with particular significance for the ex-slave population. This association has a special meaning in light of the role education played in the life of Yeargan's grandson, Max.

Yeargan's self-estimate may well have included reflection of the view, prevalent among both Blacks and Whites, that servitude in North Carolina was milder than elsewhere in the Cotton Kingdom, which led to the paradoxical notion of a "slave aristocracy," which notion was generated in one of the exceptions to the state's rural norm, Raleigh. The myth avers that North Carolina was "good" to "its Blacks," especially for skilled slave artisans like Frederick Yeargan, who were understood as having formed an aristocracy within their class on the basis of their greater marketability and relatively privileged status.

While Raleigh's Wake County was not a key point of production in the plantation economy, it was not immune from reliance upon slave labor. Before the Civil War, scores of slaves had been manumitted, some, like Julius Melbourn, becoming quite wealthy. And degree of education was probably important for a sense of membership in this aristocracy.

Education was one of the principal vehicles for "uplift" in the American South, especially for those African-Americans afforded the rare opportunity of advancing to the college level. Many drew connections between religion and education as practically and morally significant, as was explicitly emphasized throughout the nineteenth century by both literate slaves and free men and women, on the one hand, and, on the other, legions of northern-educated, mainly White missionaries who went South to spread the gospel and sanctify the "heathen," "benighted" freedmen after the Civil War.

Frederick Yeargan, deacon and trustee of the Second Baptist Church, must have given Max the august example of a grandfather who led in and supported Negro education and who concretized the notion that church ministry provided the archetype of the most honorable profession for Raleigh's responsible Black men. The institutions where Yergan attained his education both had denominational Protestant roots: St. Ambrose Academy, an Episcopal primary school, and the academy and university (or preparatory and college) branches of Shaw University.[14]

Shaw University, during Yergan's time the premier institution of Negro higher education for the entire state of North Carolina, proved vital to his professionalization. Shaw took particular pains to attract and prepare candidates for missionary service in Africa, drawing not only upon African-Americans but also among other members of Africa's diaspora.

The institution was "intended to maintain a high degree of character and scholarship, and only students who were willing to comply cheerfully with reasonable rules and regulations" were desired at the university. The curriculum followed by Shaw was a familiar blend of practicality and philosophy characteristic of nineteenth-century pedantry. The moral instruction that chapel and Bible recitation provided was augmented by daily drills in Greek and Latin—a classicist repertoire. By all indications, Yergan proved eminently successful in these subjects, making dean's list, reading sociology, law, and history, majoring in modern languages, earning a letter in football, and debating—then graduating cum laude, heading his 1914 class as valedictorian. It was an achievement many would comment on.

African Redemption, Ethiopianism, and *both* manual and academic education were strongly stressed during Yergan's era. This fact and Shaw's Africanist presence also helped shape him. The chosen vehicle through which Yergan was enabled to pursue spiritual "uplift" while preparing for Africa's redemption was the Shaw Young Men's Christian Association.

At the time, the Black YMCA was for some a potentially radical institution. The premier YMCA student association serving Negro youth appeared in 1869. Its first Black leader, William Alphaeus Hunton, ended decades of exclusively White control. He was assisted in 1898 by Ohio-born Jesse Edward Moorland, who came to be so powerful that he was able to influence the purchase and erection of almost every building used by African-American YMCA members in the United States. Moorland became a mentor and confidant of Max Yergan.

Both the English YMCA and its filial North American branch charged themselves with the tasks of providing humble, cooperative, Christian-derived (albeit nondenominational), soft leadership alternatives to the hard-edged economic and political proletarian radicalism raging through mid-nineteenth-century Europe and America. Of primary concern to representatives of each transoceanic chapter was a growing petite bourgeoisie, the emergent mediating stratum of craftspeople and educated youth preparing to join the workforce as apprentices, artisans, clerks, managers, or entry-level professionals. Following the U.S. Civil War, the YMCA attracted striving Black men, many viewing it as a way up the fabled ladder of success in American society.

Black YMCA secretaries soon became highly respected figures on Negro college campuses, powerful sources of inspiration to fellow students, whom they then exhorted to ambitiously strive toward success in Jim Crow America. They fulfilled a vital social function, for well into the 1920s very few positions stood available to most African-American professionals. YMCA role models could broaden horizons, providing faith to face up to typically uncertain futures, "each demonstrating dignity and manhood in a segregated institution."

Born into a society whose values were shaped by patriarchal traditions and institutions and into a caste for whom subaltern status was religiously reenacted in ruthless rituals, Yergan and fellow male "New Negroes for a New Era" chose Y service as a means of undoing what had been done, of pursuing perquisites prized.

By 1915, Max Yergan had become a man of mark, having worked his way up through annual student conferences, chief among which was a series of yearly Colored Work Department Summer Institutes hosted at Kings Mountain, North Carolina. Yergan's organizational gifts were initially recognized at the 1912 meeting inaugurating this summer school tradition. Dr. Mays wrote,

> Only men with a message that spoke to the needs of Negroes, and who had a point of view that enabled Negro students to look more hopefully beyond their circumscribed plight, were invited to speak at Kings Mountain. . . . It was an oasis in a desert of segregation and discrimination . . . because the conference was under the auspices of Negro executives and administrators.[15]

By the turn of the twentieth century many humanitarians of both races were sometimes chagrined at having to take sides in the looming ideological struggle increasingly separating the advocates of academic education for a classically trained Negro elite, or "Talented Tenth," including W. E. B. Du Bois, William Monroe Trotter, and Ida B. Wells, from champions of Booker Washington's Hampton-Tuskegee model of industrial education. As the moral combat between these rival schools became more keen, the foundations and local and state governments tended to take the side of the tried and true and less strident Tuskegeean. Even so, the Progressive Era did see rare southern Whites and a few Blacks working to ameliorate the Negro condition in the South— but within the confines of segregation and disfranchisement. Some of these people chose the YMCA as their instrument; in spite of its ambivalence and willingness to acquiesce in certain oppressive realities, some viewed the YMCA glass as half full rather than as half empty and did the best they could there.

One of the more dramatic illustrations of an emergent Black voice in the YMCA came at the organization's thirty-eighth international convention in Cincinnati in 1913, which proved particularly portentous for Yergan, for it prefigured the intersection of those dual ideological prongs that lent his mission its unique power: the social gospel doctrine and the allied theology of Black liberation. Walter Rauschenbusch of Rochester University emphasized the need for social activism and the duty of Christians to eliminate the exploitation of one group of human beings by others who undertook to rule them in an age shaped by robber barons and rampant, amoral industrialism, which threatened the entire human species.

This is our chance to unseat privilege, to stop the dishonoring forms of income, to insure the full income to all who work. This is the time to keep down the growth of classes in our nation, which are now springing up so rapidly. If we do not succeed in making that change toward full economic democracy today, then we shall have springing up a still firmer hold of the few on the masses, on the means of production; then we shall have property gathering in the hands of a limited class, and the control of property gathering in the hands of still fewer men.

Rauschenbusch foresaw leading roles for enlightened members of the petite bourgeoisie, the educated stratum. In his schema, the intelligentsia should be the natural allies of the proletariat, and only if they played this part would circumstances measurably improve for the laboring orders. There is a voice of class struggle here, and a voice moderating in the direction of class collaboration. Both of these voices appear crucial in contextualizing Max Yergan, for their echoes resound insistently in prose generated by him over a thirty-year period. This fact notwithstanding, little within Rauschenbusch's presentation directly addressed the singular circumstances facing Black delegates, whose material conditions were circumscribed not only by social stratum but also by race. Their advocate was Robert E. Jones, president of the Colored YMCA in New Orleans. Jones evoked the collaborative spirit of Booker T. Washington and argued for a bold commitment to forging interracial unity within the Y and America at large: "In the face of the common social evils, in the face of our city problems and other dangers that threaten, under the call of the Young Men's Christian Association of America, may not all men who desire the coming of the kingdom of God on earth work side by side, and drive back the common foe."

The YMCA encouraged Black leadership cadres through conferences sponsored at Tuskegee, Atlanta, and Hampton Universities, and Yergan voiced a first definitive commitment to the cause of African Redemption at the 1914 Atlanta conference, announcing that he had altered his career plans from the law "to some form of Christian service." Also noteworthy is that this Atlanta meeting contained a timely panel conducted by the Commission on the Enlistment of Educated Negroes for Work in Africa, whose Pan-Negro observations were clearly associated with African Redemption and Ethiopianism, though at this point, African Redemption focused on saving individual souls rather than on politically redeeming Africa from the clutches of European imperialism.[16]

After he attended this gathering, the course for the next few years of Yergan's life began to become a little clearer. After graduating from Shaw in 1914, Yergan soon registered in the secretarial course at Springfield College, Springfield, Massachusetts, where in the early twentieth century YMCA secretaries were trained.[17] This was ordinarily a three-year program, but presumably Yergan's B.A. made him eligible for advanced standing, as he entered the junior class of 1914–1915. The course was for general secretaries, educational directors, railroad secretaries and heads of departments in the YMCA. After completing the program, he returned to Washington, D.C., "for the International Director's position."[18]

After a brief period of service as a traveling student secretary in the Southwest, the outbreak of the First World War in Europe hastened Yergan's realization of the goal of Christian service in a foreign mission.

Attending the May 1916 International Convention of the YMCA in Cleveland, Yergan surprised colleagues when he answered a stirring "call" issued by E. C. Carter, national secretary of YMCA War Work in the Far East, for forty hearty volunteers to serve the "native" troops in India. Not one to mince words, Carter warned that anyone who joined would be "surrounded by every conceivable danger to life known to man," adding that "the only reward for service was likely to be a body broken by disease or death."[19]

Yergan's response to Carter's call was profound, immediate, and visceral. So moving did he find Carter's words, in fact, that six years later he told an interviewer of his reaction, which the writer reconstructed in prose evocative of love's rapture: "Afraid to trust himself—for fear he had been swept off his feet—Yergan spent an entire night in prayer before he announced his decision to enlist as a war worker."[20] By June, Yergan requested a leave of absence in order to join Carter's Indian mission.[21]

In the half-year he spent in Bangalore, Yergan was Carter's protégé. Understandably attractive to Max, the type of Yankee that Carter probably represented was the kind who had boldly gone south in the promising Reconstruction years—the militant, liberal social gospelers who had made their presence felt in historically Black institutions of learning. They invariably proved unforgettable for those optimistic masses who benefited from their tutelage.

The world YMCA movement had had a long and close identification with military service. For instance, in the Spanish-Cuban-American

War of 1898, YMCA labor was deemed vital enough to warrant creation of an Army and Navy Department in the International Committee
of the North American branch. A Y partisan characterized its stated
purpose as addressing "the needs of soldiers on the firing line, in forts,
on battleships, in national guard camps, and wherever their services
were needed."[22] Max's decision instantly made him a celebrity within
the Colored Work Department ranks.

From May 19 to May 29, he proudly attended the Colored Work
Department's annual Kings Mountain Conference, the foremost gathering of Black YMCA staffers. Years later member Ben E. Mays described
it this way:

> Only men with a message that spoke to the needs of Negroes, and who
> had a point of view that enabled Negro students to look more hopefully
> beyond their circumscribed plight, were invited to speak at Kings
> Mountain. No other organization, except the Young Women's Christian
> Association, was providing this kind of leadership for Negro students.
> They found identity at Kings Mountain. It was an oasis in a desert of
> discrimination. It could do these things because the conference was
> under the auspices of Negro executives and administrators.[23]

A month after Kings Mountain, Yergan submitted a request for a
year's leave in order to clear the way for his Indian sojourn. Then on
Sunday, July 9, at the YMCA Chesapeake Summer School in Harper's
Ferry, West Virginia, he was praised by association officials. On the dais
beside Max stood Presidents Henry T. McDonald of Storer College and
S. C. Hodges of Lincoln University, Richard C. Morse, YMCA International Committee consulting general secretary and sometime movement
historian, Dean Moorland, and Colored Methodist Episcopal bishop
Robert E. Jones. The Reverend Dr. Jones commemorated the fond farewell in an editorial reaching out to readers of his New Orleans–based
Southwest Christian Advocate. Transforming the printed page into a
bully pulpit, Jones sermonized,

> Some of us have been waiting a long time for the Negro to exert himself
> in the world movement for world evangelization and now we have a
> concrete example: A young Southern Negro educated in the South has
> gone under the direction of the YMCA of North America to India,
> where he is to work among an entirely different race than his own,

among British subjects, and is the first Negro so far as we know to do missionary work other than in Africa. The name of this young man, whose frank, open, sincere, devout, pious face we are presenting in this connection is Max Yergan.[24]

After saying his goodbyes, Yergan prepared for his overseas adventure.

Traveling on the *Nieuw Amsterdam* he had a memorable voyage, joining YMCA leader Sherwood Eddy, Carter, and other passengers en route to India via London. Max's Atlantic crossing also occurred in the company of peace campaigner Kirby Page, who made reference to him in his daily journal. Enormously impressed by the earnest African-American missionary, Page succinctly summarized their talks. On July 12, their "second day out," Page wrote this about his new acquaintance:

Early this morning Max Yergan and I piled out and had a mile run on the boat deck. The salt air was most bracing and the exercise warmed us up and after a cold salt bath we were ready for a hearty breakfast. I must tell you more about this fellow Max. He is a young colored chap, 23 years of age, a graduate of college and he also spent some time at the Y.M.C.A. College in Springfield, Mass. He has been a traveling Y.M.C.A. Secretary among his own people in the Southwest. He is going over to India for a year's work in connection with the India territorial forces. He then expects to come back and devote himself to Y.M.C.A. work among his own people. He is a very alert and wide awake chap and is really most handsome; has a very strong face and is really a strong man in more ways than one. He is a more earnest and consecrated Christian and I am looking forward to knowing him more intimately.[25]

Three days later Page again made reference to Yergan. Touching on a topic that had moved Max's colleagues before and after this transoceanic voyage, the pacifist leader wrote,

Every night before I go to bed I get up on the top deck for a little quiet time of prayer and meditation. I have had some most helpful heart to heart talks with the different fellows in the group. We are all getting very close together. It is wonderful how quickly friendships are formed when there is a unity of spirit and purpose. The young colored fellow, Max Yergan, is making a profound impression upon me. I admire him tremendously and feel that he is as fine a fellow as one could desire for a real friend. Truly Jesus Christ does transcend all racial and color lines. In him all are brothers.[26]

In their brief time together Page had been able to capture that quality of Yergan's personality, which seemed to move so many of his colleagues, Black or White, whenever they encountered him. Some remarked on a look on his face, a kind of saintly innocence; others noted his stalwart manner and muscular bearing. Similar observations appeared consistently in public and private, across the globe.

A second leg of his journey to India began as Yergan alighted in London, gateway to Britain's empire. There, with Harold S. Gray, whom Max had also met on deck, he went to the theater.[27] He also met YMCA officials and, on July 30, spoke at a Sunday rally at London's Central YMCA on Tottenham Court. A week later he was en route to Bombay on a fortnight's voyage that left from Marseilles. By August 30 he had reached Bangalore, entering a new world.

Yergan's next six months were spent ministering to the diminutive Christianized population of an ancient region whose familiarity with this foreign faith was all but inseparable from British imperial hegemony and consequent cultural colonialism, since modern Indians could view it as an alien intruder fit for only serfs, *harijan*, women, malcontents, and diverse déclassé elements whose spiritual waywardness seemed tantamount in the popular mind to treason—synonymous with a betrayal of Mother India. While Indian YMCA leaders would play a vital role in the nationalist struggle, the YMCA itself was both a creation and reflection of the colonial past and present.

Observing this reality, Max made a number of bold statements, like this frankly critical reflection:

> The Indian student is questioning the Christianity of missionaries who deny him just the very things that we have to contend for as regards speakers at our conference—etc. There is also the same endless number of churches and divisions of churches. In this respect there is a great problem. One sees at times, however, some fine examples of church federation and even coöperation and union. As to opportunities for service, they are numberless. There is a very distinct contribution our men could make, providing Christian brotherhood and coöperation were practiced by the missionaries who have come out here.[28]

The concept that paternalistic foreign missions, denominational divisiveness, and colonially rooted racial chauvinism could impede the realization of Christianity's ideals periodically recurred in Max's overseas writings from this time onward. His Indian experience marked his first face-to-face encounter with nationalism in an imperialist setting.

Beyond such references as this one, shared with a friend and chronicler in an unpublished manuscript, and some equally rare tidbits that survive buried in YMCA house organs, little has come to light about this poignant period in Max's life. It is clear from these references, however, that these months were decisive and memorable in the formation of his consciousness. They also shed light on some obscure aspects of YMCA work.

Bangalore served as an assembly center for casualty sufferers and combatants preparing for front-line duty. The Y role was to build morale for these military personnel through prayer, Bible study, and recreational activities. This was where Yergan would come in.[29] His service, inasmuch as it had Asian, African, European, and American dimensions and ranged far beyond the ordinary boundaries of war service in any one theater, had an internationalist flavor. Further, it began earlier than that of most of his fellow "Yanks" of any color (outside the YMCA, that is) and persisted longer than that of the average American Expeditionary Force doughboy. It had four components: (1) Bangalore, August–circa December 1916; (2) East Africa (principally between Dar es Salaam and Mombasa), circa January 1917–1918; (3) Camp Lee, Virginia, 1918; and (4) Paris, July–August 1919. For the moment we confine our attention to the Indian episode. Yergan's East African and ancillary auxiliary work shall be treated in the ensuing chapter.

When Max decided to answer Ned Carter's call, he became one of the vanguard members of a cadre of African-American YMCA secretaries mobilized from a score of primarily urban, racially segregated Colored Work Department branches that yielded 268 volunteers in home service and forty-nine in overseas army work.[30] In the main, these city associations, to which must be added the campus collections of historically Black colleges like Yergan's alma mater, Shaw, also financed the salaries of each sponsoree. Though these were sometimes matched to some degree by the national office, the greatest share came from local fund raising. Those entering service with foreign allied forces were granted ranks, including commissions, commensurate with regulations.

Yergan, then, was to be, for all intents and purposes, a member of the British Army—although his pay just happened to be financed chiefly by a strapped North American Black Y.

From the point when Yergan touched land in India, he was faced with powerful and pungent images. So thoroughly captivated was he by the sights and sounds of Bombay that fifty years later he confessed to having been taken with the trainside vendors hawking *pan* (a chewable betel-nut mixture encased in a betel-leaf cover) along with railway refreshments he remembered as *biri* and *metai*.[31]

Equally important is the way in which Indian audiences viewed him. In an age of expanding global color consciousness, Yergan found that earlier experiences in the historically Black colleges of the southern United States were resonant for Indian students and professors, viewed colonially as people of color. A pivotal aspect of Yergan's work, there-fore, included addressing groups of Indians about American race mat-ters, in dialogues touching both speaker and hearers, perhaps even seek-ing common cause.

In 1916, South India writhed under several overlapping, entrenched systems of group privation, prejudice, and privilege. In an era of in-creasingly vocal national consciousness, the daily indignities of the Brit-ish presence led resisters to seek solace in cultural reformation. But southerners were quite often exposed to the scorn of chauvinistic north-erners, a phenomenon not wholly beyond the ken of Yergan as a son of North America's stigmatized South. Some Indians, no doubt, may have been surprised to see this tan man, whose light-brown hue might have momentarily led a few to take him as one of their own. Around hut campfires he probably learned of the differences in perception and ori-entation of North and South, as he dined on curd rice and listened to centuries-old songs of Tamil Nadu and Karnataka.

Yergan's teaching typically took shape in the huts that housed YMCA personnel the world over. Here he conducted riveting bioscope (an early form of motion picture projector) presentations and demon-strated proper deportment for upwardly mobile peasants enraptured with the prospect of urbanism and seeking respite from the demands of family, village, and fealty to the ruling strata, as well as release from the thralldom of low caste, as not everyone was favored by fortune to be born a Brahmin. Some of those whose karma and dharma led in other directions responded to the appeal of Christianity and the Y.

In spite of the admittedly checkered history inhibiting the spread of the tradition, Christendom was no idle interloper in Bangalore. Christian proselytization in India began in earnest during the fifteenth-century contacts initiated by Portuguese mariners, compradors, fortune seekers, and fervent Jesuit friars and was continued by both fellow (and frequently rival) Catholics and Protestants. By Yergan's time a large Catholic cathedral and a Wesleyan church constituted material evidence of this activity, as did numerous "Christianized tribes," in the cultural sphere.[32]

Yergan did provide accounts of race relations while in India. In a letter to Jesse Edward Moorland, his mentor, he made reference to talks undertaken with White fellow missionaries. While concise, his description leaves little doubt about how these exchanges left him feeling. "It's funny to see here the same old color question. It reacts on me in just a bit different manner from what I get in America. I have had some solid laughs on the missionaries here. You will be interested in hearing some of them."[33]

Had he not been an American, Ned Carter might well have seemed one of the laughable missionaries Max had in mind, but it is more likely that he was alluding to those who had gone out from the British Isles, to whom a Black American in a position of true responsibility might have seemed somewhat outlandish. Either because he desired to fit in or because the situation exerted severe behavioral demands, Yergan's exposure to English classism in this colonial setting apparently "spoilt" him with a teasing taste of an enticing level of leisure for which he thirsted from those days onward. Even as an underpaid Y worker, Yergan, like so many overseas sojourners, could lounge in a *satrapy* as a *sahib*.

It would not be accurate to say that Indian service made an anti-imperialist of him, at least not in the short run anyway. The same missive that is referred to above, for example, extolled "the great liberal and wise policies of the British government," closing with the entreaty that "God grant that such principles might soon prevail in America." And it seems that this exposure during his formative years played a critical role in affecting certain habits that persuaded some subsequent acquaintances to regard Yergan as aristocratic or eccentric, such as penchants for attendance by domestic servants, for "high tea," and for daily formal dinners served at precisely the same hour.[34]

This suggests other questions, whose responses one can only guess. How did Yergan comport himself in the company of English Indian "hands"? Did he choose to eschew informal Americanisms? Might it have proven attractive to affect Anglo-Indian *Anglice*? Or did affectation merely make some see in him more of a monkeylike minstrel? It is not uncommon for Americans to cringe in the face of their Old World "betters," and it would have been difficult not to try to fit in with people who so proudly pulled the reins of power. Maybe even Carter did so.

And how might the myth of Raleigh's "slave aristocracy" have articulated with Yergan's intimate confrontation with the English crown? Was there some area of convergence between his own covetous contact with quaint customs that reinforced nascent ideas of uniqueness, now that he was a world traveler? How then could he return to the milieu that had sheltered and shaped him, after meeting the majestic maharajah of Mysore?

Yet Mother India struck Yergan in ways he probably had not anticipated. Once, upon arriving in Madras to address a Y student conference, he was shocked to find that the hall where he had been scheduled to deliver a lecture was empty. The officer in charge offered his apologies, explaining that the Indian conferees were commemorating the anniversary of the passing of Booker T. Washington. Having read a Hindustani translation of *Up from Slavery,* they wished to pay homage to the late leader. "Perhaps Mr. Yergan might be able to visit them another time," said the ranking official.[35] In a world shaped by race and racial identification, Booker Washington's example was no less powerful for legions of nonwhite colonials than it had proven to be for North Americans, Black and White alike.

The rising elite stratum of European-educated, typically Christian colonials in Africa, the Caribbean, and Asia, as well as other places, could see in Washington's autobiography a plan to achieve uplift for the masses of their own people, particularly those restricted by caste, class, race, and/or prior servile status. Wittingly or unwittingly, Yergan played a part in this process. From him, Indian youth and students could receive the story of Negro achievement straight from the horse's mouth. He, like the departed Wizard of Tuskegee (as some saw Washington), was up from slavery, having learned the tale from grandfather Frederick, who rose above it. Washington's admirers included indigenes like A. J. Appasamy, who published a two-part treatise entitled "A Challenge to India's Educators" in the leading YMCA journal, in which he attempted to acquaint local teachers with the virtues of the methodology of industrial education that had uplifted America's Negroes.[36]

In colonial India, as in English-ruled Africa and the Caribbean, imperial functionaries, settlers, and complicit missionaries all could exert a measure of ideological control over their indigenous populations by elevating selected parts of Washington's text that emphasized not merely his message of self-help but also his anxiety about politics and entering into labor combinations. Since literacy was to remain limited to a privileged, select few, already identified and under close supervision in each mission, often chaperoned through monitored ranks in the civil service, it was not usually difficult to keep track of these individuals or their allies. Thus, an argument might be made that Yergan was functioning in ways that proved pleasing to the British Empire, accommodating, aiding, or abetting the imperialistic status quo.

Other Indians were also intrigued by American Negroes and their status, however. Mohandas K. Gandhi, doubtless swayed by his South African experiences but above all by methodical and prodigious research on global racial questions, took considerable pains to acquaint himself with slavery and its aftermath in the United States, with a view toward extracting relevant lessons for India's freedom struggle. Somewhere along the line Yergan learned about him and may have been able to read and possibly encounter him, as he told Ruby Pagano in some wintry reminiscence about India.[37]

2 | World War One

Max Yergan's World War One experiences were atypical for Americans of African descent. They were also unusual for doughboys serving overseas after maturing in North America. They began in Asia, continued in Africa, and, after a return home, culminated in Paris once the armistice was declared. Max had two "bits" of overseas service, one beneath the Union Jack, another under the Stars and Stripes. Each had its own peculiar challenges and taught a particular set of life lessons. Travel also brought him closer to other lands and peoples, as a "world citizen."

Yergan's war began late in 1916, when he answered Ned Carter's call to serve in India.

Approaching mid-October Yergan's life took another turn as he prepared to leave India for East Africa, thereby coming closer to realizing his late grandfather Frederick's missionary dream. The prospect of doing African work intrigued him no end, as he indicated to Dean Moorland in this evocative passage:

> Truly am I enthusiastic over our prospects in Africa. I believe that God is opening up to us a most wonderful opportunity. When world maps are changing, Europeans becoming very familiar with all other races (for I saw thousands of black troops in France) and the present war making men more cognizant of the conditions of other people and giving at the same time a sense of responsibility—I say should we not count these evidences of God's hand as warning us to get ready for service?[1]

As if illustrating the spiritual vision he had shared with Moorland, when he landed in Mombasa Yergan wrote home with a fever of 102 degrees. Even so, he managed to convey much useful information to his Colored Work Department mentor. The inspired new arrival wrote that coming down with malaria was inevitable and reassured Moorland that it was "nothing to cause serious alarm." Then he let his great friend know that he was chafing at the bit, longing to be back in the fray once more: "I am more than anxious to get out for there are at present 'some where in Africa,' some unusually bright opportunities to serve. You would be interested in knowing the details, but I cannot give them, for military reasons."[2]

Three weeks later, Max wrote Moorland that on Thursday, November 16, he had sailed from Mombasa southward down the coast to Dar es Salaam, lately in German East Africa but now in Allied hands. By Saturday, November 25, he had had his initial chance to speak with "a group of Natives." Yergan compared the setting to a Quaker meeting, though he conversed only briefly, since he had limited vernacular language skills, being unfamiliar with Kiswahili, the lingua franca of the coastal region, which he would have encountered in Mombasa earlier and to which all military field workers were gradually being introduced.[3] Max did let Moorland know, however, that "once one gets these natives started they are keen for everything." Adopting a relaxed, conversational tone, he then eagerly went on:

> You would have been interested in an experience I had last week.
>
> I gave a moving picture show to about three thousand men and boys, most of whom had never seen such before. Their expressions and ejaculations during the show were most fitting and gave evidence of their appreciative powers. Their day is coming.[4]

A month later Yergan waxed enthusiastic about reinforcements from the Caribbean, Western and Southern Africa, India, and the far reaches of Britain's empire. But Max also reported having his hands full, ministering to a flock unfamiliar with Christianity. Detailing bouts of fever, insects, and venomous snakes, he prayed to elude illness. He described the situation graphically, in prose not meant for readers with squeamish hearts, recounting horrific scenes of battle:

> Diseases are as destructive of life and perhaps, at present, more so than bullets. For this reason and many others we shall all be glad when the struggle here is over. Men are becoming so hardened by it. Life is so cheap that it sometimes seems useless to try to save it. Even now as I write I can hear the boom of cannon; stray bullets have pierced our tent

in half a dozen places. As the men come in from the battle lines tired and wounded, swearing, drunk with blood, one realizes too clearly what a heartless thing it all is. One soon becomes accustomed to the stench of decayed bodies. Yes, one must handle half rotten human bodies. The sight of it will be with me forever. A few days ago I pulled a body out of the hot sands which had been there for days. Rats and vermin fall from the food which such a condition affords. . . . And yet out of all this there are occasions when one finds out that the big thing in life is not dead in the hearts of men. Last Sunday I saw big men who had just returned from killing other men weep when during the course of my talk they took the opportunity to reflect. Censorship prevents my writing more.[5]

Max wrote Moorland again, as the Christmas holidays approached. Exhausted, he confessed that "I need help badly." Letting his dean know that he had "absolutely poured myself out trying to meet the needs of men in the camps," Yergan added that "physically, I am far from myself. Yet there can be no let up for the needs of the troops are constantly increasing with the thousands of new ones coming in." He went on to regale his tutor with news of a projected Sunday sabbath selection geared to rein in some three thousand souls. The spiritual value of the gathering and its attendant recreational activities was clear to Max. Profoundly moved, the younger man reported seeing a delegation that had journeyed a great distance "through the tropical sun to ask me to start something for them," as he "silently prayed that God would hasten the men who are coming out from America to help," noting that despite danger, "I shall be ever thankful to God that He gave me this opportunity."[6]

By late February Moorland eagerly informed Yergan that two fellow African-American colleagues, Thomas H. Lloyd and Fred D. Ballou, had sailed on February 15 amid perilous seas, further noting that "they made a good impression upon all of us and upon the Committee in New York. They were carefully scrutinized, thoroughly examined, physical[ly] as well as otherwise and have so far, met the test. I am sure they will be a source of strength to you."[7] A fortnight later Moorland asked after them, expressing hope that Yergan would "find both of them willing to bear any burden which may be placed upon them."[8] Max then wrote Frank Sanders that he was "looking forward with joy to meeting the two men who are coming out from America to help in this particular work," adding that he knew both of them, "having met them during my visits to their colleges." He summed up his joy by saying, "Without question I feel that they should render good service. There is an opportunity here for service which none of us could afford to miss."[9]

Thomas Hezekiah Lloyd, a Howard University–educated railway porter-fireman, and Frederick Douglass Ballou, a Knoxville College printer and a native of neighboring Richmond, Kentucky, proved great assets to the Y's work. Ballou was an American Expeditionary Forces secretary. He, Yergan, and Lloyd were photographed with Major C. R. Webster, who wrote tersely but truthfully of the trio that "the men are doing admirable work among the African troops and carriers, especially in the hospital where these noble and devoted Christians bring a ray of divine light into the terrible wards."[10] By mid-July Philadelphia minister Robert S. Pritchett joined Max and company in Dar es Salaam.

Yergan's experience in the field of battle produced letters that had the searing intensity of Goya's sketches of the hideousness of war. He wrote of walking over rotting corpses, smelling the acrid stench of death, eating vermin-infested rations, and facing other horrors. These nightmarish visions and privations served to strengthen his faith in Christianity as a source of uplift and his posting to the East African war theater as a golden opportunity. Thus in his letter to Moorland describing his state of mind Yergan wrote the following:

> In our work with the Natives, we are from the outset confronted by the strong claims of Islam upon those along the coast and in many and growing instances among those in the interior. However, through our work with the men and boys in hospital and through our efforts to prove ourselves friends to them in more ways than their Mohammedan brothers, we have managed to get the Christian message to large numbers of them. You can get an idea of the possibilities when I tell you that there are several large camps of Natives brought together for military purposes. In one close there are five thousand men and boys; while in a hospital and convalescent camp a few miles away there are always one thousand or more. I could quite profitably spend all of my time with these needy ones.[11]

For seven months in 1917, Herbert Stuart toured YMCA facilities in and around Dar on a visit to historic Tanganyika, commenting in passing on the American Negro secretaries he encountered holding games, leading Bible study classes, and managing educational work. Without mentioning names, English Y official Vernon Nash sketched a portrait of a black team leader strongly resembling Yergan. Employing the literary device of an officer called "Colonel Newcome," Stuart described the hut scene this way:

> Next, Colonel Newcome and the secretary motored some miles to see the five great camps of African troops and "carriers" and labour boys. These camps are looked after by another Negro secretary, who does educational work besides similar work to what we have described elsewhere. This enormous African work is all done by one single Negro secretary, and Colonel Newcome was immediately impressed by it. He was told that on the cinema nights the amusement of the vast squatting hosts of spectators finds vent in shrieks and yells of laughter, as the cinema scenes are shewn. Unfortunately, it was impossible for him to wait to see the sight. These shows are given in a huge banda; the congregation are from every part of Africa. On a Sunday evening they meet to worship God, and that is still a greater sight. Colonel Newcome was pleased to hear that more American Negro secretaries are on their way across the ocean to help these two, who are so keenly carrying out their faith in daily service to the lowest of their brothers. The Commander-in-Chief himself urged the YMCA to send them.[12]

And it was not always the larger struggles that left an impression upon him. As much as he strove to contain and process the damage being done to his psyche from the events of the war, he also had to confront the day-to-day encounters that characterized the missionary life. One of these worked its way into a later fund-raising brochure. It was a tale based on an encounter between himself and a young African who, upon hearing him speak raised a question that would ring resoundingly in his ears for years afterward:

> When I was through, I went outside and sat on the trunk of a tree. Presently one of our boys came out and said, "You say back in America you have schools and colleges and churches. . . . And you say you are literally our brothers and sisters, that the same blood which flows through you flows through us here. If that is the case, why have so many of you remained in America so long? Why are you alone here?"[13]

Nothing about this assignment was easy. Yergan's mettle was being tested every day, along with his endurance, and whatever certitude he may have brought with him was also under siege. This is why faith was so vital to him in his effort to come to terms with the world of war-torn East Africa and his historical, racial, and present-day relationship to it.

Fortunately Max had his fellow Colored Work Department cronies to help him work through this, and from a distance he had Dean J. E. Moorland and Channing H. Tobias. Even so, the reality could not bear much resemblance to grandfather Frederick's dream.

Nevertheless, others wrote the larger story of both Yergan and his fellow countrymen. Herbert Stuart stressed the spiritual value of the labors of the African-American auxiliaries working in British service. Of their contribution he offered this appreciation:

> From the Christian point of view, this work is intensely valuable, for in these camps there are crowds of young Christian boys from their simple homes, who, without the help of these Negro YMCA men, would have none to understand or to care for their spirits or their minds during their exile from home. It is a hard life for them, plucked out of Christian influences and suddenly pitched into military life. In all Dar-es-Salaam these are the men who most need our help and love.[14]

Vernon Nash summed up the events of 1917, detailing scenarios in YMCA huts, tents, and camps in Dar and upcountry. He told of how Major Webster was incapacitated from July to August, only to be replaced by A. Perry Park, who was himself "invalided" to India in very short order. Nash also took time to devote special praise to someone else:

> The most distinctive work of the YMCA in East Africa is probably that carried on among the King's African Rifles and the natives of the Carrier and Labour Corps by five American coloured secretaries, led by an American Rhodes scholar. Three other Negroes are on their way from New York now, and the permanence of this work seems assured. Plans are already well matured for carrying on the work for Africans, not only for the garrisons of coloured troops, but among the civilian population after the close of the campaign. Chief credit for the growth of this work is given to Max Yergan, the first Negro to arrive in the

field. He is a coloured secretary for the International Committee among the Negro colleges of America, and has just returned to his work there. He hopes to arouse the coloured churches, and particularly Christian students of the coloured race, in the United States to a sense of responsibility for Africa, and to return with a party to Africa within the next year.[15]

The duties of these black mentors may have seemed modest. They showed slides and films, led prayers, served meals, and ministered to the troubled, lonely, depressed, infirm, frightened, wounded, and dying. But their presence made a great difference. For Yergan and his colleagues, the experience of "an African return" was highly emotional. That fact, combined with the trying circumstances of war, made the experience that much more poignant. And it was as dangerous for them as for the carriers and troops whose needs they served. In March 1917, Yergan was evacuated to Bombay suffering from acute appendicitis.[16]

December 1, 1917, marked the end of Yergan's British East African YMCA service. That same month, however, Moorland published an article in *Crisis* lionizing black troops. Glossing over their considerable race-specific privations, a matter of import to *Crisis* editor Dr. Du Bois, who received scores of complaints about the treatment meted out to Negro recruits, Moorland talked up the exploits of brown men in khaki, especially Max. Quoting E. C. Carter, Moorland retold Yergan's heroic saga melodramatically:

> Max Yergan, the youngest member of my staff, student secretary for the Southwest, graduate of Shaw University, only 25 years old, strong, courageous, devout, faithful in caring for every detail of responsibility entrusted to him, heard the call and went to India. Not a question was raised by our Committee regarding his race. The reports of his service to troops and of his splendid addresses at mission stations in India are most encouraging. After some months, at his own request, he went with a number of troops to British East Africa, where he had been serving East Indian, West Indian, British troops and South African troops and native troops from many parts of Africa. He suffered with fever, surrounded by every danger known to man in that region. He is now broken in health, and is on his way home; let his story be like that of Livingstone.[17]

His destination was stateside, where he looked forward to reuniting with family members and to getting some much-needed rest. Max was home just long enough to find himself wanted back in uniform in France, in American service, assisting in the demobilization of Black doughboys in Paris. February 1, 1918, thus marked the beginning of his overseas service in the city of light. Representing the Y's War Work Council, he was a recruiting officer for Black workers.

On April 21, 1918, Max regaled Hampton Institute with tales of wartime East Africa's trials.[18] He left audience members enraptured as he told of his travails and his valiant comrades, their tragedies and triumphs, exhorting his hearers to do something meaningful in life. Not for the last time, he told of battlefield horrors, as they had made their mark on him like so many others who experienced combat, though few in an African theater. But he also shared with them a message of redemption and deliverance. Leaving behind rows of admiring students, in May he returned to post, now in France.

One day, in September 1918, back in East Africa, where a few of his fellow African-American compatriots remained, Fred D. Ballou fell overboard into the Indian Ocean; his buddy, R. S. Pritchett, vainly attempting to rescue him, drowned along with his countryman. The recovered remains of both men were interred in Upanga Cemetery in Dar es Salaam.[19] News of their tragic loss would be recalled for years afterward.

The Negro troops' herculean effort almost instantly became the stuff of "Colored YMCA" legend. This is how their sacrifices were commemorated in one official record:

> The troops engaged in East Africa were by no means so numerous as in most other fields, but there was a pathos in the suffering of the ignorant African peoples, in their perplexity and confusion which was unsurpassed. Members of the colored Associations here in America responded to the needs of these Africans, and 7 American Negro secretaries were sent out to serve especially with the porters attached to the British forces. En route, two of these men were shipwrecked but rescued. Again, two of the seven were drowned, near Dar es Salaam, 1 came back so shaken by fever that he has not yet fully recovered. Of the seven, only two came back but little the worse in health for their experience. Among men whose life was reduced to its elements—where the

great question of the day was whether a man might eat or go hungry, or whether he might have the comparative comfort of a single blanket against one midnight drill, luxuries do not come into consideration; but the secretary, who went about among the sick bringing scriptural comfort to those who knew something of the Bible through mission teaching, and helping in any way possible those who were in need, experienced a reward of gratitude which made life itself seem a small thing to exchange for such an opportunity.[20]

At the conclusion of his East African service Moorland himself used the pages of *Crisis* to elevate Yergan's stature to that of a missionary race hero.

Last Christmas he went from hospital to hospital in his little Ford machine in the spirit of Christ—sometimes near the coast, sometimes far in the interior under the shelter of Kilima-Njaro, the tallest mountain in Africa, the summit of which is covered with eternal snow. Many nights he was without shelter, with small quantities of unhealthful food—yet the ring of his letters never showed any sign of dissatisfaction with the discomforts, but joy at the privilege of service.[21]

In the *Christian Herald,* an interdenominational paper based in the United Kingdom, Torrey Stearns also lionized the African-derived Max as a "missionary to his own people." Borrowing generously from official YMCA prose, he painted Yergan as a humanitarian hero in the Livingstonian mold, soon to become a familiar analogy for him:

There is a bright and encouraging side to this picture. These men are being irresistibly swept into wider and higher realms of thinking and living. They are learning to understand and appreciate each other. They are learning the dignity and usefulness of labor and the joys of unselfish service. The spirit and principles of Jesus Christ implanted in the lives of these men will be scattered far and wide as an answer to Livingstone's dying prayer.[22]

July 1919 found Yergan in London, meeting with K. T. Paul, A. K. Yapp, and K. J. Saunders.[23] With regard to the modalities whereby Max might return to East Africa, it was the opinion of the English National

Council (whose general secretary was Sir Arthur Yapp, recently named an officer of the Order of the British Empire) that Yergan would be the best choice for the first permanent YMCA secretary appointed in the East Africa Protectorate. India's Paul (who had observed Max at close range in Bangalore) and Saunders each concurred. Though there were logistical and financial concerns, they were clear about wanting him in the position. It remained for them to convince government. By September Yergan ended his service for the Y War Work Council, becoming a field secretary after the armistice.

An American Negro YMCA Secretary for Africa?

In response to the favorable reputation Max gained as a result of his overseas war work, various requests were routed either to him or to his American YMCA colleagues in the International Committee, including invitations for service in foreign mission fields. Two proved particularly noteworthy, and both came from Africa. The first and more expected of the two was from East Africa, an area with which he was familiar, having survived it at its worst, at the peak of hostilities. The second derived from a far less likely, even startling quarter: the Union of South Africa.

The East African invitation was a logical outgrowth of Yergan's recent war experience. But it is necessary to provide some background on the second appeal, from South Africa. The first call for Yergan in South Africa had come in a July 1919 query shortly after his relief of John Hope in Paris. It was initiated by Oswin Boys Bull, newly chosen general secretary of the YMCA. Born in Barnstaple, Devon, Bull was a protégé of John Mott, whose 1906 South African visit had set in train the process by which Bull was recruited from Jesus College, Cambridge, to superintend South Africa's fractious Student Christian Association.[24] He had been informed about Yergan by officials in London and, writing from Cape Town, he asked Mott for further information. Bull had himself served two and a quarter years back home during the war, before being recalled by the English National Council.

Bull had been in South Africa since 1907. Appointed in part to expand the reach of the SCA and YMCA to a previously unserved African population, Bull joined a series of earlier outsiders who had while visiting the Union championed the cause of extending the movement to all

South Africa's peoples, regardless of race. Two such sojourns had been of particular importance, that of Luther D. Wishard and Donald Fraser (founders of the World's Student Christian Federation [WSCF]) in 1895 and that of John Mott and Ruth Rouse, she representing the English associations as well as the WSCF, in 1906. Despite or perhaps because of a keen awareness of the obstacles to doing this kind of outreach, all four found it both logical and necessary for them as practicing Christians who wished to bring about what Mott had famously proclaimed "the evangelization of the world in this generation."

Accordingly, by 1916 Bull had engaged the services of the sexagenarian John Knox Bokwe, perhaps the best known African Christian leader in the country, to assist him in this endeavor. Bokwe, a Lovedale graduate who aided its principal, James Stewart, was a journalist, evangelist, and renowned composer of Xhosa-language choral classics, arranging such memorable works as *Ntsikana's Bell* and *Ntsikana's Great Hymn*. Bokwe accompanied Bull across the veld into the "Native" institutions of the Eastern Cape as they initiated what would subsequently often be termed either "Native," "Bantu," or simply "Black" work. Bokwe had volunteered on a part-time basis, prompting Bull to secure financial support for him as well as to explore the possibility of finding someone who might take on the work on a full-time basis. Bull spelled this out in a detailed letter to Mott requesting his help in finding such a candidate:

> The work demands at least one whole-time Secretary and we ought to have a very wise and far-seeing man. It will be a magnificent field for the right man: perhaps the greatest today in Africa; but it is one which in five years' time may be very much more difficult to develop. When I was in London a year or two ago [E. C.] Carter spoke to me very highly about a man called Yergan and suggested that he was a man of big enough caliber for work of this kind. I do not know at all what this man is doing at present, but I am wondering whether it is your opinion that he could be of service in this field, either for a visit or a longer period of service.[25]

Mott's response to Bull had been that he would need to make the case to Yergan personally in the strongest terms possible. At that time Max was still in France working under Ned Carter. East Africa, however, remained a strong possibility. A month later, Kenneth J. Saunders suggested to Arthur K. Yapp that England provide a national secretary for East Africa, seeking International Committee and Indian National Council support for African and Indian work. His idea was that they get a "really strong man" as national secretary, someone with "big sympathies" and a genuine missionary spirit. This person should be asked to have Yergan as an assistant national secretary, with a view toward Yergan succeeding him "when the work has become really indigenous." Saunders had in mind Herbert Bryant, who, with Indian experience behind him, would be firm enough, with Max as his aide, "to stand up to the colonial and educate him to a right attitude to the people of the country." This seemed to flow from Yergan's India experience. It would, therefore, be advisable for Max to visit England.[26]

Saunders thanked Carter for making it possible for Yergan to see him, along with K. T. Paul. On Thursday, July 31, 1919, Max talked briefly with Yapp, who noted that he would contact North American head Mott about the feasibility of a Yergan appointment for East Africa. Saunders's scheme was that the International Committee assume support for an East African post. This was his aim: with Herbert Bryant acting as secretary, the English National Council could pay his salary, the International Committee could foot Max's bill, and India's National Council could provide for one or more Indian personnel.

Aware that Yergan was scheduled to return home shortly, Saunders queried Ned Carter as to whether he might generate a letter asking the International Committee if they could keep Yergan on staff while he was in England and possibly give him a few opportunities to visit some of the colleges with a view to enlisting sympathy and "possibly U.S. support" for East African work. Both Paul and Saunders agreed that there was a great deal to be said for Max spending a few months in the United Kingdom to get in touch with the best student life there.

Saunders also reasoned that Tissington Tatlow of the WSCF could be induced to take on Yergan as a temporary staffer. Saunders considered consulting Tatlow on this but felt that such consultation would be difficult until the attitude of the International Committee was settled. Saunders was planning to go to New York in September and therefore sought approval from Carter for his proposals, which he also had been discussing with Edward C. Jenkins. The Foreign Committee of the English National Council had approved Major Watson as Nairobi secretary for two years, with the proviso that his appointment would not affect any subsequent nomination of a permanent national secretary.[27]

A week later, E. C. Carter wrote E. C. Jenkins, mentioning that Saunders had asked him to arrange for Yergan to go to London to arouse British YMCA interest in naming him to work in East Africa. Yergan, back from England, had made a favorable impression on Carter:

I do not know how Saunders' proposal will strike you. All I can say is that the YMCA ought to undertake the work for colored people in Africa. I know of few men, colored or white, who have shown finer leadership than Max Yergan and I certainly feel that he is ideally fitted to pioneer a great work in Africa. It is for you and the British YMCA to work out between you just what he will represent and by whom he will be supported if he goes.[28]

Carter's faith in Yergan was clear. His campaign continued with a letter to C. V. Hibbard indicating that as Yergan was proceeding to America in about a fortnight he hoped that after doing some work at home, followed by a period in the United Kingdom observing the British Student Movement in situ, Jenkins would make arrangements for him to go out to East Africa. Carter ended the note with his own patented rousing Y appeal:

In view of Max's intimate knowledge of our work in France, I wish you would strongly recommend to the proper authorities that he be used in speaking quite widely throughout the South soon after his arrival. He has done a great service in France just as he did in India and East Africa.[29]

Yergan reentered the United States during the first week of September 1919, arriving on the 6th. Two days later he was back at his New York desk, having resumed his prior position as International Committee secretary, a job he would continue to do through January 1, 1921.[30] All that he needed to do was prepare himself for the prospect of returning to the land of his fathers. It seemed just a matter of time, time like that he had passed while in Bangalore and then on the bloody battlefields of East Africa; time like that he had passed as he lay gravely stricken before recovering from fever; time like that he had passed when he returned to New York and then to Raleigh to visit family and friends. Time was a thing with which he had already learned how to deal. He knew what might await him in East Africa. After all, being there could not have been as hard as in wartime, so thinking it through and preparing for the task seemed a logical way to proceed. He would just have to wait.

Once back home, Yergan received a detailed follow-up letter from Jenkins. The six key questions it raised were crucial for YMCA planning in the two foreign fields Max knew best, India and East Africa. The answers could come from what in British colonial-era parlance was often called a "man on the spot," an experienced person in the storm center:

1. In your contact with missionaries in British East Africa, did you discover their attitude toward the establishment of a civilian YMCA? Please . . . give . . . details.
2. Is it your understanding with Carter that the English National Council is prepared to take aggressive steps toward starting Association work in British East Africa? What was the substance of the understanding as to men and equipment?
3. If the Foreign Committee should undertake this work, what is your recommendation as to the inauguration of it, number of men required, places where it would be established and equipment needed?
4. Estimate cost of equipment?
5. How do prices for maintenance of secretaries compare with those of India?
6. I have thought still further of the possibilities of this arrangement and believe that there is a good prospect of our doing something substantial provided we can get the whole Association Movement committed generally to a foreign policy.[31]

Yergan made an additional London visit between August and September. Aside from funding issues of a technical nature that had immediate importance, the final question about a foreign policy for the YMCA seems pivotal, not only to the movement but also to Yergan's own vision of mission in the YMCA for Africa and, perhaps, beyond. In both spiritual and temporal terms, he had already found respite from the provincialism of his upbringing, having rejected its stuffily parochial, homeland isolationism, had gravitated toward a wider sense of self, and had transcended nationality as a citizen of the world. Max would call upon every last ounce of personal resilience in those battles that lay ahead. In the end something occurred that he had not fully anticipated, due to the political climate of the times.

Ideology: The Problem of the "Two Schools"

While Yergan undertook his apprenticeship in India, East Africa, and postwar Europe, a new global ethos of social change, ranging from advocacy of reform all the way to revolution, was in full flower. Several aspects of this ethos would have appealed to him. One was the church-based reformism of the ecumenical movement that had given rise to the volunteer spirit animating the YMCA and its affiliate, the WSCF, a trend that Max was not only aware of but also helping to build. Another was the great Black migration northward from the rural and urban South to the North in the United States (in which Yergan had also taken part), a time of bold new initiatives for the amelioration of the African-American condition. Third, the optimism of the armistice stimulated a wide variety of international social, political, and cultural movements struggling to forge a more democratic world order in which dispossessed and voiceless majorities might play more pivotal roles in the workplace and the state. Many reflected new national identities.

This widely scaled militancy had particular resonance for the Black Atlantic world. In colonial Africa and the Antilles, especially, guardians of the imperial gates monitored activities and utterances of assertive ideologues they labeled as dangerous propagandists. As the Bolsheviks had challenged the old order in colonies and semicolonies, so did African, Afro-Antillean, and African-American activists in the African diaspora, for whom imperialism and colonialism had domestic analogues. For the latter particularly, the rapid globalization of the European system became seen as necessitating the creation of mechanisms capable of overthrowing colonial hegemony—the oppressive state structures subjugating Black peoples worldwide—over time by any means necessary.

For growing numbers of Africans and persons of African descent, the turmoil associated with the world war bolstered a broadening consciousness of one common condition—a wretchedness growing out of foreign paternalism, colonial disfranchisement, and cruel, callous, and crass exploitation. In their "Nonwhite" eyes, alleviation of these conditions required intense agitation, organization, and diplomacy. Such interests found expression in two complementary albeit competing strategies of Pan-Africanist propagandism, represented by W. E. B. Du Bois and Marcus Garvey. Contemporaneously, another variety of Pan-Africanism had developed that, while eschewing what it took to be the strident polemics of the political varieties, nevertheless was linked to both of them—what Kenneth King called a missionary or evangelical form of Pan-Africanism. For Max, an heir to the Ethiopianist tradition of an earlier generation, evangelical Pan-Africanism was the earliest earmark of an evolving liberationist ideology.

The international racial and political climate of 1919 was volatile. The Pan-African Congress that convened that year alerted government authorities in Britain, France, and the United States to possible dangers posed by a new Black internationalism threatening to undermine the teetering Euro-American political and economic order. At the same time, Marcus Garvey's Harlem-based, transnationally focused Universal Negro Improvement Association, active in New York since 1916, dispersed its formidable print organ, *The Negro World,* across the United States and via Britain's empire to the far reaches of the globe.

At the same time these organizations appeared, the imperialistic powers most threatened by the Pan-African idea explored ways to mollify those elements most susceptible to its appeals. One approach entailed collusion between overseas missionary hierarchies and Whitehall, with which the former were in frequent, intimate contact. This was where YMCA missionary work came in, as an antidote to fiery popular agitation. It was toward this end that George Williams had been working when he shaped the group in the 1840s, when worker agitation was sweeping across England and into continental Europe.

The Talented Tenth

Yergan was in touch with a representative sampling of the African-American intelligentsia in the wake of the First World War. He nurtured these relationships in a decade of public appearances beginning in 1915, renewing them at intervals whenever furloughs became available to him. For the most part these work-centered connections are only hinted at in correspondence. Though Yergan was an inveterate chronicler of personal and professional experience, the majority of missives recovered in this research were generated for concrete business or political purposes. Yergan was either in search of speaking opportunities, usually combined with some type of monetary hook (honorarium, donation, or other material aid for a cause), or in quest of allies in particular campaigns, especially critical for YMCA work because it was always necessary for Colored Work Department projects to raise their own funding.

Following his second period of military service, Max reached another milestone in his life. On Wednesday, June 16, 1920, Yergan and Susan Delores Wiseman were married in the Salisbury, North Carolina, residence of Dr. and Mrs. James E. K. Aggrey.[32] Their wedding ceremony was performed by fellow Colored Work Department secretary C. H. Tobias. In establishing Max's bona fides, Aggrey later made a point of noting that it was attended by some of Salisbury's "finest White ladies."[33]

By autumn Yergan was again on the road, in Atlanta on November 16, visiting Cincinnati on YMCA business from November 20 to 21, and then at West Virginia State College and Institute on November 22 as the guest of President John W. Davis and family. Clearly close to the Davis family, Max expressed affectionate concern then and later for his reception at the institute, remarking on the hospitality and favorable response to his appeal.[34] By December, while Tobias and Johnson saw their way there, Yergan's commitments in Columbus and Springfield, Ohio, St. Louis, and Kansas City precluded a hoped for return to the institute, which was especially disappointing as this marked the school's week of prayer.[35] Even though he was in absentia at year's end, however, Max's African appeal drew lucrative dividends.[36]

But 1920 also revealed the strength of official opposition to Yergan's candidacy as a permanent YMCA secretary in East Africa. Sir Edmund Northey, governor of Kenya, registered his view that he did not deem it "advisable to admit into East Africa negroes of a different caliber from those already there," thus dashing Max's hard-won hopes on the rocks of racism. Against the backdrop of the assertion of Garvey and Du Bois, Yergan become a casualty of colonialism. So while collecting funds for an African return, he had no idea where this might occur. By December South Africa resurfaced as a possibility. January 1, 1921, marked the end of Max's U.S. service with the International Committee.

The correspondence between Aggrey and Bull formed a small part of an intense debate over whether to follow Northey's lead and South African government practice by delaying and at times prohibiting American Negro or other "foreign Native" immigration or to relax the stricture and grant him an exception. In January 1921 this was the subject of conversations involving D. D. T. Jabavu and Hunter at Lovedale Presbyterian mission, members of the Native Advisory Committee, and A. D. Roberts, late of Lovedale and part of a newly named Native Advisory Council whose members also included C. T. Loram, former inspector of Native schools in Natal, and a Transvaaler, General Lemmer. Bull noted that Immigration had recently deliberately delayed AME Bishop W. T. Vernon.[37]

Bull informed Mott that "there was a pretty strong prejudice in most quarters against the American coloured man," exacerbated by recent news reports of "Martin Garvey and Co.," which, he wrote, "has not tended to weaken the prejudice." Bull himself had mixed feelings about the matter, the source of which he readily identified to Mott:

> If Yergan comes he will be doing Pioneer Work in a good many direc-tions and I find myself wondering whether that is quite the best and most acceptable thing. If we had a more highly developed work we should probably find it easier. My own personal hesitancy is perhaps in-creased by conversation in the past few days w Dr Jesse Jones of the Phelps-Stokes Commission and also w Dr Loram. The latter, as you will gather from what I have written above, occupies a very important posi-tion and also represents the modern and advanced element in the Ad-visory Council. He is eager to develop all sorts of Welfare activities on behalf of the Natives and is anxious for the development of YMCA work amongst them in any centre where opportunity offers. Also he knows something of America.[38]

Thomas Jesse Jones, a naturalized American of Welsh extraction, had by 1921 maneuvered himself into a career as an "expert on the Negro."[39] Surveying African education for the Phelps Stokes Fund, he traveled to South and East Africa.[40] Jones was politically conservative, harboring fears of Black independence. Bull let Mott know that he found C. T. Loram "exceedingly doubtful about lending his support to the matter of inviting Yergan." Without knowing him Loram had also been swayed by Jones, who was "apparently a little bit doubtful about the attitude of Moreland [sic] and your other Coloured leaders and (perhaps for want of knowing him better) classes Yergan with them." The upshot of such discussions was that Bull did not foresee a prompt decision.[41]

The next month Aggrey, landing in South Africa from Angola on the *India,* met Bull, who asked about Max. Aggrey replied that Yergan was the right man for the job.[42] A day later, on March 19, Aggrey joined the Phelps-Stokes Commission led by Jones. In the course of his stay the Gold Coast–born educator delivered some 120 public addresses.[43] A fortnight following Aggrey's entry into South Africa Yergan wrote Tuskegee principal R. R. Moton, along with M. W. Johnson and J. W. Dillard, inquiring about being delayed.[44] He also wrote President John W. Davis of West Virginia Collegiate Institute, citing Bull's February 18 letter mentioning the "strong prejudice there against American colored people" and noting "recent difficulties" in the admission of Negroes. Encouraging Davis and others to act on his behalf, Max was gathering his troops. Telling Davis his rationale for returning to Africa, he delineated these three significant points:

> First and primarily, to give our Brethren there the service of the Association and thereby make our contribution toward the coming of the Kingdom;
>
> Second, to attempt to make possible in a larger way than now obtains an outlet for the natural missionary spirit of our people here in America, and
>
> Third, and that which is doubtless the most difficult and remote, namely, to play a part in creating the sentiment on the part of Europeans who govern Africa which will be more liberal toward the Native people of the Continent and less suspicious of the motives of colored people from America who may be sent there as missionary representatives of our churches here.[45]

A second Yergan note reviewed Bull's February 18 letter and remarked that Jesse Jones had been sowing doubts "about Colored YMCA leadership in America" and had influenced at least one government official, resulting in "the legitimate missionary inspiration of our Student and City Associations [being] interfered with and its fulfillment . . . temporarily delayed by a man who has no commission whatever to represent them."[46]

The sympathetic West Virginia State College President Davis referenced a Du Boisian characterization of Jesse Jones as "the evil genius of the Negro race—a white man," scoring his action as "certainly an intensified program of suppression which the American white man is promoting. Think of Jones going to Africa interfering with the international rights of an American citizen."[47] Then Davis, incensed, as were several other Yergan familiars and correspondents, concluded with this stinging counterattack:

The immediate program of the Young Men's Christian Association as well as every thinking Negro is to dethrone Thomas Jesse Jones from his hold on so-called Negro leadership. This will discharge him from his influential position among white people. It is very clear that the white people will have no need for him when he ceases to be a dominating influence among Negroes. I shall be glad to convey to our students the point of your letter.[48]

In the same time frame Max received similarly sympathetic letters from other leaders.[49] With Aggrey in South Africa and Du Bois in the United States, Max's forces fought on two fronts. On May 3 Aggrey, giving a Booker T. Washingtonian talk to location Africans, found himself severely heckled "by a radical section of the audience." Meanwhile, a stream of letters and copies of correspondence flooded toward Du Bois from Max and his allies.[50]

The impasse finally broken in September, Yergan informed R. R. Moton of its end.[51] The Tuskegee principal offered his hearty congratulations; others soon followed suit.[52] After a stopover with Moorland, Max prepared to leave by late November, sailing out of New York, together with Susie and their five-month-old son, Frederick, on December 3.

With the combined strength of the Talented Tenth, individually and collectively, the decisive journalistic strength of Du Bois in *Crisis,* and the incessant behind-the-scenes lobbying of Aggrey, Max, the Black YMCA, and his backers claimed victory. It was the beginning of a new chapter in his life and in that of the movement to bring YMCAs to South Africa. Yergan would become the catalyst for these changes. In the rear, protecting his flanks, were scores of administrators and Black YMCA leaders, hundreds of college student branch members, and thousands of city association cadres. He returned to them again and again, by mail, by cable, in print, and in person to do what he felt they had sent him to accomplish, open a pioneer door of "Coloured" Y endeavor.

3

South Africa, Part I

On January 2, 1922, Max Yergan became the pioneer African-American YMCA secretary allowed into the Union of South Africa. The following fourteen years, the span of his missionary service, saw acute ferment within both himself and his mission field. The events he witnessed during his term occurred at a critical stage of the development of modern South Africa. His impressions of that time and place furthered his own political evolution. His gradual acquaintance with South Africa's social dilemma made Yergan view the world differently, convincing him to pursue social gospel theory to its logical secular conclusion.

Yergan's South African period must be divided into two segments, 1922–1928 and 1929–1936. This chapter treats the former time frame, while the succeeding one will deal with the latter.

Yergan's initial six years in South Africa were marked by four major developments: (1) his countrywide connection to the nascent African leadership stratum; (2) his central role in developing interracial work in local Black school and community branches of the YMCA and SCA; (3) his ascent within the YMCA, SCA, WSCF, SVM (Student Volunteer Movement), and allied institutions; and (4) his deepening consciousness as a diasporic African called to return to the land of his forebears.

Yergan brought to South Africa U.S. and colonial expertise in interracial work steeped in Washingtonian accommodationist "racial adjustment" and YMCA social gospel theory. Influenced as well by the philosophy of African Redemption, the stimulus for much of the "Back to Africa" ideology that shaped both Pan-Negroism and Pan-Africanism, he arrived prepared to devote several years to African service. Carefully constructing intricate social service strategies and becoming a fixture at well-attended public conferences, workshops, and classes at training schools, SCA or YMCA regional branches, and other learning institutions, he realized his dream, meeting black South Africa's leading lights, from families surnamed Jabavu, Bokwe, Dube, Soga, Matthews, Luthuli, and Xuma. These most advanced exemplars of modernity also held keys to doors opening to the past; most were but a generation away from rural lives they were taught to disdain as "heathen."

The Gift of Prophecy

The Eastern Cape village of Alice, where Fort Hare Native College was situated, was the community the Yergan clan chose to make their domicile between 1924 and 1936. It bore the banners of two parallel, alternately competing and intersecting prophetic spiritual traditions. The first was an autochthonous brand of revelatory wisdom, built upon men, women, and youths seeking guidance in dreams and visions and answering "calls"—supernatural signs of inspiration—providing direction for earthly behavior. These practices gave rise to a long line of indigenous avatars from Nxele and Ntsikana to the dramatic and apocalyptic sequence of events annunciated by prophetess Nongqawuse. The second was the arrival of overseas-based biblical emissaries of Christianity, beginning in the late eighteenth century and contributing to a period of unprecedented sociocultural change. In aligning himself with the latter trend Yergan also had to come to terms with the former.

The Eastern Cape province generally and its Ciskei district in particular produced legends of prophetic revelation that predated, initially competed with, and eventually absorbed, assimilated, and incorporated Christianity. So it was that a lustrous line of isiXhosa-speaking seers—Nxele, Mlanjeni, and Nongqawuse—articulated with early Christian converts like Ntsikana, legendary composer of hymns fusing sonorous isiXhosa praise songs with faith in the Christian God, some of which hymns survive to the present in John Knox Bokwe's *Ntsikana's Great Hymn* and *Ntsikana's Bell*. While cleavages arose pitting converts against conservatives, producing antinomies between "school" and "blanket" or "red" people, by the twentieth century several generations of Eastern Cape dwellers had become both Christianized and isiXhosa speaking (like their isiZulu-speaking counterparts in Natal or their Sesotho-speaking coreligionists in the High Veld). In literal and figurative lineages *amaqoboka* (converts) claimed spiritual descent from Ntsikana and his latter-day devotees, Tiyo Soga (1829–1871) and John Knox Bokwe (1855–1922). At virtually the same time when George Williams founded the YMCA in London, his countryman, William Govan, headmaster of Lovedale Seminary in Alice, Ciskei, a Free Church of Scotland institution, afforded every denomination access. Using a written examination he opened up two student vacancies, one filled by Tiyo Soga, son of Nosutu and "old Soga," who earlier attended Tyume Mission eight miles away but now became a Lovedalian. Upon his graduation, the memorably scholarly pioneer African Christian Soga studied in Scotland, marrying Janet Burnside to found a Presbyterian dynasty whose descendants gained prominence in South African letters. Max Yergan met one, Alan Soga. These transformations came as isiXhosa-speakers encountered mission-based Christianity.

The Legacy of the Mission

During the first half of the nineteenth century, Christian missionary influence and the drafting of a nonracial constitution in 1853 brought about a limited albeit substantial franchise among mission-educated Africans in the Cape province. This advance stood in striking contrast to the racially exclusionary policies of the "Boer Republics" and Natal. The Cape franchise in turn gave rise to a stratum of mission-trained Africans, or "school people," as many came to call them. Designated variously as *amaqoboka*[1] or *amakholwa*,[2] they often appeared to threaten the so-called red or blanket people, Xhosa traditionalists cleaving to pre-Christian cultural practices, principally rural-based but also migrants in towns.

School people felt mixed emotions regarding the Christianity that provided them with educations and livelihoods, yet restrained them from acting upon their own authority. *Kholwa* (converts) could face opposition from hierarchs heading the denominations they had joined. Where folkways and customary beliefs and values of the converts' aboriginal communities contravened mission and church teachings, conflicts arose. Even so, by the last quarter of the nineteenth century, mission-educated Africans, securing jobs in government, law, commerce, teaching, journalism, and printing, began freeing themselves from both missions and chiefs to act as religious, social, or political leaders in their own right. In ways Yergan recognized from his post–Civil War South, the ascendant educated stratum behaved as a *class in itself*.

The new African leadership—educators, ministers, and other Black and mixed-race (i.e., "Coloured") professionals—was most prominent in groupings established within the 1870s and 1880s especially in the Eastern and Western Cape, respectively. African organizations in this period, while often reflecting the ethnic predilections of their historical chiefs and elders, increasingly advocated a "nontribal" African consciousness. Even so, race, "tribe," and clan complicated realization of this goal. Although the recent history of wars of dispossession made the most advanced African leaders urge the pursuit of common goals, "tribal" affiliation was reinforced both within local communities and by a government alive to the potential power of the rising Western-educated Nonwhite stratum. Thus Zulu speakers, descendants of the great martial tradition of Shaka and Dingane, were at once lauded for prior military prowess and blocked in subsequent attempts to revive it.

Even more daunting was the Mineral Revolution, ushered in by discoveries of gold and diamonds between 1866 and 1886. Concurrently, the quelling of African primary (military) resistance and a rise of competing nationalisms, White and Nonwhite (i.e., Black, Asian, and "Coloured"), led to a complex and confrontative political landscape. Faced with the emergent force of the educated elite of the Nonwhite majority, expressed in nascent political organizations, propaganda, and the vote, conservative Whites, within and without government, explored even stricter methods to curb a rising tide of Black assertion.

By the turn of the twentieth century, the South African War (1899–1902) an Act of Union (1909), and a subsequent Natives Land Act (1911) made clear that African ambitions to participate in a nonracial political process would not be realized. This catalyzed a fresh territorial initiative, influenced to some degree by African-American precedents, but mostly home grown. Fired by the Land Act, luminaries of hoary "red" and novel "school" elites gathered inside Bloemfontein in 1912 to found a countrywide Native National Congress. Many who mounted that campaign were among those welcoming Yergan to South Africa. As they met, the transatlantic trajectories of their respective social formations converged. In the interwar era Yergan made his mark upon South Africa, Europe, and the United States.

African-American Influence in South Africa

African-Americans played a major part in helping to stimulate Black South African consciousness. Their influences took many forms. Exceptionally significant was the role of Afro-American missionaries associated with various Black-dominated Christian church movements, chiefly those within the African Methodist Episcopal tradition, whose zeal to broaden its base encouraged AMEs to provide support to the inchoate separatist Zionist and Ethiopianist Churches arising during the final two decades of the nineteenth century.[3]

AME interest in South Africa was part of a larger African-American thrust of missionary outreach for Africans. James Mata Dwane, leading a secessionist Ethiopian Church of South Africa, enjoyed a brief association with the AME during the late 1890s. Eventually Dwane's concern about American control over finances won out over his desire for linkage with the overseas church.[4] Dwane's curiosity and race pride were piqued by a whirlwind six-week 1898 tour taken by Bishop Henry McNeal Turner, who, in unprecedented mass baptisms and ordinations, left a legacy of Black affection and White opprobrium that was reenacted whenever Negro American clerics sought official sanction to enter the country.[5]

In 1904, for example, the General Missionary Conference of South Africa set forth the opinion that "Ethiopianism is largely a misdirected use of [the] newborn energy of [the Africans]." It also accused the Ethiopianist and AME members of displaying "an utter disregard for the principles of Christian comity."[6] F. B. Bridgman, a Johannesburg-based member of the American Board of Commissioners of Foreign Missions, was one of the participants. He was instrumental in determining Yergan's fitness for South African service. By 1916, fear of AME fury had been augmented by even greater anxiety about the Garvey movement. But even more disconcerting for government as a whole was working-class insurgency. This included both white and black labor and brought with it the specter of Bolshevism. Like AME church leaders, Black American representatives of the Baptist Church were also closely scrutinized. North American "Colored" YMCA secretaries had ties to both.[7] Yergan knew from representatives of these churches about government opposition to Negroes.

The Aftermath of World War One

Following the European armistice, Prime Minister Jan Christiaan Smuts pursued policies geared to counter labor shortages, particularly in mines but also in cities. Smuts sought to induce Nonwhite males populating outlying rural districts to move into urban areas to serve industry. The measures taken to achieve this goal, however, were involuntary, effected by coercive legislation alienating thousands from their land, effectively disenfranchising, residentially segregating, and occupationally ghettoizing Africans, who were also subjected to a pass system. The besieged populations resorted to radical activism in response to these oppressive stimuli.

The world war brought with it an uneasy truce between managers and workers. Yet postwar renewal of trade union activity among Whites, and unprecedented levels of Nonwhite involvement in politics and in campaigns to reduce wage discrimination fueled major incidents featuring civil disobedience. Drawing some inspiration from Gandhi's passive resistance endeavor of 1906–1913 and supported, in theory, by a few influential White spokesmen of the new International Socialist League, African laborers led several strikes challenging discriminatory pay and unfair working conditions.

Black sanitation workers laid down their tools in 1918. That year the women's section of the Native National Congress, led by Charlotte Manye Maxeke, threatened antipass action, protesting extension of the "influx control" system to African women.[8] A Black proletarian landmark was achieved in 1919, with the pathbreaking appearance of the Industrial and Commercial Workers' Union (ICU), founded by Clements Kadalie, a Nyasaland-born clerk. A pioneer labor combination in sub-Saharan Africa, the ICU led a series of job actions on behalf of African miners. By 1920, police brutally put down one such African mine strike. During the next two years, two African communities, the Israelites (1921) and the Bondelswarts (1922), suffered severe state violence. This level of social strife greeted Yergan on arrival.

Max Yergan arrived in South Africa on January 2, 1922, together with his spouse, Susie Wiseman, and their son, Frederick. They were met at the Cape Town wharf by Oswin Boys Bull, head of the South African YMCA, and African Methodist Episcopal Church bishop William Tecumseh Vernon. This welcoming party exemplified the multiple worlds into which the Yergan family had entered. Bull, Yergan's supervisor, represented the largely segregated YMCA, with its English and Afrikaner subdivisions, while Vernon spiritually bridged the African masses and the literate "school people" who made up an elite intellectual stratum. The two overlapped in their connections to the missionary and political establishments.

By February, Yergan's coming had been announced in *The Intercollegian*. In March he told J. E. Moorland that after "several conferences with the South African Student Christian Association," he had been asked to act as secretary for work in "native and Coloured institutions." The job required extensive travel, and he embarked upon his first journey, in the Eastern Cape, on March 4. This trip took him as far east as Transkei and introduced him to the Native Affairs Commission. While Susie and Frederick stayed behind in Woodstock in Cape Town, Yergan was on his way in his challenging, largely unknown new field.

Yergan's trekking is documented well enough to reveal the similarities between his life as a traveling secretary in America's Southwest and his travels in South Africa's rugged conditions of unpaved roads that required resort to lorries, horses, and a bevy of beast-borne conveyances. Letters hint at hitchhiking and walking, but he probably also relied on ox-drawn carts and wagons, along with the more luxurious but not always available or fully reliable motorcars. There is no hint, however, of how often he may have become stranded or even passed up by unfeeling or resentful observers. This scenario is rarely described in any detail in his correspondence or annual reports but can be inferred from photographs taken by himself and colleagues during the interwar era.

The Yergans arrived against the backdrop of one of the meanest episodes of industrial action in South African history, the mine strike called the "Rand Revolt." Covered extensively in local newspapers, this fierce combat among labor, capital, and the state profoundly impressed South Africa's residents and sojourners alike. Johannesburg-based ABCFM missionary Frederick Bridgman captured the drama of the moment in a letter to a Boston colleague:

> Last week the whites on every Transvaal coal mine went on strike. This morning the 24,000 whites on the Rand's sixty miles of gold mines went out. This throws about 200,000 natives into enforced idleness. As these natives are so far removed from home, they cannot be let loose on the community, so they must be kept in the compounds and be fed by the mine owners, so this first week of the strike the natives will cost the mines £200,000, with nothing produced to show for it. The outlook is

most serious. We shall be fortunate if industrial strife does not drive us into civil war.[9]

Starting the week the Yergans arrived in South Africa, the Rand strike framed their vision of what the country faced in the economic, social, and cultural spheres. While Max and his family searched for adequate accommodations, headlines detailing the industrial action were unavoidable. For the next two months white mine labor and their managers faced off in ferocious daily battles frequently marked by bloodshed. Africans were caught in the middle, subject to attacks from both labor and the state. In mid-March, Bridgman brought his stateside office up to date, this time focusing on an understudied dimension of the largely white job action, its effect on Africans. Querying, "But what of the Natives, especially the 300,000 [total African workers] here on the Rand?" he repeated his earlier depiction of a now 180,000 Non-white mine workers as enduring "enforced idleness," this time amplifying the problem by underlining the words. Then Bridgman asked,

> How have they behaved? The testimony of White Johannesburg is that all natives have conducted themselves in a *most exemplary manner*. They have suffered many losses and hardships from the strike, but they have kept aloof from the quarrel, have been patient and law abiding to a degree. Even when some of them were wantonly set upon and killed, yet the natives though deeply stirred and though they had it in their power to wipe out the entire white population, still they curbed their promptings for revenge. But the blacks have had another ugly revelation of the savagery of which the whites are capable. An object lesson which will bear horrid fruit some day, even as the four or five outbursts of the "superior race" since we came to Johannesburg have left a deplorable impression on native mind and character.[10]

Bridgman's dire prediction was no exaggeration. It was echoed in the initial report Yergan filed following his first year in-country. In a reflective memo he wrote home,

> In the gold mining industry it had become uneconomic for some of the mines to work on the basis of pay which white miners had drawn since the early days of the war when they took advantage of the situation to press and achieve their demands. Early in 1922 the mine owners

resolved to remedy the situation by two methods: (1) to utilize more black workers (they are hired cheaper) for semi-skilled positions; and (2) ultimately to reduce the pay of whites. One can appreciate the fear of loss of work and pay on the part of white workers (though it was fairly clear that those laid off, if any, would be absorbed in other branches, and though their pay, the highest in the world for labor, could stand reduction, in fairness). Well, the white miners went out on strike, the nearly 200,000 Natives remaining at work. The strike led to open rebellion and finally to what has been termed "the revolution." For remaining at their posts Native workers were fired upon by whites. For weeks this thing dragged on. At a meeting of strikers the government was repudiated and a declaration for its overthrow and the substitution of a republic carried. Representatives of the police, mine officials, and citizens were fired upon. It was war. Government troops were called, martial law declared and steps taken to quell the rebellion. Here are the results: Government troops called out: 19,924; government troops killed: 61; wounded: 199. On the other side and including peaceful citizens who had the misfortune to get shot during the operations, 138 were killed and 287 wounded. 31 Natives were killed and 67 wounded. Total casualties 783!! Sounds like war doesn't it?[11]

Clearly sympathetic with the African majority, Yergan was not yet fully supportive of militant labor when it confronted agents of the state and the Chamber of Mines. An extension of his view toward labor in general, this attitude was informed chiefly by the nonantagonistic stance of Washingtonian accommodation. A cardinal rule in "racial adjustment" strategy, this conservative cautiousness helped define Yergan early on.

African YMCA Work in South Africa

It would be difficult to overestimate the magnitude of the task that lay before Max Yergan. Although South Africa had been a site of YMCA branch work since 1865 when Andrew Murray founded the first Cape Town association, little attention was given to extending the movement to the majority of indigenes spread across the length and breadth of the countryside and swarming in steady streams into the urban areas, Johannesburg on the Great Gold Reef of the Rand chief among them.

At its outset the YMCA, while imported from England, was dominated by Afrikaners. For them the struggle for control over their own institutions with the Anglophone settlers and government functionaries who ruled over them was almost as immediate and intense as had been their competition with the Africans who had preceded them in peopling South Africa's lengthy, lavish, frequently lush landscape. Patterns of informal and formal racial exclusion toward Nonwhites practiced by both Afrikaans and English speakers only served to further complicate the growth of YMCAs among the nation's Black and Coloured communities.

Although there are isolated references to YMCA-type activity among non-Europeans in South Africa during the nineteenth century (including an indeterminate number of associations in Basutoland), these are sporadic and rare. Not until the much acclaimed 1896 world tour of Donald Fraser and Luther Deloraine Wishard heralding formation of the World Student Christian Federation did this alter, and then only haltingly. Wishard, an American, and Fraser, a Scot, included in their South African stops the University of Stellenbosch near Cape Town and the premier African training facility, Lovedale Institute in Alice in the Eastern Cape, thereby setting the stage for a racially separate "Bantu" or "Native," i.e., Nonwhite, Student Christian Association section. Later Fraser wrote John Mott,

> The most serious problem before the Executive will be the position of Associations in Kaffir institutions. The feeling of a great separation between these Kaf[f]ir students and the Whites naturally and most reasonably exists. I say this as a missionary and advocate of native rights. Most of the Kaf[f]ir students were themselves, a few years ago, savages, dressed with nothing but red clay and a piece of string. The intellectual and social gulf that must therefore separate them for a generation or two is necessary. There is yet little affinity of thought and ambition between the two races. The problems of the two types of institutions are poles apart—at least in the kind, and in the methods of solution. The position of the Kaf[f]ir is wholly different from that of an Asiatic. I give this as my mature judgment. After a close inspection of both classes, I think that the missionaries and certainly all the students, will agree with me. But the Kaf[f]ir field is a great and almost untouched one.[12]

Fraser went on to inform Mott that out of the five or six institutions he visited, he was only able to do organizing in two. Though he did not name them, he had in mind Presbyterian Lovedale and the Wesleyan-run Healdtown. What impressed Fraser was the size of the half-dozen Native schools he saw, which each had "a much larger population than most of the White colleges."[13] He omitted dozens.

The problem Fraser described remained largely unaddressed until a decade later when John Mott, head of the YMCA, and his English colleague, Ruth Rouse, both leaders of the WSCF, toured South Africa from April through June 1906.[14] During the visit Mott held special meetings at Lovedale where he urged White SCA colleagues to address the problem of association work among Africans. Mott had been invited annually since 1898 to the only field he had not visited. By June he had seen, among other places, Cape Town, Stellenbosch, Paarl, Wellington, Grahamstown, Lovedale, Bloemfontein, Johannesburg, Pretoria, Pietermaritzburg, and Durban.[15]

In his chronicle of the journey Mott noted that "the claims of the native African students naturally commanded our attention." The Mott-Rouse delegation visited three African institutions, Lovedale being the most significant. Healdtown sent some fifty souls to a gathering of Lovedale's 600-strong student body. In two days of revival meetings, "150 African students indicated their desire and purpose to accept Christ as their Saviou[r] and Lord," some fifty-seven from Healdtown and Lovedale declaring willingness to become "ministers, evangelists, catechists and teachers."[16] On the basis of the meetings and conferences held with missionaries, a decision was made to "extend the Student Movement to the native colleges and schools of South Africa." The aim was to send a secretary in order to undertake this work "in the not too distant future." Arguing that "Africa can never be evangelized by white men alone or chiefly," Mott contended that key to this effort was "native Christian agency."[17]

Mott's visit was memorable for the many African converts attending it, some witnesses crediting it with changing their lives. In his first year Max Yergan wrote,

> In reference to the visit you and Mrs. Mott made to South Africa in 1906, I am sure you will be interested in learning that among the most helpful and dependable native African friends I have is one Mr. Njokwene, instructor at Healdtown Institute, Fort Beaufort, South Africa, and vice-president of the Native Teacher's Association of the Cape Colony. He is one of those men one can never forget, being more than six

feet tall and having a voice equally as commanding as his height. His personality is one which makes a favorable impression upon almost any one. When I asked him, a few days ago, when he acquired his deep interest in the religious life of students, he informed me that it was during a visit which you made to his institution during your visit to South Africa, at which time he was a student.[18]

The person ultimately chosen to fulfill Mott's wish was Oswin Boys Bull, a Cambridge graduate with Canadian experience, sent out in 1906 following tours of several historically Black colleges in the United States. By early 1908, after staying in Natal during Christmastide, Bull wrote Mott of his frustrations in the new field:

Something must be done to counteract the ignorant and unreasoning prejudice against missionary work that is almost universal in this Colony. I was prepared for something bad, but it is far worse than I had expected. The whole question of the relation of the white and black races is, as you know, the problem above all others in Natal, and with no one in the country worthy of being considered to be a statesman, and this strong prejudice in addition, the prospects are not exactly promising. I doubt if the world contains a more intricate or difficult problem, but we ought to be able to make a valuable contribution towards its solution.[19]

Nominated as general secretary, Bull soon realized the magnitude of the task before him. By 1915, actively searching for an African traveling secretary, Bull acted upon unanimous recommendations of missionaries across the Eastern Cape when he selected the popular Xhosa-speaking journalist, evangelist, and composer, John Knox Bokwe (1855–1922). Bokwe was not merely a subject of history; he was history. A spokesman for his people, he was among the second generation of converts to Christianity. When he practiced composition he paid homage to revered 1815 Xhosa convert and choral master Chief Ntsikana (Sicana) Gaba. Already a sexagenarian when he began, Bokwe was a volunteer escort for Bull on his tour in 1915 and worked for him in a formal capacity from 1916 through 1920, when forced to retire for health reasons.

In South Africa Yergan projected himself as an author, speaker, and organizer. Here the African-American was in every sense a pioneer, bending and breaking the color barrier. Yergan's nascent writing career flourished within YMCA-affiliated print media both locally and internationally. These aptly mirrored his growth as a critical commentator on Christian-dominated South Africa—its proud peoples and their profound range of problems.

In February 1922 *The Intercollegian* told readers of Yergan's South African mission.[20] In the same month he let his American associates know his ideas about labor issues facing African miners and efforts at improvement by union organizing and protest:

> The most interesting and significant development in the life of the African workers has been what is called the "ICU," the Industrial and Commercial Union. This is a sort of inclusive trades union which has been developed to a remarkable degree by an African of Nyasaland, Mr. Clements Kadalie. In spite of many difficulties, he has achieved something worthwhile and his work marks the beginning of organization among African workers. I do not agree with all of his methods, and I certainly do not countenance all of his utterances but I do give him credit for having dared and partly succeeded in a field of great need and opportunity.[21]

In April, AME bishop Vernon joined the chorus of print voices welcoming Max to South Africa. Praising Yergan's selection as a triumph of liberal enlightenment supporting the "uplift" of "the native and colored people of South Africa," Vernon declared that "this courageous and humanitarian element has opened up a new avenue of progress, which can be a means of social regeneration for our people so long in need of such opportunity and aid. God is moving in the hearts of men." Writing to the AME membership, he continued:

> He will study the field, plan and direct this new movement for the betterment of native and colored men. The Young Men's Christian Association of America, through him, will bless our brethren here. All honor to them! We welcome this reenforcement. All these forces mentioned, with kindred agencies, will contribute their share in accelerating the coming of a new and necessary vision for Africa's sons, and bring to them the correct and just estimate of their relation and duty to their fellow men and to God. When this larger day comes, our spirits will have joined the silent muster roll beyond this life's hour. What matters it? The price we pay in money, sacrifice, hardship and even death, will be

small when compared with the returns in souls unfettered, in manhood and womanhood redeemed.[22]

Seven months into his stay Yergan reintroduced himself to readers of *Association Men* with is essay "The Negro in Africa—No Answer but God." Four years after his first portrait there in World War One he assessed the situation of Black South African youth in an article comparing and contrasting them with their American Negro counterparts. In diasporic voice he stated,

> The task confronting the young African student is infinitely larger and more difficult than that which faces us at home. Left to himself he might ultimately work it out along his own lines and with satisfaction to himself, but the fact he faces is an order of life not born of his own mind, and whether he will or no he must become a part of this order. He enters it with enthusiasm, but it is a hard row he has to hoe for there is a great mass to be lifted and carried—of ignorance, superstition, and poverty; a dead weight which will pull him back unless he has sterner stuff than many of us possess. It has been a great joy to me to find many of my black brothers possessing this sterner stuff and I believe they wish me to say to you that they are "climbing."[23]

In his eighth month Max graced the pages of *Manhood: Organ of the Cape Town YMCA* with a historically grounded sermonette titled "On the YMCA in North America." Introducing his South African readers to the history of the Y in the United States, he summarized its position as of 1922, described its key role in the recent world war, and devoted considerable space to comparing Black America and South Africa. Of the former he stressed the need for interracial cooperation and the salutary influence of gifts from financier Julius Rosenwald in constructing YMCA buildings in urban areas to promote "an era of interracial goodwill."[24]

Countrywide Connection to the Nascent African Leadership Stratum

Yergan's first year in South Africa had introduced him to most of the major leaders among the school people. Starting with his Teacher's Christian Association colleague, Y predecessor, and all-around guide, D. D. T. Jabavu, Max met Native National Congress (NNC) foundation member John Langalibalele Dube, Xhosa specialist A. K. Soga, and scores of instructors in the Native training institutions in the Ciskei and Transkei regions of the Eastern Cape, and the historic Zulu lands of Natal, where the string of schools founded by the American Board held sway.

The Jabavu-Yergan relationship deserves more serious attention than it has received thus far. Catharine Higgs, Jabavu's otherwise able biographer, essentially dismisses it. Yet there are clear indications that their friendship was of extreme importance to both men and, though there were apparently interpersonal tensions between them, their wives as well. The crux of the conflict and, when it worked, the comity, was their connection to America. Jabavu, like the generation of South Africa "been-to's" who were educated abroad, had in a very real sense been shaped by his American and English academic and social experiences. But of the two influences, there seems to have been something unique about his American exposure. Jabavu found familiarity made manifest in the Yergans as they at times perceived in him a kindred spirit, if not temperamentally than perhaps situationally, for he had analyzed life in America and examined the historically Black colleges and their products as closely as they had. Both men perfected affectations of British bourgeois mannerisms while reveling in "cullud" culture. And they reciprocally referred to one another singly as "brother." Moreover, they shared something even deeper, the practice of each naming a child as a tribute to the other.

On January 12, 1923, Susie gave birth to their second son, Max. In time, Yergan referred to him as Max Jabavu. Jabavu's own son, born in 1928, was christened Tengo Max. There was nothing coincidental or accidental about this juxtaposition of male appellations. Names are too important to be arrived at arbitrarily, whether in Africa or Black America. Whatever happened or did not happen later between these two families, at one point they showed the most profound and intimate connection with one another, a spiritual bonding.

Developing Interracial Work in Local Black School and Community Branches

Toward the end of 1923, Yergan took interracial work to unprecedented levels. In September he attended a gathering in Johannesburg where forty African men ("chiefs, ministers, teachers, farmers") and association personnel met an equal number of Whites in whose ranks he counted "archbishops, presidents and moderators of the religious denominations, also business, educational and professional men." There he was struck by what he saw as a "spirit of fairness and moderation," and he said as much to his mentor, Howard's Jesse Moorland, who in turn relayed it to the student body.[25]

The next month, following appearances at Tiger Kloof in the Northern Cape and Mochudi in Bechuanaland,[26] he visited Natal University College in Pietermaritzburg, thereby breaking the color barrier. Speaking directly to his audience's primal racial fears, he told students and faculty at this Whites-only institution that they had heard of the Black problem and that now he stood before them, representing the Black problem in human form.[27] Then he traveled to Rustoord (now also Rusoord) in Somerset Strand for a November weekend conference. In a widely circulated SCA publication, an observer described Max's appearance in this way:

> It was a wonderful meeting. Mr Yergan is a man who simply radiates from him the spirit of Christ. It was not so much what he said, as the spirit in which he said it, that moved us very deeply indeed, and made us feel, perhaps more strongly than ever before, our real and great responsibility to the great black races in this country. Mr Yergan pointed out that the native is *thinking*—it is for us to direct his thought into the right channels and make it *Christian* thought. Fortunately the bitterness of many natives against the whites has been changed by the knowledge that many of the white people are in sympathy with them—this was especially so at a recent church conference at Johannesburg. We ought to seek to know the black people, said Mr Yergan, to visit their institutions and learn what their ideals are. They are, he said, very patient and very easily satisfied. The keynote of the whole meeting was the word, "good will," and the prayers which followed showed a very sincere desire to fight down race prejudice, that we all may be one in God, who made us all.[28]

Having made his way through all four provinces and Bechuanaland, he then went to Basutoland.

A second year took the African-American missionary even further afield as Yergan saw Basutoland's Morija Training Institution at least twice, in 1923 and 1925. The earliest recorded references to Max's presence within the mountain kingdom dated from November 1923, when he was mentioned in the Thabeng Normal School[29] vernacular Sesotho house organ, *Leselinyana la Lesotho*. Then Yergan guided visiting Swiss guests M. and Mme. Henry-Louis Henriod of the World Student Christian Federation across what some call the "Switzerland of Africa."

Founded by the Paris Evangelical Mission, Morija afforded Yergan an opportunity to share his messages of uplift, Christianity, and cooperation with Basotho youth, students, and community members. Max and Henriod spoke or preached at Morija Bible School, the Progressive Association of Lesotho (Morija Branch), Thabeng School, and Morija Church. Yergan's subjects included temperance, patience, hard work, and an active belief in Jesus. A Morija Bible School talk, after Henriod, treated slavery. *Leselinyana* recalled it this way:

> As I am standing here I feel at home. I do not feel this way because of the resemblance of Lesotho to Switzerland, the country of origin of Mr. Henriod, in its topography. But what reminds me of home is seeing you and I find you are black as I am. It is now three hundred years that my grandfathers were taken to America as slaves. They left Africa by being sold. I mean they were sold just as one could sell his cow. When a husband was sold to a client going to Mechachane [to the north] the wife would be sold to a client at Quthing [in the south] and the child to a client at Qacha's Nek [in the southeast mountains], one to one place and the other to a different one. There were whites who saw this trade in human beings from Africa to America as a great commercial advantage. For two hundred years these slaves were leading a heavy and painful life.[30]

Leselinyana went further as Yergan cited God as a remedy to the slave's dilemma.

To the Progressive Association, a farming cooperative, Yergan delineated a five-point prescription for progress: food, domestic hygiene, education, thrift, and what he termed "the fullness of personality."[31] The quartet of agrarian themes was borrowed directly from Booker T. Washington's *Up from Slavery*. The reference to "personality" appears to be Yergan's innovation, a device often employed exegetically.

On November 11, Yergan stood in the pulpit of Morija Church. Max's text was Luke 19 on Zaccheus, commander of the tax collectors.

Aiming to show the universal redemptive power of Christ, *Leselinyana* had Yergan speaking these words:

> There are people who seek to procure certain things for the sake of hav-
> ing them and not with an intention of saving them but to destroy them.
> Herod once did the same. He looked for children not to save but to
> destroy them. There were some whites, who have looked for and are
> still looking for new countries, not looking for these countries to save
> their citizens but only to make a living for themselves and to oppress
> the citizens of other countries. It had been so in my nation three hun-
> dred years ago. Whites came to Africa and caught some black people,
> took and sold them as slaves in America, the slaves of whom I am a
> descendant. In those three hundred years these slaves toiled without any
> remuneration or salary.[32]

Yergan's panacea for this oppression was God's grace, which he felt
helped slaves learn manual trades, attain educations, and do the hard
work that allowed them to improve their situations, individually and collectively. In a style generously mixing parables, proverbs, anecdotes, and
scripture, he drew upon recent and past history and contemporary social
movements like temperance, counseling patience, piety, resilience, humility, and mindfulness in service to God and humanity as paths to glory.

Founding a Basutoland Native SCA chapter, Max would return to
see it in 1925.

Leselinyana saw Yergan's tour as successful. One may wonder what
this meant. Lacking the language skills that would enable him to speak
directly to his audiences, Max had to rely upon intermediaries. Only a
handful of his hearers could have comprehended his speech. Yet Negro
American missionaries were not wholly unknown in Basutoland;[33] subaltern references would have resonated with them.[34] Between the symbolism of his American background and his own attempts to build support for himself as a "returned African," Yergan represented with some
skill his overseas people, their diasporic lived experience, and their historical connections to Africa.

Combined with the imprimatur of Christianity and the permanence
of print, Max's personality left tracks in the soil of the mountains of the
"Rooftop of Africa" that remain visible. Overcoming barriers of language and the mediation of interpreters, not to mention the watchful eyes
of White missionaries and government officials who were terrified by the

specters of Marcus Garvey and Ethiopianist nationalism, he made a mark that reveals the power of the presence of an evangelical pan-African personality. In an insular environment among a particularistic people, Yergan told stories that could not have appeared more remote but that left space for him to return. Against all odds, he saved a place for himself and his saga in oral tradition, the heroic poetry, or *lithoko,* of the Basotho.[35]

Yergan's Basutoland adventure paid clear dividends. It permitted him to forge bonds with Henriod, which increased his influence, now reaching toward the higher circles of the World Student Christian Federation, and it also enabled him to connect with the land and people of another place whose lives and customs were both intertwined with and yet distinct from those of the mass of Africans living and working in the Union. Reciprocating some of the hospitality they had experienced, during the Christmas vacation Susie and Max hosted Reverend and Mrs. Casalis of the Paris Evangelical Mission, the order that ran Morija.[36] By late February Cape Town YMCA Secretary Bull wrote E. C. Jenkins, "Yergan is doing excellent work and making splendid impressions—and the passing of time only serves to make more clear how sound—(I almost said 'white') he is all through."[37] It may have been early to note a Freudian slip, but Bull made one. No wonder it proved so prudent for Bull to encourage Mott to pay Yergan's way from Cape Town to Europe to attend a series of international meetings the following year.

In January 1923 Max had participated in the third national conference of the ICU (Industrial and Commercial Workers Union of South Africa), in April he published "The Native Students of South Africa and Their Problems" in *The Student World,*[38] a vehicle of the World Student Christian Federation, in August and September he met and chaperoned WSCF luminary Henry-Louis Henriod across South Africa and far into historic Basutoland, and throughout the year he had been written up regularly in *Imvo Zabantsundu* ("African Opinion") the King William's Town newspaper founded by John Tengo Jabavu. *Imvo* provided a running commentary of Yergan's feats.

Ascent within the YMCA, SCA, WSCF, SVM, and Allied Institutions

In 1924 Yergan entered the ecumenical speaking circuit, attending major overseas conferences in Swanwick and High Leigh,[39] England,

Saarow, Germany, and Holland. Along with his growing family he had also moved from Cape Town to the Alice, Ciskei, campus of Fort Hare Native College in the Eastern Cape. In early February O. B. Bull asked E. C. Jenkins if the Y's National Council would fund Yergan's attendance at the August WSCF meeting in High Leigh, England.[40]

The next two months found Yergan the focus of laudatory articles in *Imvo Zabantsundu*.[41] By mid-April he was elected to the WSCF Executive Committee. Later that month Bull thanked Mott for letting Max attend the High Leigh conference, adding that "Yergan is doing really well." Bull felt that Max possessed "the gift supremely needed in South Africa, a far-seeing patience," a phrase in the letter that Mott underlined. Bull went on, asserting that "even the most stand-offish soon find him out for the charming fellow he is. He is creating some new precedents in addressing audiences of students in the European colleges."[42] June found Thomas Jesse Jones and J. E. K. Aggrey returning to South Africa for their second Phelps Stokes tour.

During September Yergan brought Fort Hare principal Alexander Kerr up to date on his participation in recent Holland, Swanwick, and High Leigh conferences:

> On the day of our arrival we went to Holland to attend the student conference and from Holland went to Swanwick. After Swanwick he went to the General Committee Meeting at High Leigh. The student conferences were of immense interest and help to me, but the General Committee meeting was of far more significance. It is significant in the first place in that it had two Negroes as members, the other being a woman representative of the Negro section of the student movement in America. In the second place a precedent was established in electing me as a member of the executive committee of the [WSC] Federation, thereby giving Negro students in America and Africa as well (for I think it was on the strength of my African connection that I was elected to the executive committee) a larger share in the full life of the whole student movement.[43]

The High Leigh conference precipitated another at Le Zoute, Belgium, that sparked the inauguration of the International Institute of African Languages and Cultures.[44] Yergan's contributions to this conference were noted by an Aggrey biographer.[45]

Midway through 1925, Yergan claimed not to have lost any of the inspiration that led him to the Southern African subcontinent. In fact, he seemed to overflow with new projects and dreams, proudly telling Moorland that he still retained "a head full of plans and ideas." Chief among these stood the vision of a structure on the Fort Hare campus that would take advantage of the ethnic and religious diversity of the college, which he felt was "the one seat of learning for Africans South of the Equator which has already some of the marks of university rank and which will without doubt be the recognized African University for the entire sub-continent." Adopting the practical logic of his prior sociological training, he proposed grooming future African leaders using a scheme with "three or four" major components:

a. We want to weld together these members of the great Bantu section of African peoples (roughly speaking, all the peoples South of a line running irregularly across Africa North and South of the Equator belong to this family) by helping to give to their leaders common ideals of service

b. Under conditions of increasing secularization of education we want to contribute towards the very much needed spiritual foundation of the people.

c. We want to have a share in making possible a Social Vision for each student, and

d. We wish to demonstrate among the heathen masses for the benefit of the students, what may be done along lines of social improvement.[46]

After having surveyed the length and breadth of the Union Max determined that what he and association work needed most was a structure that could house a new research institute for African social service workers on Fort Hare's campus:

This building will make each one of the above desires directly possible, for it will serve as the common rallying point for the entire college, thus breaking over tribal, denominational and all other walls of separation. It will also be a community building—a sort of human laboratory, if you please, for experimenting and discovering, for the observation and instruction of students as well as the Christianization and social improvement of the masses of needy people in the neighbourhood of the college. The building would also serve as national headquarters for our movement and give us facilities for a much needed literature depot where we can become the distributing center for the much needed printed page among our people. The building will cost at most $20,000 with I suppose another $1000 for a movie machine and extra equipment. We may have to wait until my return from furlough before we see this building erected, but we need it, we want it, and I believe God is going to give it to us.[47]

In 1925 Max traveled extensively in Natal[48] and the Transkei, detailing his reflections to his Colored Work Department mentor, Howard University dean of men Jesse E. Moorland. The Yergan-Moorland correspondence captures Max's mind eloquently and candidly at that historical juncture. In July he taught in the All Saints Mission Winter School for Natives and attended the SCA's Pretoria General Conference, in August speaking to the Cape Teachers Association on "The Art of Living."

The SCA Native Department held its first conference at Inanda Seminary February 26–28, 1926. Sixty-one student delegates attended from Amanzimtoti (Adams College), Edendale, Mariannhill, Ohlange, St. Chad's, Umpumulo, and the host institution. Zululand's Archdeacon Lee convened, tackling the topic of "The Spiritual Life, the Basis of Service." J. Sandstrom, J. Dexter Taylor and John Dube spoke on social service, and O. B. Bull spoke on the Student Christian Movement (SCM) and WSCF, while the American Board's H. A. Stick led Bible study. African educators also figured:

> Another gratifying feature was the splendid influence exercised by Messrs. Matthews, Lut[h]uli, Bokwe, Guma and Mbamba. Most of these men, now teaching, were at one time, and that not so long ago, forceful student leaders in their respective colleges. It is a sign of our vitality and growth that their devotion to the Movement has continued.[49]

By April 1926 Max had registered two thousand students in the SCA's African branches. Within that year Yergan had also made three significant contributions to landmark European ecumenical gatherings. First was the August 1–6 World's Conference of YMCAs at Helsinki, Finland, while the second was the General Committee meeting of the WSCF at Nyborg, Denmark (August 16–25), and the last was the key September Le Zoute, Belgium, conference. Each appearance granted Yergan and his South African mission keen exposure, establishing him as a critical thinker with a scholarly bent and as a missionary with a flair for formal theological discourse.

In September 1926 Yergan attended the International Missionary Council's Le Zoute Conference in Belgium to discuss "The Christian Mission in Africa." Yergan boldly challenged the faith assembly, declaring, "The test that the Africans I know bring to Christianity as they see it is the social teaching of Jesus. They say, 'What you White men do speaks so loud that we cannot hear what you say.'"[50] He left a vivid impression, further strengthening his ecumenical position. In October C. T. Loram, addressing the Tuskegee Institute, publicly invoked his name, saying,

> Max Yergan—You should know him; if you don't know him you should get to know him. He is one of God's good men. Yergan has done it, by common sense, real goodness and by his wisdom. He is doing in our country what Booker T. Washington and Dr Moton have done for you.[51]

Furlough

During 1927 Yergan took his first U.S. furlough. In January he received the first Harmon Foundation award for religious service. Soon after, his print output increased to include a brief but pertinent profile in *Men of New York* called "Seeking Greater Justice," the key two-part series "Race Currents and Conditions in South Africa" for the Hampton Institute journal, *The Southern Workman* (April and May), where his earlier World War One exploits had been mentioned a decade earlier.

However, it was in 1927 too that the Yergans lost their great friend, Gold Coast educator J. E. K. Aggrey, who died in Harlem Hospital on April 12. Dr. Aggrey had exerted the most profound influence upon both of them. Not only had Max and Susie been married in Aggrey's Salisbury, North Carolina, home, but Aggrey's South African speaking tours in 1921 had also helped lay the groundwork for Max's own YMCA/SCA travels. Aggrey had also spoken up for him when YMCA and SCA officials shared the government's fears of admitting an American Negro into the Union. The ironic conjuncture of bidding farewell to this confidant and role model while being touted as his successor in many quarters marked a passing of the baton.

The year 1927 also was the occasion of his first *New York Times* coverage, coinciding with his introduction to the philanthropic financial nexus via Rev. Anson Phelps Stokes, administrator of the African- and African-American–inclined family fund bearing his surname, and via Edward Clark "Ned" Carter, who facilitated his introduction to both the Rockefeller and Carnegie Foundations. These funding arms of big business claimed a religious base, and Yergan made pitches to all three about his South African work, to great effect.[52]

Yergan's *Times* mention came in connection with a talk he gave to the twenty-fourth annual Northfield, Massachusetts, Women's Foreign Mission Society Convention, chaired by Lila Mansfield (Mrs. Henry W. Peabody). Yergan, as principal speaker at the meeting, discussed legislation then being contemplated that would remove laborers' freedom of movement and would also remove literate, enfranchised Africans' right to vote for government officials. Responding to a query regarding his views on efforts to return various races to their original geographic locations, Yergan said, "That question goes quite far back, and you must be the first ones to decide. . . . I think I would rather have to ask you that question. Could you do away with all these beautiful buildings and return to crowded Europe?"[53]

That summer the Yergans also met the wealthy White socialist writer and NAACP member Mary White Ovington. Immediately taken with them, Ovington was sufficiently impressed by the YMCA secretary to include him in her latest literary creation, a volume of biographies of Negro notables entitled *Portraits in Color*. To be assigned a place along with such luminaries as tenor Roland Hayes and baritone Paul Robeson was a coming of age for Yergan. Of her decision Ovington wrote fellow NAACP member William Jay Schieffelin, "It seemed to me that nothing would help the Negro more than to have the white people look upon him as an individual, not as a type, so I have chosen twenty individuals whom I know and admire."[54] Ovington and Max would continue to correspond over the next few years, especially concerning South Africa. The publication of each of these compendia greatly enhanced Yergan's public profile.[55] By the end of the year Yergan also had been invited, with WSCF editor and author Basil Mathews, to a luncheon "to be attended by people primarily interested in various international publications for the purpose of meeting [Yergan] and perhaps securing some advice" from him.[56] Thus opened a new set of doors to periodical publishing.

Deepening Consciousness as a Diasporic African Called to Return to Ancestral Lands

The year 1927 was therefore the year when the reputation Yergan had been cultivating within the missionary and philanthropic nexus on the basis of his overseas endeavors had begun to pay local dividends within North America itself. On its board of advisers sat Rev. Phelps Stokes and African-American sociologist George Edmund Haynes, Urban League founder and Federal Council of Churches race relations specialist. All of these accomplishments increased interest in the nationwide speaking tour he had undertaken to raise funds for the continuation of his South African work. Even so, it was unlikely that the vast majority of people aware of his overseas activities were fully aware of their scale, let alone the degree to which Yergan exerted influence. He himself had begun to reveal some of the strain of operating in a relative vacuum.

Toward the end of 1927 Yergan addressed the Student Volunteer Movement in Detroit on "The Strength and Weakness of the Missionary Movement in Africa." On the heels of securing funding pledges from the Rockefellers and expanding contacts within the philanthropic world, he used this talk to reflect upon what he had seen in South Africa and its linkage to the broader global challenge to Christian missionaries.

Assuming the position of critical support, Yergan emphasized four problems posed by contemporary Christian practice. These included denominationalism, or competition within Protestant churches; failure to support the growth of indigenous African leaders; and race, described in two distinct contexts, as "racial identification of missionaries with governing powers" and as "the existence or recognition of class or racial differences." Regarding the latter, Max shared these choice sentiments:

> Many Africans maintain, and in many instances not without real justification, that some missionaries share with other whites their feeling of racial superiority or something of racial snobbishness, and that this is exemplified in some instances by the absence of an ordinarily courteous attitude. And in other instances the African Christian complains because he is made to feel by his missionary leader a difference which under the circumstances takes on the stamp of inferiority. The financial relationships between some missionaries and their African workers are sometimes responsible for this, and one admits that unless the missionary is

particularly and constantly careful, a relationship of employer and employee between himself and his African associates is liable to come into existence, to say nothing of a more strained relationship between himself and the masses of people among whom he is working.[57]

While he may have appeared to blur the distinction between class and race, their interdependence in South Africa made this a logical approach. As a conciliator Yergan was addressing an audience whose appearance and attitudes mirrored the vast majority of Whites in South Africa; they too, either consciously or unconsciously, identified with the ruling race and class. Yergan gently chided them, admonishing,

> There are certain social relationships, or sometimes the absence of such relationships, which are responsible for this idea of superiority and inferiority entering as a great weakness. In the opinion of some people, this is a very delicate point, but, notwithstanding that, one submits in all seriousness and out of real concern for the great cause in which we are interested, that it is a great stumbling block in the way of a full, untrammeled advance of the Kingdom of God in Africa.[58]

In roughly the same time frame Yergan addressed a European audience on a related theme. Using analogies in the style of Dr. Aggrey, Yergan treated racial prejudice with the parable of a man who hated dogs and then was faced with a wounded animal whose broken leg had to be set. Despite his prejudice and the inconvenience of tending to the despised beast, he did so and found himself changing his mind to the point that he actually went out and bought one. Yergan used this story to show the ways in which human beings, particularly young boys, could learn to get along in spite of their preconceptions of one another. Writing in 1927 against the backdrop of rising anti-Semitism in Europe, he also included Africa:

> The present writer has had the interesting experience of hearing boys, to say nothing of men, of at least six different countries and races swear most completely and contemptibly at or about men and boys of other races simply because they belonged to other races. In Africa I have also talked with European boys of two countries who conscientiously believed that the black boys of Africa are in the world solely to make life more pleasant for Europeans. These are but evidences of the existence

of racial prejudice or wrong racial attitudes, world wide in extent and supported by otherwise quite intelligent people. Our attitude toward the boys of other races is therefore a very pressing question and we do well to examine very frankly some of the reasons for these manifestly evil relationships in order that we may discover how they may be improved.[59]

But Yergan did not talk about prejudice outside of its social or economic context. In fact, he made a point of connecting it to the expansion of Europe and America and the various relations and factors of production to which this gave rise.

Moreover, in contrast to social thinkers who treated prejudice as purely psychological, he delineated some of the material consequences of institutional racism:

But the manifestations of race prejudice go infinitely beyond the uttering of words. For instance, in some countries it expresses itself in the laws made by the legislature. By such laws, people against whom there is strong prejudice are denied the right to engage in work for which they may be or may become fitted, also the right to study in public schools, colleges and universities as well as the right to improve their living conditions in keeping with accepted standards. There are countless other petty annoyances such as the inability to get food to eat in public restaurants, or, in some places, to get decent accommodation in public carriers. Race prejudice also manifests itself in what are supposed to be courts of justice. There are communities in some parts of the world where persons who belong to races against which there are strong prejudices find it almost impossible to get a fair trial especially in the lower courts of such communities.[60]

As in his "Strength and Weakness" article, Yergan here too touched upon the problem of identification with the ruling race. Here he warned his audience not to lull themselves into smug complacency by believing they were free of this malady:

Let not those living in countries where this dread disease does not openly obtain regard themselves as free from it. Nor can they look with a "holier than thou" attitude upon those guilty of prejudiced practices and thank themselves or God that they are not as others. Parts of Africa and America which have been settled by people from all sections of Europe as well as countries of Europe and Asia bear eloquent and awful testimony to this fact: that, thrown under circumstances where it is apparently to one's advantage to join with others in exploiting a minority or otherwise weaker group, one must be of exceptional qualities not to join with the oppressors, the ignorant or the misguided.[61]

Max's remedy for racism in its economic, social, and political manifestations remained righteous Christian practice. Without wishing to judge others by what they felt, did, or did not do in this regard, he offered five suggestions:

I.   Let us make use of the best that has been said or is being said today through books on this subject of racial relations and attitudes.
II. Let us seek and encourage personal conduct, fellowship and friendship with members of other races.
III. Let us learn more of the mind and spirit of the Jesus we love whom we profess to follow, on this particular question.
IV. Let us get a new glimpse of what surely must be the will of God who made all people for to dwell together upon the face of the earth.
V.   And then, conscious of course, that our goal will not be reached overnight, that the long weary road of arousing and educating sluggish public opinion must be trod,—conscious of these and the other prices that must be paid as was the case for instance with human slavery and the drink evil, let us with a courage born of our belief in God and man set ourselves afresh to the task of understanding, of loving friendship, of service, of a world of God.[62]

In these articles from late 1927 lay the core of Yergan's most dynamic and difficult challenges to his consciousness and career. These concerned his relationship to the spiritual and the social, the political and the personal, faith and finance, theory and practice. Shaped by the segregated South of North America, chastened by Indian, Eastern African, and now Southern African experience, he could not ignore the relationship between economics and ideology. Still viewing himself and his salvation in terms of his Christian missionary labors, he also came in contact with other theoreticians whose notion of the social gospel included taking stands to make life on earth more livable for workers and peasants, and between and among Christians and others of different backgrounds.

Meanwhile, Yergan's national reputation within the United States was soaring. In February he learned that Howard University would award him an honorary M.A. in absentia in June; spoke at Northeastern University on the New Africa; and sailed from New York harbor bound for the Holy Land to attend the International Missionary Council's Jerusalem meeting from March 24 to April 8.[63]

In March, long-time Yergan aide Edgar Thamae wrote him from Basutoland. Having served as "a book-keeper and typist for a trading store" in Thabaneng during Yergan's furlough, Thamae mentioned having seen Professor Jabavu during a recent visit on invitation from Basutoland's government to speak to the Basotho on agriculture.[64] Missing the Yergan family, E. J. Thamae expressed keen anticipation of their return. That this eagerness was largely motivated by his own career concerns cannot be doubted, but the genuine affection Thamae communicated toward the Yergans was unmistakable. Not merely an employer, Yergan clearly functioned as Thamae's mentor as well. Thamae's obsequious note opened with the servile salutation, "My dear Master." In view of Max's own hereditary relationship to black slavery, this is at least ironic.

Halfway through 1928 Yergan received a letter from a Xhosa doctor who had recently returned from twelve and a half years in the United States, Alfred Bitini Xuma. Born in Manzana, Engcobo District, Transkei, in the Eastern Cape, Dr. Xuma had studied at the Wesleyan mission of Clarkebury and then Edinburgh before acquiring further schooling in America.[65] Destined to make a major mark upon Black South Africa, Xuma had learned about Yergan from Chicago African-American YMCA secretary Grover Little.[66] Writing Yergan in June, the physician initiated a friendship that would become important for both families. Citing a letter from Chicagoan George Arthur,[67] Xuma had glimpsed Yergan at an international YMCA convention in Des Moines, Iowa. Then, in his no-nonsense fashion, Xuma sought the advice of Max and Susie W. Yergan on the former's choice of a prospective spouse.[68] From this direct and critical inquiry, their relationship developed. Strongly influenced by his lengthy American residence, Xuma sought a bond with these African-Americans.

As was true in the case of the Jabavu-Yergan friendship, Xuma was drawn to Max because of his North American experience, along with the reputation Yergan had gained for his work in both the United States and South Africa. Like Jabavu, Xuma had been impressed by the achievements of those Black Americans who would have fit W. E. B. Du Bois's definition of the Talented Tenth, equivalent to the "school people." Accordingly, they arranged to meet when Xuma returned to his Johannesburg home.

But Yergan had also on more than one occasion shown either openly or in a more indirect fashion that his connections to Africa and Africans were not historical alone. Challenged, often even hamstrung by his American upbringing and his conflicted desire to establish his bona fides as "civilized," as what literate francophone Africans were taught to call *évolué*, or "evolved"—or, later, assimilated (*assimilé*)—he too struggled with what Du Bois had termed a double consciousness, a "twoness" that derived from being a Negro and being human, a state more trying perhaps in Africa than stateside for now it meant determining how he should relate to Africa and Africans *at home*.

While in later years it became fashionable to disparage Yergan for imperiously flaunting the trappings of empire, those who do so should think back on what their own intellectual and sometimes literal foreparents did upon receiving Western educations. What did they wear? How did they comport themselves? How did they choose to communicate? How did they outfit their dwellings? Yergan did no more nor less than any "school person" would have aspired to do in that place and time. He wore fine clothes, he enjoyed his bourgeois entertainments, and, yes, he tried his best to live as well as a White man, for was this not the standard of that time?

Yet deep down, perhaps in the recesses of his soul where no one else could go, there had to be some other sense of longing for kinship with the people of this land. He hints at this possibility in the occasional passage from his correspondence with Moorland, Tobias, and others, and it comes up in the "brotherly" banter he exchanged with Jabavu—or even stiff and stuffy Xuma. All struggled to find out how to be modern, Western, and African at the same time. Who perhaps more than the American Negro better personified these paradoxes? No wonder that Africa's gift to America could become at once envied and scorned, and why, therefore, would not this cause the crassest confusion?

But Yergan could stand up in front of White audiences and tell them that he too was Black, using a word he was instructed to despise in a continent called dark, among comrades several skin tones browner than his. He dared on many occasions to identify himself with his African compatriots, as when he wrote to Henry-Louis Henriod, "We Natives especially . . ." He and Jabavu could jest about "cullud" culture, could be loud and raucous and howl and guffaw and stamp their feet and backslap one another when in private as they were when on the road crossing the veld, camping out and debating for hours. They could be Nonwhite together, New Negroes but also ancient, authentic Africans.

Somewhere down deep was this link that may have begun with his grandfather and that tied him not merely to brown folk back home but also to the Aggreys and those African students who passed in and out of Shaw, then to those Africans like Sol Plaatje who made their New World and diasporic sojourns, to Dube who lived in Brooklyn, to Xuma who made his way from south to north, to the leading lights who founded the Native National Congress, many with North American and specifically Negro experience, to the Semes, and to so many others then and afterward. So why not speak of oneself in the same breath as every other "Native"? How could he represent his brethren if he did not at some level try to make common cause with them?

By the close of 1928 these influences led Yergan to compose a monograph, *Africa, the West, and Christianity,* prepared for distribution to the meeting of the General Committee of the World Student Christian Federation in Mysore, India, in November. In this, his first time back to India since the world war, he spent over a month on the road. While we do not know his precise trajectory at that time, there are indications of where Max went. There is almost no question, however, of what Yergan thought going into the conference, as his extended work amply revealed. It was truly the culmination of the growth he had undergone during the 1920s, in South Africa, in Europe, and, finally, upon returning home during the period of his furlough. It foretold a new course for the next decade, the main themes of which were now laid out before his readers. In no sense was it possible to view him exclusively within the framework of either the Student Christian Association, the YMCA, South Africa, or the United States. Yergan was now firmly establishing himself as a world citizen in the Black Atlantic.

At the same time, Yergan had also been exposed to a wider world in which race, while still critical, no longer was the only major challenge that mattered to him. In his time and location it was inescapable, but it also articulated with other factors, most prominently class. This was something that had been on his mind for many years. It had been crucial in his own development as an educated professional. It was fundamental to the Du Boisian notion of the "Talented Tenth" who saw as their charge the "uplift" of their racial fellows, and for those working as missionaries in foreign lands where they fought "heathen ignorance." In each instance he had local allies in the "school people" who helped him succeed in South Africa—the Jabavus, Dubes, and others who welcomed him as part of their metaphorical extended family. As he faced the end of his sixth year of service these variables would coalesce in new, unforeseen ways, giving Yergan a fresh awareness of himself and his world.

His travels had dramatic consequences, internally and externally, in his life and mission. A hint of what lay ahead for Max came in a June letter to Mary White Ovington written on his return to South Africa from Jerusalem. Recovering from the flu, Yergan reentered South Africa in the wake of a drought broken briefly by fairly heavy March rains but followed by more drought, leaving cattle and people without water. On his mind were two other matters, the political scene and an upcoming South African missionary conference scheduled for the next week. Of the former Max wrote,

> You have doubtless learned that the Government has decided not to proceed with the proposed Native legislation which it had introduced in Parliament here this year. I am not yet able to say why this step was taken but I am inclined to think that it is due to the tremendous protest made in this country as well as in Europe and America against such patently inadequate and unfair legislation. I have reference to the segregation, franchise and land bills which have been before the Parliament of the country. I have not yet been able to gather up the threads of political developments but it does seem apparent that the Government realizes more than it did two years ago a sense of responsibility towards the temporarily defenceless and largely voiceless Natives of the country.[69]

On the same day Max wrote Ovington, Thomas Jesse Jones wrote Anson Phelps Stokes. Citing C. T. Loram, Jones claimed that Yergan's request for funds to help Fort Hare students was unnecessary in view of lavish bursaries available to them from Basutoland, Natal, the Transvaal, and the Transkeian Territories General Council. Jones argued that "the drought has hit many Natives hard but not those who would send their sons and daughters to Fort Hare. What is needed much more than bursaries to Fort Hare students is money to give the hungry Native school children at least 2 decent meals a day."[70]

The conclave Yergan wrote Ovington about was the SCA General Conference held July 5–9 on the theme of "Which Way Is Youth Headed?" In a summary of the meeting Max described four impressions that it made upon him. First was the vitality of youth itself, which he described as "religious, enthusiastic, idealistic, courageous and hopeful." Second, he found the conference itself to be courageous, both individually and in terms of the participants' public expressions of willingness to apply Christian principles to social questions, notably that of race. Next, the meeting was one where hope was evident. Last, it was challenging.[71]

Ovington's response to Yergan's lengthy June missive was an interesting one. In reply to his description of the land, its people, and their problems, she played an old tune. Responding to a reference Max made to African labor leader Clements Kadalie, she sighed,

> How I wish I could talk to you about the Labor Movement and the Missionary and the Y.M.C.A. I think the Y.M.C.A. is at its best in its local work. I mean the direct work in the field such as you do. Here in New York we don't think very highly of National Headquarters. They are too political for one thing. Why do they need so many highly salaried men? Sometimes I hope that there will be as big shake-up here which will result in more power to the workers who are really in the field.[72]

Within days of Ovington's answer, Yergan was en route to India, for the WSCF General Committee's Mysore meeting, taking an offprint called *Africa, the West, and Christianity.*

4

South Africa, Part II

The Road to Radicalization

Max Yergan's public identification with radical left politics surfaced around 1931. Until then he balanced three sets of interests: one local (his overseas-based South African YMCA mission work); one transatlantic (lingering concern for North America); and one increasingly internationalist, shaped by the YMCA, SCA, and WSCF. Christian and secular "witness" aided the transformation, as did trips to Europe, Asia, and North America. These brought new friends and renewed old ties with Black YMCA allies J. E. Moorland, C. H. Tobias, and John Hope. Together they faced a hopeful new era.

More conservative Christian colleagues found Yergan's growing leftism sudden and surprising. In fact, however, it was a deliberate transformation performed by a man with global interests, movements, and contacts after a decade of observing, researching, and discussing the theoretical and practical requirements of a changing age. All of these factors coalesced at a time and in a way common for the era within his cohort, progressive churchgoers. Change finally came when Max urgently needed a fundamental intellectual and spiritual breakthrough.

Yergan's new course crystallized during 1927, while he was on his two-year U.S furlough. In January 1928, on a tour in Cleveland, he made a stopover there en route to a Student Volunteer Movement convention in Detroit. He attended the National Alpha Phi Alpha Convention, spoke at the Cedar Y, preached at Mt. Zion Congregational Church, and was interviewed by a local YMCA paper, the *Cleveland Red Triangle*. "The mind of the European is slowly awakening to the magnitude of the African situation," he told the reporter, then added,

> Wealth is pouring into that vast territory, and the world is turning there for the products which Africa yields. This has created a startling economic and social problem. By force of circumstances, the natives find

themselves living in a civilization which is basically European. They are daily faced with the necessity of adapting themselves to the standards which surround them.[1]

Yergan stressed the salutary effects of YMCA work in the difficult South African field:

The Young Men's Christian Association has been responsible for bringing the claim[s] of the natives before the white inhabitants. Our work has been principally among students, who will be the leaders of the next generation. Where formerly we met suspicion and opposition, the doors are now open to us everywhere. More and more the whites are taking up a serious study of the interracial problem which confronts them.[2]

On February 15, secretary Yergan told of "The New Africa" at a mass meeting at Northeastern University (the YMCA College), where he was a guest lecturer sponsored by the Sigma Delta Epsilon honor society. The campus newspaper welcomed Max's appearance and address, praising his oratorical skill and eloquent, restrained message.[3] The reporter noted that he had "emphasized the purpose of African leaders today as raising up additional leaders of character and zeal by modern educational methods."

Mr. Yergan won the decided favor and interest of his large audience because of his fair and broad-minded treatment of the problem. Throughout the address, he maintained an admirable dignity and high level of approach; never did he resort to petty prejudices and undue racial consciousness.[4]

Evidently equally moving in Yergan's appeal was his timely reference to a recent cable from Professor Jabavu at Fort Hare detailing the enormity of a drought in the Eastern Cape. Jabavu wrote,

The drought this year beats all known records[,] exceeding even the previous worst, that of 1861, for since January (1927) it has not been wet enough for a plough to enter the soil! Folks have missed out two ploughing seasons, the June and the November, and the sun is that hot that we seem to be living inside a stove or oven day after day! Therefore I cannot hope to be able to raise any funds locally.[5]

Northeastern then launched a schoolwide Max Yergan Fund campaign aimed at its five thousand students.[6]

As Max returned to Fort Hare, following the International Missionary Council's April 1928 Jerusalem meeting, the South African Communist Party was rethinking its strategy toward millions of Nonwhite workers. That year the Communist International had changed its general line to call for a "Black Belt Republic" in the American South and a "Native Republic" of workers and peasants in South Africa, both seen as consistent with the principle of self-determination. This controversial new emphasis spurred recruitment of Africans in South Africa and "Negroes" in the United States.

Its membership and effectiveness peaking by the mid-1920s, the ICU was by 1928 plagued by external and internal difficulties that hampered its effectiveness. The Communist Party sought to fill the vacuum created by the union's eclipse. Yergan noted the linkage between the South African and North American "Negro questions." Connecting the two proved logical for a Black American with African experience pursuing a personal commitment to social change that was informed by a transatlantic diasporic sensibility.

The late 1920s were marked by widespread interest in socialism. This was true globally, especially after the rise of Italian fascism, followed closely by German Nazism. In both the United States and the Union of South Africa, a vital question of the diverse working-class movement was where to locate racial oppression in the struggle against capital and the state. Socialist parties emerging in each of these milieux stumbled when facing the "Black question." This became one of the greatest ideological tests for socialist revolutionaries. Comintern action forced the issue in both the African and American Communist Parties.

These concerns were on the radical Christian agenda as well. After the Bolshevik revolution social gospelers strove to come to grips with the first socialist state. YMCA director John R. Mott had helped lead the Hoover Refugee Relief Commission after World War One. Edward Clark Carter (the "Ned" Carter who facilitated Max Yergan's overseas postings in Bangalore and British East Africa), was by the late 1920s secretary of the American Council of the Institute of Pacific Relations (IPR). The IPR grew out of a Honolulu meeting organized in 1925 by YMCA alumni to foster better racial, cultural, and social understanding among North Americans and Asian-Pacific peoples.[7] Already active in a collective originally called the National Conference on the Christian

Way of Life (later, the Inquiry), Carter began his IPR tenure the next year. His self-ordained charge as IPR head included rapprochement with the USSR. He saw himself as an "honest broker," as did Yergan in South Africa.

Yergan's communications with fellow Black YMCA veterans J. E. Moorland, C. H. Tobias, and John Hope revealed growing interest in communism and the USSR. Wondering whether revolution was necessary in South Africa, he considered whether socialist theory was compatible with Christian doctrine. After South Africa's 1929 election and the global economic depression, he moved ever leftward. Back in May 1928, Max's jottings home showed anger with Union government actions, as he wrote, "There is a sense in which there is always a crisis here. I do not say this for rhetorical or any other effect; it is true because of the very nature of a situation created by a vast complex of factors and forces sometimes uncontrolled, often in conflict, always active."[8] He then went on to detail the social, political, economic, and spiritual challenges with which the citizenry grappled.

By mid-1928 Yergan's view of Africa generally and South Africa in particular had changed greatly. His talks with people of divergent backgrounds permitted him to explore the new world that Africa and Africans had forged between the world wars. These he presented in preacherly prose, in language still showing his religious calling. More and more, he opened with invocations ritualistically debunking the myth of African heathen ignorance, which he himself had previously accepted, as in the following passage:

Please put out of your mind most of your previously acquired pictures of Africa if they represent only wild beasts, savages, the witch doctor and other aspects of "darkest Africa." Witch doctors, superstition, ignorance and cruelty we have, and sometimes in abundance, but along with this aspect of African life there is another equally as engaging and much more difficult to deal with. The true picture that you must have of Southern Africa must include mines, railways, work shops, highly commercialized agriculture and many other aspects of modern life as you know it.

With this fresh view of Africa came a novel vision of the Africans themselves, whom Yergan portrayed as sentient, self-actualized, resilient human beings able to take upon their shoulders the burdens of bettering their own living, working and social conditions through education, religious training, and progressive labor combinations. In his annual brief to his stateside colleagues, Yergan commented on a stirring example of this new spirit, that of a nascent secular, working-class consciousness in Africa:

> The most interesting and significant development in the life of the African worker has been what is called the "I.C.U.," the Industrial and Commercial Union. This is a sort of inclusive trades union which has been developed to a remarkable degree by an African of Nyasaland, Mr. Clements Kadalie. In spite of many difficulties, he has achieved something worth while and his work marks the beginning of organization among African workers. I do not agree with all of his methods, and I certainly do not countenance all of his utterances but I do give him credit for having dared and partly succeeded in a field of great need and opportunity.

His rediscovery and embrace of the ICU leader provides a key to Yergan as well. That year Kadalie had made a potent enough impact upon him to warrant his hosting the controversial unionist at a major missionary forum, much to the chagrin of some of Yergan's "European" colleagues. Acquainted with Kadalie since at least 1923, when, as Kadalie's honored guest, Yergan addressed an ICU public meeting, the secretary of the "Bantu" section of the Student Christian Movement now reciprocated by issuing an invitation of his own, news of which he trumpeted in June 1928 to Mary White Ovington:

> Just now I am busy in preparation for a South African Missionary Conference which is to be held next week. This gathering will be watched by the country in general for its programme is certainly a departure from all previous gatherings of this nature. We are going to devote our whole time to a discussion of the full range of Native life. You may be interested in knowing that Mr. Kadalie who is the efficient leader of a Native Labour Movement called the I.C.U. is to be one of the speakers at this gathering. I mention this because there was a very strong protest on the part of some missionaries and church leaders against appearing on the same platform with this man? [*sic*] I think it is a distinct advance to have made it possible for missionaries and church people to be

exposed to the point of view of this very significant Movement which Mr. Kadalie is leading.[9]

Kadalie's movement was noteworthy for the presence within its ranks of a small but prominent set of African and "Coloured" active members of the Communist Party, most notably Jimmy la Guma[10] and John Gomas, both widely known Cape Town militants. Yergan almost certainly knew of them and had opportunities to notice them in action. He also read Communist literature, especially the party organ, *Umsebenzi* (*The Worker*). Given his personal contacts and awareness of local and international news, he may have read of the Sixth World Congress of the Communist International, held in September 1928. However, responding to liberal and state pressure, by 1928 C. K. Kadalie was expelling Communists from the ICU ranks.

While the "Negro question" in the United States was of keen concern to social radicals after the Bolshevik revolution, class distinctions separated middle-class or petit-bourgeois elements from working-class African-Americans. As early as the Fifth Congress of the Communist International in 1924, Black U.S. delegate James Jackson reflected this stratification by criticizing a Chicago conference of Negro organizations held that February that was dominated by an ecclesiastical and professional elite. Jackson ended his critique on what party stalwarts would have felt was a triumphal note: "Nevertheless we were successful in the last two days of the congress in provoking a split."[11] The matter was placed under consideration by the Fourth Enlarged Plenum of the Executive Committee of the Communist International (ECCI).[12] It recurred at the ECCI's Fifth Enlarged Plenum one year later. But few anticipated the centrality of this aspect of class struggle before the Sixth World Congress.

Learning from the accumulated experience of fraternal socialist parties in addressing the vexing nationalities question, certain Comintern operatives launched trenchant attacks on particular parties for their alleged failure to regard oppressed national groups with sensitivity. Japan's Katayama Sen[13] (a resident in several historically Black colleges) took the occasion of the Sixth World Congress to criticize the Communist Party of Great Britain for its "criminal neglect" of Ireland and India, and laid into the parties of the Netherlands and North America for similar crimes against Indonesia, the Philippines, and African-

American toilers in the United States. Together these groups warranted consideration as colonized peoples.

Thus the North American "Negro" and South African "Native" questions became connected. South Africa's delegates helped draft a protocol beginning,

> In the union of South Africa, the Negro masses, who constitute the majority of the population and whose land is being expropriated by the White colonists and by the State, are deprived of political rights and of freedom of movement, are exposed to the worst kinds of racial and class oppression, and suffer simultaneously from pre-capitalist and capitalist methods of oppression and exploitation.[14]

The document then proceeded:

> The communist party, which has already had some successes among the Negro proletariat, has the duty of continuing still more energetically the struggle for the complete equality of rights for the Negroes, for the abolition of all special regulations and laws directed against Negroes, and for confiscation of the estates of the landlords. In drawing into its ranks Negro workers, organizing them in trade unions, fighting for their admission into the trade unions of white workers, the communist party is obliged to struggle by every means against racial prejudice among white workers and to eradicate such prejudices entirely from its own ranks. The party must vigorously and consistently advance the slogan of the creation of an independent Native Republic, with guarantee for the rights of the white minority, and translate this fight into action.[15]

Yergan's comments from late 1928 reveal a further frustration that a furlough may have both relieved and inflamed, especially when he returned to a seething cauldron from which only he had escaped. This was clear in his remarks on the deteriorating position of the African majority in South Africa, especially that of the small, vibrant stratum of Christian-educated, property-holding "school people," middle-class African professionals whose social backgrounds, aspirations, and painful experiences with formal and informal racial discrimination so mirrored his own. Elite African freeholders in Cape Province, voters since the nineteenth century, now risked losing the right to vote. In the peculiar way in which words have often been used to mean their opposite in South Africa, in the middle to late 1920s the Nationalist-Labour Pact government struck at the last vestiges of African autonomy in landholding, labor, and the franchise. The semantic deceit of the Pact government was clear in the ironically titled "Representation of Natives in Parliament Bill," a maneuver intended to disfranchise black voters. This was met by universal African outrage, spurring Yergan to report home heatedly:

> The Representation of Natives in Parliament Bill, whereby those Africans of the Cape Province (that province of the Union in which Africans vote) will cease to exercise the vote on the present basis, and in its place a new system will be instituted whereby certain Africans throughout the country will vote for seven Europeans to represent them in Parliament. Very strong, almost unanimous, objection has been registered against the last two of the above proposals by the Africans themselves. In addition various groups of Europeans as well as individuals have protested against the last two measures as being retrogressive and unjust. The Bills are now in the hands of a Parliamentary Select Committee and it remains to be seen in what new forms they will be brought before Parliament when it convenes early next year. The effect of this proposed legislation upon the entire life of Africans is extremely vital and they are watching it closely.

This trend, and the severity of the Depression, led Yergan to evoke the plight of the African masses.

> The economic condition of the Native population according to careful observers is not improving. Dr. James Henderson, Principal of Lovedale Institution, states as the result of a survey made in a given district that "over the greater part of South Africa the Native population is economically losing ground, that, relative to its members, its resources are shrinking, and becoming exhausted, and that the means at the disposal of many African communities have normally ceased to be sufficient for sustaining healthy life." There is no longer any doubt about the grave economic condition of Native Africans; and it is equally as clear that its improvement must be undertaken from almost as many angles as there are in life here.

Africa, the West, and Christianity

By the end of 1928, Yergan was on the move again, this time to greet the General Meeting of the World Student Christian Federation in Mysore, India, where he reconnected with the leaders of the Indian YMCA, K. T. Paul and Surendra K. Datta. The previous May, Paul had asked that WSCF authorities release Yergan to spend an extended period in India, suggesting five to six weeks, during which time he could investigate the major regional YMCA centers in such cities as Madras, Calcutta, Delhi, Lahore and Bombay.[16] Also representing South Africa were D. D. T. Jabavu and Z. R. Mahabane.

On the eve of Yergan's departure, Fort Hare principal Alexander Kerr took advantage of the opportunity his latest sojourn provided to write a reminder of what he saw as Yergan's fitness for this mission. To do so, Kerr recapped the history of Yergan's South African work. Beginning by telling the origins of Student Christian Movement (SCM) work in South Africa in 1896, Kerr mentioned early contacts with Native training institutions. Describing the problem of recruiting an American Negro as "an affair of some delicacy," he revisited the saga of "stringent immigration restrictions" leveled at Black Americans. Then Kerr shifted to Yergan, indicating precisely what he faced and how he discharged his duties:

> The man sent out, therefore, had to meet a very exacting test. First of all he had to possess the qualifications of character, of scholarship, of training in, and experience of, work among students, of sympathy with men belonging indeed to his own great race, but separated from him by language, customs, outlook and awareness of modern civilization. Secondly, he had to have such breadth of Christian sympathy as would allow him to work hand in hand with missionaries of many Christian denominations, each with its own peculiar approach to the heart of the African. Thirdly, he had to possess such tact as would enable him to commend his work to a European population not at large impressed with any grave necessity for the uplift of the Native people and by no means convinced of their capacity for progress in the ways of civilization. Fourthly, he had to have such a fund of sound doctrine and appreciation of the realities of the situation as would make it easy for a government traditionally nervous, not without reason, of movements of native opinion, to countenance his activities amongst the more educated

section of the Native people. In the providence of God, as it now seems to us, the choice of the American Committee fell upon Max Yergan.[17]

Yergan's Mysore address proved detailed and erudite. Building upon the firm foundation of his presentation to the Enlarged Meeting of the International Missionary Council in Jerusalem in March, he presented an extensive survey of challenges facing committed Christians in South Africa, later published as *Africa, the West, and Christianity*. Drawn from a close reading of some of the best available literature on European colonization, the text showed impressive command of source material for someone who was essentially a self-trained Africanist.[18] It bore the earmarks of Yergan's prior writings, as well as profiting from his lecturing acumen. Following Parker Moon, he saw the rationale behind imperial expansion as principally economic, a response to the need for new markets, but also as influenced by the revolution in communications, desire for raw materials and surplus capital. Quoting C. J. H. Hayes, he then stressed the decisive role played by the growth of nationalism. From Leonard Woolf he derived the notions of the "beliefs and desires" of Western peoples, which, according to Basil Mathews, were powerful forces in the successful realization of the aims of the occupiers.

In considering instances of direct occupation and control, he analyzed Eastern and Southern Africa, raising a few pointed queries. Presenting the issue of the clash of cultures in terms of competing claims laid by Africans and European occupiers in these regions, he gently stated that "from the point of view of the African, rights of personality, rights of previous occupation of the land, the right to live and grow in terms of the new life in the midst of which he finds himself, are involved." But then he judiciously added that "European interests on the other hand demand the black man's labour and land; and sometimes the land which the black man himself needs."

The remainder of Yergan's text concerned South Africa, which historically resembled the United States. The South African problem pivoted around race, culture, and land. Race mattered not in the abstract but as a mechanism whereby social inequality was mandated and enforced by a body of legislation and institutions. Competing cultures and claims led to intractable conflict. Maintaining an accustomed and practiced, evenhanded stance, Yergan gave weight to the views of both sides in this combat, measuring but not judging the African or the European, acknowledging where the power lay—within White-created structures of dominance—but also emphasizing the primacy of the issue of land.

> There is deep seated dissatisfaction and real unrest among Africans because of the inadequate extent of land to which they have access. This dissatisfaction is by competent authority recognised and admitted as justly based. Africans and many Europeans contend that there can never be the basis for right racial relations until there is a provision whereby Africans may purchase more land. Indeed it is argued that the absence of opportunity for purchasing or leasing sufficient land is very largely responsible for most of the disabilities under which Africans live. The land question then, in the opinion of most Africans and many Europeans, is the root of the larger question affecting the relations between the two races.[19]

Assessing the effects of the European presence upon Africa, Yergan saw mixed results. Unable to state categorically that Africa's encounter with the West was in every sense an evil one, he balanced his scale of objective achievement with a counterweight of chaotic erosion of preexisting structures, beliefs, values, and societal controls, painting a picture at once subjective, subtle, and sharp:

> With family life very largely broken up wherever western industry has touched, the old restraining influences of the African social code no longer serve. The simplicity of village life of yesterday has been destroyed, never to return again.
>
> Nothing so solid and so well understood as their own ideas and customs of the past are available for Africans of to-day. New diseases against which there is built up no immunity beset Africans as a result of the penetration of outside forces. Strange food and new living conditions have lowered the vitality and power of resistance to disease on the part of large numbers of Africans, especially those engaged in industries. The power and authority of their traditional rulers, their chiefs, have been shaken and in many instances destroyed by the power of the white man.[20]

Having diagnosed the ills afflicting occupied Africa in general and South Africa in particular, Yergan proceeded to his prescription, an application of the Golden Rule. This uplifted the "personality" of Africans,

ceased color stigmatization, and led to increased "European" cooperation and acceptance in policies directed toward Africa and African people. Max was especially hopeful about the force of public opinion, embodied in institutions like the International Labor section of the League
of Nations and within colonial governments. Lastly, he lauded the
younger generation:

> In South Africa, for instance, the youth and student sections are becom-
> ing rapidly acquainted with the great social questions of that land and
> are not only seeking the facts but are progressively arriving at right con-
> clusions about responsibilities and relationships. The Church of South
> Africa is likewise acquiring an increasing conviction of its social mis-
> sion and function and is undertaking to fulfill its responsibilities in these
> respects.[21]

Yergan arrived in India late in November, remaining for the entire
month of December and well into January 1929. We do not know much
about his movements during his sojourn there, but it is likely that he
traveled extensively across the country, perhaps by rail and motorcar,
possibly revisiting old haunts in the Bangalore of his youthful World
War One years, but also taking note of the progress of the appeal of
Gandhi's *satyagraha* movement, about which he would have read for
years.

Back home in the United States, Yergan's star continued ascending,
as his fund-raising efforts to match Rockefeller and Carnegie grants
stirred the imaginations of both anonymous masses and thoughtful,
well-heeled individual donors. In March, pharmaceutical magnate, Tuskegee University trustee, and Black YMCA supporter William J. Schieffelin reported that the great tenor Roland Hayes was permitting the
proceeds of the sale of box seats in his final Carnegie Hall recital to be
given to benefit the Max Yergan Building Fund.[22]

Yergan's extended WSCF stay in India greatly stimulated his thinking
on the direction of his work in the federation's Executive Committee in
general, and in South Africa in particular. In the latter his first order of
business was to attend Fort Hare's Governing Council, where he revealed his plans for a YMCA building and dwelling house, where the
Executive Council was empowered to act in concert with Yergan in
connection with these intentions. Upon finishing this business, he contemplated decisions relative to other parts of Africa as well, notably

Rhodesia, Central Africa, Eastern Africa, and even the Gold Coast and Sierra Leone in West Africa. Anxious to share his short-term plans with WSCF leader F. P. Miller, he wrote,

> The remaining portion of 1929 must certainly be given to a most intensive strengthening of our associations in South Africa. Visits must be made to Southern Rhodesia and to Portuguese East Africa, but as I see things now, my main emphasis must be in South Africa. At the same time I must carry certain responsibilities in connection with the South African Missionary Conference and give some attention to the building project which we have on involving our new National headquarters and the Students' Union at Fort Hare on which about £10,000 will be expended. Time must also be found to respond to the quickened interest among European students in a new approach to the racial question—a task to which almost all of one's time could with ample justification be given.[23]

After his note to Miller, Yergan wrote David R. Porter of the International Committee. This missive, unlike the one to Miller, differed on the scope of WSCF work. The crux of the dispute was this:

> I appreciated your insistence at Mysore upon the necessity of the Federation definitely committing itself to projects in parts of the world other than those in Europe. I think it was helpful for you to make known the fact in the article which you wrote at Mysore that the Federation had committed itself to some such undertaking in relation to our work in Africa. Following this decision I have taken the liberty in one or two communications to headquarters, especially to Francis, to outline for them what I think they should do.[24]

This, then, was the raison d'être of his Miller letter, a copy of which Yergan enclosed, while revealing confidentially to Porter his broader aim, namely, to push for greater integration of extra-European work. Yergan did this "so as not to embarrass Francis." Then, he enumerated his objections:

> (1) The decision taken at Nyborg did not in my opinion contemplate the formation of a Council for the purposes which are true of the pre-

sent European council; but rather an all European conference somewhat along the lines of the Pacific Area Conference; (2) Our concentration in Europe will greatly handicap the Federation in pursuit and in achievement of its world wide mission. (3) . . . My conception of the Federation's task is to make for the largest exchange between nations and races and to give its aid to gatherings of the largest possible international and interracial nature. This point is the more real to me in view of one reason for the formation of this council as stated by Pastor Lilje at Mysore, namely, the necessity on the part of Europe to organize in order to combat a threatened religious invasion from the outside.[25]

Yergan wanted to place the WSCF firmly on a platform of nonracial internationalism. Doing so was not consonant with the organization's Eurocentric leadership, which had little feeling for the world beyond Europe's borders, save as adjunct to Christian civilization. In any case, fewer still could accept that there may have been any lessons worth learning from these backward, backwater areas. In his own way, then, Yergan threatened their hegemony. This shows in his memorandum's concluding point:

(4) Finally I pointed out that if the movements of Europe feel it necessary to act in concert some of us at least in other parts of the world cannot afford to be cut off or to be out of anything that affects us so vitally as theological and international trends in Europe. A case in point is the relationship between Europe and Africa. In every way politically and economically and certainly in the religious realm, Africa has been tremendously influenced by Europe, and this will continue to be the case for many, many years. In view of this we in Africa desire to see Europe's point of view influenced as largely as possible by other sections of the Christian family, namely, the East as well as America. For this reason I have favoured a council which would attend to minor routine and administrative questions common to the European movements. But in regard to larger theological and international questions my view is that what is required is an all European conference emphasizing of course the questions and difficulties of the European movements, and kept within reasonable size, but organized to be representative of the entire Federation, in order that it might serve the entire Federation and in turn to be served by those parts of the Federation outside of Europe.

Porter's response was diplomatic in the extreme. Noting the importance of this communication, he replied that he felt "glad" Yergan was "keeping in touch with Francis," stressing that "we must continue to uphold his hands." Sharing a few items of current WSCF and International Student Service interest, he closed with a soft but unsubtle admonition for staff to close ranks:

> We must continue to think together on various points of the Federation policy. A guiding principle in the European Council will be what will facilitate their work, and at the same time, not interfere with total Federation loyalty.[26]

The following two months brought with them complications in the health of the Yergan family. In April, their eldest son, Frederick, was bedridden, struck down with what appeared to be appendicitis. Ever the missionary, Yergan rationalized that this was "rather hard, but it is a part of the price one must pay for our privilege in Africa."[27] In mid-June, Fort Hare principal Alexander Kerr, responding to a request for information concerning Yergan, submitted references to the Alice magistrate and to the Government Trade Commissioner.[28] Later on in the month Max also revealed that, learning of Susie Yergan's mother's illness, he and Susie had decided that she would travel to the States by late July, leaving their three children in his care, an unprecedented parenting experience for Yergan.[29]

Yergan demurred upon receipt of Porter's May letter, agreeing "with Francis that the period immediately before us is one within which much of the future policy will be settled" and emphasizing that he was "in full accord with your desire that we give him every help possible and hold up his hands in every way."[30] But this may have also been a tactical retreat. Yergan could not press on single-handedly; he needed movement allies. At the moment, he had his hands full, taking care of the children alone for the first time. He had just returned from the extreme north of South Africa, at the border of the Limpopo River separating it from Southern Rhodesia. These travels made him even more anxious to share his knowledge.

The South African elections of July 1929 gave Yergan much to think about, prompting him to reestablish contact with NAACP leader Mary White Ovington. Informing her of the Nationalist Party victory, Yergan detailed the effect of the elections upon the people with whom he worked most closely:

> As a result of the elections Africans are more discouraged than I have observed them to be in a long time. In my recent travels I have discussed the situation with a number of our leaders and I find that they share this general discouragement. Running through it all, however, there is a gleam of optimism. There is a growing consciousness that our way is to be a long and hard one in view of the new circumstances which obtain here as elsewhere in Africa, as a result of historical processes of the past century or so. Personally I have encouraged this point of view on the part of some of the leaders at least for I am convinced that we have simply got to dig ourselves in and lay as solid a foundation as possible. This of course is very complicated, for how can one lay a foundation when one is by law prevented from buying land or selling one's labour wherever one desires, or when one is denied facilities for advanced education, or even good elementary education as is the case here with a few exceptions? It is a recognition of these facts which leads me to say that there are many other approaches to the solution of our difficulties, for instance, the approach by way of labour organization, political education and organization, and doubtless other ways and I never withhold any help or encouragement that I can give to my friends here who are undertaking to deal with our situation from these points of view. I wish you could be here to use it all, get the threads of it for yourself, help us understand it and use your pen about it.[31]

Yergan's reference to a "growing consciousness that our way is to be a long and hard one in view of the new circumstances which obtain here as elsewhere in Africa as a result of historical processes of the past century or so" is subject to varying interpretations. In a direct historical sense the remark may refer to the manner in which the vast majority of Africans lost control of their land to Europe. This did occur roughly within the period of the preceding one hundred years, with some distinction depending upon the area under consideration. But it is also the case that the time frame Yergan referred to saw the emergence of several movements trying to improve conditions for working people. One effort, with which Ovington would have been quite familiar, was the trend toward socialism, to which Yergan may equally as well have been alluding. This movement could attract religious as well as secular radicals, each of which type could be encountered within South Africa; indeed, scores of radicals were both. The key to finding comrades lay in reaching impressionably youthful elements, who had the energy to battle over the long haul. And it is precisely such a group of young militants that Yergan describes thus:

> The most encouraging development that I can write you about has to do with the youth of this land both European as well as African. I have just come back from visits to two of the large University Colleges for Europeans at Johannesburg and Bloemfontein. At each of these places I had a very cordial reception and while all of the people did not agree with my point [of view] they were at least more or less open minded and were willing to discuss questions from a factual basis. In October I am going to have 30 or 40 European students at the South African Native College for a three or four day conference, where we shall give more time to a discussion of the economic and general social aspects of the Racial question here with the hope that we may discover a number of ways whereby there may take place much more cooperation between African and European students.

While the impact of Yergan's solitary activities may easily be overstated, it is vital to give them the weight they merit. Yergan had been active in the Joint Council, as well as in the SCM and its SCA and YMCA affiliates, and posted himself advantageously at Fort Hare. He was thus part of a circle that included teachers and heads not only of Native training institutions of the Cape and Natal but also of the many Whites-only schools and colleges in the Transvaal and Orange Free State, the heart of Afrikanerdom, to which over time he gained entry. On several occasions he appeared before crowds of students, faculty, and staff at such institutions, to great effect, if he and others are to be believed.[32] Perhaps it was his unique status as a "foreign Native" that made it possible to extend courtesies to him which homegrown Africans, irrespective of their accomplishments, were not permitted. Nevertheless, his positive reception reinforced his faith in the power of interracial work.

It is also evident from his letter to Ovington that he was in no way shy about how his work might be regarded, particularly with respect to

its interracial dimension. Here he pulls no punches when informing
Ovington about what he contemplated for the next year:

> In June of next year we are planning for a large National Conference to
> be attended by 150 well chosen African students from all over the
> Union of South Africa as well as Basutoland, Bechuanaland and per-
> haps Southern Rhodesia. There will also be present 50 European stu-
> dents and about 30 teachers both European and African. The confer-
> ence will therefore be interracial. It will also undertake to deal with two
> questions in a rather comprehensive way: (1) What is the real content of
> the Christian Gospel for the life of Bantu students and people today?
> (2) What sort of future have Bantu students and people a right to look
> forward to, and what is the nature of the cooperation that they have a
> right to expect from Christian Europeans? While we shall emphasize
> the religious basis of this conference, we shall in every way seek to place
> equal emphasis upon the whole question of implicating Christian prin-
> ciples in every realm of life. Our conference therefore is bound to be of
> a radical nature, and, I hope, of far reaching consequences.

Yergan also informed Ovington of the larger plans on which he had
been working. They had been broached in prior grant proposals to
Rockefeller, Carnegie, and Phelps Stokes and were now outlined in their
fullest dimensions. Yergan wrote Ovington about an idea similar to
rural YMCA work done in America, but closer to that of India and
Korea, which sought to combine social, religious, and economic needs.
In a three-step process, he had embarked upon organizing a national
committee to help advise him on the project, doing field investigation
and starting to train selected African youth in a social service regime.

> What I am most anxious to do is to station in parts of the country a
> number of young, well chosen men with a social passion and vision and
> with definite ideas and methods for realizing their vision. Our task is
> nothing less than reconstructing the foundation for the life which the
> years ahead of us will demand. That to me is one of the tragedies which
> our people in South Africa and I fear all over Africa are facing and will
> increasingly face. Whether we like it or not, and I am sure we do not
> like it, we are passing through a period not unprecedented in the history
> of Europe and perhaps not in parts of the Far East, whereby strong

forces from without are crowding in upon us in such an overwhelming way that it is impossible for us to withstand them on the basis of our own indigenous strength social, economic or political. The inescapable observation to be made all over Africa today is that the social fabric of this continent is breaking under the impact of Europe politically and America, Europe and Asia economically. There is much talk of the desirability of our not becoming Westernized. But this process is [already] taking place everyday as witness the rapid progress which is being made in political and economic developments here, and as witness the break down in African home life, in the larger social spheres and in the true inwardness of African religious life which in times past was related to and controlled almost every act of the individual African as well as the life of the tribe. I have stated all of this in order to let you see how involved the situation here is and consequently how complicated our task is. In spite of all I have said above, however, the way that I am trying to follow is quite clear and I propose to push on.

As the American autumn began, Susie Wiseman Yergan, back stateside on family business, spoke to students at Bennett College for Women in Greensboro, North Carolina, in October 1929. Sounding a note that would resonate loudly among YMCA and YWCA partisans, she excoriated the infamous tot system whereby African workers were remunerated partly in alcohol. Later on the Black press quoted her as saying, "The liquor traffic is playing havoc with some Africans. In some of the rural districts [where] wages are exceedingly low, some of the men receive only so many drinks of wine for their labor." Wiseman Yergan hammered home the problems of morality, economics, hygiene, disease, and poverty, further stating that "one of the paramount problems is to take care of the rural people and especially the non-student group. We are hoping soon to have out there people who are doing the same type of work as your farm demonstration agents. There is plenty of work for them to do."[33]

The final year of the 1920s brought Yergan both renown and disappointment. The reputation his work achieved, both inside South Africa and beyond it in Europe and North America, brought acclaim; by June, for instance, he was already planning for a monumental Fort Hare interracial conference slated to take place the following year. On the other hand, there remained profound limits to what he as one individual, even "exceptional," American Negro could do. It was clear, for example, that in spite of having at one time met with a number of influential leading figures in the South African YMCA movement, and after seven years of touring and seemingly ceaseless sermonizing before audiences of every conceivable description, the lily-white, separatist nature of the "European" Y movement stubbornly remained intact, with Native and "Coloured" branches on their own. Though he was allied with the system, Yergan's frustration was growing.

The same year saw the reintroduction of the acts of Parliament that had been tried by the Pact government to further dilute the already tepid participation of Nonwhites in political, social, and legal arenas. The effect upon Yergan of these apparently irresistible trends would be great, yet another test of his mettle as a dedicated racial adjuster. Why was he faced with the task of adjusting? Why could not others try to adjust themselves and their own aspirations to fit the needs of building life cooperatively? Was that not the object of Christianity?

Further evidence of Yergan's uneasiness with the state of affairs in 1929 came in his reactions to several talks delivered in England late that year by General Jan C. Smuts. After his general electoral defeat of that year, Smuts accepted the invitation of the Oxford University Rhodes Trust to revisit his alma mater as part of its lecture series. During November, General Smuts presented six public addresses. As Yergan's reply was dated shortly after the second address, it was probably a response to either the first, on "African Settlement," or the second, on "Native Policy," but it was equally as likely a response to both together. Smuts's first talk praised Africa's white rulers, extolling Afrikaner virtues while identifying two rival schools of thought on African development: the imperialist, represented by Cecil Rhodes; and the humanitarian, exemplified by colonization's liberal critics, like Lord Olivier. Separating them, Smuts shared his personal viewpoint on Native character. For him Africans possessed many virtues, but required firm supervision to find and stay on a straight and narrow path. He thought Africans lacked initiative, were happy-go-lucky, were easily satisfied, had little foresight, and were good subordinates when led by masterful white employers.[34]

For Smuts, the solution to the Native "problem" was to recognize how to respond to the Native's specific characteristics by providing needed guidance to allow efficient production to occur, while limiting external influences that would add stress to societies already suffering the ravages of industrialization, by "allowing them to develop along their own separate lines." The reasons behind Smuts's statement were logically spelled out in his second Oxford address about "Native Policy," where he claimed that "the negro and the negroid Bantu form a distinct human type which the world would be poorer without," proclaiming the infantile features of Africans in psychology and outlook.[35]

Having thus painted a portrait that dovetailed neatly with his earlier address on African settlement, Smuts took his conceit of the reputedly easygoing, uncomplicated aspects of "Negroid" demeanor to what he considered its logical conclusion, which was that "wine, women, and song" were valued by Africans, but they lacked art, literature, and religion.[36]

In Smuts's schema, the essential differences in culture and mentality that separated Africans from Europeans needed to be recognized in distinctive approaches to policies governing the two. Incorrect application of policy could lead to a situation whereby an African might be "de-Africanized" and turned either into "a beast of the field or into a pseudo-European." Smuts argued that this had occurred as a result of the ways in which Africans had been treated in the past, first as subhuman and then as equal.[37] This was a phenomenon that other Europeans often called "detribalization."

Smuts, portraying himself as reasonable and progressive and cloaking himself in the garb of a protector of African institutions (not unlike colonial contemporaries in British-, French-, Belgian-, and Portuguese-ruled Africa), was really outlining a plan of marginalization and unprecedented restriction. As he emphasized fostering development along separate lines, the larger purpose of his theory came into focus. The climax of his presentation was reached when he considered the end of policy to be the creation of "separate political institutions for the two" i.e., territorial and institutional segregation.

Smuts was proposing nothing less than turning back the clock on the very social processes that had produced the "school people" who exercised limited but powerful symbolic authority as educated exemplars of ways of life fertilized by the Afro-European encounter. While pretending the opposite, Smuts would arrest this development, dividing rural folk from their urban counterparts by emphasizing African traditional life over Western education.[38]

This notion of limiting the influence of school folk was, in a nutshell, everything that educated Africans, and those committed to making common cause with them, dreaded reading from a head of state in

South Africa's Union. Such sentiments, while hardly unfamiliar to Yergan as an American of African descent and a missionary, still struck him as immoderate. Soon after learning the contents of these addresses, Yergan fired off this enraged reaction to WSCF official Henri-Louis Henriod in Geneva:

> I must also write you and some of the British Student Movement people what I feel about the Rhodes lecture which General Smuts has just given at Oxford. Frankly, I am very much disturbed for his address is of the type which carries so much truth in it that people may not detect the serious fallacies in it and the very dangerous policy which it advocates. Moreover his address is given at the time when it may have the most harmful effect upon the decisions which the British Government may make in regard to the Hilton Young Report. I have observed what seem to be most favourable press reports in England. I am anxious to know what the German and French press have to say about it. In South Africa the most liberal papers like the *Cape Times,* and I am told, even the *Johannesburg Star* have given him most favourable reports, all of which distresses me. It is a strange fact that just now I must turn to the most reactionary Dutch papers like *Ons Vaderland* for a criticism of what they term his shrewd imperialism. Of course it is clear that this stems from their jealousy of and bitterness toward General Smuts.[39]

These Smuts Oxford addresses happened to coincide with the Hilton Young Report referred to in Yergan's letter. Hilton Young had been charged with determining how administration would proceed in East Africa, where competing land claims fed friction between European settlers and African indigenes, in an era during which Britain had resolved that it would protect what it termed the "paramountcy of native interests." Attempts by Smuts to show South Africa's governmental segregation as progressive thus had a dual purpose: first, to project himself as a global statesman; second, to buttress his shattered position at home, resulting from his postelectoral defeat, as he began laying the groundwork for future domestic legislation. Good public relations were thus essential to a wider comeback plan.

Also toward the end of 1929, Yergan met another interesting individual, a student leader at Fort Hare named Donald M'Timkulu.[40] When they met, M'Timkulu led Fort Hare's Student Council and was responsible for helping to stimulate campus interest in and handle arrangements for the major Bantu-European Student Conference that Yergan was then in the process of organizing for the college for the following academic year. Every single detail had to be carefully attended to because its inter-racial atmosphere was not to be restricted to the conference and work-shop areas but extended into previously private and strictly separated spaces—dining areas and dormitories. Participants, White and Black, were to be housed in the same living quarters at a 98 percent Nonwhite institution. While some efforts had been made to introduce Whites and Blacks to common learning and conferring situations, these had still respected the conventional context of social segregation. Yergan's idea was new.

M'Timkulu found Yergan "very acceptable to us black students," re-calling how the African-American's "addresses constantly played on the tune of harmony."[41] M'Timkulu also recalled that Yergan was touted as a symbol, an example to be emulated, by Professor D. D. T. Jabavu, as well as others in his social circle, like future Fort Hare faculty force, Z. K. Matthews; all of these Fort Hare African community members saw Yergan as theirs. Of the pioneer African Fort Hare professor, M'Timkulu said, "Jabavu was very jocular. Now and again in remarks to groups of students, he would point to Max Yergan as the kind of hero figure that we should emulate." Matthews, for M'Timkulu "a dominant student figure" at Fort Hare, also "was a great admirer of Yergan."

At around the same time as he began to take note of Yergan, M'Timkulu also became aware of the active administrative assistant handling Yergan's affairs, friendly Frieda Neugebauer. So approachable and down-to-earth was she, in fact, M'Timkulu recollected, that at first "I didn't realize she was a South African." Only later did he alter that idea. M'Timkulu long thought that Neugebauer hailed from the United States. M'Timkulu added, "Yergan travelled a great deal at various African schools." By 1930 "Student Christian Movement [administra-tive] work in general . . . was mainly done by Frieda Neugebauer." Of her clear uniqueness, M'Timkulu added,

> My impression was simply that she was so easy to get along with. We had only a few—two—white lecturers—women—at Fort Hare, and they were sort of standoffish, but she was not. With her it was easy to establish fairly friendly personal contact. She came to Fort Hare with Max Yergan.[42]

So, between 1929 and 1930, a new helper became prominent in Max's professional and personal life.

Self-Determination: Linking the Two Great "Negro Questions"

The racial and ethnic segmentation of the South African social formation imparted a peculiar character to workers' movements that arose within that milieu. Left-wing radicalism consequently grew at different rates among different sectors of the population and came to assume ethnic and regional overtones. Socialist agitation informed by the Marxian tradition tended to appear overwhelmingly "European" in the period preceding World War One and bore a filial relationship to radicalism in Britain. Inroads were made into African ghettoes or "locations" in the years after 1919, quite phenomenal efforts being made between 1926 and 1929, a period of unprecedented growth. This expansion of socialist sentiment was presaged by the relationship that tied the International Socialist League (ISL) under David Ivon Jones to the Industrial and Commercial Workers Union from 1919 onward. After 1921, a South African Communist Party (CPSA) entered the picture. Communist ideology was often transmitted in study circles and night schools.

Marxist study circles figured prominently through the 1920s but had a particularly profound effect after 1926, receiving a setback in 1928 when the CPSA—following the separatist precedent set by its American counterpart, which had adopted a policy of "self-determination" in a "Black Republic" based in the "Black belt" in the southern states— itself called for a "Native Republic" of workers and peasants. It was in this period that unique emphasis was placed upon cultivating African cadres who might then function as working-class leaders.[43] Beginning with the inauguration of a Ferreirastown experiment in 1926, Communist Party night schools played a major role in aiding African workers to attain some level of fluency in English while also acquainting them with a socialist tradition.[44] Among Whites, while a small number were English speakers, the vast majority were Jews who had recently emigrated from Eastern and Central Europe, a trend that had been occurring throughout the decade and would continue thereafter.

Some of the early formulations that took shape in these schools were, for linguistic reasons, frequently extremely awkward, and look theoretically rudimentary for their naïvely crude reductionism. The Ferreirastown school founder, Edward Roux, a White dedicated to stimulating the growth of African cadres, provided an example. In 1926, T. W. Thibedi wrote an article in his native Sesotho in the *South African Worker.* Its English translation included this description of class struggle:

> There are only two groups of people on the earth and they are as follows:—
>
> 1. The group of the capitalists who stand only to govern the workers and make laws by which they succeed in robbing the workers of the product of their labour power.
> 2. The second group is that of the workers which is the one that makes everything necessary for life.
>
> These two groups do not agree, but face each other like a cat and a rat. . . . Now it is the duty of all workers of all countries to unite and fight against the capitalists and their laws and against the robbery that is made by the rich. If you workers wish to live in nice houses and get all the necessities of life, you must overthrow the capitalist government and start a government where capitalism and poverty shall not be known, as they have done in Russia.[45]

In the vernacular this was very effective. No doubt many working-class Africans received not only invaluable instruction in English in these schools but also exposure to the theories of class struggle, of capitalist exploitation, and of the relationship between class divisions and racist oppression. Recalling his experience in one such school, Moses Kotane, a participant who later rose to become a Communist Party general secretary, shared the following vivid remembrance:

> One thing struck me very deeply and that was the Native study class. Here the real wage slaves are being enlightened in the direction of literacy. Here in the slum area, in a "hall" fitted with benches and so-called tables, gather big, hefty pupils to listen to, swallow and digest the words of their teachers. In the vague and gloomy light of a few lamps and candles there sit those dark masses before whom one day the great capitalists will tremble and beg for mercy. With backs bent, intent on study, with a craving and desire for knowledge not equalled among whites, they are gaining the knowledge which is power and which will one day help them to accomplish the social revolution in conjunction with their white fellow-workers.[46]

Unlike the older African National Congress and the Industrial and Commercial Workers' Union, whose prominence and mass appeal were based upon attempts to overcome the intra-ethnic contradictions of a brutally divisive, race-conscious social formation, the South African Communist Party, fueled by the "Native Republic thesis," embraced, in theory and aspiration, *racial* integration, even though introducing new African cadres into its ranks had almost destroyed it during the late twenties. Despite tokenism in many instances, it was clear that among the most visible party militants stood men and women of African origin, especially by the decade's end. Openly defying law, custom, and prior party practice, these recruits were now political comrades and, at least nominally, potential social equals. While theoretically problematic, the policy did spur Black recruitment.

Coming fresh from a meanly segregated North America during the 1920s, Yergan would have found this unprecedented interest in attracting members to the CPSA striking. In addition, Yergan's work in the interracial Joint Council Movement eschewed the ethnic nationalism of most "race" men and women of the period in favor of work within ostensibly interracial (although certainly not integrated) settings. There was thus a degree of continuity between Joint Council participation and association with Communist members professing nonracialism. But Yergan had to have been impressed by the differences between the Whites he encountered in the moderate but apolitical Joint Councils and the more openly combative, fearless, outspoken, and uncompromising White Communists engaged in trying to fight racialism in ways that even liberals considered irresponsible.

However, the racial dimension of the matter should not obscure the fact that the "Negro" and "Native" questions emerged as subsets of the broader national and colonial question. While Black membership was first considered in 1920, not until the Third Congress of the Communist International in 1924 were Comintern members from colonial territories able to influence the direction of debates on this key issue. By 1927, a full-fledged League against Imperialism appeared. Among its representatives were two South African militants, African National Congress (ANC) leader Josiah T. Gumede and "Coloured" Communist Jimmy La Guma. Prior to this Congress, colonial delegates, mostly Nonwhite, swallowed their national and racial pride as their situations and struggles were trivialized by specialists who often treated them in a patronizing, high-handed, and arrogant manner. With forbearance, tact, and a quiet determination not unlike that required of Yergan in South Africa, such colonial cadres as India's M. N. Roy, Vietnam's Ho Chi Minh, Sen Katayama of Japan, and Semaun of Java eventually made their presence felt. The racial side of the South African national question delayed African participation in its solution until the middle and late 1920s. While Yergan's awareness of the debate is not known, he knew some of its principals.[47]

The Comintern's line change, which tied struggles of Black South Africans to those of African-Americans in the South, is thus of great interest. This could be both convenient and challenging for someone in a position like Yergan's. Although South Africa differed from the United States, racism, the color bar, and a parallel segregation system made it more familiar terrain for a Black American than many non-Africans wished to acknowledge. This was certainly a factor in the attempt to block Yergan and other Negro missionaries from entering the country. By the 1930s, using the messianic tradition of activist, liberatory interpretation of biblical texts, Black South Africans and Black Americans sought, on several occasions, to achieve convergence. In responding to a revitalized Communist Party actively courting darker constituencies in both countries, Yergan heeded yet another call—a mission he seemed uniquely qualified to fulfill—rooted in the ecumenical social gospel.

The Social Gospel Trend within the Ecumenical Movement

Max Yergan was not the only ideologue in his theological cohort who was moved to think differently by the events of the Depression era. Mention has already been made of John Mott's internationalism, along with Ned Carter's leading role in the Pacific Relations Institute. George Haynes, founder of the Urban League and race relations head for the Federal Council of Churches, did racial adjustment advocacy. Yergan was in close touch with all of these men, in addition to others of a more philanthropic bent whose support for the YMCA was great. If not radicals, they were at least tolerant of radicalism.

Among the three, Haynes's relationship with Yergan was unique. Haynes, like Yergan, was at heart a social gospeler; moreover, by academic training and overall reputation, he was securely tied to the foundation nexus, trading on postwar links to the Russell Sage Fund. As a

logical outgrowth of his respect for Yergan's achievements as a conciliator and his interest in the race relations field, Haynes was drawn to
South Africa. He attended a conference planning meeting organized by
Yergan with ten White clerics in Cape Town in May 1930. Haynes
asked, "What would be the attitude of the churches to the projection of
work among the colored and the Bantu population of the City?"

Quick to respond was Congregationalist cleric Ferguson, who said
that as a body "the churches had a genuine interest in the welfare and
development of the colored people and would welcome any work that
would help them." When one minister queried the reason behind
Haynes's question, he stated that "the Y is an arm of the church, [that]
its fundamental policy is to place the controlling voting power of the
organization in the hands of those who are active members of churches;
[and] that the experience of the Y in other lands indicated that the
progress of the work hinged on the cooperation of the churches."
Haynes's retort prompted the question whether the YMCA "had a plan
and a program which it proposed to bring into the area." Haynes
turned a challenge into an opportunity, relating that each territory's
plan is "worked out by those in the country, [and] that the criteria by
which our survey is to judge the work begun among Natives by Yergan
are drawn from . . . the ideals, purposes, policies . . . which have been
undertaken, the result achieved and the conditions and needs which
confronted the movement in S.A." Referring to the Y recruitment effort,
Haynes concluded that "the churches would rally to such an effort."[48]

A sobering note was sounded as "old Meiring" of the Dutch Reformed Church ventured a warning, his fellow Afrikaner constituents in
mind.

> He said he would offer me one caution. In traveling through the coun-
> try and speaking, especially to people of Dutch extraction, but also to
> others, bear in mind that there are those who have the liberal point of
> view but there are many others and what I may say may make the task
> of the progressives hard or easier.[49]

Haynes's response was very like what might have issued from Yergan:

> I assured him that my main work is observation and inquiry; that
> speaking was only to be done where it could not wisely be omitted; that

I should then speak only of what I knew about in America; [and] that I would be cautious even in that.[50]

Though Yergan was credited as having cohosted the interview, he carefully played his familiar behind-the-scenes role, presumably to guarantee the White religious leaders maximum exposure to yet another American Negro dedicated to cooperative racial adjustment. He delicately allowed them to draw their own conclusions regarding Haynes's fitness to conduct his investigation of African Y work. This statement facilitated a seamless, genial closure to their talk, as the collective emphasized this point within the context of a hearty endorsement by participating Cape churches. A spirit of "observation and inquiry" led Haynes through his address to and record of Fort Hare's June interracial meeting.[51]

Bantu-European Student Christian Conference, June 1930

The universally acknowledged zenith of Max Yergan's career as a YMCA secretary was reached in the unprecedented interracial SCA gathering he organized at Fort Hare, June 27–July 3, 1930: the Bantu-European Student Christian Association Conference. The meeting was noteworthy as a rare opportunity for Whites and Blacks to interact on a nonracial level. Such a conclave would have been a major event anywhere in the world at that time—including the segregated United States—but that it occurred in South Africa was astounding. The participants who assembled constituted a veritable who's who of South African liberalism, but also included racial moderates from outside the country as well.

On Friday, June 27, Max Yergan dedicated the new structure in remarks carried by the press.

> This is the building for the Christian Union, which has crystallised in brick and stone the dreams of our students for several years. This building is to serve a threefold purpose. It is to provide a common centre for the Bantu students of the Union, to furnish a community centre for this area and to offer training for those students who come to Fort Hare for preparation as leaders in YMCA work and in social service among the Bantu people in the urban and rural areas of the Union.[52]

Susie Yergan unlocked the doors to the new Fort Hare Christian Union Building and welcomed the delegates to enter, at which time Francis P. Miller, chairman of the World's Student Christian Federation spoke of the gathering as one intended to express a common faith, exemplified in the symbolism of a nascent edifice but also dependent upon concrete spiritual endeavor. Other speakers were E. H. Brookes, Howard Pim, D. D. T. Jabavu, Principal Alexander Kerr, Charlotte Maxeke, Ray Phillips, A. B. Xuma, W. G. Ballinger, George E. Haynes, and R. V. Selope Thema. Jan Hofmeyr, M.P., delivered a keynote address before an integrated audience of nearly four hundred, the flower of South Africa's youth, Black and White alike. Max considered the assemblage a demonstration of Christianity in action. Analyzing the gathering's significance, Yergan later wrote,

> This conference was undertaken with three definite purposes in view: first to clarify for ourselves the meaning of the Christian gospel and ascertain more deeply the truth of God which is in Christ; secondly to discover more effective ways to implement in our full corporate life the fullest content of the Christian faith; and, thirdly, to bring together representative students and senior people of the European and Bantu races of Southern Africa in order that together we might face the needs and facts of our common life and together seek a way out of our difficulties.[53]

White participants in the conference were not always able to transcend the limitations of time and race. Howard Pim read a paper later printed under the title "Introduction to Bantu Economics," the central thesis of which asked whether "African economics" was not a contradiction in terms. For Pim, Africa's collective ethos had both strengths and weaknesses. The latter could be glimpsed in what he took as "tribal" power, whose effects Pim summed up as antithetical to Western thought and practice:

> In fact then the "Science of Economics" as we Europeans understand the term is a feature and a consequence of individualism, and only to the extent that the Bantu are individualists, and this means only since they have met the European and followed his lead, have they any "Economics" at all.[54]

Of relevance to Yergan is that whatever hope Pim held out for the improvement of the Bantu lay in their ability to imitate those he saw as salutary exemplars, America's Negroes. In making this argument, Pim followed not only the lines laid out by late governor of the Gold Coast, Sir Gordon Guggisberg, but also a widely held belief among both Blacks and Whites from which Yergan benefited. For all its ethnocentric faults, Pim's argument did lead to this point:

> I do not claim that this remarkable advance made by the American Negro proves that the South African Native is capable of bridging the gulf that in South Africa divides him from the European, but I do say that it shows quite definitely that people of Negro and Bantu race are capable of prospering under a social system that is individualistic in the extreme, and if they have done it once I see no reason why they should not do it again. There is no justification whatever for refusing them the opportunity, especially as if they fail no one can be worse off than if opportunity had been denied, while their success will redound to the prosperity of all.[55]

Even if Pim seemed to be speaking above all to himself and other "Europeans" and was certainly excluding the Nonwhite audience, his comments concerning this emulative road to progress were revealing.

A great irony of this situation was that it represented an attempt to transcend racial barriers by the Bantu Student Christian Association—the very embodiment of the South African form of racial segregation.[56] Such an effort had not been undertaken by White liberals or White institutions; it was left to Black people, those lethally oppressed and toxically disadvantaged by the color bar, to create a remedy that acknowledged the cruelty with which racism victimized masters and minions alike by rendering it impossible to recognize the ways that each depended upon the other, the inextricable ties that bound them. Fort Hare Professor Edgar H. Brookes praised Yergan's effort as follows:

> Max Yergan has done an unobtrusive but wonderful work in South Africa. He more than any other individual, conceived and planned this Conference and carried it through to success. We are grateful to America for the gift of this modest Christian gentleman, a true knight who

has achieved the conquest of his own soul and is ever ready to conquer others for his Lord.[57]

Here then, "Bantu" Christians demonstrated to their "European" co-religionists, with whom they could not even share full membership in one body pledging to promote Christian comity, how genuine Christianity should be practiced. With one audacious stroke, Yergan took complete advantage of this extraordinary opportunity, creating conditions for a temporary suspension of segregation in dining halls, sporting arenas, and meeting rooms. This brought Black and White students, faculty, staff, and guests closer to one another than either group had ever dared dream possible. Barely a week long, this social experiment had great ramifications, its resounding echoes reverberating past Fort Hare, Alice, and the Cape into the countryside, penetrating as far as Afrikaner Stellenbosch. Again, a Black American seeking common cause with Africans had shown the way to a revolution. As Don M'Timkulu recollected,

> Stellenbosch was there, Pochefstroom was there, and Pretoria was there, and, of course, we had the English—Anglophone—universities: Cape Town, Rhodes University, Natal, they were also there. So it was—from the point of view of anyone interested in inter-racial harmony—it was a tremendous success. But as I say, it aroused real tremendous hostility, as for the first time I should think, the Afrikaners took seriously the whole question of interracial mingling, which before, I mean, the general attitude of the Afrikaners, as far as the blacks are concerned was that "they're nice fellows and not too troublesome"—that's all. But now they were faced with the fact of a kind of equality between black and white for which they were absolutely unprepared. So as far as the South African angle was concerned, the conference at Fort Hare, and the fact that Max Yergan was the main organizer of that conference, sent up his reputation very high, particularly amongst the blacks.[58]

The repercussions of the conference were immediate and far reaching. As soon as the meeting began, it garnered coverage in the local news media, Afrikaans as well as Anglophone. The *Cape Times* accorded it first-page space for three days straight. But nothing said could approach the physical facts of the case for causing controversy. Helen

R. Bryan, secretary of the Committee on Race Relations for the American Friends Service Committee, who interviewed the Yergans in 1931, reconstructed the most delicate part of the scene as follows:

> After two meals at which the students had been divided according to their race, a group of European students accosted the conference leaders with the inconsistency of their methods saying they had been summoned to the conference to think together but that this purpose was decidedly retarded by the artificial division in the dining hall. The system was arranged so as to conform with the students' suggestion.[59]

Some commentators felt that a dire precedent had been set. Not surprisingly, many such opinions came from Afrikaner conservatives and fearful Anglo South Africans. Yergan's greatest regret was that the conference was not attended by more "Dutch" speakers. To his mind they would have had the most to gain from a chance to actively experience Christian fellowship with their African peers. On the other hand, White conservatives felt that they also had the most to lose by rubbing shoulders with people they believed to be their social, racial, cultural, intellectual, and spiritual inferiors. Judging by the responses of commentators critical of the event, it was widely believed that Yergan's gamble had been a major fiasco, several considering it a provocative but counterproductive exercise exceeding the bounds of good taste. The controversy snowballed.

Given reportage of the event, M'Timkulu's memory that the Afrikaner press and public proved totally unprepared for what transpired at friendly Fort Hare appears to be an understatement. In a letter to the tendentious *Die Burger,* a correspondent published this provocative account:

> The place is the sitting-room of a public boarding-house, not far from Worcester. The speaker, a prominent member of the staff of a European training school in the Western Province, and, as he insisted with emphasis, a member of the Head Committee of the Union Students' Christian Association. The audience, white Afrikaner school-going boys and girls with parents and friends. After preliminary religious performances, the speaker said that he was just back from the Christian Students' Congress at Fort Hare, and wished, Oh, so much, to tell of the wonderful

development of the Kaffirs and the brotherly atmosphere of their community there. First he told them of the wonderful learning riches and high birth of the American Negro who is apparently the head of the Fort Hare Kaffir School or "College" as he called it—a gentleman, who, when he had come out from America was at his (the speaker's) house and shook hands with his wife in a truly gentlemanly fashion, and how at that time, though some of the Europeans were at first against it, the Church Council at last gave the hall for an address by this Dr. —— to a packed audience of whites.[60]

The riotous reaction to the Fort Hare fellowshipping was by no means confined to journalists' reports. "European" students, particularly those from institutions in the Afrikaner heartland, were the recipients of all kinds of abuse. M'Timkulu recalled, "Some of the students faced some really hostile criticism when they got back to their home areas."[61] The reason for this was not difficult to determine as Afrikanerdom fought fiercely for the hearts and minds of its sons and daughters:

Some of them [the conference attendees], particularly those that came from the Dutch Reformed Seminaries [were exposed to this because]—I might say it was even more important in South Africa because the white universities which were involved were some of the biggest and most well known universities.[62]

Even the otherwise bold principal of Fort Hare, Dr. Alexander Kerr, virtually uniformly revered for fair-mindedness and probity, became positively timid facing the furor that his African-American friend and fellow missionary's nonracist fearlessness had fueled. Forty years later he still addressed the controversial subject of integration nebulously:

At the opening of the hall in 1930, a conference for the discussion of matters religious, social, racial and economic was attended by 300 delegates under the presidency of the Chairman of the worldwide YMCA Organization. Papers were read by authorities in the separate departments and lively discussions followed. More than local interest was taken by the Press, not so much in the subjects discussed, as in the fact that European students and guests had been accommodated in the College hostels and all meals had been served in the College dining hall without segregation of the races. In retrospect, this was an early exhibition of the climate of opinion which foreshadowed a policy that was to become much more prominent politically in later years.[63]

But those within the orbit of the WSCF, SCM, YMCA, and YWCA, as well as their philanthropic and humanitarian supporters, also noted Yergan's achievement. One of these was Thomas Jesse Jones, who gave a copy of the August 1930 South African *Outlook* commemorating the event to his colleague Anson Phelps Stokes, commenting, "As you will note, the Bantu-European Conference was organized by Mr. Yergan. From all accounts it has been a real achievement in the direction of interracial relations and the effective development of the Native People."[64]

Seeking to capitalize on the achievement of the conference's goals, Yergan wrote Rockefeller Fund executive Thomas Appleget that the building was functioning and that the daring Bantu-European interracial experiment had truly proven successful. In his letter, Yergan summed up the meeting's threefold significance. It was important, first of all, in that it occurred; secondly, in that it was a religious gathering that showed the power of Christianity in action; and thirdly, in that it was a manifestation of the possibility of finding a middle road. Appleget responded,

> Certainly the information which you send me is very encouraging. No wonder you are so enthusiastic after such a conference. You are performing a highly useful and courageous function in one of the most delicate and complicated of fields. For that reason you must not be discouraged if things do not always go as well as the meetings which you describe in your letter. Every step can not be forward, but I am certain of the inevitable progress of your march.[65]

Yet in spite of the sage counsel provided by Appleget, the vituperative attitude of local White conservatives toward the Fort Hare conference deeply wounded Max. While he often evoked it in his WSCF correspondence, he proved unable for months to write at length about the gathering. It must have been painful for him to comprehend how something on which he had labored for so long, marshaling all available resources, could yet have been received so thoroughly unsympathetically. This did little to ease his troubled mind; rather, it intensified his sense of uncertainty about the value and propriety of the burden he had committed himself to share in South Africa, for people imprisoned within a state and society impervious to even the smallest, least threatening efforts to bring about change. At that very moment when he should have been able to celebrate, to take a much deserved rest, to celebrate a job well done, fate dealt him another bitter pill.

The year 1931 brought Yergan to the United States, where he engaged in a number of lengthy discussions with his old mentor, Moorland. Early that year he shared a YMCA panel with Ethan Theodore Colton, a Y partisan worriedly captivated by the Soviet Union, having recently published a treatise entitled *The XYZ of Communism*. Yergan left the States in August of that year, en route to Cape Town via London. One of the sojourners Yergan met while in London was Morehouse president Dr. John Hope, with whom he spent several days in London before permitting himself to be coaxed into accompanying Hope to France. They motored through the Bois de Boulogne, then went by rail to Versailles. President Hope would travel to Russia that winter, and this trip may have come up in conversation.[66] Indeed, several of his London days were passed conversing with people who either had traveled to or were considering visiting the Soviet Union. Yergan became so enthusiastic about what they had to say that he spent three weeks seeking a visa so that he, too, might savor the great Soviet achievement. However, her was foiled by interminable delays. At this time, his thoughts turned to the pressing need for a thorough, fundamental transformation of the prevailing social and economic order. In a frank letter to Moorland, Yergan bared his soul:

> I have never been so aware of theories. My days in England during the time of the political and financial crisis there, and even my limited understanding of the absence of any plan or courageous programme for dealing with these problems as they touch practically every country in the world all lead me to believe that it is a revolution we require in order that a large part of the past may be blotted out forever and a new chance given to man to try again for a life better than the one we live today. That is really my belief and state of mind just now; and coming back to Africa has only confirmed it.[67]

Hope's invitation to Yergan to meet him in Paris extended to attending the large French Colonial Exposition then underway there, an exhibit that received much international attention and acclaim. However, the show struck Yergan as anything but positive. As he later frankly informed Moorland,

> I was greatly disappointed with it. It revealed to me the subtle and callous nature of French colonial policy. While pretending to make French subjects of their colonial population, and lift them to the advantages of French civilization, this exhibition made it quite clear that the French like all European colonial powers are interested in one thing only—the exploitation of the country and the people whom they profess to desire to civilize. The French are just now carrying on an energetic campaign to unite all of the colonizing powers against what they call "the communist terror"; this is aimed really at fastening further shackles upon millions in Africa and elsewhere.[68]

Central to solidifying this inchoate yearning for revolution was Yergan's friendship with the performing artist and political activist Paul Robeson and with Robeson's spouse, the writer and former chemist Eslanda Cardozo Goode. Unable to secure satisfying outlets for their multidimensional talents in the United States, the Robesons, like so many other African-American artists and intellectuals, sought more fertile fields on foreign shores. For Paul Robeson this included not just the unique charm of aesthetic endeavor and a broader range and number of employment opportunities but also the ideological stimulation provided by the presence of a lively corps of tough-minded, anticolonial, and antifascist intellectuals and trade unionists in London, many of whom were of African and Caribbean extraction. Essie Robeson, who studied anthropology under Bronislaw Malinowski and sociology under Raymond Firth at the London School of Economics, wrote several valuable books treating this vibrant era.

Robeson and Yergan would have had lots to converse about in 1931. They traveled in concentric circles. Both had been subjects of chapters in two pioneering studies of African-American achievement published in 1927, *In Spite of Handicaps* and *Portraits in Color*. Both had been awarded the Spingarn Medal, the highest laurel conferred by the NAACP for accomplishments within the field of race relations. They were also active members of the Alpha Phi Alpha fraternity, as was W. E. B. Du Bois. Robeson and Yergan were especially concerned with the colonial situation and its effects on Africa's scions and were united in their conviction that Americans of African descent had more than a nominal interest in the conditions faced by their kith and kin who yet resided in the ancestral continent. Finally, both men shared strongly religious backgrounds in which Christian practice included a commitment to working for social change. These common interests and Robeson's links with radical activists would have provided many opportunities for Yergan to expand his senses and sphere of contacts.

The Robeson-Yergan relationship, however, as crucial as it may have been, was not the sole factor in this "second conversion" of the African-American missionary. No less decisive was his receptivity to South African radicalism. By the 1930s an oppositional landscape in South Africa had emerged. Growing Communist Party influence caused Yergan to devote close attention to its activities and led him to make contact with party militants and sympathizers. The root of this lure is based in part upon ideological changes Yergan had begun to manifest during 1931.

Crisis in the World's Student Christian Federation

The upbeat outcome of the landmark Bantu-European Student Conference at Fort Hare should have seemed sufficient to guarantee even greater renown for Yergan and his innovative endeavors. As it happened, however, Yergan's public triumph only presaged a private trauma with profound professional and personal consequences. In the course of the deliberations undertaken by conference members, Yergan was frequently observed in the company of Mrs. Rena Datta, née Rena Carswell, a secretary in the WSCF office in Geneva and the spouse of another federation official, author Dr. Surendra Kumar Datta. S. K. and Rena Datta had joined the WSCF after lengthy service in the Indian YMCA, where the Dattas were each well-known leaders.

Rena Carswell's connection with the WSCF began in 1911 when she was named personal secretary to Ruth Rouse of the federation. Carswell, who had previously been prominent in the British Student Christian Movement, toured North America and southeastern Europe with Rouse between 1912 and 1914. She subsequently served as general secretary of the YWCA in India, Burma, and Ceylon before becoming a WCSF official in her own right.[69]

Although Yergan and Rena Datta had worked intensely on this and other WSCF business during the months preceding the Fort Hare conference, the official who noticed them began to suspect that there may have been more than merely federation matters on their minds and suggested as much to Dr. Francis P. Miller, the chair of the federation. Miller then undertook what may only be described as an investigation, in order to determine the seriousness of the allegation and, if necessary, devise a remedy allowing the concerned parties to salvage the situation.

In his autobiography, *Man from the Valley,* Miller outlined the events that transpired in the wake of the Fort Hare conference.

> I was about to take my departure from Fort Hare when a conversation occurred which introduced me to a personal scandal within the organization whose ramifications eventually reached out to three continents and threatened the very integrity of the World's Student Christian Federation itself. The crisis continued for the next two years, involving American Negroes, British, and Indians who were all members of the inner group of the Federation. Eventually, it was resolved through the withdrawal of the main characters from Federation work.[70]

This reflection, made almost forty years after the event described, indicates the degree to which the WSCF was able to contain the scandal to which Miller referred.

Max Yergan's situation was certainly conducive to an affair. As has already been mentioned, he spent significant periods away from home. With the passing of the decades, he came increasingly to be viewed as a valuable addition to interracial ecumenical meetings for both his ideas and the disarming, witty, and nonantagonistic way in which these were usually presented. It must be added that, from the earliest days of his appearance as a public figure, his photographs reveal that Yergan cut a profile strikingly handsome, which made him keenly popular with audiences wherever he went. A world traveler, an articulate speaker, projecting a bright, genial, engaging, ostensibly easygoing manner and winning smile and affecting a glowing, perennially youthful visage, Max Yergan easily drew attention and admirers; little evidence suggests that he did much to discourage either. He used his appearance to wield extraordinary personal power. Even when he began showing his age, this magnetic appeal remained—and surely had an impact on Rena Datta.

The friendship Yergan and Rena Datta struck up was clearly an outgrowth of their work. Both were confronted by the relentless challenges of doing interracial work with moderates and liberals on a daily basis. They saw each others as allies in this often lonely struggle. It didn't hurt that Rena knew India well and Max retained fond memories of his months in strife-torn Bangalore during World War One. They were both far away from home—she based in frigid Switzerland, he in temperate but culturally alien South Africa—each seeking some respite from the ceaselessly rigorous demands of racial leadership.

Yergan probably knew S. K. Datta from his Bangalore days, since Dr. Datta was then second in command of India's YMCA. Yergan appears to have met Rena Datta in 1928 at the time of the Mysore conference. Extremely impressed by her, he communicated this to Chairman Miller in a letter. Yergan asked S. K. Datta to attend the 1930 Fort Hare Conference, but conflicting scheduling commitments rendered this impossible. Both Yergan and Datta were seen as WSCF race relations specialists.[71]

However innocently it began, over time hawk-eyed observers within the federation began to speculate about the flowering of an inordinate degree of mutual interest between these two fellow WSCF workers. It is uncertain when this scrutiny started, but it gradually ensnared Edgar Thamae, Yergan's personal secretary, Fort Hare's principal, Alexander Kerr, Oswin B. Bull, Francis Miller, John R. Mott, Susie Wiseman Yergan, and others. Thamae was implicated after he revealed that he had been issued instructions to personally deliver any messages from Geneva directly to Yergan. Shortly thereafter, an unusually heavy amount of WSCF cable traffic was perceived as having been exchanged between Geneva and Alice. But it was the offhand remark by the unidentified person at the conclusion of the 1930 Bantu-European Fort Hare meeting that ultimately led Francis Miller to consider taking action.

For six months, Miller and several associates in the federation exchanged memoranda on the Yergan-Datta affair. Because Miller was WSCF chairman, any disciplinary measures that might be warranted would fall upon him to formulate and enact. Miller had evidently hoped that, upon being confronted with the matter, the principals would recognize the extent to which their relationship might have been misconstrued, would recant, and would go on with their lives in a manner consistent with Christian mores.

In fact, however, this proved a massive miscalculation on Miller's part. Far from accepting responsibility for untoward behavior or for permitting others to draw such inferences from detailed observation, both Yergan and Datta launched virulent counterattacks on Miller. In Datta's case, this was done with the support of her husband, who was personally insulted at what he stated was undue familiarity with his wife, not from Yergan but from Miller, who routinely greeted her by her given name. Yergan's response was that Miller ultimately proved unable to overcome the prejudice inherent in his aristocratic Virginia upbringing and had leveled at him baseless, racist, personal attacks.

As Miller's investigation unfolded, it seemed that the accused had destroyed the evidence. Whatever letters, cables, or printed messages might have been conveyed back and forth between Datta and Yergan, no paper trail could be found. Yet, this was not the end of the matter. Intent upon pursuing his inquiry to the bitter end, Miller constructed what he must have envisioned as an air-tight case against Datta and Yergan, making mention of "divorce" to state what one or the other "estranged" parties would perforce contemplate—a highly charged, ill-chosen term having divergent legal and informal implications in English and American usage and custom. The reality remained that there was no conclusive proof that divorce was viewed as either inevitable or desirable, although it might be inferred that Mrs. Susie Yergan entertained the idea. The divorce reference further incensed S. K. Datta, who then heatedly threatened legal action against Miller.

The affair became notorious, news reaching Channing Tobias, Yergan's long-time friend and colleague from his Colored Work Department days, and others in the WSCF's New York, London, and Geneva offices. Miller is correct in indicating that the situation took two years to resolve, and then only with the departure of the principals from the group. This case was hanging over the head of Max Yergan like some sword of Damocles all the time that he moved to the left. To a great extent, his life and future career within the federation clearly depended upon a successful outcome in this treacherous case—one that could lead either to complete exoneration or abject ignominy.

For this and other reasons, 1931 contained many challenges for Yergan. As January opened, New York–based Y officials wired Yergan urging a sudden recall stateside, ostensibly to resist the dire straits of steadily deepening Depression and its effect on YMCA finances. Accordingly, Yergan booked passage on a ship that sailed on March 11, on what was designated as a "special trip," arriving, after some delay, in New York by the end of April. He wrote Phelps Stokes to inform the philanthropist of an upcoming speaking engagement at Howard University slated for the midpoint of the forthcoming month. Telling Phelps Stokes of having received an emergency call home, he sought to arrange an in-person interview with the fund's director.[72]

Within days of Yergan's New York landing, F. P. Miller also cabled two WSCF officials, Martin and W. A. Visser 'T Hooft. At about the same time Yergan was meeting with Phelps Stokes, Miller zealously pressed his investigation through WSCF channels.[73] Meanwhile, Yergan got word from Phelps Stokes that he would try to arrange an appointment for Yergan to meet the South African minister, Eric Louw. Phelps Stokes added that "Louw has recently visited Tuskegee and was impressed."[74] Phelps Stokes was then planning a Carnegie South Africa lecture tour.[75]

Max's status had continued to ascend in the corporate offices of the Phelps Stokes, Rockefeller, and Carnegie funds. A week prior to Yergan's Phelps Stokes meeting, Rockefeller secretary Thomas Appleget had spoken highly of the young man to Dr. Edmund E. Day, director of social sciences for the Rockefeller Foundation, and urged Yergan to pursue this contact on his own when feasible.[76] In short order, Appleget wrote Phelps Stokes in response to a Stokes communication mentioning their commitment to aid Yergan's work. This occurred close on the heels of Yergan's Phelps Stokes meeting. Appleget mentioned writing Carnegie Foundation head Frederick P. Keppel along similar lines. Then Appleget shared a compelling idea that may have had a bearing upon Yergan's future plans:

> Incidentally, I have been wondering lately if Yergan might not eventually be a man to consider as president of some southern educational institution. It seems to me that a man who can deal so successfully with the Dutch and the English and the natives in South Africa might have some hopes of succeeding with a board of trustees, a faculty and a student and alumni body in America. I should deeply appreciate your opinion as to what Yergan should eventually do with himself.[77]

Phelps Stokes, preparing to see Yergan again within a fortnight, then received an invitation from three Yergan YMCA associates to attend a special luncheon honoring Yergan and YMCA author Ethan T. Colton.[78] Three days later Phelps Stokes replied to Appleget's career suggestion for Yergan with characteristic tact and promptness. Giving the matter the time it merited, Phelps Stokes declared,

My impression is that Max Yergan is doing a work of such great significance in South Africa that it would be inadvisable to call him back to the United States unless conditions are such that he cannot wisely continue there. As you know, the race problem in South Africa is probably the most complicated in the world. I make no exceptions. Now Yergan is one of the few Colored men who has tackled the problem wisely and constructively and who has the confidence of the best elements in all groups. I am inclined to think, therefore, that although he would be well fitted for certain types of work in the south, it would be wiser for him to remain where he is if he can continue to carry on in a reasonably effective way.[79]

Rockefeller and Phelps Stokes Foundation staff members were present at Yergan's May 18 luncheon appearance with YMCA partisan and writer-lecturer on Soviet affairs, Ethan T. Colton. Rockefeller's A. W. Packard evaluated Yergan's performance in brief but strikingly sensitive minutes:

> Mr. Yergan's talk covered in general the points already brought out in his presentation here. We were further impressed with the earnestness of his own efforts and the significance which is inherent in his undertaking. We asked him afterwards what success he was having here in raising funds. He seemed to be rather blue and discouraged.[80]

It may have been the case that pecuniary problems were not the only problems plaguing Yergan at that moment.

Yergan remained in the United States through August, when he took leave of his old friend and mentor, J. E. Moorland. Thereupon he quit the country, originally intending to spend a week to ten days in England. Once there, however, he found that he wandered restlessly, lingering a month during which he came into contact with unnamed and unnumbered people who had been to the Soviet Union. So moved was he by having met them that he tried to obtain a visa for himself but was prevented from doing so by bureaucratic delays. That same month Yergan ran into Dr. John Hope, his old Colored Y colleague, whom he had relieved in France in July 1919. Hope invited Max to meet him in Paris. They drove to the Bois de Boulogne, then had dinner. That Sunday they visited Versailles. In the same time frame Yergan and Hope saw France's Colonial Exposition.

In April 1932, Yergan communicated with Miss Una Saunders of the Geneva office of the WSCF on the subject of "Bantu" work for girls and women within the YWCA of South Africa. Having already unofficially entered into deliberations along these lines in response to a previous letter from the same correspondent, Yergan outlined his views on the prospect of affiliating a Black branch of the YWCA in South Africa to the World Committee of YMCAs in Geneva. Saunders had visited the country on an ill-fated fact-finding mission with this aim prior to that time, either late in 1931 or early in 1932. From his conversations, Yergan got the impression that "nothing is contemplated whereby a separate YWCA organization will begin to serve Bantu women and girls."[81]

Yergan's vision of African YWCA work was an extension of his training scheme, devised to address the needs of women and men, rural and urban, as well as boys and girls. Max continued, stating that he saw this as a five- to seven-year commitment by the conclusion of which it should be evident whether the idea was a workable one. He then reminded Saunders that he already had a small fund of a little over two thousand pounds with which to begin the course. As far as Y recruitment work for women was concerned, a woman needed to be sent out as a secretary from overseas, he affirmed.

Outwardly at least, Yergan's public relations project proceeded apace. He made profitable use of his time in the next six weeks. Given the way the philanthropic network functioned, informally as well as formally, it is doubtful that rumors about his alleged affair were kept fully under wraps. In any event they seem not to have deterred him. By mid-June, Yergan had sent Patrick Duncan, Carnegie Corporation trustee and minister of mines for South Africa, a memo on his training project, along with a revised proposal:

> The work which we have developed in South Africa and the assets which we have gained have, I firmly believe, reached the point where we are fully justified in utilizing them in the practical service of one of South Africa's greatest needs, viz: the social and economic improvement of the Bantu population. Indeed I believe that we cannot avoid facing and undertaking to improve these conditions. In the attached memorandum I have barely referred to the situation which the Bantu face and even to that extent I have hesitated to write on a subject with which you are so thoroughly acquainted and for the improvement of which you have such long years of service behind you.[82]

In his explanatory remarks to Duncan, Yergan went on to state,

> While I have drawn upon my observations and experience and have put some thought into the preparation of the memorandum, I recognize its limitations. At the same time I believe that it sets forth a scheme which is practicable and, in its development, capable of coming to successful grips with the realities of Native social and economic needs. I believe further that it is in line with tested educational procedure and at the same time will permit of whatever adaptation to our need in South Africa that may be required.

Here Max was using the humble voice of the lowly addressing the mighty. He knew that Duncan as a minister and Carnegie Corporation official would not react kindly to anything that seemed to threaten his prerogatives, so he adopted a self-effacing, supplicative tone. Even so, Yergan could not conceal what he took to be the singularity of his scheme, revealing this to Duncan in all its grandiloquent glory:

> The proposal will not have a single competitor in the whole of Africa; it will be one effort to provide a leadership which may cooperate with Europeans in helping Africans to face intelligently and solve constructively some of the most difficult human problems that a community could possibly be confronted with in our time.

But was this, indeed, what Duncan and his fellow White South African men of power really wanted? Did they desire a self-conscious African petit bourgeoisie with whom they might one day find themselves sharing and the next, competing for leadership? Was Yergan naïve about this or was he some kind of radical rascal? Or, worse yet, was he a revolutionary masquerading as a moderate? Answering these questions requires close study of the proposal. What seemed so exciting at first sight now struck some as sinister. This appears to have proceeded along a two-tracked path. On one side stood those like Duncan, who knew Yergan only by reputation; on the other stood Phelps Stokes, F. P. Keppel, Jones, Loram, Oswin Bull, and Fort Hare principal Kerr, who had more intimate knowledge of the man, his mentality, and his local and international career profile.

Accordingly, as August opened, Charles Loram, upon receiving his own copy of the memo that Yergan posted to Duncan, wrote Frederick

Keppel, head of the Carnegie Corporation in New York, enumerating his preliminary responses to the memo:

1. There can be no question as to the desirability of and even necessity of training Natives as social workers in South Africa.
2. The South African College at Fort Hare being the centre of Higher Education among the Bantu is the most suitable place for such training.
3. Mr. Yergan is quite the best man in South Africa to undertake this training. Moreover in Mr. Alexander Kerr, the principal of the South African Native College, he has one of the wisest and shrewdest white men in South Africa as a colleague and advisor.
4. The complete scheme is somewhat ambitious but Mr. Yergan is wise enough to proceed one step at a time.
5. If the scheme is carried through there is need for a governing council of the proposed institute to ensure the support of all the mission and other bodies engaged in social work among the Bantu.
6. It seems to me to be imperative to make certain that other employment is available for the men and women trained at this Institute. Mr. Yergan's memorandum is more optimistic on this point than I should be at present. There is no organized YMCA movement for Non-Europeans. I am certain that the Union Government would engage such men although the Directors of Native Education might prefer to appoint as inspectors of schools or supervisors men who received this additional training. I am not as optimistic as Mr. Yergan regarding the employment of urban workers.

   The general idea is a good one and Mr. Yergan deserves every support but there are innumerable details to be settled before I could recommend the scheme for financial support.[83]

In Loram, Natal's chief inspector of Native Education, Yergan received the most sympathetic hearing he was likely to get from any official in or close to government in South Africa, but even Loram conceded that Max Yergan's proposal faced certain practical and technical obstacles. Loram spoke both to and for government—and Carnegie. It is evident, then, that all concerned took the scheme seriously.

A month later, Phelps Stokes, on tour in South Africa, told a colleague that he had great confidence in Yergan, though temporizing that the present hard times might make it difficult to carry off the plan. Phelps Stokes took pains to point out that in his view "Yergan is a man to tie up to."[84] As an illustration of this, Stokes asserted that the African-American was held in respect everywhere he had visited, including Stellenbosch, St. Cuthbert's, and other schools. To amplify this, Stokes jubilantly trumpeted that "wherever I show his picture it is vigorously applauded, indeed, next to Aggrey, there is no picture that brings out anything like the enthusiasm with both audiences as a picture of Max Yergan, unless it be that of Abraham Lincoln."[85] But by then, massive changes involving Yergan were well underway. Eventually, Mrs. Datta quietly relinquished the secretariat; Yergan, however, went out with a characteristic rhetorical flourish. Defiant, unrepentant, and maintaining his stance as the aggrieved party, he unsparingly lambasted Miller in a note scorchingly abdicating office.

In the summer of 1932, "at a special meeting of officers and members of the Federation Executive called upon [his] request," Max Yergan tendered a verbal resignation from the Executive Committee of the WSCF. This was followed by a letter charging Chairman Miller with gross misconduct regarding his personal and domestic affairs and unauthorized interference into his official position in South Africa. As earlier letters make clear, Miller and Yergan had been quite close. This friendship was one of the casualties of the Datta-Yergan affair. Unable to extract a face-saving apology from Miller, Yergan fumed,

> Notwithstanding the nature of his actions and my firm conviction that Mr. Miller has also been actuated by racial prejudice in what he has done, I had hoped that a suitable recognition of his wrong and an apology for it by him would make it unnecessary for me to sever my connection with the Executive Committee to which I had just been re-elected. On the very last day of the General Committee meeting, therefore, I took the initiative, sought Mr. Miller and gave him the opportunity to make the required apology and amends. The result of my effort was as stated above. I still hope that the chairman . . . will be led to recognize and apologize for the wrong he has done my family and myself and thereby heal this breach in the official life of the Federation.[86]

Because of the lag between August and early September 1932, the period between his oral and written resignations, Yergan's star might have still seemed in the ascendant when David R. Porter wrote his friend from Oberlin. Writing in his official capacity as executive secretary of the National Council of Student Associations, Porter told Yergan of the accomplishments of the body's most recent meeting. The timeliness and poignancy of the letter must have been heartening for Yergan, in light of the doubts he had been confronting in preceding months. Porter opened in the spirit of genuine fraternity:

> No meeting of the National Council of Student Associations can be held without frequent reference being made to you and other members of our fellowship who are in work in other lands. Your name and work have been mentioned several times in this meeting, enriching our lives because the very calling of attention to the significance of your position of leadership of thought and action with the students of South Africa takes us out of our concerns at home and into the larger concerns of the Christian world task. Those of us who know you personally cherish your friendship; the rest of us are eager to begin friendships with you when you make your next appearance in the States.[87]

Irksome questions remain about this scandal. When Porter's letter was first uncovered, little else concerning this curious episode could be determined. Any reference files that contained information on it had either been expurgated or kept in perennial confidentiality. At that time, only Yergan's interpretation of the events referred to in Miller's cryptic autobiographical allusion could be located. It steadily became evident that something of a potentially compromising nature was rather obviously and even uncharacteristically being concealed. In view of later evidence, some of the reasoning behind this concealment can be seen as sound. But it does not explain Yergan's reelection to his WSCF position. If he was viewed as a scoundrel, a rake, or a common adulterer, it should not have been difficult to ease him out of office, unless perchance there was another dimension—a division of opinion on the question—and Yergan, and perhaps Rena C. Datta as well, capably marshaled their own forces, who believed their counterinterpretation of the events and sided with them against Miller. From Porter's letter, drafted after the August meeting but in advance of the formal written resignation, it is clear that Yergan had many committed friends in the WSCF who kept faith in him and in the sincerity of what he said he was doing.

What seems remarkable in the Datta-Yergan correspondence that survives, notably that part of it still housed in the federation's Geneva archives, is how well these two cooperated, especially in the planning of the 1930 Fort Hare conference. There certainly was a great deal of cable traffic, but it is not inconceivable that this was caused primarily by the exigencies of their strategizing process. Few if any of the surviving cables seem sensitive in any way and several were signed off by other federation officials operating in Geneva. While a romantic affair may well have grown out of this work, it could also have had political overtones that Miller and others found equally objectionable, since Yergan wrote quite frankly about South Africa as his stand was becoming more and more openly radical, especially after 1928. Had a link between radical thinking and the appearance of impropriety in a relationship with Rena Datta prompted a coup against him?

Early in 1931 Yergan wrote Rena Datta, replying to a note she had sent the previous November expressing support. Its carefully chosen prose, full of emotion, reflected the kind of spiritual depth one would associate with an evangelist of his stripe. Yergan wrote,

> I am sure you, and I trust others, realise that there is much more involved in our situation here than the mere question of relationships. I said in a letter to Cockin a few weeks ago that we are faced with the task of establishing the fact that in its final analysis the racial question for us involves a great spiritual fact. Frankly I have no interest whatever in facing it except from this point of view. I think one might develop interest from an altogether different point of view and this may doubtless come to pass but for the past years and for the present I have been throwing myself into this task from the conviction that God's will is involved and God's way is the way. It has been and is difficult going and that is why the sort of help which you and others have given is so much appreciated. One's hands have really been upheld.

Two weeks after delivering his formal resignation note Yergan wrote David Porter, thanking him for a September 11 letter written after his Oberlin Student Division meeting tribute of September 6. Having found Porter's missive upon returning from visits to SCAs in the Transkei, Yergan opined,

> These are times when everything within us is being tested by the actual circumstances of life as well as by the forces which are creating circumstances. . . . I think it is also true that, to an unusual extent, severe strains are being placed upon us personally and that the reality of all

the truly spiritual powers, which we are capable of possessing, are being tested by our human relationships. Coming therefore, at such a time as this, your letter is very much appreciated, and I write to thank you for everything you say in it.[88]

Then Yergan opened up to Porter, as only a friend might dare. He showed Porter his utter vulnerability and honestly bared his soul. The armor of his seemingly unflappable exterior had been breached, leaving Yergan deeply wounded in the regrettable federation affray. Thus, seeking consolation, he struggled to attain psychic equilibrium:

> I rejoice in the fact that it is possible for us to break through great distances and every other barrier even more real and find something of reality in what we speak of as universal Christian fellowship. I have been finding this fellowship exceedingly shallow and meaningless when put to any real test, and I have been brought to the point where, for my own spiritual future, I must examine it almost ruthlessly in order to make sure that it really exists. It is therefore with all the more joy that I welcome your letter and the meaning which I can believe is behind it. It is always a tremendous encouragement to me to know that I have relationships with you, and a few others in America, which fall within the realm of spiritual reality.[89]

It is likely that the disposition of the alleged affair with Rena Datta will never be known, particularly inasmuch as it indeed seems plausible that the correspondence that would have given concrete proof of its existence was, in fact, shredded. There are snapshots of Yergan with Mrs. Datta during the Mysore Convention, and no spouses are in evidence at that moment. Yergan certainly had a fondness for magnetic women—of that there can be no doubt. Even though circumstantial evidence suggests some salacious possibilities, there are other attractive women with whom Yergan was linked who were high-minded enough to conduct an extremely deep, intellectual relationship with him; that such relationships occurred indicates that Yergan's own interests in dynamic women and in the spiritual underpinnings that animated the ecumenical movement went far beyond the superficial. One indication that this was so was his acquaintance with Juliette Derricotte, an extraordinarily engaging woman who was among the most brilliant leaders ever produced within the context of the YWCA.

Juliette Derricotte

In the interwar era, Juliette Derricotte was a national figure in the Black YWCA, sister movement of the Colored Work Department. In the same way that the male leaders of the Black YMCA kept each other apprised of the progress of the struggle against discrimination in the larger organization, their spouses were also often involved in parallel activities within the YWCA. At roughly the same time when Yergan began to cultivate a constituency that was international in scope, Juliette Derricotte was doing likewise. As with Rena Datta, Yergan had an ally in Derricotte. Derricotte and Yergan spent a considerable time together at Mysore, and one letter from her to him treats at length the problems common to interracial student work among young women and men. Their relationship was professional, businesslike, and scrupulous in its attention to the fact that Derricotte knew the Yergan family. At the same time, the two had serious, tender concern for one another, and, whether seen in terms of Christian comity or as a product of their common struggles, both her writings to him and, later, his poignant eulogy of her following her death were abidingly and publicly affectionate.

Derricotte and Yergan met on a number of occasions. The Black leadership stratum within the YMCA and YWCA was small and tightly knit, particularly among nationally known figures. The two movements functioned complementarily, and it was not uncommon for YMCA men to marry YWCA women. These structures had tremendous importance during the segregation era, as alternative sources of professional authority, status, and rank. Derricotte's cooptation by the WSCF gave her international stature, as happened for Yergan. They compared notes about their respective experiences since it was clear that within the context of the WSCF both were being used as guinea pigs in a social experiment examining the feasibility of racial integration within the federation on a token albeit meaningful basis.

In the summer of 1929, Derricotte sent Yergan a letter, belatedly answering his request that she document some of her impressions of the efforts made by the Student Christian Movements on behalf of Black students in the United States. It began by indicating the degree to which the historically Black colleges were hamstrung by the findings of the 1916 Thomas Jesse Jones report on Negro education, which emphasized Hampton-Tuskegee-style industrial training over academic institutions like Talladega, Atlanta University, Wiley, and Shaw. Black schools, already suffering from limited fiscal endowments and inadequate equipment, still strove to provide liberal educations. The Association of College Presidents in Negro Schools consequently pushed for a reexamination of the colleges.

Derricotte pointed out the significance of the reorganization of particular educational centers—principally the merger of Atlanta University, Morehouse, and Spelman College—for President John Hope. Other topics touched upon included a congressional bill granting a permanent appropriation to Howard University, the creation of Dillard University, and the emergence of Hampton and Tuskegee as degree-granting institutions. Derricotte took special interest in indicating the growing numbers of Black college students: twenty thousand enrolled, three thousand of whom attended White schools. She noted changes in racial composition among historically Black college faculties. Once heavily White, they were now increasingly Black, showing a growth of educated Black professionals at high levels. The new Black Ph.D.s, however, were often hampered by their relatively narrow scholastic interests, which caused them to neglect the old concern for "personal relations" that had once marked Negro education. She also lamented the rise of athletics and fraternities as new sources of privilege, often with great political consequences.

But it was the religious underpinnings of the work of the Student Christian Movement, the YWCA, and the YMCA that brought out the best in Derricotte. Obviously, the mission of these groups had been on her mind for a very long time. Nostalgic perhaps for the old days, she mourned the passing of a disciplined, sober, religiously formed attitude to life. In ways that resembled some of the attitudes expressed about urban life in general, greater freedom was equated with lax discipline, yielding myriad problems. Her thoughtful summation brought all of these ideas together:

Now when you couple with this religious lethargy on campuses the general disinterest in religion among colored people in the United States right now, you can see very clearly what our position as Student Christian Movement workers is. I know that there isn't a colored church in most of our cities which would not be packed to the utmost every Sunday morning, but you and I know that the younger generation of colored people, our young business men and our young professional men, have got so involved in their thinking on this question of race and religion that the old time religion, for which our racial group was noted, can no longer be credited as a part of the experience of the younger group. The YMCA and YWCA among colored people are not religious organizations, and I think we fool ourselves if we keep thinking they are. I will not presume to speak for the YMCA in detail, but I know that for the majority of colored women in the United States the YWCA is an organization which offers them a chance for a kind of leadership that they may find difficult to get in other organizations, and that it serves mostly as a tool with which they handle certain racial situations in the United States, and of course in too many of our cities it has become a purely commercial enterprise.[90]

Derricotte echoed many of Yergan's concerns about the nature and significance of Student Christian Work. Through letters like hers he kept pace with some of the major changes in American society and reflected upon these to an extent that might not have been possible had he remained in North America. South Africa afforded him an important critical distance from the U.S. battlefield. The deterioration of the YMCA and YWCA and the diminution of interest in religion among younger people were also apparent in South Africa, in Fort Hare and elsewhere, and this had to affect Yergan's thinking. Finally, Derricotte made a keen aside concerning WSCF chairman F. P. Miller that deserves consideration in light of the Yergan-Datta episode. While Derricotte's remark need not have portended the scandal, it provides food for thought. This is what Derricotte wrote about him, whom she knew from her WSCF position:

> Francis Miller came in the office just for a few minutes during his recent visit to the United States. He is most enthusiastic in his new relationship to the Federation. I was a little disappointed that he was not as frank as I had believed he would be in this position, especially on the matters of the Federation and International Student Service. We do not find ourselves so clear, as men and women go, in working out our relationships as national movements to both of these interests. I hope you are going to stick by the Executive Committee and help steer us through to a very honest attitude.[91]

Derricotte was not fully at ease in Miller's presence, and she did not find him forthcoming. Neither observation could bode well for the

WSCF, as far as interracial and interorganizational work between YWCA and YMCA leaders was concerned. Her decision to gently prod Yergan in a favorable direction may have a larger significance not readily apparent. Derricotte was extraordinarily diplomatic in her treatment of controversial issues, a characteristic quite necessary for YWCA and YMCA secretaries, particularly if they were persons of color. John Mott, Miller's predecessor as WSCF chairman, seems to have been far more able to put Black people at ease than his Virginian successor. Derricotte here also apparently wondered about Miller's ability to work cooperatively with women, something Yergan might facilitate. If this is an accurate reading, it might show yet another Yergan skill.

On November 7, 1931, Derricotte suffered major tissue damage sustained in an automobile accident and was in effect assassinated by racism. She had been driving from Nashville, Tennessee, to Athens, Georgia, intending to visit her mother, when her car crashed near Dalton, Georgia. Gravely injured, she was cruelly denied admission to a nearby White hospital. She was then forced to endure an agonizing ten-mile ambulance ride to a local "Colored" hospital in Chattanooga, where Fisk University's dean of women expired. The tragedy of Derricotte's premature, mortifying demise shocked and saddened not only her Y colleagues but all who had known of her. In a tender appreciation introducing a 1936 monograph about her, Yergan inscribed this modest but impassioned expression of remembrance:

> I shall, above everything else, remember her for her quality of true friendship; such a quality is so rare, so necessary, and so seldom found in any real and enduring sense, that Juliette Derricotte's conception and practice of it constitute one of her unique gifts to our time. Our race could ill afford to lose such a gifted member; the larger human and spiritual cause, which she served transcending race and nation, is now without one of its strongest and proved advocates; the realm of friendship has in its ranks an empty place because we mourn the untimely death of this sweet and gentle soul.[92]

A Double Life

Over the course of the 1930s Yergan began leading a double life. On the surface he continued to discharge his day-to-day duties as a YMCA secretary in the service of the SCA. After hours, however, he coached young Africans in the socialist tradition, introducing them to radical concepts and revolutionary literature in night schools and on guided tours. One of these pupils was Govan Mbeki, released from Robben Island in 1987, after twenty-three years of imprisonment. On several occasions during his life Mbeki had gone on record crediting Max Yergan with his radicalization. He has stated that in his presentations to Mbeki and other young colleagues, Yergan was "utterly convincing." So complete was Yergan's mastery of this double role that the majority of people, including even Mbeki, who were familiar with him as a YMCA worker had little awareness of his extracurricular activities until years afterward.

Precisely when this radical activity began is unclear, but its effect upon Yergan's professional persona was evident by 1932. Concluding an annual report for that year, surveying the events, travails, and accomplishments of the prior twelve months, he wrote openly and at length about something new:

> No one will be surprised to learn that communistic propaganda is finding fertile field in South Africa. Efforts have been made in the courts to stamp out such propaganda, but these efforts have not succeeded because of the reality of the legal provisions for the freedom of speech. The communist paper [*Umsebenzi, The Worker*] a clipping of which I attach to this report, is circulated weekly throughout South Africa, and is read by most Africans to whom it can be sent or who themselves may obtain copies of it. It is remarkable that such a paper is permitted, but it is more remarkable that there are no more serious outbreaks than we have. I do not mean to say that there are not frequent uprisings on the part of labouring Africans against government officials and sometimes their employers, but the striking fact is that while a number of Africans are exposed to such propaganda, they have not in any large numbers acted precipitately. The communist appeal is being discussed in almost every village, for the workers from the mines take back with them news of what they have heard, and it is safe to say that the most remote part of Southern Africa as well as other sections in the North from which South African labour is drawn are being affected in thought by those whose mission it is to propagate the new ideas. . . . I have no desire to contrast Christianity with communism, but I cannot refrain from observing that communism offers to Christianity its supreme opportunity

as a force for social regeneration, and there is no place in the world where this is more true than here in Africa.

Yergan may not have openly desired to contrast Christianity with communism, but he was familiar with at least one contemporary theologian who dared to do precisely that, Episcopal bishop W. Montgomery Brown, heretical author of the controversial *Communism and Christianism,* a notorious social gospel tract that purported to relate and reconcile the precepts of Christ, Darwin, and Marx. *Communism and Christianism,* widely read in the 1930s, influenced many religiously inclined progressives in South Africa. One, Albert T. Nzula, a pioneering African Communist Party general secretary, went on record as having learned a great deal from it and was fired from a teaching position for his candor, precipitating a truly meteoric radical career. In this sense, the passage above reflects even further the contradictions inherent in Yergan's position. Unable to openly state his support for what was officially considered subversive albeit marginally legitimate conduct, because the "communist appeal" was so vital a force during his time in South Africa, Yergan was compelled to comment upon it. His concluding sentence shows that he felt moved by this request. It is thus vital to consider what motivated Yergan to follow in the footsteps "of those whose mission it is to propagate the new ideas."

South Africa during the 1920s and 1930s was a haven for political refugees fleeing from European ferment. After the Bolshevik revolution and throughout the consolidation of Soviet power, revolutionary activists of every stripe, ranging from Russian émigrés to Labor Zionists, poured into the country in great numbers. Among these were many highly politicized Eastern European Jews fleeing religious, ethnic, and official persecution. Several of these new emigrants also had extensive experience in labor agitation, having fought against tsarist police and challenged oppressive regimes like that of imperial Germany. The most politically sophisticated of these migrant militants initiated instruction for workers, often in Marxist study circles taught in evening schools. Along with their predecessors in South Africa, mainly those associated with the tradition of left-wing industrial radicalism in Great Britain, these instructors stimulated dissemination of socialist literature and facilitated party building.

Yergan's activity so closely resembled the work of these militants that the similarity could not have been coincidental. Because his activity was clandestine, however, evidence detailing how he politicized African youth and students is very scarce. Indeed, if such documents ever existed they may never come to light, due to the precautions necessary for this work. But select personal testimonies bear witness to his influence, chiefly those of Wycliffe M. Tsotsi, "Roch" Fanana Fobo, and Govan Mbeki, each of whom attended Fort Hare in Yergan's final years of YMCA service in South Africa, from his 1932 WSCF resignation on.

Wycliffe Mlungisi Tsotsi was a Fort Hare student during the 1930s. He met Yergan in 1932. Tsotsi remembered Yergan as having been a resolute foe of segregation, a stance apparent from their very first encounter. Two points impressed him about Yergan, his intensity and his profound commitment. The former was manifested in Yergan's frequent exhortations to "cut deep," meaning to delve beyond the surface of things and not to approach them superficially. Yergan's dedication prompted Tsotsi to join the All Africa Convention at its inception in 1935, a decision that became crucial to his career. It was only later that he learned of a trip Yergan made to the USSR. Consistent with other sources, Tsotsi also recollected that Yergan was secretive and did not want the authorities to know his real feelings.

Yergan left South Africa with his family early in 1933, arriving in the States in late April. There he embarked upon a series of public speaking engagements timed to coincide with his receipt of the NAACP's highest accolade, the Spingarn Medal. Capping a decision-making process dating from the close of January, Yergan's selection was a subject of an internal memo composed by Dr. Du Bois:

> The Committee feels that Max Yergan of the YMCA in South Africa is the logical candidate for the award this year. He has done an unusual and self-sacrificing work covering a number of years and succeeded year before last in assembling the first South African Interracial Conference. The results of this Conference during the year 1932 have been very encouraging. We feel that this is the high mark of Mr. Yergan's career and that on account of his family and other conditions, he may be leaving South Africa in the near future.[93]

The NAACP announced the choice in March, singling Yergan out as "a missionary of intelligence, tact and self-sacrifice, representing the gift of cooperation and culture which American Negroes may send back to their Motherland" and acclaiming his feat of having "inaugurated last year an unusual local movement for interracial understanding among black and white students."[94] Arriving in New York, he garnered considerable attention in the African-American press through the ensuing month.[95] Toward late May Yergan sat on the dais as one of the speakers at an interracial dinner on the subject of South Africa given at the George Washington Hotel, sponsored by the Department of Race Relations and the African Welfare Committee of the Federal Council of Churches (FCC). Appearing alongside Yergan were Oswin B. Bull, formerly YMCA head at Cape Town, now director of technical education for the Basutoland government, and the FCC's Dr. George E. Haynes, who acted as emcee.[96] On June 11, at its annual Sunday commencement ceremony, Yergan was awarded an honorary Master of Humanics for his South African service, from Springfield College, the YMCA's degree-granting institution. At the time the Master of Humanics was the highest degree offered there. Yergan had attended the school from 1914 to 1915, during which time he took the secretary's course. As he presented Yergan with the degree, Blake Hoover, secretary of the Springfield Y, spoke of Yergan's accomplishments, singling out his contribution to racial understanding between South Africa and America.

On Saturday evening, July 1, he was awarded the Spingarn Medal. Two weeks later colleague Channing Tobias praised his performance and that of sociologist Ira de A. Reid, at an annual Y lay conference.[97] Early in September, South African–born educator, humanitarian, and sometime adviser on Native affairs, Charles T. Loram, wrote F. P. Keppel of the Carnegie Corporation to convey his impressions of Yergan's revised African training institute proposal, expressing out his view that Yergan "makes a very good case" and hoped for funding.[98] Late in October, Yergan addressed the Kiwanis Club of Boston.

In early December, Yergan was the honored guest at the Founder's Day celebration for famed Gammon Theological Seminary in Atlanta. Before he exited New York, however, he made contact with Robert M. Lester of Carnegie, providing Lester with a followup on his proposal. Yergan's note to Lester contained a report, dated December 1, 1933, appended to a cover letter, which included the following information:

> I should like to take the liberty of enlarging upon the reference in my
> report to a memorandum which I have submitted to the President of

the Carnegie Corporation, embodying a description of the proposed Institute for Training Social Workers in South Africa and a request for a grant towards the support of the Institute. As stated in my report, while certain progress has been made under the corporation's grant to us, the bulk of the grant remains unexpended in view of the fact that we have felt it unwise to give effect to a program, which would have called for the expenditure during the past two years of the entire grant, before we could know definitely of our ability to secure the funds required to give effect to an inclusive program. This inclusive program involves the strengthening of our present service and the addition of the Institute already referred to. As soon as information reaches me with regard to action of the Trustees of the Corporation, we shall be in position to go ahead with the sort of inclusive program possible in the light of the awaited action of the Corporation's Trustees.[99]

The next few months saw Yergan traveling and giving sermons and speeches at local YMCAs, churches and academic institutions, still collecting funds to augment his foundation grants-in-aid. At the same time, his training institute was dissected and discussed in both New York and South Africa. He, his work, and the institute came up in a variety of contexts. Prior to leaving South Africa, Yergan had assisted Howard Pim in planning a study tour of the Transkei, made under Carnegie auspices. The tour's report, published late in 1933, was circulated and read by January 1934. Loram was underwhelmed by Pim's effort, to say the least, writing,

> The report is somewhat slight and does not add materially to our knowledge of the social and economic situation in the Transkeian territories. As you will have noticed, much of the information is already contained in other reports and there is a regrettable absence of the real research which is needed to check up on current generalizations about the condition of the country.[100]

In contrast to other similarly critical reactions, Yergan approached Pim's work with a wholly different spirit. Whether this was affected by his own relationship with Pim or his lack of graduate certification as a Ph.D. (unlike Dr. Loram) is uncertain. Nevertheless, his pithy, more charitable critique, cabled to Carnegie president F. P. Keppel, appeared as follows:

Have read Transkei enquiry carefully and understand it does not purport to be exhaustive document it is of specialized rather than general usefulness and presupposes considerable knowledge of South Africa by average reader chapters on education and economic commission report are very helpful and justify publication to which I do not think any South African community or government can take exception stop mailing document today.[101]

Late in April 1934, South African–based Carnegie Corporation trustee Patrick Duncan reported that the corporation's South African Advisory Committee, after consultation with Joint Council head and South African Institute of Race Relations director J. D. Rheinallt Jones regarding Yergan's institute proposals, concurred with the latter that the scheme was too ambitious. The fund's trustee went on, stating, "I am informed that Principal Kerr of the South African Native College is in entire agreement with Mr. Jones's criticism and suggestions."[102]

By mid-May 1934 the *Boston Evening Transcript* reported that Yergan was spending much of his furlough in Beantown. While YMCA leader John R. Mott was touring South Africa and surveying his work, Yergan was speaking to audiences about life in the embattled Union. Harping on themes he had developed in earlier writings and public talks, he emphasized gold and its effect upon the political penetration of Africa by foreign invaders, coupled with the development of the productive forces of these lands by the same elements and the simultaneous emergence of an intractable race problem. Of the latter, Yergan told his Boston audience,

> These Europeans consider themselves permanent residents of South Africa, but they are very much aware of their European historical and cultural background. It is this background which has made them develop the modern and progressive cities of Cape Town, Johannesburg and Durban, to construct modern railroads, to establish promising leather, steel, chemical and furniture industries, to provide universities, elementary schools, women's clubs and child welfare societies.[103]

Yergan contrasted the growth and development of economic relations yielding wealth for powerful Whites with the abysmal man-made social and political handicaps faced by the mass of Africans. Acknowledging the Africans' numerical superiority and the rising pressure to conform to changes forced upon them by industrial life, he asked his Boston audience to carefully consider this question:

> How many members of various classes, races and cultures who find themselves in the same community live together with a measure of mutuality and common effort toward the common good, without violence being done to the personality of one group by the other?

The measure of his achievement in South Africa, Yergan contended, was in the efforts undertaken by the YMCA to build character as a prime ingredient in the creation of leadership, as well as reconciliation between Africans and Europeans, an illustration of which was the fact that while previously proscribed from the White universities, he now claimed to have more invitations to these than he could accept.

Barely a fortnight after Yergan's Boston appearance, he heard from Carnegie Corporation head Frederick Keppel. Keppel informed Yergan that, having been in contact with Patrick Duncan and having examined the comments prepared by Rheinallt Jones regarding his training institute proposal, Carnegie's South African Advisory Committee offered its opinion that the institute should be mounted by Fort Hare under the control of the institution's council and senate and directed by Principal Kerr. The Advisory Committee also wished for the government to be asked to contribute toward salaries, while Carnegie's funding would be used for equipment, scholarships, and organizing purposes, and suggested an application of four thousand dollars per year for a period of four years.[104]

Yergan's response to Keppel, sent one month later, noted Keppel's letter and stated Yergan's willingness to act upon the Carnegie Corporation Advisory Committee's suggestion regarding Fort Hare connections.[105] It is doubtful that the sensitive Yergan failed to discern the all-too-subtle undermining of his authority that had taken place, however.

Among many of the generation of students who like Yergan himself had been products of historically Black colleges, however, the YMCA secretary was often viewed as a formidable figure at that time. The future historian John Hope Franklin recalled this image of him:

> When I was at Fisk University between 1931 and 1935, Max Yergan was one of our heroes. The stories of his work in Africa as a member of the staff of the YMCA captured our imaginations, and I can still re-

member his visit to Fisk, at commencement time in 1934 I believe. It was the first time I saw him. . . . The impression was favorable, and we placed him in the category of Du Bois, McDowell, Mordecai Johnson, and Howard Thurman. It was not that we knew all that much about him. It was that he had performed "good works" in Africa.[106]

In 1934 Yergan had also begun to impress Govan Mbeki, then a 24-year-old student from the Eastern Cape. Mbeki, a former pupil at Healdtown, had entered Fort Hare as a matriculant in the high school section in 1933. No stranger to radical militancy, Mbeki, at a very early age, had acted as an interpreter for a cousin who organized for the ICU. By 1933 he came into contact with Edward Roux, a botanist who founded the Communist Youth League and edited *Umsebenzi (The Worker)*, the party's newspaper. Roux had pitched a tent at Sandile's Kop above Fort Hare and delivered a number of stirring lectures to students. The following year, Yergan and Mbeki, who had met earlier, became close friends. Having formerly known Yergan primarily as a YMCA missionary, Mbeki now became aware of Yergan's militancy.

The year 1934 was the one in which Yergan returned to South Africa from his second furlough. Mbeki noticed profound changes in him. When Yergan resumed the campaign for the construction of a Christian Union building at Fort Hare, Mbeki noted, "he was no longer the Max Yergan we had known—concerned only with church work." Mbeki attributed this change to a trip to the USSR allegedly undertaken that same year.[107] Yergan's new persona was quite different from the one he had presented during the 1920s. As Thami Mkhwanazi related after interviewing Mbeki in his prison cell,

> Yergan, who remained at Fort Hare for another year, was invited to deliver lectures on communism and fascism to the political science class. At the time, Mbeki was reading the subject as one of his two majors for a Bachelor of Arts degree. Mbeki became friendly with Yergan who, he said, invited him to his home and "fed him" with literature. One of the first books his friend gave him was Lenin's *The State and Revolution*.[108]

Mbeki actually became a protégé of Max Yergan, accompanying him on trips to the countryside, the "study tours" mentioned earlier. In the course of these sojourns, Yergan provided a commentary that made a lasting impression on the youths who feasted on his analysis. In a 1990 interview with Robert Edgar, Mbeki shared his recollection of vivid field trips across the Transkei and Ciskei. When Mbeki first encountered Yergan, the African-American was an extremely religious man. Although he was always a powerful speaker from the pulpit, in the early 1930s the content of his sermons was rather typical—much the same as that of the other preachers at Fort Hare's chapel. Around 1933, however, Yergan went on leave; upon his reentry, "he was a changed man. He was no longer the Max Yergan that we knew."

> Now, I don't quite remember how we came to be close together, but on one occasion I do remember that he was asked by—the lecturer who was in charge of psychology and political science and philosophy—he was brought into our lecture room to give us a talk on Nazism. He gave us a comparative talk on Communism and Nazism, and I think it is from that date that he and I took on. After that, he invited me quite often to his home in the evenings, and by then he had a section of his library, say, from here to there—but it was all Marxist-Leninist books there. I remember on one occasion, just shortly before he left Fort Hare, he turned round to say to me, when he left Fort Hare he would donate all those other books, you know, those American books—he would leave them here at Fort Hare—"But, comrade, that portion—that library—I will take with me, because I value it." That's what he said.[109]

Mbeki became a beneficiary of the type of learning laboratory that today would be termed the "open university." When asked to join Yergan on his circuit, he found himself transported to another realm, one in which even mundane observations contained within them the seeds of profundity. For him Yergan proved every bit as inspiring outside the classroom and beyond the pulpit as his stated reputation. Yergan took advantage of this teaching opportunity. Mbeki recalled,

> Now, when he went out on his missions sometimes he took me along as far as Cathcart. We would drive over the[re] [on] horse back—we would drive out over to Cathcart and we would come back with his youngest son who, I think, was Charles, his youngest boy, and all along the road he would be talking. You know, there are big, large expanses of farm land—whether on occasion it was over the mountains—it was, I think, for a mile, or even more than a mile, it was just sheep, sheep, sheep. And he turned around and he says to me, "Comrades, look at

that. All of that belongs to one man, and the most [rest?] of the people around here have no land, have no sheep. Why should that be?" And he related it to Marxist-Leninist teachings.[110]

Perhaps the most telling of these remembrances comes from the time after the merger of the private and public personas, when Max had decided, for good or for ill, to be as consistent as he dared in the exposition of his views. This occurred not only within the context of the classroom but also, finally, in that holiest of holy places, the pulpit itself. Yergan, whose name was often preceded by the title "reverend" in both official records and publications, never outgrew—in fact, did not seem willing to end—his relationship with missionary Christianity. He did, however, consciously seek to alter the ways that the work to which he had dedicated his life should be viewed and understood by those it was intended to uplift. This also appeared inspiring to Mbeki.

Then on a special occasion—which was the last time he appeared on a Fort Hare platform, as a preacher, at the [Student] C[hristian] A[ssociation] Hall—he preached from there, and I still remember the text of his sermon, to this day. And he says—and again, I'll try to put it in the accent in which he gave it—he says, "I am come that you may have life, and have it more abundantly." That was his sermon. And he developed from that to talk about the conditions under which men lived, and especially in South Africa, and the answer he gave was the adoption of Marxist teachings. That was the last time he was allowed to appear on a platform or a pulpit to preach. That was the last time. So that was Yergan.[111]

Yergan's changes of mind and heart did not go unnoticed at home. Even Mbeki was aware of the degree to which Yergan and Susie had come to view the world differently and, as an occasional guest, was sensitive to the stress this added to the Yergan household. These recollections revolved around the central question of Yergan's life thus far, the principles to which it had been dedicated and with which it was linked. In many ways this related to every conflict he had faced since 1928. While this could not have been known to Mbeki, he was observant:

Now I was very often at his house in the evenings. Now there was, his wife—I don't know if she's still alive—she used to sometimes talk to me and say, "All right, have your ideas with Max, but why does he discard religion?" Well, I don't know if in his personal life he had discarded religion, but as far as I knew, that sermon which he preached was the last sermon which he preached at Fort Hare. And I think for some two years after he was at Fort Hare and then never again preached. And then, well, his wife would tell me that—she would first want to discuss religion with me—and, of course, I had no interest; I showed no interest. And then she would start talking to me seriously about that. And so, that's that. And then Max left.[112]

It is critical to add, too, that Yergan was also influencing and being influenced by fellow Colored Work Department associates closer to home, some of whose conversations and letters have not surfaced but who were surely in either direct or indirect contact with him through the 1920s and 1930s, among them James Ford, Mordecai Johnson. and the Guiana-born George T. N. Griffiths, subsequently T. Ras Makonnen. Each knew Max from the Colored YMCA days and was about his age. Ford, Johnson, and Yergan shared southern upbringings, had attended Negro colleges, and had then participated in the Great Migration north. Though some particulars of their relationships in the interwar years are somewhat cloudy, each was destined to interact closely with Max. Each also symbolized the starkly diverging career pathways that lay open to Yergan within and beyond the boundaries of the Black YMCA.

Johnson, an ordained minister, followed Yergan as Colored Work Department traveling secretary in the Southwest, later becoming Howard University's first Black president. Using Howard as his bully pulpit, Johnson made himself a national figure in Black theological circles. Moreover, he consistently carved out a radical position, reflecting his *engagé* social gospel orientation. Outspoken in opposing segregation and other forms of racial discrimination, Johnson made public pronouncements that were clearly left of center in the interwar era, precisely the time when Max moved in a similar direction. Further, Johnson was one of a handful of left-leaning Black Christian intellectuals devoted to Africa.

In 1928, Johnson appeared on a panel with colonial critic R. L. Buell at Williamstown, Massachusetts. Both lambasted the West for exploiting Africa and Africans. Johnson was later paraphrased as asserting that, apart from a handful of missionaries and other altruists, "up to the present the development of Africa has been dominated by economic and imperialistic groups for the benefit of the capitalist class." Then, after criticizing the Garvey movement, he was cited as having said the following:

> He declared that the conflict in Africa was not between the white and black races, but was the same conflict which exists in every country between a comparatively small group of capitalists and the great mass of people. What he hoped for the development of Africa was that the Christian element of the white world would get the upper hand over the selfish exploiters, so that the natural resources could be developed by modern scientific knowledge for the benefit of the people as a whole, both white and black.[113]

James Ford represented the other end of the spectrum from Johnson. Son of an Alabama sharecropper and grandson of a lynch victim, he was a scion of the soil and a "colored" college man. Attending Fisk University on the eve of World War One, Ford put off receiving his degree in order to enlist.[114] Protesting discrimination while still in uniform in France, Ford returned to a series of dead-end jobs in Chicago's post office. Frustrated yet fighting for social change, he joined the Communist Party, where he rose steadily in the ranks, becoming by 1932 its vice-presidential candidate, alongside William Z. Foster.[115] Yergan knew Ford from his college days. Both had YMCA connections.

Two months after announcing his vice-presidential candidacy, Ford gained notoriety during the July 28 Bonus March, when he and thirty-five other communist veterans were arrested as the alleged ringleaders of the march, under orders issued by Herbert Hoover and carried out by Douglas MacArthur. By then Ford would have been well known to the FBI, having spent two years in the USSR from 1930 to 1932 and reemerged as the second most visible communist functionary in the United States, and *Black* at that. Both Hoovers, John Edgar and Herbert, undoubtedly fumed.[116]

Though unsuccessful in his bid for the vice-presidency, Ford rose in Communist Party ranks. In 1936 he transferred his headquarters from Chicago to New York City as the new head of the party's vital Harlem Section. This was the year planned for a broad-based National Negro

Congress, which provided a chance for Yergan to become reacquainted with Ford, whom he had met during his Colored Work Department period.[117] A year later Max selected Harlem as his base of operations.

The trio's third member, George Griffiths, revealed a subtler side of Yergan's personality but a vital part of his persona, his Christian internationalist-cum-Pan-Negro-nationalist charisma. This had been critical to his success in South Africa as a source of inspiration to fellow Blacks of widely differing backgrounds. Griffiths, like other foreign-born Afro-Caribbean and African sojourners in the United States during the 1920s and 1930s, had depended on the Colored YMCA for lodging and fellowship, and there occasionally heard Max in appearances at Black college campuses. Until about 1934 Griffiths viewed Yergan only from a reverent distance. That year, however, the two had a memorable encounter, later recounted to Kenneth J. King. Noting the rise of radical interwar thinkers in the YMCA, Griffiths stated,

> He told me something of the tragedy of the Bantu students, and possibly when he met these great thinkers in the "Y," and saw the drift of the period, he expected some really powerful support. Quite likely it was the contact with the rebel element in the churches—people like the Presbyterian A. J. Muste, that made him more rebellious on his return to South Africa, and helped to bring about his break from the YMCA as international secretary.[118]

Griffiths's re-creation dovetails nicely with Govan Mbeki's for a similar period, giving both testimonies added weight. Taken together with Johnson's profile, their remembrances show Max's deepening involvement with a liberation theology he shared with John Hope and George E. Haynes.

The end of Yergan's 1933–1934 furlough was marred by a series of professional setbacks. His efforts to fund the projected Fort Hare social work study course met considerable opposition. J. D. Rheinallt Jones of the Joint Council Movement and the South African Institute of Race Relations criticized Yergan's proposal for a social service institute for Africans as too elaborate and ambitious, too costly, and inconsistent with extant realities. The idea for an African Social Service Center marked a concretization of a previously more generalized social concern animating his Y work. Reasserting faith in Christianity, Max advocated altering teaching policy to respond to the immediate necessities of African students, whom he viewed as being in need of grooming, if not for eventual control at least for some sort of leadership role in South Africa. This necessitated unusual boldness:

I believe strongly that in our policy and service of the present and future there will be required certain changes of emphasis and points of view. These changes will make our movement less respectable in the conventional sense, may make us less popular with those in authority and may cut us off from some of our present friends. That I think would be taking the way of the cross; and it seems to me to be the only way consistent with the meaning of the life and death of Jesus.

Whether or not these changes were indeed consistent with "the way of the cross," they did, in fact, contribute to a loss of respect, not so much for the YMCA movement as a whole as for Max Yergan the man —at least within conservative church circles, for reasons that were probably rooted in the crisis of confidence that appeared in his WSCF controversy. Yergan had begun to reveal even more of himself. His public and private identification with radical, uncompromising, leftist friends and comrades was becoming embarrassing to some of his White South African YMCA associates, who had come to feel that the charismatic Black American was exceeding the limits of tolerance.

Since 1932, a year after Yergan had begun to confront his own need to delve more deeply into social theory, he had contemplated a new program designed to inspire social consciousness by means of a course curriculum emphasizing the teaching of sociology. The curriculum would address changes in the African "family and custom, the techniques of social surveys in African communities, [and] African urban life, examining the effects of industrialisation upon African communities and economies," each of which topics seemed valuable additions to his usual recreation and religious instruction. He justified the need for such a curriculum by referring to the report of the 1932 Native Economic Commission, quoting the following passage:

"[The curriculum] should aim at freeing the mass of Natives from their reactionary conceptions—animism and witchcraft, certain phases of the cattle cult, the 'doctoring' of lands as an alternative to proper cultivation, the insistence on a large amount of leisure, and all the mass of primitive fears and taboos, which are the real reason for their backwardness. The removal or transformation of these is the first great problem of Native education."

The commission's report had been careful to add, however, that such measures did not seek to make "the Native" dissatisfied with his background. Rather, they were intended to help individuals build upward from the foundations of "Native society," developing within themselves a sense of pride in their people and a desire to improve what was good in their own traditional institutions, pointedly adding, "and of this there is a good deal." Yergan's plan was not implemented. The reasons for this are not entirely clear, a fact whose significance grew over the next few years and may have had some bearing upon Yergan's subsequent decision to pursue a very different career path.

Alfred Bitini Xuma

For at least a decade Max Yergan corresponded with Alfred Bitini Xuma, one of the most famous opposition figures in interwar South Africa. Considerably more militant than Jabavu, Xuma presided over the African National Congress (ANC) in the years of its rejuvenation, when a revitalized Youth League permanently altered the direction of the organization. Yergan's relationship with Xuma shows old patterns of caution, caused no doubt by his lengthy surveillance experience. The Yergan-Xuma correspondence brims with cryptic encoded references to mutual acquaintances and ostensibly sensitive conversations. Yet it is virtually impossible to detect from what survives of the letters of these two men how either felt about the ANC between 1928–1945.

The earliest available letters from Max Yergan to Dr. Xuma date from June 1928. Written to respond to two of Xuma's letters—one of June 4 and another of June 7—they accepted the doctor's invitation to friendship. The physician was asking for the Yergans to help him find a spouse.[119] (This they did, though it took some eighteen months to finish the task, with Xuma's marriage to Amanda Mason in October 1931.) Though Yergan promised to write Xuma again within a few days, there is a break in the surviving correspondence of almost two full years. The next available missive, dated June 1930, concerns the upcoming Bantu-European conference at Fort Hare, to which Xuma had been invited to make a presentation on "The Christian Approach to the Race Question." Max had also asked Edgar Brookes to discuss the same subject, but Brookes wished to do so from a psychological and religious point of view, highlighting ways in which Christianity might combat race prejudice. Xuma was asked for something else.

> I had thought that you could be a bit more personal by making known to the gathering some of the disabilities which we as an educated class live under. I had thought also that it would be possible for you to make a number of constructive suggestions which would show to the Europeans who will be present how we may cooperate in removing both the causes and the manifestations of race prejudice. Here, of course, you should be free to deal with various aspects of the cause of such prejudice. I thought also that you might bear your witness in regard to your belief in the power of Christianity to displace prejudice between the races. While I do not wish to have you restricted in regard to what you are to say, it does seem to me that an address along the lines I have indicated, coming from your own cultured personality, will go a long way towards inspiring our own students who will be present, as well as towards helping the Europeans who will be present to acquire an altogether different idea of an educated, cultured black man. I might add that in my own address I have the same thing in mind.[120]

Two years later, Xuma was inviting the Yergans to visit his family. Even more than had been true for the Jabavus, an American connection was a feature of Xuma's education and personal life. Xuma had received some schooling in the United States before becoming a medical doctor in Scotland. Upon the premature death of his first wife, Xuma married Madie Hall, an African-American socialite. For these reasons, a close relationship was a logical possibility, something that Xuma suggested, expressing his hope that Mrs. Yergan, Xuma, and educator and social worker Charlotte Maxeke live as neighbors. Yet Yergan replied that his wife was "still very tired and in need of a change." Susie Wiseman's schedule appears to have been impossible, as she was raising a third baby and "teaching the children with no break in their school period" while also remaining involved in a club she had started—the Unity Home Maker's Club. Yergan hoped she might be able to visit the Xumas in Johannesburg the following month.[121]

The tenor of Yergan's Xuma letters changed very profoundly by 1935, obviously affected by the gravity of the Hertzog Bills and local reaction to them. Evidently unable to conceal the full intensity of his revulsion to these, he used guarded, cryptic, stifled prose.

> I note your reference to our conversation here relative to what is passing through my mind both with regard to what is happening in South Africa and my attitude towards these developments. While I had a reason for talking in some what extreme terms with you I am very glad and appreciate the fact that you recognize that I should do nothing rashly and that I shall consider all sides before I take any action.[122]

Having been treated to Xuma's hospitality shortly before the letter was written, Yergan indicated his intention of visiting them in Johannesburg "within the next month." Obviously combining business with pleasure, their respective families, including children, were able to spend an enjoyable time together, leaving the Yergans exhilarated. After pointing out the many ways in which serious and frivolous matters had been combined during the visit, Yergan reassumed his confidential, cabalistic tone:

> With regard to your personal matter, which we discussed, I appreciate the confidence which you placed in us which led you to take up so vital a matter with us. With regard to the person in New York whose name I first mentioned to you and about whom you so correctly understood me as being very much impressed I am frank to tell you that I consider that person a very splendid person indeed, and it was for that reason that I was so emphatic in what I said. I wonder if you wish me to take the liberty of writing there? With regard to the other two, I shall send you whatever information I can get you about them and I shall be glad to advise you in any possible and desired way. So please feel free to call on me and in the meantime I shall keep my own mind at work on the matter.[123]

By October 1935 Yergan had seen Xuma again, informing him that he planned to leave the country around midmonth.[124] By then, having been helped considerably by Yergan over the years since their first contact, Xuma was now in a position to reciprocate. Xuma's reply came in a deeply compassionate five-page handwritten letter in which he tried to reassure his African-American friend of the value of his work. Writing with the utmost candor, Xuma spoke directly with keen insight. Filled with sage advice, the letter ranged from the avuncular ("Keep friendly with all even those with whom you may differ in opinion and outlook") to the brotherly:

> You know, Max, your position here is a diplomatic one. It is not a mere personal matter that ends with you. You have the reputation of a rising great people [American Negroes] who must use their most meagre opportunities to serve their African cousins most guardedly.

Then he waxed eloquent, writing,

> Your last ten years in this country have not been in vain. You won the confidence and good will of many intelligent people. From time to time your mind may shift to different directions and to different camps but you must remain courteous and friendly even with those with whom you may not see eye to eye. . . . Many of us may not see eye to eye with you as far as you see, now, and even for my own part it may be best and wise that they do not. I say that because any extreme action at the present juncture would only tend to victimize the African. In other words, it would be only destructive for us with nothing to gain or in its place for the benefit of our people. It would do much worse than even that. It would give our high authorities here [an excuse] to stand firmly in the way of any minister giving permission for Afro-Americans to enter this country for service. That would be used as an excuse of branding them all as radicals who incite hostility between black and white.[125]

The next months brought travails, making letter writing difficult. Those written were often terse and hurried. Their principal purpose was to inform Xuma of Yergan's return and to express the wish that the two would have an opportunity to meet soon.[126] The next month, May, found the two trying to arrange a meeting, showing even greater urgency than before, again due to the dizzying pace of the Hertzog Bills. At this time, Yergan abandoned customary caution:

> I am most anxious to talk with you, aside from personal matters, about the convention which meets in June. I have heard something of what has already happened and I have taken the trouble to acquaint myself with the actual state of affairs with regard to the Bills that were passed.

What I am most anxious about, however, is the steps which the proposed convention may take with regard to the bills and it is this I wish to talk about with you. In case it is not your plan to visit Alice en route to the Transkei or on your return to Johannesburg, I will send you a note to inform you of the time I shall come to Johannesburg.[127]

From then on, the key feature of their correspondence is its attention to politics, first concerning the All African Convention and later concerning Max's work in the International Committee on African Affairs.

Frieda L. M. Neugebauer

As stated earlier, around 1929 someone else came into Max Yergan's life who was to make a lasting impression. Frieda Neugebauer was fully equipped to teach zoology at Fort Hare during Yergan's final years in South Africa but appears not to have done so. Instead, she appeared somewhat suddenly as Yergan's stenographer. Who she was and where she sprang from seem the stuff of mystery. Rumors abound. Some thought Neugebauer to be of Jewish extraction.[128] If so, she might have emigrated to South Africa seeking refuge from Germany during the early Nazi period, as many Jews did. What this tale did suggest, along with the impressions of a more simpatico Black contemporary (Don M'Timkulu), was that she was much more favorably disposed toward dealing with Black people in general and Black males in particular than commonly was the rule for any White women in South Africa, even and perhaps especially for those who worked at Fort Hare Native College, for whom a proper social distance between the races seemed de rigueur.[129] More daring is the fact that she appears to have been brought to Fort Hare expressly to assist Max Yergan as a corresponding secretary, a role she was to fill for several years thereafter on both sides of the Atlantic. During the 1930s and afterward she was very close to the Communist Party of South Africa. Neugebauer had earned a B.S. in zoology from the University of Cape Town (UCT) in 1933 and an M.S. in 1936, and was briefly employed at UCT as a demonstrator in the Zoology Department from May 1, 1936, until the end of January 1937. Also in this period she taught at Fort Hare, where it is likely that she met Yergan. The two became fast friends and occasionally were observed in each other's company. Their relationship would have turned heads anywhere but raised eyebrows not only due to its interracial character but also because Max Yergan was a person whose every move was already noted.

Neugebauer is recalled as possessing a vibrant, very confident, even willful personality, as being strikingly militant, and as being unwavering in intensity. She talked of the USSR and in particular of Litvinov. Quite possibly once associated with the *Guardian,* a progressive Cape Town–centered weekly formerly edited by Brian Bunting, Neugebauer often confided in Mary Dick, an erstwhile staff member at Fort Hare whose septuagenarian sister, Nancy, later lived in the United Kingdom. Nancy Dick credited Neugebauer with changing her from a "confused liberal to a radical" and starting her on the path of committed trade union activism. Although Nancy did not recollect Neugebauer having mentioned Max Yergan, her sister Mary told her that they "had a close relationship."[130] Among mutual acquaintances it was almost an article of faith that Neugebauer had played a decisive role in Yergan's radicalization, some claiming that she steered him to the left. This hints at Frieda's extreme orthodoxy, particularly if she had genuinely extolled Litvinov.[131] Even if Frieda lit the spark to kindle the flame, however, it would be wrong to ignore the fact that Max had been gathering fuel since the 1920s.

The Neugebauer-Yergan relationship persisted well beyond the American's departure from South Africa. Neugebauer not only joined Yergan in New York, assisting him in brainstorming about what later became the Council on African Affairs but also, on some occasions, was a traveling companion. She aided Ralph Bunche in facilitating arrangements for travel and accommodations prior to his 1937 fact-finding South African tour. That April she dined at Bunche's London flat in Yergan's company. In his diary, Dr. Bunche cited Neugebauer as Yergan's "South African girl friend," a highly perceptive notation.

Although a moderately shadowy figure, Neugebauer's linkage with Yergan became notorious among people within his orbit. Gossip must have caused each of them great discomfort because informants who survive from that time almost invariably mention it critically. Only two did not do so: Nancy Dick and Govan Mbeki, probably because each had high regard for both partners personally and politically and may, therefore, have seen something beneficial in an unconventional, deeply idealistic coupling of suspect moral value. It was, of course, no secret that "Reverend" Yergan was a family man. Whether motivated by curiosity or other exploratory urges, the relationship lasted far longer than most casual affairs, well into the early 1940s. The persistence and character of their association, however, illustrate that much more was going on between this pair than met the icy eye. From 1937 until some time in 1942 Yergan and Neugebauer acted as each other's alter egos, undertaking most work efforts cooperatively, she drafting his letters, both giving lectures and interviews together.[132]

When Yergan's relationship with Neugebauer is considered alongside his collegial bonds with Rena Datta and Lena Halpern (yet another leftist woman who was to have a lasting impact on Yergan in a subsequent period), it is safe to state that his relations with partners, whatever forms these took, affected Yergan politically. It is not necessary to inquire into the nature of these relationships to find evidence that substantiates this hypothesis. The chronological sequence alone, coinciding as it does with quantum leaps in thinking and behavior, shows definite and direct links to women Yergan knew. How this articulated with Yergan's marriage to Susie Wiseman is not easily ascertainable at this time; our only evidence is indirect, drawn from those who knew each of them, primarily during their Fort Hare years, undoubtedly a most challenging venue for anyone's marriage.[133]

All African Convention

The most significant event during the period following Yergan's return to South Africa was the promulgation of a draconian draft of legislation that would fundamentally alter reality for Black South Africans. In 1935 J. B. M. Hertzog introduced the subsequently named Hertzog Bills. Prime Minister Hertzog's strategy was built on furthering processes that had their origins in the time of the Native Land Act of 1913, the foremost piece of expropriational legislation in the modern era, forcing 85 percent of the African population to reside on 15 percent of the land. The Native Land and Trust Act of 1936 extended African residential segregation. Then, a Native Representation Act struck Africans off the Cape common electoral roll, substituting a fully revised polling system for "qualified" Africans to "elect" three White "Native" representatives, annihilating the vestigial "Cape liberal tradition."

The African majority's response to these dire measures, most evident within the elite stratum, was shock, outrage, and wide-scale mobilization. As had been true when the Draft South Africa Act of 1909 was being promulgated on the eve of the creation of the Union, mass meetings were mounted across the nation to discuss and counter the Hertzog Bills. According to W. M. Tsotsi, Yergan played a behind-the-scenes role in this agitation, the most visible outcome of which was seen in a new All African Convention. The historical parallels between the anti-Union movement of 1911 that sparked formation of the Native National Congress and the emergence of the All African Convention were clear. By now, however, the political landscape had narrowed considerably, and had at the same time become muddier.

Though the African National Congress had sustained itself in the decades since Union, protesting injustice and otherwise catering to its essentially petit-bourgeois Black professional constituency, it was not prepared for a salvo of such an enormous magnitude as Hertzog's, even though there had been signals from 1926 on. Native replies to Hertzogism, therefore, required a coalition. Despite ethnic, linguistic, and regional cleavages, the South Africa of 1909 had been one in which Africans could raise, with effort to be sure, a national congress that might represent a wide range of authoritative personal opinions on the vexing "Native problem"—opinions that were based on daily life. Such an organization contrived ways of accommodating antinomies of commoners and royals, Christians and pagans, and educated and uneducated, and, over time, it even began to pay at least some attention to problems of gender relations and economic democracy. However, the world may have been far simpler in 1909.

The South Africa of 1935 was racked by worldwide depression. Wretched poverty, earlier the exclusive province of Africans and so-called Coloureds, plunged into the heart of Afrikanerdom. Indigent Boers joined persons of color in homelessness and abject penury. In a world increasingly challenged by a rising fascism that complemented the *Herrenvolk* philosophy of what T. Dunbar Moodie has termed the "Afrikaner civil religion" as well as the hundredth anniversary of the "Great Trek," government was susceptible to a host of new pressures that no one opposition organization could possibly counteract alone.

Appealing to the frustrations of Afrikaners cast adrift by forced migration from their rural countryside farms to cold, cruel cities like the vastly overcrowded Johannesburg, Hertzog promised to uplift his benighted Boer brethren by debasing Blacks. The spate of legislation fashioned to achieve this end was presented in 1935, to take effect in 1936.

It must have provided added impetus to Yergan's desire to visit the Soviet Union. It convinced Max that his effectiveness in South Africa was coming to an absolute end. Hertzog's disfranchisement of the besieged "school" stratum was the last straw.

Departure from South Africa

The 1935 furlough, with its secret Soviet interlude, was topped off by the stateside emergence of the National Negro Congress. From its inception this umbrella organization caught Yergan's attention. Its guiding light, John Davis, issued Yergan an invitation to participate in its inaugural meeting in February 1936, less than a month before his South African return. Such a concatenation of events proved decisive.[134]

On May 8, 1935, Yergan, back in South Africa, met with F. P. Keppel of Carnegie Corporation in Durban as a belated in-person followup to Keppel's letter to Yergan of May 29, 1934, relating the series of recommendations offered to revise his Fort Hare–based African Training Institute proposal by the South African Advisory Committee.

In March 1936, following upon two of the major events in his life thus far, implementation of the 1935 Hertzog Bills and the deepening of his magnetic bond with Paul and Eslanda G. Robeson in London, Yergan reassessed his situation, concluding that it was now time for a change from the sacred cause to which he had devoted the last fifteen years. After great and apparently painful reflection he submitted a letter of resignation to YMCA headquarters in New York. This is how it began:

> The government in South Africa is not only not interested in the development of Africans but is quite definitely committed to a policy which is destructive of any real growth among Africans of that country. This I believe to be true not only of the present government but of any government expressive of the basic political and economic principles upon which South Africa as a state is founded. I believe the serious evils to which I refer are inherent in the type of imperialism and its local manifestations operating in South Africa. In terms of the effective arrangements operating there both the material resources as well as the great mass of the population are exploited by and in the interests of the overseas imperialist power, Great Britain, and the local governing class. To

make this possible, Africans have been robbed of their land, deprived daily of their labor with exceedingly inadequate compensation and are being reduced to a level worse than serfs. And the business of any government, representative of the theory and practice of imperialism and the deeply rooted convictions of the dominant class in South Africa, is to maintain the status quo.[135]

From his preliminary materialist analysis, Yergan concluded by confessing the basic impropriety of the work he had been conducting on the grounds that it did not meet the urgent demands of the social and political situation. Instead, the type of cooperation fostered by institutions like the YMCA and the Student Christian Association not only refused to challenge the wrongs of South Africa but also, by its silence, showed complicity, in effect allying itself with the state's repressive apparatus and leaving him with no other alternative but disengagement:

> It therefore seems to me that any organization, movement or institution at work among the natives in South Africa, is necessarily political. Under the circumstances there can hardly be any such thing as practical neutrality. In practice, to varying degrees, of course, most such organizations, institutions, etc., owe their existence to the same forces and policy from which South African governments spring, and therefore, by any real test or analysis, more or less reflect towards native Africans the fundamental political and economic point of view of those who control South Africa.
>
> For me, an alien in South Africa, to be identified with those who constitute the exception and do not reflect the governing South African point of view, would be clearly impossible. This I know from my observation and I see no other conclusion but that I must take the only course which seems to follow.
>
> The service which I could now render to Africans would be considered by government to be of a political nature which it is hardly possible for a South African government, or those institutions under its control, at work in African life, to approve. It, therefore, seems to me that I am not justified in running the risk of possibly embarrassing the International Committee by that course of action in South Africa which I firmly believe to be right and in the interest of the good life for Africans as well as the mass of non-ruling Europeans in that country.[136]

On the face of it, Yergan had completed a momentous ideological transformation. Having seen the light about the classist and racist South African system, he had outgrown the limited, collaborative neutralism of YMCA work. There was a contrary interpretation of his action, however, this time from Oswin Bull, a Y official instrumental in allowing Yergan to initiate his mission. Bull had had ample opportunities to observe Max closely over the years. Bull conveyed his own reading to the New York office, endeavoring to explain Yergan's behavior in a rather different context, as he candidly confided:

> No doubt this opinion is due mainly to the breakdown of Yergan in his private life. There can be no doubt that the facts of this are more widely known among the Africans than we realise. They will say nothing about it, unless asked point blank, and probably very little even then, but many must know. For instance, for a long time Thamae, who was Yergan's secretary, was receiving letters from Geneva every week addressed to him, but he was instructed not on any account to open them but to hand them over at once to M.Y. for whom they were intended. That sort of thing does not remain hid even though the man concerned says nothing about it at the time.
>
> I want to stress also the sense of urgency of taking definite action. Our African leaders and the sympathetic White people have been living for so many years on the promises about the development of the Training Scheme and Yergan has done nothing to set it forward, that they are growing sceptical; while at the same time the need for the services of trained Africans is greater than ever. If things had not gone wrong we should have had several trained workers in the field by now and the value of their work would have been demonstrated convincingly.
>
> Yergan himself is a very pathetic figure and my heart is very sore for him. He is taking the line that the basis of the service which he can render must be much more radical than is possible in our conditions, that work under your and our auspices is only palliative and not really Christian. Consequently he has felt compelled to resign. At the same time he talks guardedly to me about expecting to be coming back to work here, under auspices unspecified. As a matter of fact it is most unlikely that the Government will let him into the country again once he has gone. I do not know exactly how much they are aware of it, but his close relations with Communist leaders out here are known, as also his visit to Russia prior to his return last year. I am astonished that he is,

apparently, under the impression that he is going to be able to come and go as he likes.

As for Mrs. Yergan, who has done a really first-rate piece of work here, our hearts are very sore. We may be reading the situation wrongly but we anticipate a separation when they get back home. She carries with her the very deep sympathy of those who know anything about the situation in her home, and she has shown a fine dignity through all her bitter experience.

We have been sitting on the top of some very explosive material for some years now and it is God's mercy that we have not been sent sky-high, work and all.[137]

Unanswered questions remain after one reads Bull's analysis of the impasse. While the record provides ample justification for the letter of the charges leveled against Yergan, the justification for their spirit is not so evident.

Visit to the Soviet Union

Clearly Bull alluded to the Yergan-Datta "affair" and Yergan's visit to the USSR to make his point. If the Hertzog Bills and the All African Convention represented two-thirds of the reason for Yergan to resign from the Y, certainly the trip to the Soviet Union completed the circle. Almost no detailed data are currently available on the trip. Like so many other things in Yergan's life, its timing is in dispute. Colin Bundy, following the lead of the mature Govan Mbeki, has suggested that it took place during 1934. Although this is plausible, the theory seems to rely most heavily upon Mbeki's own fragile memory of an event from five decades ago that even then would probably have been deeply shrouded in secrecy. He could certainly be forgiven if he was off by a year or two. At this writing there is no paper trail corroborating this hypothetical voyage. By contrast, there survive certain cryptic but much richer references to a trip taken during the months immediately preceding a return to the field in 1935–1936. While no diary or journal references to the trip are found among the documents in Yergan's Howard University papers, fragmentary written impressions make at least some reconstruction possible. These were latter-day reflections prepared with a very different purpose and for an inquisitional audience. In one instance, for example, Yergan reconstructed this twenty-year-old encounter with a Soviet official:

> In the winter of 1936, while living in South Africa, I visited the Soviet Union as a tourist. In a conversation with a Russian official, Mr. Lozovsky, I was naively amazed at his detailed grasp of facts about social and educational conditions in Rhodesia and the Union of South Africa. Although he had probably never visited these countries, he talked about persons in Africa, both European and African, as though he had conversed with them the day before. He really interested me when he described vividly and accurately the condition of the road between Thabanchu, in the Orange Free State, and Maseru, capital of Basutoland. His command of details was astounding.[138]

However much time Yergan spent with the man many foreign friends of the Soviet Union knew as "A. Lozovsky" or "Lozovskii," the man was also known as Solomon Abramovich Dridzo (1878–1952). Comrade Dridzo-Lozovskii was in charge of the Red International of Labor Unions (RILU), the policymaking body for the trade union arm of the Communist International. He functioned as something akin to an official greeter for many foreign delegations touring the USSR.

The Robesons and/or Frieda Neugebauer may have had a hand in Yergan's Soviet sojourn. In 1931 he wrote of conversations with people who had toured the Soviet and had tried, without success, to secure a travel permit. That year he traveled to France with Dr. John Hope (a later visitor to the Soviet Union). By then Yergan had met Frieda Neugebauer, who was familiar with the USSR and who "spoke of Litvinov."[139]

About the same time, Yergan and Mbeki rekindled their acquaintance, transforming it into a full-blown mentor relation. Mbeki became more aware of Yergan and the change he was undergoing as Max became more vocal about socialism and the need for fundamental social change in South Africa. Yet, unless Mbeki was privy to Yergan testimony that no other of his confidants heard, there is no proof that Max visited the USSR in 1934. This would seem much too momentous an event for him to have soft-pedaled it and should have surfaced amid a copious corpus of private and professional tricontinental letters. No such missive has so surfaced. But a 1934 trip was by no measure either implausible or impossible. Consequently, it *appears* that either Bundy or

Mbeki, or both, were slightly mistaken about the chronology. However, they are certainly accurate about Yergan's *sensibility*, as he had probably been preparing himself mentally years before the actual Soviet trip became a reality.[140]

Such confusion is understandable. Yergan did make a dizzying series of trips in 1933, 1934, and 1935, any one of which could have led to the USSR. The one most worth considering occurred when Yergan sailed for New York City, arriving there during November 1935. His YMCA record makes it seem that Max kept close to New York through late February, lingering long enough to attend the inaugural meeting of the National Negro Congress. On March 1, Yergan shipped out of New York, arriving back in South Africa by late April. It must have been in this two-month period that he explored the USSR.

All of Yergan's previous voyages to South Africa had taken two to three weeks. Even in the roughest weather, in the days of steam, a fortnight was commonly sufficient for a traveler to reach Cape Town. On no account would two months be required. Anywhere from two weeks to a month are unaccounted for, and within that time a European, and specifically Soviet, excursion would have been a distinct possibility for Yergan. In his later elliptical allusion to the trip, he pointed out that he made it in winter 1936.

Leading the small quantity of "evidence" about the tour is the hearsay testimony of journalist Dorothy Gilliam, who provided her perspective on Yergan's USSR trip, seen from a special vantage point. Her reconstruction took shape in the England flat of the Robesons in 1937 in this flashback:

> Among the blacks who came to see the Robesons in London in 1937 were William Patterson, their old friend, whom Essie had met on her trip to Africa a year earlier, and Max Yergan. Yergan, who was destined to have a long, close and ultimately explosive association with the Robesons, had been an official of the Coloured YMCA in South Africa. Shortly after Essie's visit he resigned that post because he found it "too conservative" and "opposed to the forces of peace and brotherhood." He returned to New York by way of Moscow, where Patterson said he introduced him to Stalin and Molotov.[141]

Back in South Africa in the concluding days of April, Yergan wrote Ralph Bunche, briefly mentioning a few subjects that were of concern to him. One was the current situation in South Africa, which he viewed somewhat dismally. Another concerned what appears to have been a recent excursion:

> My visit to the Soviet Union was in every respect revealing and infinitely more than I could possibly have thought of before I left America. I regard it as the greatest experience of my life so far as the results of travel are concerned.[142]

However much he intended to act tight-lipped about this trip, in point of fact Yergan proved quite unable to contain his exhilaration. How else could Oswin Bull have learned about his tour? Even had Yergan not told him, a mutual acquaintance would have. If so, the revelation was less a product of indiscretion than of ebullient naiveté. Other letters from the time betray his pro-Soviet obsession.

If Yergan kept a diary or date book of his Russian tour, it apparently has not survived. It would have been uncharacteristic for Max not to have done so, particularly about such an inspiriting and singularly moving personal travel experience. Moreover, in an era in which letter writing and journal jottings were prized as marks of civilization, he was the type to keep such a record.

Many observers have suggested that if bronzed skin were not the norm in Moscow and environs during the 1930s, Black folk there were not as a rule objects of the scorn so familiar to residents of most southern localities and several northern sites in their natal United States. In outlying areas, whose inhabitants were often olive hued, some Black Americans cited encountering kindred complexions. This absence of overtly racial discrimination, coupled with a cheerful curiosity about the coloring and culture of these atypical Americans, who, most Russians knew, had suffered privation in their homeland, convinced many impressionable sojourners that they had seen the racial future.

Paul Robeson, a notably vocal exponent of this viewpoint, was in no sense alone as an African-American impressed by Soviet experience. Scores of Negro professionals saw Russia in these years, vast numbers of whom neither professed nor embraced socialism but were hard pressed to ignore the power of such race-neutral imagery. Few Black tourists left the Kremlin unmoved. This is palpable between the lines in Yergan's correspondence with Negro National Congress (NNC) national secretary John P. Davis, whom Yergan met before and during the

NNC and with whom an intense working relationship developed very shortly thereafter. Davis was, in early 1936, a friend of the Soviet Union. Yergan impressed him. In January, a few scant weeks before the NNC, Davis invited him to the gathering, reserving a prominent speaker's spot for him on the program.

In the mid-1920s, despite diminutive numbers, Moscow's African-Americans functioned as an expatriate community. Many had some relationship to the Communist Party, though by no means were all "politicals"; one, Emma Harris, the so-called Mammy of Moscow, had actually arrived in tsarist times—for which she was nearly executed after the October revolution. But Harry Haywood [Hall], his brother Otto Huiswoud [Hall], Oliver Golden, Lovett Fort-Whiteman, and Jamaica-born author Claude McKay all spent time in the Kremlin's shadow. Many of these Black Americans forged friendships with African and Afro-Caribbean militants, typically politicals studying at KUTVU (Universitet Trudyashchiysya Vostoka Imeni Stalina, or the University of the Toilers of the East Named for Stalin). By the mid-1930s this cohort also included émigrés like Frank Goode, brother of Eslanda Goode Robeson, engineers Robert Robinson and Richard Williams, reporter Homer Smith, and agronomist George Tynes. Some, like Smith, Haywood, Harris, and Coretta Arli-Titz, married Russian spouses. Interwar-era African-American visitors were directed to these folks. They would share the arcane lore of Blacks in Russia, beginning with the great author Alexander Pushkin, telling tales little heard outside the country. However brief his sojourn, Max would have brought back unusual and surprising information from Moscow, facts to give even ardently anti-Soviet listeners pause. Consequently, even while living in the frightful face of Stalin's bloody purges, several Black visitors found it hypocritical to be shocked at the cruel carnage around them, as neighbors disappeared, given what might await them at home. This may have been on Yergan's mind when he met Essie Robeson after his Soviet journey.

In 1936, Eslanda Robeson toured Africa, camping down south for several weeks, during which time she and son "Pauli" were guests of Yergan and Dr. Roseberry Bokwe, whose wedding they planned to attend. Yergan and Essie surely exchanged their impressions of the Soviet Union. Each knew people who had been to the USSR, some of whom had met Yergan in London and some of whom Max may have met through Neugebauer and other acquaintances. In 1931, for example, U.S. cadre Eugene Dennis became a Comintern rep in South Africa, where he functioned under a nom de guerre but was revealed by name to local Communist Party officials like Edwin Mofutsanyana, who knew Yergan in this time.[143] It is not known whether Max knew Gene Dennis. Finally, Paul Robeson had also traveled to the Soviet Union, and Yergan had to know this well. Essie's trip held clues to Max's evolving state of mind.

Eslanda Robeson's South African Sojourn

Late in 1936, Eslanda Cardozo Goode Robeson, along with her adolescent son, Paul Junior (aka "Pauli"), sailed to South Africa as part of a broader personal fact-finding mission that was also related to her field research in pursuit of a doctorate in cultural anthropology at the renowned London School of Economics. Reaching Port Elizabeth on June 19, she and Pauli were met by Max and R. T. Bokwe, a recent Edinburgh medical graduate. Almost every day of the next two weeks, Essie and Max spent days sightseeing, shopping, and communicating about Africa and the world, in meetings of the minds uniting Susie Yergan, Z. K. and Frieda Matthews, Dr. James Moroka, Seretse Khama, and others.

Though Essie had heard about Yergan, largely from her spouse, "Big Paul," she had not herself met him. From the start she, Pauli, and, in her words, "guardian angel" Yergan got on well. Yergan and Dr. Bokwe guided Essie and Pauli through Port Elizabeth, lunched with them at the adjacent African "location" of New Brighton, and went on to Grahamstown and to Alice, site of Fort Hare, where Essie was reacquainted with "Zack" Matthews, his wife Frieda, and their children, alternating between them and the Yergan clan for accommodation and spirited evening conversation. Much of the driving, upwards of two thousand miles, was done by Max in what he rather uncharitably described as his "aged Dodge."

Yergan took pains to show Essie the full range of South African reality, emphasizing the brutal irony with which Africans purchased a bag of mealies for their own consumption for five times the price the identical quantity would fetch from Whites for cattle feed. Repeatedly she saw not only the effects of racial oppression but also how Africans had to pay for the "privilege" of segregation.

After the daylight sights and sounds of countryside and city, contrasting the hustle and bustle of European Johannesburg and Bloemfontein with the Native townships upon whose labor the city dwellers fed, the nocturnal hours were taken up with discussing prospective solutions to the problems that so fully and sadly occupied their waking hours—solutions not only for Africa but also for the wider, certifiably wilder world outside.

Essie provided an illuminating description of some of these sessions that suggested that they were not entirely of the ordinary variety. Starting by contrasting the states of African and African-American education, they moved to politics, again in a comparative framework, and then into the arena of ameliorative strategies. This led them to India (where Yergan had recently met Nehru) and its independence. Next the scene shifted to Italy's Ethiopian adventurism, Japan's assault on Manchuria, Spain, the possible restoration of Germany's former African holdings, and the bland inefficacy of the League of Nations. Then the conversation built up to a striking but not wholly unanticipated climax:

And the one hopeful light on the horizon—the exciting and encouraging conditions in Soviet Russia, where for the first time in history our race problem has been squarely faced and solved; where for the first time the words of the poets, philosophers, and well meaning politicians have been made a living reality: Robert Burns' "A man's a man for a' that"; France's Liberté, Egalité, Fraternité; America's "All men are created equal" and "are entitled to life, liberty, and the pursuit of happiness." All these grand ideas and statements have been hauled down from the dusty reference shelves at the back of men's minds and have been put into active, vigorous, successful practice by the Russians, so that men and women and children of all races, colors, and creeds walk the streets and work out their lives in dignity, safety, and comradeship.[144]

William Patterson, James Ford, and Ben Davis, who seem to have played a part in Yergan's Soviet sojourn, were three of the most influential African-American office holders in the Communist Party. All had spent time in the Soviet Union and would have shared their impressions of the Soviet experiment with Yergan. They would build upon this personal and professional relationship for the next decade. Together they were able to facilitate Yergan's post–South Africa entry into the U.S. Left.

Whatever ambiguity lingered in Bull's mind regarding the authenticity of Yergan's conversion, his voice was a minority opinion. It was not insignificant, however, and probably carried considerable weight in the YMCA, whose International Committee trusted him. To the outside world, and especially to the Left, Yergan was taken at his word. In a pointed paragraph, he was quoted as sharply saying,

> "I cannot go on as I am in the face of this failure of so-called liberalism which is condoning the increasing political and economic repression of the Africans. The time has come when the African Natives must be assisted in their open fight to organise themselves whereby they can act unitedly in resisting the powers that exploit them."[145]

Yergan received a vote of confidence from Paul Robeson, who lauded him for having the courage of his convictions, whatever the short-term cost. In a response that set the tone for the way Max's resignation would be seen for years afterward, Robeson was, as was customary for him, formidably eloquent.

> Max Yergan's stand is one of the finest and most important things that could have happened. His taking the only honest way out of a false position should show the light to many so-called leaders who want to be blind and who have not the courage, honesty and manliness of a Max Yergan to speak out boldly and to defy the powers that be, or to strike a note of discord against those who pay the piper, and, consequently, call the tune. The YMCA, a supposedly Christian organization and religious institution, has long befuddled and betrayed the Negro people. Yergan's admirable stand provides a fine lead for other Negro intellectuals who are occupying false positions from which they may wish to escape, but who are wavering.[146]

Another indication of the way posterity would honor Yergan's departure from South Africa came from Carter G. Woodson, editor of the *Journal of Negro History*. Woodson, a champion of Yergan's efforts since the 1920s, stressed the larger ramifications of what he construed to be a major sacrifice:

> Certainly Max Yergan, though not an African, but a Negro American casting his lot wholly with those people, deserves much credit for his recent decision. After working under the auspices of the Young Men's Christian Association in South Africa [for] fifteen years he learned from

experience that such Christian teaching as is permitted the natives in South Africa without any mention of their oppression is mere mockery. He has come out of Africa in protest against such an ineffective method, hoping in a more direct way to prepare and to arouse intelligent natives to work against this injustice and ultimately deliver themselves from serfdom. In thus taking this stand Yergan will make it difficult for Negroes to enter South Africa even as missionaries. There is today considerable objection to the program of certain missionaries and only with extreme difficulty can Negroes enter the country. The Government of South Africa seriously objects to the teaching that all men are brothers and that a Negro before God is the equal of a white man. The Government has decreed that all men are unequal, and the blacks must remain content to be the serfs and wage slaves of the whites. No law to bar evangelization has been enacted, but certain economic imperialists believe that it must be done ultimately if their program of exploitation is to continue with success.[147]

Both Oswin Bull's criticism of it and Max's cover story had merit. Each played a role. Yergan had been in personal turmoil since the summer of 1931 and probably before. Bull was correct that missives exchanged did not go unobserved by Yergan's secretary, Thamae, nor others with whom he came in contact. Thamae's wife recollected that Susie Yergan upbraided Yergan for his lengthy and unexplained absences, and both the Thamaes and Govan Mbeki sensed tensions in the Yergan home. In 1930 these impressions of Yergan's private life had entered the very public record of both the WSCF and the YMCA. With the furthering of his ideological growth, controversy increased. Bull, whose acerbic reactions were clearly recorded, even suggested that Max did not have a bad time of it in South Africa. He probably felt this way by judging from Yergan's extraordinary standard of living.

In a curious off the cuff remark to an itinerant Ralph Bunche in 1937, Bull issued a parting shot at Yergan. In his notebook, Bunche jotted the following entry after a revealing chat with Bull:

November 7, 1937:

—Bull says he thinks Yergan exaggerated the physical inconveniences he suffered here—he thinks that Yergan was treated very well in that respect, tho he added piously: "it is not for a white man to say what spiritual suffering a colored man undergoes in such a situation."

Bull emphasized that Yergan underwent a change after his trip to Russia —he wanted everything to be "more radical" in the union after that.

—Said Yergan lacked organizational ability, tho he was a good contact man. Said Mrs. Yergan's work would be more lasting than Max's and both Mr. and Mrs. Bull had more praise for Mrs. than for Mr. Yergan.

—Said Yergan cooked his Y.M.C.A. goose in South Africa when he wrote a stinging, discourteous letter to the international Secy., charging that as a white southerner he was prejudiced and blacking Max's work (re Denmark conference).[148]

In the months following the departure from Alice, it is unlikely that Yergan thought much about Oswin B. Bull. The South Africa that concerned him was less the one "adjusted" by the YMCA and more the one envisioned by the All African Conference, responding to activists like Xuma and Robeson, whose voices, with Frieda Neugebauer close by, helped shape an International Committee on African Affairs.

What may have been the last straw for Yergan was described by the late controversial founder of the Unity Movement of South Africa, I. B. Tabata, a resident of the country during Yergan's term of service. In his inimitable fashion, "Tabby" once said that at a certain point after his movement to the left, Yergan took the unprecedented and powerful step of torching his theology texts.[149] No one else has written or spoken of this; yet it has a profound symbolic value as an action that most would consider irrevocable, not only for his missionary career but also for his relationship with the Gibraltarlike Christian, Susie.

5

Progressive Leader, 1936–1948

Upon returning to the United States Max Yergan fully dedicated himself to a life of left-wing activism. This took three forms. First, he deepened his connection to the National Negro Congress, becoming first its Harlem and then its national representative. Second, he concentrated upon building the new International Committee on African Affairs (ICAA), both domestically and internationally. Third, he sought to build a base in academia, using his adjunct position as instructor of Negro history at City College of New York as his anchor.

By 1936 Max Yergan was by most estimations, including his own, a revolutionist. He had said as much to Govan Mbeki, both explicitly and implicitly, but it was also quite evident from his public utterances and whenever his personal correspondence strayed into political affairs, as it had been doing since 1931. He had presented himself in this way to Ralph Bunche and John Davis, but also to Quaker pacifist Clarence Pickett.[1] The question remained for him of how to move forward with his principled ideological transformation yet still maintain his connections to his prior constituencies and backers.

As Max prepared to leave South Africa he was already setting up a strategy that would ensure a smooth transition from his previous decade and a half of service abroad. Using his transnational network of contacts, he combined expertise gained in the YMCA both nationally and internationally with experience of foreign travel to carve out a unique approach to race leadership that fused progressivism with a bit of rhetorical Pan-Africanism. Thus he became accomplished in three different arenas, as NNC administrator, as ICAA executive director, and as City College faculty member employing sophisticated publicity strategies. The prime and perhaps most pivotal of these platforms was the National Negro Congress.

The National Negro Congress

The National Negro Congress grew out of a Howard University conference on the "economic status of the Negro" held during May 1935. Cosponsored by the university's Social Sciences Division and the Joint Committee on National Recovery (JCNR),[2] the meeting had originated with Ralph J. Bunche, chair of Howard's Department of Political Science, and JCNR executive secretary John P. Davis. The Howard meeting identified a need for closer collaboration among Black organizations, political, fraternal, or religious, and for a central coordinating authority to articulate objectives for racial struggle. The body envisioned was a broad-based National Negro Congress that would "give strength and support to all progressive programs of all Black groups" without duplicating or replacing the work of any already existing structure.[3] Secretary Davis sought race leaders, Max among them.

The first NNC took place in Chicago's Eighth Regiment Armory in mid-February 1936. Attending were 817 delegates representing more than 385 political, laborite, and religious organizations and more than five thousand visitors, including several Communist Party sympathizers of both races. In the course of the week preceding the founding Congress a committee led by Adam Clayton Powell Jr. drafted a reluctant Asa Philip Randolph as the group's president, acknowledging his stature as chief spokesperson for Black labor.

The NNC meeting was noteworthy for balancing national and international issues, paying special attention to the Italian fascist "Rape of Ethiopia," a sensitive racial issue for African-Americans, within whose communities antifascist sentiment intensified.[4] Lij Tasfaye Zaphiro, special envoy of Ethiopia's London legation, addressed the gathering, countering European colonial allegations of Abyssinian barbarism with news of the savagery of fascist Italy's invasion.[5] Black Communist leader and vice-presidential candidate James Ford tied Ethiopian resistance to Italian aggression to the African-American fight "against lynching and for civil rights and decent human relations."[6]

Then Congress attendees heard a missionary recently arrived from Cape Town[7] who linked Italian imperialism in Ethiopia to the expropriation of African land in South Africa, describing conditions in that country resembling those afflicting Black folk in the United States. Bringing the NNC into the picture, the speaker ended by saying that "this Congress has the opportunity and responsibility to make it possible for all organizations here represented to subscribe to a minimum program—to fight for those things on which the organizations are in agreement."[8] Max had entered the National Negro Congress. His introductory speech garnered attention from both national and international reporters.[9]

Yergan's NNC position was extremely strategic. When he appeared as an intense bystander at the first National Negro Congress, catching the eyes and ears of John Davis and Ralph Bunche, architects of the NNC, he came with another potent recommendation. Not merely an individual, he was also of keen interest to the Communist Party. Known to former YMCA member Communist Party leader James Ford since his student days, Max met Party leader Abner Berry, later quoted as having thought, "look at the big fish we caught."[10] He was not alone.[11]

Yergan brought the new group his YMCA expertise, along with fresh familiarity with the campaign waged by the All African Convention (AAC) in South Africa. As its external secretary he was well placed to keep its goals and needs before his American comrades. It was logical and consistent for him to do so as the African National Congress, part of the AAC, had been influenced by the NAACP, and the AAC's aims resembled those of the NNC.

Max's initial NNC speeches emphasized his strengths as a specialist in African affairs by connecting Africa's struggles to one another as well as to those of African-Americans. At the first congress in Chicago in February 1936, Yergan stood at the podium and said,

> I have spent the last 15 years in Africa, traveling and working in all parts of the continent. However, I will speak today mainly of Ethiopia. Through the attack on this small country we are becoming aware of the aggressive nature of Fascism, and of the necessity for an intelligent, organized resistance. This thing called Fascism is the outgrowth of a larger force—imperialism. Imperialism has reached such a point that it controls much of finance capitalism.[12]

Yergan went on to zero in on "capitalist trusts." In a section referred to by later descriptions of the Congress, Yergan, implicitly invoking Marx, linked land, labor, and capital:

> The capitalist trusts divide up the spoils and partition the territories of the world among themselves. This phase of imperialism has manifested

itself in every part of the African continent. Britain, France and other European countries have taken much of the land; the French colonies alone have a population of 50 million. In the taking of land a labor market is set up. Various new forms of labor are forced on the people, and labor is drained out of the country.

He then provided a further analysis of the effects of the imperialism he described:

> Imperialism, then, means annexation of land and confiscation of labor. . . . It destroys the culture—the basic social fabric of the people's life. In South Africa through the color laws, Africans are kept out of many phases of skilled labor, and on the lowest level, industrially. Laws limiting freedom of assembly make it difficult for them to organize to defend themselves. Other legislation prevents their moving about freely.

The platform provided by the NNC made Yergan better known to a wider and more secular audience. It also provided him with the support needed to embark upon a new venture, the establishment of an information and lobby group about which he had been communicating with Paul Robeson. Out of their collaboration was born the ICAA, or International Committee on African Affairs. It grew directly from recent experience.

International Committee on African Affairs, 1937–1941

The principal transnational activity in which Yergan became engaged during his militant period was the International Committee on African Affairs. Founded with Paul Robeson in 1937, it profited from the energy of its skillful secretary, Frieda Neugebauer. Taking its cue from the International Committee of the YMCA, the ICAA was an idea to which Robeson contributed in large measure. Despite his critical reassessment of the Y, the new group's title and personnel indicated Max's persistent desire and intention to replicate YMCA achievements. Yergan's African connection did not end on his exit from Fort Hare. Continuing as AAC external secretary, Max went public in a series of exposés excoriating Y "racial adjustment" policies; in interviews conducted in London during his spring 1937 European tour, he questioned the use of local YMCAs to mitigate Native oppression. Scrupulously quoted by African-American reporter Homer Smith, stringer for Black and White U.S. gazettes (one of a handful of correspondents accredited to the Soviet Union), who wrote as "Chatwood Hall," Yergan explained why he had quit South Africa.[13] The Hertzog Bills were uppermost in his mind; called upon to bear witness and testify, he saw the problem as caused by colonial finance and settler capitalism and its remedy as being popular democracy.

Before leaving Fort Hare, Yergan told Smith, he had gone out to Africa believing social service and Christian teachings would lead Africans to "the good life." Twenty years later, "I am convinced now that there will have to be fundamental changes, striking at the very roots of political and economic conditions in South Africa, before the African can be assured of even the beginnings of a good life." He illustrated this point with mining salaries:

> Since 1932 profits in the gold mines around Johannesburg and in the Transvaal increased 100% and dividends over 70%. Wages of white workers measurably increased. But not since the war has there been a single increase in the wages paid to over 200,000 Africans working in these mines.[14]

To Yergan this disparity resulted from the fact that Nonwhites were afforded neither access to organized White workers nor recognition for their own labor combinations. Previously, under Clements Kadalie, "a militant African," the Industrial and Commercial Union voiced the demands of African workers until government and coopted "European" labor collusion undermined it, outlawing future endeavors like the ICU. The Native (Yergan preferred to use "African") National Congress consisted of "detribalized" (Western-trained) professional Natives, teachers, ministers, and lawyers who were intended to find token spaces in a Eurocentric schema, but, Max opined, "There is no place for them under European imperialism." He amplified this comment by adding,

> The greatest need of the masses of Africa today is organization along industrial lines. It is necessary for the Africans to organize and to educate in order to give each child and adult a firm, deeply-rooted conception of the good life for him and the community.[15]

Seeking to cultivate left-leaning Howard politics professor Ralph Johnson Bunche, then preparing a research tour of South Africa, Yergan shared his enthusiasm about Russia following his winter 1936 tour, noting that Bunche, too, had thought of visiting Russia. Yergan offered to help Bunche in South Africa, giving Bunche his take:

> Developments in South Africa will be familiar to you: legislative repression on the part of the government; increasing poverty on the part of the people; and groping blindness on the part of the middle class. Meanwhile underground movements are becoming more active. I hope you and your family are well.[16]

Bunche's response suggests some discomfort. He demurred, citing with arctic elegance a simultaneous note from mentor-sponsor Isaac Schapera, University of Cape Town anthropology professor, who insisted on arranging his trip. Feigning interest in Max's continental junket and recent thoughts on fascist Italy, Bunche professed eager anticipation of a "long pow wow" with Yergan upon his return.

In June 1936, a second All African Convention convened, with Yergan and Essie Robeson in attendance. It elected fresh officers: former ANC president Professor D. D. T. Jabavu, now AAC president; Dr. A. B. Xuma, vice-president; Dr. J. S. Moroka, treasurer; H. Selby Msimang, general secretary; R. H. Godlo, recording secretary; and Professor Z. K. Matthews, adviser. Max Yergan remained as secretary of External Affairs, his most visible connection to the AAC in the country itself, although this was his final conference appearance. The convention lasted from 29 June through 12 July; by 30 July, Fort Hare said goodbye to Max and Susie Yergan. On 9 August, they sailed aboard the RMS *Windsor Castle*.

While Yergan struggled unsuccessfully to meet Bunche personally prior to his departure, he heard from a perturbed Xuma, who questioned, "Why are you so silent?"

> Politically, things do not look too bright. The Government are advancing with their policy of control without hindrance and have even succeeded in electing one of their own as Governor-General in the name of Mr. Patrick Duncan. One can see how farcical a position of Governor-General is becoming. It is purely a political reward to one of those who have defended the policies of the government.[17]

In a lengthy letter, Xuma relayed the sad story that "the Convention has not made any spectacular moves yet," adding more optimistically, "but I hope to be sending you some interesting news about its activity as a result of certain lines of action that I have suggested." Of Jabavu Xuma wrote, "Our old friend D. J. as usual is apparently holding the trump card that nobody can guess as yet." Irksome too was the AAC's lack of a printed organ to publicize its programs, leading the physician to lament,

> I have been much concerned about the future of our Organisation, as we have no organ with which to popularise our propaganda. As you know the so-called African papers, the "Umteteli," "Imvo," "Bantu World," etc., are controlled by interests that would not be too happy if the Organisation were to be a success. The attack is either a silent boycott or the usual paternal advice to our African leaders. It would have served the interests of our people greatly if we could have had means to equip and finance an independent African paper. I hope I can find encouragement in that direction during my short visit over there.[18]

Xuma expressed anxious concern about "the establishment of a scholarship and Research Fund for Africans to study overseas and get new contacts and also to do research work here at home and overseas." Echoing themes previously explored with Yergan (sentiments Max shared), Xuma urged, "If we could make it possible for such selected men and women to have advanced training overseas, we would be creating a broader base and a more intelligent leadership and guidance for our people." Critical to this was finding an overseas backer to "give Fort Hare a modern and up-to-date library" and buy "complete equipment" for the college's underfunded "Scientific laboratories."

Yergan's reply to Xuma's letter took almost three months to materialize, coming as Bunche prepared to leave and brimming with news of the status of the International Committee on African Affairs. Yergan urged Xuma to bring him up to date "as soon as possible about your plans," adding, "My own plans are taking very definite shape and I shall be writing you about them both personally and in your official capacity." Pledging to do so within a week to ten days' time, Max went on:

> Will you further say to the officers of the convention, as well as to Messrs. Thema, Msimang and others, that you have heard from me, that there are some splendid developments about which I shall be writing

them shortly, and that my desire is that they meantime hope, notwithstanding this very long delay in writing them. I hope you will make it
clear to them that illness has been responsible for the delay.[19]

Yergan made one more attempt to reach Bunche before his Union
field trip. The final predeparture letter to Bunche had two aims: first, to
arrange a London encounter; second, to provide preliminary information on work currently in progress involving the International Committee on African Affairs. Max pronounced the new committee "under
way," identifying Raymond F. Buell, Mary van Kleeck, Hubert T. Delaney, and Mrs. John F. Moors of Brookline, Massachusetts, as having
accepted his invitation to join. Repeating some language used in a letter
to Xuma the day before Bunche sailed, Yergan set forth the ICAA's
three principal purposes: researching policy and legislative enactments,
finding and training selected Africans, and connecting with the cooperative movement.

Since some of his postresignation public pronouncements sparked
controversies in quarters where he was known, one of Yergan's first
steps in laying the groundwork for a new career was to reestablish ties
with former friends and associates from his YMCA days. They required
reassurances of steadfastness where Africa and the association were
concerned. He gave this in a note posted in February 1937. Replying to
critics, it began,

> The idea seems to have entered the minds of a few of my friends that I
> am no longer interested in the work which I did for fifteen years in
> South Africa. Nothing would be further from the truth. While I know
> that most people are aware of my continued interest in our African
> work, it occurs to me that I should send this letter in order that there
> may be no misunderstanding whatever.[20]

Adopting an earnest narrative tone, Yergan reiterated the centrality of
the cause to which he had dedicated decades of his life, emphasizing
that he extracted from his previous work inspiration for his present
endeavor. Readers could still sense the spiritual animus sparking his
mission labors:

> Within its established principles the International Committee of the
> Y.M.C.A. gave me more or less a free hand in my capacity as Senior

Secretary of the South African work. It was therefore possible for me to give expression to my own ideas and to utilize my efforts and energy as I thought best in the year-to-year promotion of the Association work in that field. It is therefore inconceivable that I could suddenly lose interest in what is, after all, the expression of years of service. For this and other reasons it is possible for me to say to you without reservation whatever that I am not only interested in the work which we have developed in South Africa, but interested in the sense that I want to see that work continued. With this in mind, it is my hope that our South African work will still be a channel through which the Association movement here will find means of expressing its interest in the world-wide program.[21]

Then, making a special plea to his YMCA family, Yergan showed that he had not abandoned them. This reminded them of what they still meant to him in spite of his now attenuated relationship to the Y. Since Y service and Africa were closely tethered for those who knew him, he carefully cinched both connections in such a way as to counter rumor mongering:

The same reasoning which has led a few people to imagine that my interest in the African work has become less has caused some to think that my relationship to our Associations here at home is less than in the past. May I, with all the emphasis possible, state that this is in no sense true. Not only do I feel as close to the Association movement here as I have always felt but, in view of my continued though somewhat changed relationship to Africa, I have every reason and desire for maintaining and strengthening my Association relationships here in America. There is no basis whatever for any misunderstanding between myself and the Association movement here; and I am particularly anxious to make it perfectly clear to the secretaries and the laymen with whom I have had long years of contact and between whom and myself real friendships have developed that I desire to be thought of always as one of their number.[22]

He closed his letter with the promise that he would be "glad to send shortly a statement" about his "new relationship to Africa," underscoring his aim of clarifying "that the work in Africa is *our* work and should be supported and that I am always one with my Association workers."[23] In fact, the YMCA network was Max's core constituency and would so remain thereafter.

The note elicited a favorable response from Xuma. Yergan's plan grew directly out of his Fort Hare experience of identifying and training "a select number of Africans." This was the scheme that found expression in the institute that he held had been "blocked by government" and other opponents. Still holding out hope for such training to occur in the Union, Max argued that an alternative was to bring Africans to the United States and Europe. Their study "would be broadly based," with emphasis on "scientific training in economics and sociology."[24]

Xuma was enthusiastic about this idea, telling Yergan, "It made me feel quite happy and hopeful for both of us and those in whose cause we are interested." Xuma was high on the ICAA's potential. He and Yergan were at one in planning and envisioning aims:

> I doubt if there is any scheme I would welcome more to be associated with than that outlined in your last letter. As a matter of fact, in it I find much realisation of my hopes and plans. Nothing, therefore, would give me more pleasure than to play my little part in the furtherance of the aims and objects of the proposed committee.[25]

Xuma wrote as if the ICAA might fulfill his own dreams regarding data collection, documenting and disseminating his own vision of African elite formation. Seeing both scholarly and political value in the ICAA, he replied,

> It should give close contact between us and scope for research, and exercise of our intellectual powers in gathering and giving the necessary information on this Continent. It would also necessitate close and more frequent contacts between us by going to and fro, writing or reporting about the findings.[26]

Max next headed for Europe. He first went to London, knowing this colonial metropole had always attracted guest workers, students, and countless other emigrants, many from Africa and the Antilles, and while there he met leaders with a wide range of political leanings. The Robesons knew many of these leaders, especially those involved in progressive political and cultural work. They frequently were the Robesons' guests and attended his performances. Paul and Essie in turn had reciprocated by supporting their work in every moral and material way possible. En route to Europe, Yergan contacted Xuma again, praising his New Year's address, which had been printed in *Bantu World,* and expressing faith in the All Africa Convention.[27] A day earlier he had written Bunche, who with his spouse Ruth had been visiting London since February.[28]

As he had done with Xuma, Yergan indicated to Bunche that he had had other meetings prior to leaving New York. This time he told Bunche of a talk with Margaret Wrong of Edinburgh House in London. Wrong, a missionary literacy specialist with considerable African experience, had already published *Africa and the Making of Books: Being a Survey of Africa's Need for Literature* (1934) and *The Land and Life of Africa* (1935). In spite of his impatience with some missionaries, Yergan's impressions of his time spent with Wrong provoked a ringing endorsement:

> She will be back in London late in April and she will be desirous of seeing you, if you can find the time. I think it will be especially nice if Mrs. Bunche could meet her and the people she knows. Her connections are missionary but she is a splendid person herself and her friends are worth knowing.[29]

Despite recent criticisms Yergan clearly had not cut all ties to the moderate missionary and philanthropic establishment. His ongoing relationships with them were consistent. In Paris he spent at least a day visiting Afro-Antillean author René Maran (1887–1960), whose novella *Batouala* had won the French Academy's Prix Goncourt in 1921. A friend of Howard's illustrious Alain Locke, Maran was enlisted by Yergan to join the ICAA.

Maran had spent thirteen years as a colonial civil servant in French-ruled Ubangi-Shari (now the Central African Republic). His prize-winning work portrayed an African prince criticizing pseudocivilizing colonialism, a stance influenced by the negritude movement. By 1928, however, the same work lauded seven years earlier was banned in the colonies. Yet Maran himself, like Yergan, was ambivalent on the colonial question. Writing from London on May Day Yergan quoted Maran (whom he misidentified as African), saying, "For the first time in my life I have enthusiasm for the policy of a French government."[30]

Yergan's circuit included Marseilles, then Belgium and the Netherlands, where he met Mary van Kleeck and Mary Fleddérus. These women were associated with the International Institute on Industrial Relations, under whose auspices he would deliver a paper at the Hague during the summer on "Standards of Living in Colonial Areas."[31] He enlisted both for the ICAA.

Yergan and Neugebauer were in the British Isles by April 20. Alone and together, Frieda and Yergan called on the Bunches. Having encountered each other here and there around NAACP and NNC sites, Yergan and Bunche now met each other via Eslanda Robeson, although, as previously established, the two had arranged this earlier. Bunche, whose papers contained a 1928 clipping on Yergan's efforts to secure a Rockefeller grant for his Fort Hare job, made other diaristic jottings concerning the former YMCA secretary, the tenor of which occasionally seemed to vary in tone from that of the correspondence exchanged between the two men, perhaps motivated in part by Bunche's critical reaction to Max and Frieda. Neugebauer assisted Bunche in securing accommodations via South African sources.[32]

Bunche's record listed four contacts with Yergan and Neugebauer and a private meeting with the latter concerning Cape Town lodgings. A week before their initial get-together, the *New York Times* duly reported that Max had been recommended to teach Negro history at City College of New York. On the same day, April 14, his likeness appeared in the Communist Party's *Daily Worker,* a detail noticed by America's federal intelligence community.[33] Yergan and Bunche had their first London confab on April 21. Bunche found him "young but pleasant enuf [*sic*]," noting Yergan quipped that his father was "a prize s.o.b."[34] Max was keenly soliciting Bunche's aid. Yergan's manifest affection for Robeson was evident, leading him to write of him and other allies:

> I know of no person more constructively effective in the international life of peoples of African descent than Paul Robeson. He has given me several hours of his busy time in London. He is a power in many ways, and as we talked and planned together, I became increasingly aware of the significance of his membership in the International Committee on African Affairs. Paul Robeson, René Maran and Leonard Barnes, a noted writer on African problems, constitute the European membership of our committee. The African members will be announced shortly, and our Bulletin issued upon my return to New York by the middle of May.[35]

Two days later, Max and Frieda had tea with Ruth and Ralph Bunche and "Nyabonge" (Toro, Uganda, prince Akiki Nyabongo), Johnstone (Jomo) Kenyatta, D. G. S. (Don) M'Timkulu, WASU (West African Student Union) head I. T. A. Wallace-Johnson, Robeson, George Padmore, and "Ras (Teferi) Makonnen." Bunche's daily log read,

> Max explained his African Committee and Geo [Padmore] explained the African Bureau and Journal project. Max suspicious of George's Trotskyist sympathies but they got on okay. . . . Max may go to Spain and may be able to arrange for me to go. . . . Miss Neugebauer is going to aid me in finding accommodations in South Africa. Yergan and Neugebauer stayed for dinner.[36]

The collective considered the projected aims of the ICAA, though Padmore and Makonnen kept aloof. Padmore, born Malcolm Nurse in Trinidad and a former Bunche student at Howard, had from 1927 to 1934 overseen the Negro Bureau of the Communist International but had broken with it by 1937, becoming persona non grata. Both Padmore and Makonnen the British Guiana–born man formerly known as George Griffiths, a former American sojourner and Colored YMCA patron who recalled Yergan from his earlier years, were now stalwart Pan-Africanists. Yergan, whose position was more orthodox in supporting the Soviet Union, seems to have adopted the Party's view on the "heretical" Padmore. At the same time, Max did provide Bunche one pound for Padmore's IASB (International Africa Service Bureau), if it materialized, but instructed him to destroy the check if the project did not materialize.[37] Those assembled in the Bunche household represented some of the leading members of the African and Afro-Caribbean intelligentsia based in London; Max had to be impressed.

This London trip was a homecoming of sorts for Yergan. While we lack detailed information, it is clear that Max traveled there in 1931, and it is possible if not probable that he may have encountered Robeson and some of his comrades at that time. Robeson would then have been close to both Padmore and Kenyatta. Kenyatta was involved with socialism, the Communist Party, and Padmore, and Padmore, as head of the Negro Bureau, held the brief for Black subjects, including struggles by Negro toilers in Africa and the Caribbean. Indeed, he published a periodical called *The Negro Worker*. The colorful Makonnen, then a

London restaurateur, recollected Yergan in this choice passage from his autobiography:

> It was all the more necessary for us to take a hard line on communist maneuvres at this time, because they had just recently had an important acquisition in their ranks. This was Max Yergan who had served for many years in the YMCA movement in South Africa; it wasn't so strange, as I knew myself, to move from YMCA radicalism into left-wing politics, and now he was touring round Europe making contacts for his organization, the Council on African Affairs. He formally inaugurated the Council in the early forties, along with Paul Robeson, but already in the prewar period Max had been touring Europe, working among the student element. This put us in a terrible mess, because we knew very well that whoever got signed up by Yergan would then simply become part of the Russian axis, and would proceed to move according to whatever the line from Moscow was. We were particularly concerned to prevent the many South Africans from being used to this end, but I think the only man they did partly manage to use for a time was our old friend, Marco Hlubi, a Zulu, who worked as a dancer in the Negro Theatre Company at the old Unity Theatre near King's Cross. Yergan and the communists behind him preferred to make advances towards indigenous Africans like Kenyatta or straight black Americans or West Indians.[38]

Sierra Leonean leader Isaac Theophilus Adunno Wallace-Johnson was a KUTVU enrollee in 1931–1932 whose movements were monitored by British intelligence. A Nnamdi Azikiwe ally, he authored a 1935 treatise on the Ashanti Confederacy and, as founder-editor of the *West African Sentinel,* he had been charged with sedition and was deported from Gold Coast after publishing an *African Morning Post* article in 1936. In a polemical reply to Italian atrocities during its invasion of Ethiopia—his *Has the European a God?*—Kwame Nkrumah was moved to reproduce the offending passages in toto, including the following:

> He believes in the god whose name is spelt Deceit. He believes in the god whose law is "Ye strong, you must weaken the weak. Ye 'civilised' Europeans, you must 'civilise' the 'barbarous' Africans with machine guns. Ye Christian Europeans, you must 'Christianise' the pagan Afri-

cans with bombs, poison gases." . . . In the Colonies the Europeans believe in the god that commands "Ye Administrators, make Sedition Bill to keep the African gagged, make Deportation Ordinance to send the Africans to exile whenever they dare to question your authority. Make an Ordinance to grab his money so that he cannot stand economically. Make Levy Bill to force him to pay taxes for the importation of unemployed Europeans to serve as Stool Treasurers. Send detectives to stay around the house of any African who is nationally conscious and who is agitating for national independence and if possible round him up in 'criminal frame up' so that he could be kept behind the bars."[39]

His Highness Prince Akiki K. Nyabongo was also well known to the Robesons. In 1936, he had guided Essie during her East African travels as Yergan had done in the South. An author, the prince penned *The Story of an African Chief* and *Africa Answers Back*. Cousin to the ruling Omukama, monarch of Uganda's Toro, Nyabongo (an Oxford anthropology fellow student of Essie's when she attended the London School of Economics), was like Kropotkin a rebel-aristocrat, a royalist dedicated to democracy. His books argued for relativism and rationalism in dealing with Africa. Essie might have felt he would be a good fit.[40]

Don M'Timkulu met Yergan in his dormitory days at Fort Hare, after graduating in the class of 1927—that is to say, well before he was the Marxist-Leninist Govan Mbeki befriended in 1934. He, along with Essie Robeson and Kenyatta, was studying at the London School of Economics. Sharing church background and social gospel leanings with Yergan, M'Timkulu had a different relationship to the Bunche gathering. A Bunche acquaintance, he and the politics professor had met a year earlier as students in the States, M'Timkulu at Yale, Bunche at Harvard. Having received the same scholarship, they were both in England, and they had much to discuss. As M'Timkulu was still living in "student digs," he was pleased at Bunche's largesse in sharing hearth and hospitality. Prior to this meeting, Bunche's invitation had stated that he would have a few guests, including Padmore, which piqued M'Timkulu's curiosity. He viewed Pan-Africanism as being of "academic interest," and so was pleased to have been included. The fact that Max Yergan was there proved an added boon, since he had not seen the ex-Y man in some time and was extremely excited at having an opportunity to catch up on things with him. In contrast to Bunche's writeup of the conversation, he remembered Yergan listening very intently to the day's proceedings but not saying much himself.[41]

M'Timkulu's attitude toward the Pan-Africanists, and that of his crony, Z. K. Matthews, was skeptical. They viewed the movement not in the abstract but in terms of the concrete situation facing them as Black South Africans. M'Timkulu and Matthews, while sympathetic to the causes of their colonized continental cohorts, nevertheless saw their own social formation as a mixed society—albeit a grotesquely unequal one. For them the priority was not throwing the "Europeans" out (despite the fact that their Xhosa-speaking colleagues had seen this as an article of faith for more than a century) but effectuating participation in a democracy. M'Timkulu, while elated at hearing these debates, was moved just as much by the prospect of meeting Pan-African personalities, orthodox and unorthodox, Robeson in particular. In this he may have shared something with Bunche, whose views on Pan-Africanism were broadly similar, if, as Bunche biographer Brian Urquhart suggests, Bunche saw the trend as a distraction. Also like M'Timkulu, Bunche was moved by Robeson's gift with children.

Following closely on the heels of conversations with Maran in Paris and Bunche, et al., in London, Yergan further prosecuted his campaign of recruiting members of the African, African-American, Afro–West Indian, and left-liberal White intelligentsia for service in the ICAA. On the last day of April, he even reached the Lion of Judah. As he informed followers and friends, Yergan journeyed from London to Bath to arrange an audience with aides of an eminent East African monarch exiled by fascistic dogs of war: "Yesterday I went back to Bath in England, to the estate where the Emperor of Ethiopia has temporarily retired. My talk there with a member of the Emperor's staff is a story in itself."[42] His efforts were richly rewarded in late May with a check for fifteen hundred dollars of "seed money" from aide-de-camp Paul Robeson.[43] Yergan's twenty-one days in Europe had been both eventful and productive, leading him to issue the following brief to his constituents:

> Three weeks in Europe have brought me into touch with a number of effective people, here again revealed to me something of the nature of the fast-moving history which each day unfolds, and have made clearer the forces behind that history. It is not enough, for instance, to say that the fascist forces in Spain yesterday rained death from the air upon hundreds of civilians in the Basque country; it must be added that the very

nature of fascism whether in Spain, Ethiopia, America or Japan leads to precisely these results, effect inevitably following cause. The connection between men and events is the lesson of all history.[44]

As mentioned earlier, after the 1936 National Negro Congress Max traveled to Moscow on a tour that might have reached all the way to the fearsome head of state. One author wrote that he joined William L. Patterson, who introduced him to Molotov and Stalin.[45] The next year, 1937, permitted Yergan to deepen his interest and involvement in the National Negro Congress while also constructing another organization. With Paul Robeson he laid plans for an International Committee on African Affairs. Taking part of its name from the globalist trend to which he had devoted one-third of his life, the International Committee of the YMCA, Max, with Robeson, strove to create a lobby group intended to influence U.S. Africa policy in a favorable direction. Pivotal to the ICAA's organizing strategy was the network of African-American intellectuals he had met in two decades of YMCA visits to historically Black colleges and universities. Assisting in this was Frieda Neugebauer, who relocated from South Africa to work as Yergan's secretary.

The demands of the ICAA and NNC often overlapped, giving free rein to the many facets of Yergan's personality. In the same way that Max's African expertise won him an NNC platform, his global interests found expression in the International Committee. He surrounded himself with persons of diverse ethnic, racial, and national backgrounds, and this made the ICAA an unusual site in interwar-era North America. While South Africa had a central place in its work, the ICAA was a clearinghouse for information on the continent as a whole; its Africana library was among the best in the country, perhaps in the Western world, reflecting the wide network of contacts of its founders and those they recruited. Between them, the ICAA and NNC presented a striking panorama of modern African history.

Max's first targets were people inside or close to South Africa, including Ralph Bunche,[46] ANC president A. B. Xuma, and AAC leader Professor D. D. T. Jabavu. Invited too were Europe-based progressives like colonial critic Leonard Woolf, Afro-Antillean Parisian novelist René Maran, author of the prize-winning *Batouala*,[47] and U.S. residents Mary van Kleeck and Mary Fleddérus, who collaborated on works of political economy, dividing their time between America and Europe. In the spring they arranged for Yergan to participate in a conference sponsored by the International Industrial Relations Institute (IIRI). A year later, a revised version of his IIRI paper was published as *Gold and Poverty in South Africa*. This European junket, beginning in London and extending into the continent, cemented the foundation of the International Committee and buttressed Yergan's career. The year 1937 also marked a reunion with A. B. Xuma, who sailed to the United States in May. On September 7, Max fêted guests Xuma and Jabavu at New York's International House.

For Max, being in their presence must have seemed like old times. In an event sponsored by the ICAA, both Jabavu and Xuma spoke frankly about South Africa, with Channing H. Tobias presiding.[48] Their candor so upset Thomas J. Jones that he fired off an angry letter.[49] Jones's reaction notwithstanding, this was an auspicious beginning for the committee. By spring Max had also managed to secure an adjunct appointment at New York's City College to teach Negro history, the first Black American so honored.[50]

City College of New York, 1937–1941

As shown above, a large part of the reason for Yergan's rapid rise in New York after fifteen years in Africa lay in his connection to the Harlem branch of the National Negro Congress, which maintained regular contact with the Harlem section of the Communist Party. The Party sponsored a cultural thrust of its own, extending to students in area schools, notably those attending the City College of New York (CCNY). In mid-April 1937, CCNY's Frederick Douglass Society, a campus body interested in studying Negro life and history, lobbied in-tensively to recommend Max Yergan for an appointment to the instructional staff.

They were assisted in their campaign by a handful of leftist instructors, including historian Philip Foner and English teachers Morris Urman Schappes and David Goldway. Foner, Schappes, and Goldway had seen some of Yergan's writing[51] and found him impressive as a speaker.[52] Progressive CCNY faculty, staff, and students had by then been pressing for the hiring of African-American faculty for some time.[53] The Teacher's Union and some campus Communists played a vanguard role in this campaign.[54] By spring 1937, the fruits of that agitation were partly realized as news articles announced Max would teach Negro history at the college in the fall semester.[55]

When Max appeared on campus on a Wednesday that autumn, Schappes, Foner and Goldway, wishing to show hospitality to the new faculty colleague by taking him to lunch, found him refused service by dining room staff in the Main Tower overlooking the Harlem River. Their response to this was immediate and vociferous—the trio held a demonstration, loudly accosting other diners until the college food staff, embarrassed, made an exception.[56]

A similar disturbance was generated by the issue of accommodations. Having resided in rather commodious quarters on the Fort Hare campus, Yergan took an unprecedented step shortly after his repatriation home by purchasing a house in what had theretofore been an all-White block on Hamilton Terrace, just off the City College campus. His move was met with a very disquieting, although not unfamiliar, local reaction. A group of neighborhood hoodlums, thought to be parishioners at a neighboring Catholic church, allegedly hurled projectiles through his windows, smashing several of them. When progressive supporters of Yergan's candidacy learned of this unexpected act of vandalism, a demonstration was organized at the college campus. The demonstrators marched to the scene of the crime, chanting appropriate slogans along the way, and then, pausing to survey Yergan's damaged domicile, resumed their trek to the Catholic church, where they repeated the display. The depredations came to an end, but thereafter, an observer suggested, White residents began moving out of the area.[57]

The circumstances surrounding Yergan's appointment, his public allies, and the way he conducted himself all gave Yergan the appearance of a high-profile left-wing instructor.[58] In a place and time where such ideology mattered greatly, that had both positive and negative effects.

The syllabus for Yergan's course, "Negro History and Culture," tells us much about his approach to the topic:[59]

THE COLLEGE OF THE CITY OF NEW YORK

History 168   Dr. Yergan

NEGRO HISTORY AND CULTURE
Assignments I–V
Prehistory, General Background
Continent of Africa
Schmucker, Woodson, Delafosse, Boas, Mair, Soga
Journal of Negro History (as indicated)

Attention is directed principally to the African continent in studying the background of the Negro peoples. Stages and characteristics of cultural development in Africa in many aspects resemble cultural developments elsewhere. Indeed the early and subsequent advances of man in Africa were a part of the general human experience. We shall examine man's experiences in the Nile Valley as well as cultural development in other parts of the continent including the Bantu of Southern Africa and other groups in Central and West Africa.

    I. ORIGINS—Man in general—Man in Africa Schmucker, pp. 12–23; 24–42; 257–259 Delafosse, pp. 1–26; Woodson, I 3–19; II—1–21

    II. BASIC FACTORS INFLUENCING AFRICAN CULTURE, Schmucker, pp. 165–168; Delafosse, 149–161; Woodson I—pp. 22–36

        A. Environmental Surroundings

            1. River valleys, mountains, deserts, plateau areas

            2. Geographical isolation

            3. Soil conditions—vegetation

            4. Climate—heat, rains

        B. Equipment—human, natural

            1. The African—a man

            2. Stone, copper, iron, gold, etc. and their uses

            3. Tools and implements

        C. Adaptation to environment

            1. Finding food and shelter

            2. Pastoral movements

            3. Domestication of animals

            4. Agricultural Development

    III. THE ORGANIZATION OF SOCIETY IN AFRICA Woodson I—pp. 149–156; Mair pp. 30–77; Delafosse pp. 162–171; 172–193

        A. Life in the family—Mair, pp. 30–77

            1. Organizational beginnings

            2. Power of parents

            3. Position of children; their training

            4. Customs and their significance at birth, adolescence, marriage

        B. The Tribe and Clan—Mair, pp. 173–204; Soga, pp. 15–19; Delafosse 162–172

            1. The chieftainship

            2. Political organization

3. Tribal authority
4. Custom enforcement
5. Ownership of property; inheritance
C. Land in the life of the tribe—Mair; pp. 154–172 Delafosse pp. 162–72; Soga, 383–5
   1. Theories about land
   2. Land ownership
   3. Use of land

IV. MENTAL MANIFESTATIONS

Schmucker, pp. 127–135; Delafosse, 214–245; Woodson I, 149–167; Soga, Chap. VII to X inclusive
A. Concepts of good and evil
B. Art representations of mental concepts including plastic and graphic mediums, dance and music
C. Primitive religious beliefs and customs and theories of life

The syllabus as represented in this excerpt suggested that Yergan had a keen familiarity with contemporary currents in African studies, as each title referenced in this syllabus offered up-to-date information and ideas. It is also certain that Max's orientation would have been shaped both by missionary readings, on the one hand, and his more recent immersion in Marxist-Leninist theory, on the other.

In the same season, Yergan's association with the National Negro Congress grew. Between his connection to the CCNY Left and his office in the NNC it was just a matter of time before Max's prominence in pro-Communist circles would attract government attention. While government scrutiny may have begun as early as 1936 with his Soviet tour, the firmest evidence of surveillance dates from the next year. In his capacity as assistant to John P. Davis, Yergan wrote to President Franklin Roosevelt requesting a meeting to talk about Scottsboro, proposed antilynching legislation, and other potential legislative enactments "affecting Negro people."[60] He sought an audience with the president around November 16 or 17.[61] As with any letter to the White House, this one set off security queries about the writer's identity and history. The prominent reference to the Scottsboro case was duly noted. Several attempts to arrange a meeting with NNC representatives proved unavailing.[62] This created a paper trail that eventually led to the FBI and its director, J. Edgar Hoover.

In December, responding to Black YMCA veteran and Lincoln University dean of men Frank Wilson, Yergan undertook a speaking tour. Wilson had asked Max to give three presentations: a Saturday supper meeting for thirty students, faculty, and staff, focusing on ethnic minority groups around the world, including South Africa; a Sunday morning service stressing the importance of religion in facing the world's great challenges; and a Sunday afternoon faculty forum on South Africa.[63] An article in the school newspaper stressed that Max had quit South Africa YMCA work upon realizing "that the problems of the Africans were mostly political and economic, and the policy of the YMCA was not formulated to meet the needs of these millions of subjected people."[64]

Following Oval Office snubs to requests for meetings and the successful Lincoln visit, Yergan sent out a circular to presidents and secretaries of state of all the American republics, the League of Nations, and the Pan-American Union, to all diplomatic representatives in Washington, D.C., and to all consular representatives in New York City condemning the callous killings and deportations of Haitians in Dominican territory by strongman Rafael Trujillo.[65] A fortnight later he received a cable from Undersecretary of State Sumner Welles in response to a letter he had sent concerning American policy in the Caribbean, centering on Haiti, that had sparked off an NNC mass rally. Welles made clear his displeasure in what he probably took to be meddling in his affairs.[66] However insignificant Welles may have considered Yergan's action, it was added to the catalogue of Yergan-related correspondence now under close scrutiny by State Department and White House officials. Without knowing it, Max was attracting attention within the highest circles of government. The response to this informal investigation was that the organization was "not reputable."

With the beginning of 1938 the House Un-American Activities Committee began amassing material on the National Negro Congress, listing it as subversive. Its rationale for doing so was based upon three premises: (1) Some NNC members were also members of the Communist Party; (2) the NNC supported the right of the Communist Party to exist; and (3) the NNC endorsed statements on behalf of some Communists.[67] At the time, however, Yergan and Davis were far more preoccupied with NNC matters, ranging from the printing of the proceedings of the second congress to a January 23 Yergan address on fascism at Leigh Street Methodist Church in Richmond, Virginia, to an invitation from Quaker Helen R. Bryan to speak at a February 6 afternoon gathering of the Friends on a topic Max had identified as "The Negro—A Determinant in the Future of American Labor."[68] In late January he spoke at an NNC forum at the Detroit YMCA.[69] A week later Max, with Mary van Kleeck and Mary Fleddérus, met Quakers Clarence Pickett and Helen Bryan in Philadelphia to consult about an October conference presentation on Negro standards of living and labor conditions throughout the world, sponsored by the North America– and Europe–based International Industrial Relations Institute.[70]

During late February Yergan spoke against Jim Crow in the colleges at a CCNY meeting sponsored by the Frederick Douglass society, the Meroë Society, the Teacher's Union, the American Student Union, and the Communist Youth League.[71] When in May the League of Nations Council, meeting in Geneva, discussed fascist Italy's claims to Ethiopia, the International Committee on African Affairs sent telegrams of protest. Yergan met with Carnegie Foundation representatives seeking aid for a November ICAA conference run by Pickett, van Kleeck, and Yergan.[72] In late July he set sail for Europe.

Thanks to van Kleeck and Fleddérus, orders had been coming in for *Gold and Poverty in South Africa* before and after Yergan's summer European trip.[73] By autumn, the publication garnered a favorable review in the prestigious British journal *International Affairs*.[74] Near Thanksgiving Yergan polled Bunche seeking information and his opinion regarding a British proposal to settle Jewish immigrants in Africa, a proposal that complicated the land question by setting it against the urgent need to relieve refugees from Nazi persecution:

> Undoubtedly, imperialist Britain and its allies elsewhere will seek to turn to their own advantage this proposed settlement of Jewish immigrants. It is likewise easily conceivable that propaganda from fascist countries will be promoted on a wide scale in Africa w/ the possible result that some Africans may be so misled as to look to the fascist powers as their protectors under the circumstances.[75]

Bunche's response, posted a month later, offered a detailed and incisive analysis of the statement in a way that reflected the quality of his acute mind:

> It seems to me that this offers no decent solution to the problem, particularly in view of the fact that the hands of the imperialistic countries which are now thinking along these lines, are not at all clean. As usual

the English are seeking a way out at no cost to themselves. If England and her dominions showed any inclinations to let down the barriers against Jewish immigrants, my attitude might be less severe, but this they do not propose to do; consequently they are seeking to make another Palestine out of the congested areas in Africa in which Jews may be settled. The central question in such settlement will of course revolve about the problem of land. In east Africa, particularly in Kenya, this problem is already in the acute stage. The most desirable land areas have already been alienated—the natives have seen their most desirable land, which was the White Highlands, alienated to whites at terrific costs to their own welfare. The introduction of more whites, Jews or non-Jews, will certainly aggravate the situation, and of course, the natives as always, bear the costs. In none of the reports that I have seen, has there ever been any suggestion that in the alienation of further native land areas, would there be any compensation for the natives in terms of increased control over their own country as a means for protection against continuing encroachment.

The suggestion relative to Tanganyika is particularly unhappy in my estimation. Tanganyika has a considerable German population and during my recent visit there, I was impressed with the extent to which pro-German and pro-Nazi propaganda is being disseminated among the natives. The natives, with no basis for understanding the full import of Nazi doctrine, and with many grievances against the British administration, would fall easy prey to this insidious propaganda. For these and many other reasons, such as the inevitable conflict that would arise in East Africa, not only between Jews and natives, but also between the established Indian traders and new Jewish traders, always at the expense of the native population of course, I do not think that the proposed settlement of Jewish refugees in Africa could be endorsed.[76]

By year's end, *Gold and Poverty* had been assessed by the *International Labour Review*.[77] In January 1939, Rose Wright, in charge of missionary education for young people for the Indianapolis-based United Christian Missionary Society, endorsed it.[78]

That same month the *Journal of Negro History* published Yergan's article, "The Status of the Natives in South Africa," which buttressed his position as an informed scholarly observer of the South African scene. Reprising some of the earlier statistics cited in *Gold and Poverty* and other prior works, it also helped strengthen Max's case as a historian in two senses: first, it showed his African expertise and, second, it helped to reinforce his selection as a serious teacher of Negro history, as this was the subject of the journal.

By the start of 1939 *Gold and Poverty* had been widely disseminated, reaching nearly seven hundred recipients throughout the world. This probably accounts for why it is still easily found in libraries today and remains high among Yergan's better-known printed writings. Review copies and sales alike continued unabated well beyond the first quarter of the year.[79] On August 31, Max delivered an address on "Standards of Living in Colonial Areas as Influenced by Governments" to the IIRI's annual Hague Summer Study Conference.[80]

October found Yergan back at Lincoln University speaking on "Man's Struggles in the World of Today" for a Sunday morning chapel service and then for an afternoon forum on the condition of Africans in South Africa.[81] The same campus newspaper issue that described this talk featured a Sunday interview with Max's eldest son, Fred, a CCNY mechanical engineering student. Fred indicated that he was contemplating changing schools and had considered Lincoln.[82]

By late November 1939 Yergan had written Franz Boas an ICAA form letter that began, "On my recent visit to Europe I heard or saw nothing that impressed me more strongly than the desire and effort of Africans and other colonials to improve their living conditions." Inviting Boas along with his other correspondents to share his concern, he continued, "I recognized also the great importance of the growing knowledge among sections of the English, French and other people that injustice in the colonies is a chief enemy of democracy in the home country." Then he continued, using familiar language:

This question of the status of millions of Africans and their right to a better life is at the heart of the present world struggle. The good life and world peace to achieve that life are goals which turn our thoughts to Europe and its relation to the struggling and oppressed everywhere.[83]

Yergan's goal was, of course, to interest Dr. Boas in the work of the ICAA. Boas responded in the affirmative, expressing his willingness to discuss the matter, but he also indicated that "it will not be easy to convince Europeans or Americans that people on lower stages of civilization are not there solely for purposes of exploitation."[84] While no other correspondence exchanged between the two appears to have survived in this period, Yergan did contact Boas again about African affairs and an equally pressing career concern two years later. In the meantime the ICAA focused upon its own growth.

The ICAA on the Move

Buoyed by the momentum of recent transatlantic successes, Yergan concentrated on building his new coalition. Among luminaries cultivated for ICAA membership and a leading light on the masthead of the group's fresh stationery was Raymond Leslie Buell, a popular, prolific political scientist who had written extensively on a range of territorial and international administrative subjects. Buell published monographs and analyses for the Foreign Policy Association and a Boston-centered pacifist collective, the World Peace Foundation. Africa scholars knew Buell for his 1928 work, *The Native Problem in Africa*.

Three years before *The Native Problem* Buell had compiled *Problems of the Pacific: A Brief Bibliography Prepared for the American Group of the Institute of Pacific Relations*. The IPR was launched precisely the same year by a zealous board, most of whom were ex-YMCA officials. Its first director, Edward C. ("Ned") Carter, supervised Max in India. A building later housing the ICAA was owned by Frederick Field, the second director of the Institute of Pacific Relations and a close Carter associate who was later active in both the ICAA and its 1941 successor, the Council on African Affairs. Carter, Buell, and Field were each internationalist in outlook. Carter had also built a following from *The Inquiry*, an anti-isolation journal. Previously called the "National Conference on the Christian Way of Life," the *Inquiry* circle was a liberal, social gospel–influenced collective. Much like the IPR, it was rooted in the YMCA, even using Y print facilities. Thus the ICAA sprang from both the YMCA and the Institute of Pacific Relations.

Like Carter and Yergan, Field had overseas experience, in Asia. Field was a first cousin of itinerant recording producer and jazz impresario John Hammond (who later joined the Council on African Affairs). Field and Hammond were left-leaning heirs of the Vanderbilt family. Throughout Yergan's term, Field corresponded regularly with John Davis and George P. Murphy of the National Negro Congress, directing the American Peace Mobilization while IPR American Council head Carter presided over Russian War Relief.

From the start the ICAA was interracial in its composition. At least half of the membership was Black, the other half White. Males predominated, but there was rarely a time during which women did not occupy visible and prominent roles, wielding considerable influence. One such woman was Frieda Neugebauer, he previously mentioned activist secretary. At one juncture, Mary van Kleeck, director of Russell Sage Foundation's Industrial Studies Department, held sway. In its heyday, the ICAA represented a cross-section of the interwar intellectual Left. Neugebauer and van Kleeck had IPR ties, the former as a stenographer, allegedly from 1934 to 1949,[85] the latter intermittently contributing to *Pacific Affairs*. At its inception key board members were situated in colonial capitals, notably London and Paris. Although little else beyond surviving memoranda, press releases, letters, and news articles points to their effectiveness, the members maintained regular contact for two decades and were able to mount and sustain a powerful sequence of well-publicized actions and campaigns.

Pioneer ICAA members were, besides Buell, Robeson, Bunche, Howard University president Mordecai W. Johnson, rising Howard trustee Channing H. Tobias (both Black YMCA officials), René Maran (aforementioned Paris-based, Afro-Antillean originator of *Batouala*), Leonard Barnes, Mary van Kleeck, Hubert T. Delaney, Mrs. John F. Moors, Ferdinand E. de Frantz, and Norman H. MacKenzie. Prominently named on its letterhead as director, Yergan commonly signed memoranda or news releases.

Neugebauer and van Kleeck proved pivotal in this period of ICAA development. Individually and together, they seem to have accepted a major share of responsibility for its day-to-day operations. If Oswin Bull's estimation of Yergan as an "idea man" had merit, office workers with detailed follow-through skills helped him look his best. Effective at generating concepts, speaking publicly, chairing meetings, and pressing the flesh, Max participated in far too many groups in any given week to stay abreast of his duties without assistance. Despite the very public role he played in many organizations, Yergan relied to a great extent on behind-the-scenes support from Neugebauer, van Kleeck, and other auxiliary personnel.

Van Kleeck was then a seasoned scholar and respected foundation consultant. A Russell Sage associate since before World War One, she authored pioneer studies linking occupational-safety, workplace, and gender issues. An ardent social democrat, van Kleeck brought impres-

sive progressive credentials and stature. From about 1925 on, she cultivated a discerning concern for Negro labor. She and Max both knew
George Haynes, whose collaboration with Russell Sage dated from the
fund's first decade. Urban League founder, Federal Council of Churches
Race Relations Bureau doyen, and 1930 Yergan Fort Hare Bantu-European Conference invitee Haynes, van Kleeck, and Carter all cooperated
in creating an innovative 1928 National Interracial Conference for the
Study and Discussion of Race Problems in the United States in the Light
of Social Research.

The year 1935 saw van Kleeck extensively furthering her contacts
with Joint Committee on National Recovery (JCNR) triumvirs Ralph
Bunche, John Davis, and George Haynes. In February Bunche and Davis
invited van Kleeck to make a presentation to the upcoming three-day
JCNR May conference on "The Position of the Negro in our National
Crisis." She had been asked to speak to the query, "For What Type of
Social Planning Should the Negro Technician Work?" but this oppor-
tunity was precluded by previous commitments in the West Coast.[86]

Van Kleeck also counted Quakers Helen R. Bryan and Clarence Pickett as cordial colleagues. She may have met Max through them, or
maybe through mutual JCNR heads Bunche, Davis, or Haynes. Van
Kleeck was also clearly of the Left as well. Davis, for example, had
known of her work from winter 1935, when she served as one of seven
expert witnesses testifying at City College before a labor subcommittee
of the National Committee for Social Insurance.[87] Her activist reputation estranged van Kleeck from the Russell Sage Foundation, leading it
to distance itself from their employee's "radical" social studies.[88] More
critically, late in 1935 van Kleeck's chairing of the Interprofessional
Association for Social Insurance brought accusations of communism
from a New York City publication, *Equity,* prompting her to aver, "The
Interprofessional Association is not and never has been a 'communistic
group.'" Such charges were to dog her for some time to come.[89] At different points in the decade, Yergan and van Kleeck crossed one another's paths. By June 1937 van Kleeck and Max had conversations in
the course of which she decided to join the ICAA.

By 1937 Yergan adroitly used his African expertise to fashion a new
position in the National Negro Congress, that of a vice-president for
International Affairs. It is likely that these credentials impressed van
Kleeck, whose entrance into the ICAA came quite early in its life. She
moved comfortably in those same circles that had facilitated Max Yer-

gan's rise: social gospel–minded liberals, corporate philanthropists, and left-wing militants. Together with her colleague and collaborator Mary L. Fleddérus, van Kleeck was positioned to help Yergan's career. In June, for an upcoming meeting of the overseas International Industrial Relations Institute, van Kleeck interviewed Yergan on his draft on "Standards of Living of Native Workers in Africa." Given her Dutch name, van Kleeck could also have had a special interest in South Africa, particularly regarding Black labor.

Although neither a professional social scientist nor a degreed researcher, Yergan brought fifteen years of practical social service experience to bear on erudite discussions of conditions affecting Black South African labor. He had regularly published articles on the subject and now held an adjunct professorial position within a reputable New York university. In missionary, philanthropic, and ecumenical circles he won acceptance as an authority in this sphere of study, commanding respect from lay and specialist audiences alike on both sides of the Atlantic. In his time relatively little written on African labor in South Africa was accessible to nonspecialists—maybe deliberately so; knowledge was power, and the more the oppressed knew about the nature of their oppression, as Xuma saw, the closer they might come to power. Finally, few Black Americans had positioned themselves as pivotally and adroitly as Yergan had managed to do thus far with regard to acquiring African expertise. Since Fleddérus and van Kleeck devoted considerable energy to keeping their Hague-based International Industrial Relations Institute alive, Max Yergan could bring a critical global dimension to the Negro industrial question. This motive took Max to Europe to teach the IIRI about black burdens and white wealth in South Africa.[90]

Yergan pursued a two-track strategy, providing Ralph J. Bunche with a lengthy IIRI document in order to interest him in the group and its activities. This he undertook during a June vacation spent in North Carolina.[91] The second track involved direct contacts from van Kleeck. During the first week in July, van Kleeck corresponded with Ralph Bunche (probably at Max's suggestion), informing him of the upcoming IIRI Hague conference on "The World's Natural Resources and Standards of Living," slated for August 30 and 31 and September 1, at which Yergan was scheduled to deliver a treatise on standards of living among Africans in South Africa. In her missive to Bunche, van Kleeck identified five main areas under consideration by the group: (1) the raw materials of the world and their distribution; (2) the work of the League of Nations Committee for the Study of Problems of Raw Materials; (3) natural resources and disasters; (4) the effects of power development in economic organization; and, as the focus of all the preceding papers, (5) economic organization and standards of living, considered with special reference to such areas as Africa and the United States. Yergan's paper would fit into this last-named area.[92] Within days of van Kleeck's invitation, Bunche received a letter from Yergan, requesting that he be sent notes of periodicals of merit, as Bunche found them during his Eastern and Southern African travels, governmental and nongovernmental, as well as news on consumers' and producers' cooperatives. Max paused to "wonder if you plan to make your proposed trip to Eastern Europe before you go to South Africa." Relative to the Union, he offered to serve as an intermediary in visa acquisitions and introductions.[93] Then van Kleeck, knowing that Bunche had mentioned visiting Holland encouraged him to do so, communicating the possibility to Mary Fleddérus, pressing him to meet her at IIRI.[94] Van Kleeck followed this with a letter from the Hague reminding him of the invitation.[95]

In mid-August Yergan wrote Bunche telling him his comrade Louise Thompson Patterson of the International Workers' Order had just set sail for "France, England, and perhaps other countries in Europe," intending to attend a "Conference on Racial and anti-Semitic Affairs" in Paris in September. Max explained that he had told her to see Bunche in London after a visit to Spain, "for there are serious matters which she will also wish to discuss."[96]

By late August, Yergan and the ICAA had arranged a gathering at Manhattan's International House featuring AAC leader D. D. T. Jabavu and ANC head A. B. Xuma. This meeting was scheduled for Tuesday, September 7, with Channing Tobias presiding and various Black and White dignitaries attending. The flier Max sent out a week in advance was a masterful piece of public relations, capably balancing drama and commitment:

> If Africa is not today in the headlines, it does not mean that life there has ceased to be full of tragic problems. There is a real sense in which Africa's ills have become chronic. Italy in Ethiopia; France, Britain, Portugal and Belgium in the rest of Africa; Germany's demands for colonies and the consideration given to these demands by the powers; the ruthless exploitation of the people and resources of Africa; repressive legis-

lation of the most destructive type, and the growing poverty and misery of Africans—these are the facts of African life which constitute first-class headline material. Imperialism is still the menace, the wrecker of human welfare that it always has been and we must not lose sight of its fact and effect.[97]

Writing on the eve of the conference, Yergan let Xuma know that Jabavu was to speak on the last ten or fifteen years of South African legislation, under the title "Africans and Modern Politics." His next charge would be to put forward the claims of the AAC. Max then asked Xuma to expatiate on "The Basis of Repression in South Africa," or a subject of his own choosing.[98] He had had in mind *Grondwetism*[99] and imperialism.

Nearly six hundred audience members attended the International House forum. Each presenter followed Yergan's plan. Thomas Jesse Jones of the Phelps Stokes Fund (with whom Max had had a lengthy and checkered history) took offense at the Black criticisms. The next day Jones dressed down Channing Tobias for his association with this event:

It was inevitable that the American audience should be depressed by the completely discouraging outlook. Practically nothing was said to show that in South Africa there are white and Native people who have been working together, for the improvement of conditions and that progress has been made. The devoted and really heroic services of many white people for the Africans were never once mentioned. This left colored Americans, already acutely conscious of white injustices, still more deeply resentful toward white people. While I entirely understand the distrust of white people by colored people and emphatically regret the prejudices and injustices for which white people are responsible, I know that you share my conviction that many white people are sincerely devoted to the full development of colored people in every part of the world. What a tribute Dr. Jabavu, Dr. Xuma, and Mr. Yergan could have paid to the able and devoted missionaries from Europe and America who have labored faithfully and effectively for the Native people of South Africa. They could have told of the increasing concern of many British and Dutch people in the welfare and in the rights of the Native people. Despite the very unfair division of educational expenditures, Fort Hare Native College is probably the best college for Natives in all

Africa, and the school system for Natives is constantly being enlarged and improved so that it now ranks above the school systems of other parts of Africa.[100]

Jones's criticisms notwithstanding (indeed, partly because of them, as he indicated to Dean Frank Wilson), Yergan pronounced the International House event a resounding success.[101] This could cut both ways; Jones had shown himself to be someone not to be trifled with, but in that triumphal moment Yergan thought mostly of the palpable victory the ICAA had won.

Yergan proceeded to plan for an appearance at Lincoln University later that fall.[102] At this point in time he began to link the two great "Negro questions," the problems of Africans and the problems of African-Americans, arguing that "indeed, it is because of the similarity between African and American problems and an historic relation be-tween Africa and America that millions of Americans are deeply interested in the African situation."[103] In what might easily be taken for a Pan-African progressive argument, Yergan makes the case for political parallelism:

> Whatever we may think about the larger issues of peace and war must, of necessity, include Africa and her millions of inhabitants. If we are interested in the industrial struggle in terms of the C.I.O.–A.F. of L.– employer set-up as known in America, we must be informed about the half million workers in the gold mines around Johannesburg, the thousands in the Rhodesian copper mines, and the millions at work on European-owned farms and plantations in Eastern, South Central and Southern Africa. We must know of the low wage levels maintained by industries that pay large profits, of the legal handicaps under which Africans strive to organize their labor, and of the disruptive forces at work in African society due to invasion from without. Repressive legislation, economic handicaps and lynchings, as these take place in Africa, have a familiar ring to Americans.

Second NNC, Philadelphia, 1937

On October 15–17, when Yergan was one month into teaching Negro History at City College, the NNC held a second congress at the Metropolitan Opera House in Philadelphia. Introduced there as associate to the national secretary, Yergan gave an address entitled "The Historical Struggle of the Negro People." As in so many of Max's projects, this one operated on multiple levels. He thus presented himself in three roles simultaneously: (1) as a leader in the NNC, whose position in its Harlem branch had enabled him to exert influence upon the national executive; (2) as cofounder and executive director of the ICAA, whose interests were both national and international; and (3) as a historian who was both teaching and seeking to make Negro history. There in the shadow of the Liberty Bell, Yergan and the assembled delegates celebrated the seventy-fifth anniversary of the Emancipation Proclamation. In a rousing speech spelling out the centrality and vitality of "Negro" activism, Max presented his leadership credentials.

> The National Negro Congress looks back over seventy-five years upon four million freed men. Today the Congress voices the deep needs of fifteen million workers for freedom. That span of three-quarters of a century is full of importance. It shows that Negroes were and are aware of the meaning of freedom; it reveals their determination to struggle for that freedom. In 1862 and 1865 Negroes had a share in the human forces which were on the march; today that share is larger; the role of the receiver, of beneficiary, has become less; the job of struggling for one's self has increased, and that is as it should be.[104]

At roughly this time, Yergan was making other friends as well. One was Louise Thompson, who by 1937 held national office in the International Workers' Order (IWO), a fraternal society with sixteen different national groups designed to aid the laboring masses. Mention has already been made of a Yergan-Thompson meeting that occurred as she prepared to travel to Europe during August 1937. Because IWO national headquarters were located in Manhattan, Thompson occasionally traveled there from her Chicago base, where she undertook to fulfill the bulk of her district organizing duties. In the challenging circumstances facing these national groups, IWO locals served as homes, functioning as cultural centers while promoting solidarity. Occasionally, Thompson would run into Max, whom she and others found to be quite appealing, exuding personal magnetism. The striking picture Thompson paints of him reinforces several contemporary reminiscences:

So, I would go in for [IWO] board meetings after I went to Chicago— come into New York for board meetings and I think it was during that time period—the Council [on African Affairs] was established in 1937 —that I met Max Yergan. Now, it's interesting, for, most of us, I guess, not only young women, but older women—we looked upon Max as like a saint. He was a very charming man. He did have a way with women, and we all loved him. It was almost like he was a saint. He had this face, this [visage] that was, well, you know what I'm talking about? And we loved him. As a matter of fact, many people adored him.[105]

Max wrote a foreword to Martha Millet's edited IWO volume, *Fight the Fifth Column.*[106]

Rapp-Coudert

Yergan's adjunct position at CCNY, while the source of both attention and praise, was also inherently unstable. As temporary faculty he and others always operated under threat of dismissal or replacement. As a politically vocal instructor he managed to bring attention both to himself and to the various causes he represented, but these features of his public life did not necessarily strengthen his position. At the same time, he regularly wrote and published articles in a variety of media, enough to satisfy the requirements of journalism. The problem arose, however, when he and other left-wing faculty members became the focus of attention from two conservative Albany, New York, lawmakers. Rapp and Coudert feared the increase of communist influence on school and university campuses as a threat to the security of the state and nation. They thus began a campaign to root out such activism by targeting the activists around which it tended to revolve. As the only African-American faculty member, Max Yergan had become a prime candidate.

Since 1937 Yergan had been able to count on his CCNY position to enable him to test ideas in the classroom and enhance his stature through his university connection. Indeed, he had passed up other positions in higher education in order to enjoy the benefits of his CCNY connection. He had previously been encouraged to think about an administrative position in African education, and more than once his allies in the liberal philanthropic establishment suggested him for the position of president of a Negro college. The CCNY position seems to have trumped the others, even though it was not as secure as either of these alternatives. Taking the CCNY job was a calculated risk and the stakes were never clearer than they became in 1941 as the United States inched closer to war.

A year earlier Rapp and Coudert had taken aim at campus radicalism, not merely at colleges and universities but across the board, including into elementary and secondary schools. Rooting out students as well as faculty, they sought to bring about a "clean sweep" of the institutions of higher learning, then worked backward toward their feeder schools. It would have been impossible for them not to have considered Yergan a worthy adversary.

By 1941, Yergan had been informed that his contract to teach at City College would not be renewed. The public rationale for his nonreappointment was that he had made no distinctive contribution to scholarship in the field of Negro history. Within the campus Left, however, this was interpreted as part of the "purge of the profs" who were associated with the Communist Party. Even though Yergan was not formally charged as a Rapp-Coudert defendant, there was little question of his political alignments, making it difficult to separate his removal from the political circumstances pertaining under Rapp-Coudert. Yergan's dismissal was covered in both the establishment and left press, and precipitated an extensive letter-writing campaign directed at the City College administration and officers of the New York Board of Higher Education. Over one hundred letters were sent on his behalf. This support puts him in a somewhat special relationship to Rapp-Coudert. Unlike Morris Schappes, who was indicted for perjury, and Foner, Goldway, and others, who were clearly targeted and terminated by action of the Rapp-Coudert committee, Yergan suffered what might be called "collateral damage." Nonetheless, his fate should not be viewed as unrelated to that of his other more credentialed, more established left-wing colleagues. It was also an object lesson in the costs of taking stands on the Left, adding to his prestige within the progressive movement, on the one hand, while also raising fears within the intelligence community of his political radicalism and what it might portend. The letters were written by a mixture of former students and rank-and-file friends of Max Yergan and what he was taken to represent. They were generated by men and women of all educational, racial, and class backgrounds and indicate the way in which "the Dr." was viewed both on and off the City College campus. But these letters could not save his position.

Harlem Nocturne, 1942–1944

Between 1942 and 1944 Yergan became one of the most familiar faces in Harlem. Fame, however, had a price and, when combined with outspokenness, dissent, or deviation from prevailing opinion, mainstream or governmental, especially in time of war, could be costly. At such times constitutional freedoms so often taken for granted might be imperiled. Max and his allies operated on their belief in the protections of the Bill of Rights; at the same time, the combined forces of government, the state, and its police arms viewed him with enmity.

In late January 1942 Yergan held a Council on African Affairs (CAA) meeting; within weeks he set Robeson's schedule for March and April appearances. On February 14, a new joint venture, the *People's Voice* weekly newspaper, hit the stands in Harlem. Led by Rev. Adam Clayton Powell Jr., it was intended, according to the Baptist minister, to become "The Lenox Avenue edition of the *Daily Worker*."[107] Buoyed by black businessman Charles Buchanan, Powell's foray into journalism was part of a larger strategy to broaden his base beyond Harlem's limits. It was an idea to which Max would contribute, fiscally and conceptually. Starting in very gradually, virtually imperceptibly, behind the scenes, Yergan became more and more visible in the *Voice,* as an added name on its editorial masthead, as a face in the crowd of luminaries and speakers quoted in its pages, and, on occasion, as a columnist who penned opinion pieces and investigated an array of African subject areas. The *People's Voice* stands as a definitive piece of material evidence of an ironclad Powell-Yergan partnership, with consequences for both. It was a lightning rod. Four days following the first appearance of the *People's Voice,* Yergan wrote Robeson upon returning from a brief respite spent at a Northfield, Massachusetts, hotel. Waiting for him upon his return were arrangements for a "large public meeting concerning Africa in the wake of the Singapore fiasco, and the present predicament of India." Engaging the urgent issues, arguing that "two points were immediately apparent," Max enumerated them as follows:

> First, the strategic military importance of Africa[,] since all shipping to the USSR and to the Far East must pass Dakar as well as the Cape of Good Hope at the Southern tip of Africa; and second, the defenceless condition of the African people. As is true in Britain with regard to the

cause of allied defeat in the Far East the American people are more eagerly interested in the significance of Africa to the entire allied effort. As you already recognize the American public knows practically nothing about Africa, particularly the internal conditions.[108]

Max believed that "the Council should hold a large public forum," preferably in Manhattan Center "or some other place which will seat about 4,000–5,000 people." He felt that Robeson could be one of two or three speakers. Robeson's task, as Yergan saw it, drawing implicit analogies with the aggrieved masses of subject Singapore and embattled India, would be to "deal with the importance of the African people in the same sense that the Chinese and the Indian people are important," adding that, "In this connexion we could stress the resolution passed at the Council meeting calling for the arming of the African people and extensive utilization of African resources." Further, Max advised, another speaker could be *PM* editor Ralph Ingersoll, "who with the aid of large maps and stills portraying the strategic military importance of Africa could talk of the military importance of Africa to the whole cause of the United Nations." This was a timely gambit. The Allies were just then advancing toward Northern and Eastern Africa. This attention to Africa encouraged a reminder to Robeson that "Africa is increasingly in the news." For Max, due to the Council meeting and a press release to which it gave rise, as well as an assembly addressed by Frieda the prior Saturday, "it was clear that there is tremendous interest in Africa just now." He felt they should derive maximum benefit from the situation. That same day, Max gave Robeson added insight into the United Spanish Aid benefit at the Commodore Hotel.[109] Yergan also referred to Robeson's "sound action" with respect to what he termed "the Kansas City matter," about which he enclosed press clips. Yergan's closing, almost an afterthought, told Robeson of cabling Stephen T. Early, secretary to President Roosevelt, requesting "an immediate appointment to confer on the larger aspect of 'Negroes and the War.'" Again, Max's rationale was implicitly Pan-African. He argued,

I wish in my conference w/ him to refer not only to this question in terms of its national but also in terms of the international importance of the Negro people, particularly with regard to Africa and our strategic relation to the Chinese and Indian peoples just now.[110]

Indeed, on the same day, Yergan had in fact wired this to Stephen Early:

TELEGRAM YERGAN TO STEPHEN T EARLY
SECRETARY TO THE PRESIDENT
  EARNESTLY REQUEST APPOINTMENT WITH YOU TOMORROW OR
FRIDAY IF YOU CAN GRANT IT, REGARDING LARGER ASPECTS NE-
GROES AND WAR AND PROPOSED DELEGATION TO THE PRESIDENT
                                        MAX YERGAN
                                        PRESIDENT
                      NATIONAL NEGRO CONGRESS[111]

Again, a Yergan White House telegram immediately garnered high-level attention, more perhaps than he ever realized. Secretary Early, as if facing an office blaze, requested assistance straightaway. Yergan may have even unwittingly exacerbated matters when his initial wire was not answered as expeditiously as he had expected. He reflexively sent a second cable to FDR's secretary, Maurice McIntyre: "REFERENCE MY TELEGRAM FEBRUARY EIGHTEENTH MR STEPHEN EARLY AS FOLLOWS EARNESTLY REQUEST APPOINTMENT WITH YOU TOMORROW."[112] The combined effect of conveying two urgent telex messages to Oval Office watchdogs in as many days probably ranged somewhere between constituting a nuisance and posing a menace to U.S. national security. McIntyre, taking no chances, hastily contacted the head of the Works Progress Administration, as a handcrafted addendum coyly disclosed: "MHM called Aubrey Williams to check on this man + outfit + was informed 'not reputable.'"[113] All the while, it seemed essential to maintain the appearance of a more routine approach to the entire matter. After all, presidential staffers received communications exactly like this every single day. Seen superficially, McIntyre's reply looked rather matter of fact:

WIRE JUST RECEIVED. MAY I SUGGEST YOU WRITE ME FULLY
REFERENCE MATTER YOU WISH TO DISCUSS. IF QUESTION OR
APPOINTMENT FOR DELEGATION TO SEE THE PRESIDENT
GENERAL WATSON, SECRETARY IN CHARGE OF PRESIDENTIAL
APPOINTMENTS, ADVISES ME IT IS IMPOSSIBLE AT THIS TIME.[114]

Then, as if to reinforce the first telegram, Early finally got around to Yergan:

TELEGRAM RECEIVED. THE PRESIDENT'S SECRETARY, MR MARVIN
MCINTYRE, HAS BEEN GIVING HIS TIME AND ATTENTION TO
PROPOSALS AND REQUESTS SIMILAR TO YOURS. THEREFORE I
SUGGEST YOU SHOULD SEE HIM. SCOPE OF MY WORK EMBRACES
VERY DIFFERENT MATTERS.[115]

Early, McIntyre, and Williams, all southern "good ole boys," held no brief for "colored" correspondents conspicuously connected to communist causes or colleagues; each wire added grist to their mill.[116] Ten days later, on February 28, NNC president Yergan was back on the speaking circuit, this time stumping before a crowd at an All-Harlem People's Conference at Mt. Olivet Baptist Church, where he went on record as backing full participation in the war effort among native, foreign-born, and Spanish-speaking Americans. The following Saturday, the weekly *People's Voice* reported the event.[117]

In the interim, something else had been happening that bears mention. On March 2, the Executive Board of the Council on African Affairs held a business meeting about the present publicity campaign. Shortly after, Yergan wired Dick Wright, entreating him to "please telephone me immediately."[118] By now Richard Wright was widely known within the Left, having earned renown for novels, essays, reportage, short stories, and artful verse. Max continued to contact him at odd intervals, and they often crossed paths inside the circle of vanguard cultural workers who clustered around the *Daily Worker* and the *New Masses,* and elsewhere. Yergan was given promotional copies of Wright's works and in return apprised Wright of various NNC and CAA jobs. The two shared something else. Neither knew that others were monitoring them. Wright's biographers have recognized this, and this gives texture to their later treatments of the talented, tormented literary titan.

By March 1942, surveillance of Yergan was intensified by the intelligence community, which was probably influenced by his renewed contacts with the White House, closeness to Robeson, and highly public identification with critical views on the war, both domestic and international. Nor should one overlook the matter of his confidants. At that juncture—if not earlier—FBI agents ebulliently traded with other agencies—in this instance, opposite numbers in the navy—index cards on "subject[s]" whose "name[s] appear[ed] on a list of persons who are in varying degrees associated or sympathetic with the Communist Party."

These card were consistent with the preventive detention cards issued previously.[119]

The FBI never fully relinquished control over their files. While at times they donated copies of portions of these files to other agencies, it was vital to them to retain authority over all potential evidence for any possible future criminal investigations. Even at the risk of duplication of effort, Max's Bureau file expanded. On March 19, the FBI noted that files bearing Yergan material were "reviewed for the purpose of making a custodial detention card in connection with the custodial detention program." Then an arresting addendum: "Though the practice of making custodial detention cards has been discontinued, this information is being placed in the file for possible future use."[120]

On May 27, Green H. Hackworth posted a letter to Sumner Welles, undersecretary of state for Latin America. Hackworth was responding to a press release dated May 25 that he had received from the Council on American Democracy, to which was appended an open letter to Acting President Ramon S. Castillo and the ambassador of Argentina in the District of Columbia, criticizing Castillo's alleged pro-Nazism. Signers included Ruth Benedict, Adam Clayton Powell, Ferdinand Smith, Vito Marcantonio, and Max Yergan. Hackworth's note to Welles told that Hackworth wondered whether this open letter was a possible violation of the Logan Act, Section 5, Title 18 of the U.S. Code.

This section of the statute made it illegal for a citizen of the United States, either directly or indirectly, to commence or carry on any verbal or written correspondence with any foreign government or an officer thereof "with an intent to influence the measures or conduct" of that government or officer in relation to "any disputes or controversies with the United States." Conviction for this infraction brought a penalty of five thousand dollars and imprisonment of not more than three years. Upon closer consideration, however, Mr. Hackworth luckily relented, chillingly conceding that it was not worth it to bring up the matter to the Department of Justice lest it stir up adverse publicity. An expert who literally wrote the book on international law, Green Haywood Hackworth had given a reprieve to Max and his fellow citizens of which they had not even the slightest inkling.[121]

On June 6, the *People's Voice* ran a message headed "This Is Our War. Wipe Out Discrimination. Let Negroes Fight Equally." Initially a press release issued by NNC president Max Yergan that was sent to President Roosevelt, this message read as follows: "The Council on Af-

rican Affairs hails the decision of the US government to send a special
economic mission to the Union of South Africa which will seek means
to develop the vast material resources of that country to aid the war
effort of the United Nations." Yergan further informed the chief executive of his organization's view that "the Council urges the appointment
of Negroes to this mission which is headed by Colin Wickersham of the
War Production Board, and Hickman Price of the Board of Economic
Warfare." The *People's Voice* coverage of the story ended by stating
that "Dr. Yergan pointed out that the government's sending of such a
mission would stimulate the whole war effort by bringing the resources
of that country behind the United Nations."[122]

In November 1942, the *Daily Worker* ran Max's photo above a caption reading,

> As an American Negro, and I know for millions of Negroes, I join you
> in hailing the Soviet Union on this its 25th anniversary. The normal,
> magnificent achievements of the Soviet people . . . draws forth the
> unstinted admiration of all honest men. . . .
>
> But it is on the battlefields against the Hitler fascist beasts that the
> Soviet people have shown their truly great qualities. They have envel-
> oped themselves in everlasting glory. As long as man can write or sing
> he can have no greater theme than the matchless conduct of the fighting
> men and women of the heroic Red Army.[123]

As 1943 opened, NNC officer Edward E. Strong, employing the letterhead of the New York Committee to Aid the Southern Negro Youth
Congress, wrote to Mary McLeod Bethune of the National Youth Administration (NYA) in reference to an upcoming NYA conference. Yergan, as one of the sponsors of the Southern Negro Youth Congress
(SNYC), had been interested in securing the support of Mrs. Bethune
within the context of the CAA, though this looked unlikely in the short
run, given her commitments both to the government and to her other
roles as Bethune-Cookman College president and head of the National
Council of Negro Women. Because she was a federal employee there
were limits on the political alliances or causes with which her name
was linked, especially in view of her alliance with First Lady Eleanor
Roosevelt.[124]

Should matters change, however, Bethune might become available.
She was known to have been willing to back a number of worthy race-

related uplift ventures, particularly those connected in some way to education, self-improvement, and Negro empowerment. She had backed such efforts not only locally but also in Africa, for which she retained a soft spot due in part to an unrequited dream of being a missionary. Yergan gleaned some knowledge of her affection for Africa, which could come in handy; soon he drew ever closer to Mrs. Bethune.

On January 11, the Council on African Affairs held one of its regular meetings. Its most important piece of business was the sobering fact that the resignation of vital CAA administrator Mary van Kleeck had then become effective. Van Kleeck had been with the Council almost since its inception, having supported it through thick and thin. She had helped to formulate strategies and plan events, and, after Max's ostensible destoolment of NNC president Asa Philip Randolph, strove mightily to mediate between Executive Director Yergan and an irreconcilable Ralph J. Bunche.

It is unclear whether van Kleeck's resignation was influenced by factors other than the stated reason she provided her colleagues at the Russell Sage Foundation—that she'd been beset with too many competing claims upon her time, and, therefore, needed to cut back. Van Kleeck had herself been under surveillance, at least from 1941, if not earlier, due to her association with liberal and radical causes. The council was just one of several groups for this *engagé* woman. It is uncertain whether she may have been forced to step down by growing pressure emanating from within the intelligence community.

But the CAA had commandeered untold hours of her time and energy, and it is likely that she had private anxieties regarding the value of what she had been putting into the organization balanced against what it did and what the outcomes of its campaigns had been. If van Kleeck did discuss such anxieties with anyone, confidante Mary Fleddérus would have been a safe depository for her brooding fears. Of course, this could not stop acquaintances from advancing theories. At any rate, again it proved necessary to fill a CAA vacuum.

On Monday, January 25, Ralph W. Close, Carveth Wells, Yergan, Anson Phelps Stokes, and Edwin W. Smith addressed a town hall meeting concerned with the topic of "Africa and the World War." Smith and Phelps Stokes had each known Yergan for years within the context of the philanthropic and missionary community, Smith having been a missionary himself, best known for his biography of Gold Coast educator and Yergan colleague James Emman Kwegyir Aggrey. Rev. Smith's chronicle of the International Missionary Council's 1926 Jerusalem meeting had pronounced Yergan's positions praiseworthy. Described as an "author and anthropologist," Dr. Smith was reported as having "outlined the history of Africa's development," while Yergan was, in the next day's coverage of the event by the *New York Times,* said to have "listed the social, economic and political reforms that, he said, should be carried out for the benefit of the native population."[125]

In early February, van Kleeck resigned. This had to affect Max deeply in view of all the aid she had provided him. Max soldiered on, however, inviting Langston Hughes to an NNC function, appearing alongside Adam Powell at a Negro People's Committee rally on April 4, and participating in an Eastern Seaboard Conference on "The Problems of the War and the Negro People" on April 10–11 at Powell's Abyssinian Baptist Church. Yergan spoke on a panel called "A People's Victory —A People's Peace." In the audience were FBI informants who reported his opinions on the international situation this way:

> Max Yergan, President of the National Negro Congress, related his experiences working among the African people and the evil policies practiced by the European nations upon these people. England, Belgium, and Italy were pointed out as being the chief oppressors of the Africans. Yergan predicted that the day is not far away when these people will shake off their chains of bondage and unite with their brethren overseas for greater democracy and good will. Yergan stated that Great Britain is reluctant to arm the natives, even when she is engaged in a bitter struggle for her existence. She is afraid that they will turn their guns on their oppressors—the British.[126]

Toward the close of April, Yergan wired President Roosevelt, in part to chide him and in part to exhort him to strengthen the new, fragile Fair Employment Practices Committee created to adjudicate racial grievances. Unaware of how the FBI and Army had been scrutinizing his speeches and photographic and written appearances in the pages of the *Daily Worker,* the National Negro Congress president pulled out the stops and stipulated,

MR PRESIDENT THE NATIONAL NEGRO CONGRESS HAS SINCE THE ISSUANCE OF YOUR ORDER 8802 AND THE CREATION BY YOU OF THE FAIR EMPLOYMENT PRACTICE COMMITTEE BEEN FULLY AWARE

OF THE TREMENDOUS IMPORTANCE OF BOTH IN THE STRENGTH-
ENING OF NATIONAL UNITY AND OUR WHOLE MACHINERY OF
WAR PRODUCTION WE HAVE HOWEVER RECENTLY BEEN GREATLY
ALARMED BY THE CHARACTER AND THE STRENGTH OF THE
ATTACKS MADE UPON THIS VITALLY IMPORTANT COMMITTEE WE
BELIEVE THAT UNLESS DRASTIC STEPS ARE TAKEN THE COMMITTEE
WILL BE DISMEMBERED AND THE SPLENDID POSSIBILITIES IT HAS
FOR CURTAILING DISCRIMINATION BASED UPON RACE CREED AND
COLOR WILL BE NULLIFIED ALREADY SEVERAL OF ITS LEADING
FIGURES HAVE RESIGNED AND THERE ARE RUMORS THAT A
NUMBER OF OTHERS REGARD THEIR EFFORTS TO ACTIVIZE THE
COMMITTEE AS USELESS UNDER PRESENT CONDITIONS WE ARE
CALLING UPON YOU AS THE INITIATOR OF THE COMMITTEE TO
IMMEDIATELY TAKE SUCH STEPS AS WILL PLACE THE COMMITTEE
AGAIN UNDER YOUR DIRECT JURISDICTION SO AS TO GUARANTEE
ADEQUATE FUNDS AND POWER WE BELIEVE THAT THE RETENTION
OF EARL B DICKERSON OF CHICAGO AS A MEMBER OF THE
COMMITTEE IS ONE OF THE GUARANTEES OF THE PROGRAM
ENUNCIATED BY YOU WILL BE CARRIED INTO LIFE THE REMNANTS
OF THIS STRONG COMMITTEE MET IN WASHINGTON APRIL
NINETEENTH LAST WE BELIEVE THAT THE ACTIVITIES OUTLINED
AT THAT MEETING SHOULD BE CARRIED OUT IMMEDIATELY AND
THAT THE REQUEST THAT THE RAILROAD HEARING POSTPONED BY
THE WAR MANPOWER COMMISSION SHOULD BE RESTORED TO THE
CALENDAR FOR THE SEVENTH AND EIGHTH OF JUNE NEXT MUST
BE VIEWED AS OF THE UTMOST IMPORTANCE AND CARRIED OUT
IT HAS BEEN RUMORED THAT DR WILLIAM EARL COLES OF THE
UNIVERSITY OF TENNESSEE HAS BEEN SLATED TO HEAD THE
REORGANIZED COMMITTEE WE REGARD SUCH AN APPOINTMENT
AS FRAUGHT WITH DANGER EFFORTS TO DESTROY THE COMMIT-
TEE HAVE ADVERSELY AFFECTED THE MORALE OF THE NEGRO
PEOPLE WE BELIEVE THAT IF THE PROPOSALS OUTLINED ABOVE
ARE CARRIED THROUGH IT WILL STRENGTHEN THE UNITY OF THE
NEGRO PEOPLE AROUND THE NATIONS PROGRAM FOR VICTORY.[127]

Two days later Ralph Johnson Bunche submitted his resignation from the Council.[128]

As indicated earlier, Harlem was Yergan's base. After establishing himself in the Harlem Council of the National Negro Congress, the

Harlem Section of the Communist Party, and the Harlem-headquartered *People's Voice,* he must have been regarded by some as one of Harlem's own. At the end of April he visited Chicago to speak on "The Darker Races in World Affairs" at Jean Baptiste Point Du Sable High School for a world service program sponsored by a centennial committee closely affiliated with the YMCA.[129] In early July, an anonymous adversary sent to New York's City Council a letter that eventually reached the desk of Mayor Fiorello LaGuardia. Its writer held that the *People's Voice*

> was the brain-child of Dr. Max Yergan, an avowed Communist, who two years ago was ousted from the faculty of City College for his Communist teachings. At first Yergan remained in the background of *The People's Voice.* Now he sees no reason to hide his connection. He is boldly listed on the paper's masthead as treasurer, and no issue of the paper goes to press until he and Powell approve the treatment and handling of every story.[130]

In the enervating opening days of August 1943, responding to years of grievances against police brutality, Harlem erupted in a paroxysm of rage that was exacerbated by the war. Following earlier precedents, notably in 1935, police violence, intercultural and social misunderstandings, and community rumors combined in volatile ways to create a perception of disturbance within the state apparatus. Since this occurred against a background of heightened fears about security brought on by the war, local authorities were being monitored by military and federal intelligence agencies. Of great immediacy was the fact that African-Americans in Detroit had risen up to protest war discrimination two months earlier, a series of events that had been watched closely both nationally and locally, not least by New York city's mayor. Therefore, when Harlem exploded in the summer of 1943, the mayor's office called on local leaders Ferdinand Smith, Hope Stevens, and Yergan to walk through the streets appealing for calm alongside him, using the radio as well.[131]

Even though Yergan's role in the aftermath of the disturbances was documented as a palliative one designed to defuse communal tensions, his presence was construed as somehow contributing to the danger that both the FBI and Military Intelligence suspected still lingered in the area, and for which they considered him at least partly responsible.[132]

Blind to these intrigues, he went about his business, inviting Walter White to a Harlem Cultural Committee meeting[133] and issuing a non-threatening nationwide appeal to La Guardia and thirty other mayors "to establish immediately local interracial committees."[134]

Council on African Affairs, 1941–1948

From 1941 to 1948 what initially had started out as the International Committee on African Affairs was transformed into the Council on African Affairs. Among the persons closest to Yergan during this time was stenographer Frieda Neugebauer, who continued to handle his daily correspondence in both the CAA and the NNC, though not always alone. Between 1942 and 1943 Max's profile grew considerably, aided significantly by Frieda, operating both within and beyond each office, organizing media and travel appearances.

Although there had been losses, there were also significant gains, not always from active participation but from the standpoint of name recognition on the CAA's masthead. From its inception in 1941 this successor to the ICAA boasted such luminaries as Franz Boas (until his death a year later); sociologist and author of *Black Bourgeoisie,* Dr. Edward Franklin Frazier; record producer John Hammond; and educator Mary McLeod Bethune. While Yergan's travels were as a rule neither as extensive nor as frequent as Robeson's, there were times when the two had overlapping speaking schedules, including tours in the United States and, in at least one case, in 1944, a major junket conducted within Canada.

After a regular CAA January meeting, Yergan and Robeson set off to tour the far North. In early February Yergan spoke from Toronto on the CBC's Trans-Canada network on "The Atlantic Charter and the Colonial People in Africa." In remarks relayed by the NNC print organ he said,

> Within the framework of the Atlantic Charter there exists today the re-alistic possibility—indeed, the necessity for carrying forward a broadly-conceived plan for meeting the education and health needs, providing the economic development, and insuring speedy advancement toward complete responsible self-government for the African people.[135]

That month he invited Eleanor Roosevelt to a Robeson testimonial.[136] Back from Canada in March Max met for two hours with State Department chief of African affairs, Henry S. Villard, on lend-lease, Ethiopia, Liberia, jurisdictional and territorial problems, Africa's place in the postwar planning, world security, and Negro personnel and public relations in the department. Accompanied by CAA members Edith Field and Alphaeus Hunton, the delegation met Villard and assistant Charles W. Lewis.[137]

In mid-April the council held a widely publicized conference on Africa. Clark M. Eichelberger, director of the League of Nations association since 1934, asked Ralph Bunche's opinion of the conference and its sponsors, receiving a detailed critical reply:

> The Council followed the party line during the days of the Stalin-Hitler Pact and switched back when Hitler invaded Russia. It wasn't very active, however, and little was heard of it until about a year and a half ago when it started sponsoring meetings. Paul Robeson is used primarily as the "big name" to attract attention; Yergan is the Council. Hunton, who has been a consistent fellow-traveler if not a party member at Howard for years, and who knows absolutely nothing about Africa, was taken on as Educational Director about a year ago. Edith Field, the Treasurer, is the wife of Fred Field, formerly of the IPR, and follows Fred's line, which is strongly partyish.[138]

Giving Eichelberger Yergan's CAA history, Bunche indicated that the conference might be interesting but warned him not to be drawn in by Max, calling him "a very clever article."

The timing and subject matter of the conference on Africa attracted dignitaries galore, including Francis Nwia-Kofi Nkrumah (later known as Kwame); Ibango Udo Akpabio, president, African Students Association; Mary McLeod Bethune; Joseph Chamberlain, Columbia University professor; National Maritime Union president Joseph Curran; Rayford W. Logan; J. M. Obermeier, president, Local 6, Hotel and Club Union, AFL; Cecilia Cabaniss Saunders, executive secretary, Harlem Branch Y; Bishop David H. Simms; and Dr. Henry Sigerist of Johns Hopkins University. Convened to discuss compulsory labor, the industrial color bar, wages and working conditions, mechanization, and the disposition of ex-Italian territories, among other topics, the meeting was well publicized.[139] Max's timely analytical essay, "The Future of Africa," appeared scarcely a week later.[140]

Both the conference and the writings that framed it made the point that it was time for Africa and Africans to be viewed differently, as economic actors in their own right deserving of dwelling in a world that transcended the nations of superior and inferior races, a world that could come in the postimperial, postcolonial, postwar world. At the conference in particular Yergan proposed an international agency to supervise and improve all colonial territories. Max then involved himself in planning an NNC "I am an American Day," helping out in the organization of a National Council of Negro Women testimonial for Mary McLeod Bethune, publicizing his African Affairs observations, and urging FDR's reelection.[141]

Vox Populi, 1945–1947

Yergan played a very important role within the *People's Voice* from 1945–1947. In a position of power facilitated by his association with Rev. Adam Clayton Powell Jr., he gradually became one of the power brokers behind the popular newspaper. Yergan having been scrutinized by the FBI since *PV*'s inception, his links to the tabloid had been noted in his dossier, along with his *Daily Worker* photos and columns, NNC letters to the president, personal telephone conversation logs, and, occasionally, even detailed summaries of his movements.

PV had played a major role in publicizing Council on African Affairs campaigns, including a later controversial effort to relieve South Africa's Middledrift drought in 1943. A key to Yergan's evolution lay in events that took shape during 1945. This was when he intuited that things had begun to change, though if others noted it they did so in whispers. As the year opened, Max maintained his profile as president of the NNC and executive director of the Council on African Affairs. Advocating maximal postwar economic inclusion, the NNC sponsored a Reconversion and Full Employment meeting devoted to predicting problems facing African-Americans after demobilization. The conclave followed a War Manpower Commission report presaging that peacetime production conversion, seniority, and veteran preferences would all be bad for Black labor in a postwar world.[142]

Although this major NNC campaign took up considerable space in the *People's Voice,* references to President Yergan, frequent occurrences whenever the Congress was mentioned, were now strangely lacking for most of January and February, when the NNC National Board met, declaring unity in action among Negro groups its dominant theme for 1945.[143] But by February 27, at least part of the reason for his omission was made clear. On that date news broke of his divorce from Susie Wiseman, his spouse since 1920.[144] Together they had had three sons and a daughter, all but the first born while the Yergans were domiciled in South Africa. Upon returning to North America in 1936, however, the couple had become estranged. Yet it was not until nine years later that their contract was formally dissolved. A fortnight later, *People's Voice* announced the schism.[145]

The end of any marriage is always some kind of milestone, as the failed union had become a millstone. It was preoccupations with personal matters that tore Max's attention away from both the NNC and the Council on African Affairs. Those close to him knew he had been seeing a New York physician, Lena Halpern, a socialite who was said to have once had a radical background. In the short run, Yergan's public appearances and pronouncements appeared much as they had in the past. But then, the week after he and Adam Clayton Powell addressed an April 6 NAACP conference on colonial problems chaired by Dr. W. E. B. Du Bois and held at the 135th Street branch of the New York Public Library,[146] President Franklin Delano Roosevelt died suddenly. In his official capacity as NNC President, Max hastened to cable the new chief executive:

> In this hour of great responsibility you have our complete confidence, and we shall continue doing our part for the achievement of the great goals to which our country and its allies are committed.[147]

Max eulogized the beloved New Dealer in the next issue of the *People's Voice.*[148] Close on the heels of FDR's passing, Yergan was in San Francisco for the opening of the World Security Conference out of which the United Nations organization sprang. Max had struggled to obtain observer status, attempting to secure credentials through the offices of Ralph J. Bunche, whom he had once tried to recruit for the Council on African Affairs. Bunche, however, had other ideas. Not wanting to seem intimately associated with a man widely known as a friend of the Communist Party, Bunche gave Max the cold shoulder. Incensed at this rebuff, Yergan revealed as much to their mutual acquaintance, Archibald Macleish. The terms used to communicate his displeasure with his one-time acquaintance proved intemperate. Neither Macleish nor Bunche kept silent about Yergan's remarks, as indicated by this telling report of their interviews with him, which turned up at the FBI's Washington office:

> Max Yergan has had a number of discussions with ARCHIBALD MAC-LEISH of the US State Department on the Council [on African Affairs]'s program, and has expressed confidence of being successful in gaining the support of RALPH BUNCHE, Division of Dependent Areas, US State Department, of whom he said, "He knows we can do a job on him any time we like. He also knows we are not subservient to the State Department." Yergan, according to a confidential source has also conferred at length with Liberian and Haitian delegates and representatives of negro pressure groups in respect to the colonial problem.[149]

Within the preceding year, Max's FBI file had grown considerably, prompting Bureau director J. Edgar Hoover to order installation of technical surveillance devices, i.e., wiretaps, in his work site and residence. It is unclear but highly unlikely that Yergan was alive to this.[150] The flippant quip from Jonathan Daniels to a White House colleague overstating Max's status as a high-ranking Negro "red" surely did not help matters any. Taking care to send back regular reports about the activities of himself and CAA leaders W. Alphaeus Hunton, Du Bois, and Robeson, Yergan kept his name before the *People's Voice* audience. All the while his dossier remained high in the minds of spywatchers in the intelligence community. They traced his interpersonal encounters, the dissolution of his marriage, his travels, public or private utterances, and actions, scrutinizing all of his moves. Without fully knowing it, he had reverted to the position he had had in South Africa.

Max was concerned to stress the linkage between the domestic needs of Negroes and the international triumph over fascism. He also retained his concern for Africans and other colonized peoples. In this regard his concerns were not very distant from those of Dr. Du Bois. Yergan still saw the needs of both colonized Africans and American ethnic groups as benefiting from the alliance that had won the war in Europe. In May he wrote,

We won this war through the unity of all the progressive forces of America in support of the Anglo-Soviet-American coalition which alone made victory possible. That same unity—among the democratic peoples of America, and between our country and our powerful allies—can secure in peace the goals for which we fought this people's war. As a necessary force in the coalition of national unity to win the war, the Negro people have made great strides toward freedom. As a still necessary force in the even broader coalition of national unity to win the peace, we shall consolidate and extend our wartime gains until full democratic rights have been attained.[151]

In his estimation of the world situation, Max still followed the Soviet Union's lead. This was especially evident in relation to plans being forged for United Nations trusteeship. Such a prospect, aimed at updating the late League of Nations mandate system, was being considered for territories previously under German control just prior to World War One, and subsequently administered informally by Allied powers like Britain. Yergan saw this plan as containing certain pitfalls, in mid-May 1945 admonishing that "the central issues involved in the American proposals for international trusteeship over colonial territories are being obscured by the dangerous emphasis being placed upon the protection of national interests, military or economic, as opposed to collective security." To strengthen his point, Max praised a statement made by Soviet foreign minister V. M. Molotov as indicating more genuine understanding of the colonial trusteeship problem.[152]

Yergan continued to push this line through May and June. During the week of May 11, 1945, while delivering a self-government speech for Chicago's branch of the Council, he said cautiously that while the world conference proposals on dependent territories did not go far enough, they formed a basis for real progress for colonial peoples. Stressing constant vigilance, he said of the California United Nations conference, "Out of San Francisco will also come the organizational machinery backed by agreement and power which will enable peace-loving peoples to proceed along the paths to be charted in San Francisco."[153] He followed this up with a telegram to leaders in San Francisco criticizing Britain's trusteeship plan:

We regard the British proposal for regional commissions for international cooperation as a departure from principles already projected for the world charter in that there is deliberate exclusion of independence for colonial peoples as one of the commission's objectives. . . . Regional commissions which evade the goal of self-government will be regarded by colonial peoples as instruments of foreign domination.[154]

Late in June 1945, Max joined a National Conference of Negro Leaders called by Mary McLeod Bethune. Representing the NNC, Yergan sat on two committees, one on Colonial Problems chaired by Rayford Logan, with Walter White, Wyatt Dougherty, and Eunice Hunton Carter, and a Drafting Committee, led by William Hastie, with George L. P. Weaver, Rayford Logan, Doxey Wilkerson, Charles Browning, Estelle M. Riddle, R. O'Hara Lanier, and Ted Poston. Channing Tobias convened the assembly.[155]

The following month, however, a dramatic event occurred. French Communist Party head Jacques Duclos, widely believed to be acting upon Stalin's orders, sent an open letter criticizing Earl Browder, his U.S. counterpart and a close Yergan acquaintance. Browder was purged from the Party's leadership, and the war-era Communist Political Association was reconstituted as the Communist Party, USA. William Z. Foster replaced Browder. This change of line and personnel exacerbated extant tensions within the NNC. Overtly this was difficult to detect, but Max was slightly modifying his stance. Yergan had felt good about Browder, and his ouster undoubtedly stung him. By August, he was exulting in the victory of the British Labor Party, arguing that this win far surpassed in significance a North American change from Republican to Democratic administrations; for him it was tantamount to a scenario in which "true liberals" in the southern states, in alliance with Negroes, turned out the plunderers who had misruled those states. This was its import:

1. Since slave trade days Great Britain has plundered, robbed and oppressed Africa, the West Indies and other colonial areas; now decency has a chance;

2. A Labor Party win may presage colonial independence; though not yet anti-imperialist, Labor is moving in that direction, stripping British robber barons of their might. . . .

3. A Labor victory can serve to reopen quickly and correct the highly unsatisfactory action of the San Francisco conference on the rights of colonial people.

Above: Kings Mountain, N.C., YMCA Conference 1916, faculty and leaders. Yergan stands in top rear. Jesse E. Moorland seated third from left. Reprinted with permission, Moorland-Spingarn Research Center, Howard University. *Left*: Max Yergan en route to or in East Africa, circa 1916. Reprinted with permission, Kautz Family YMCA Archives, University of Minnesota Libraries.

Above left: YMCA Secretaries, German East Africa (Dar-es-Salaam), circa 1916–1917. Standing left to right, Frederick Douglass Ballou, Thomas Hezekiah Lloyd, Max Yergan. Major C. R. Webster seated. Reprinted with permission, Kautz Family YMCA Archives, University of Minnesota Libraries. *Above right*: Student Christian Association gathering, South Africa, n.d., circa 1920s. Student leaders unidentified. Reprinted with permission, Moorland-Spingarn Research Center, Howard University. *Left*: Max Yergan, Susie Wiseman Yergan, and son, Frederick Yergan (born July 4, 1921), circa 1921. Reprinted with permission, Kautz Family YMCA Archives, University of Minnesota Libraries.

Professor Davidson Don Tengo Jabavu addresses gathering in Christian Union Hall on Fort Hare "Native College" campus during landmark Bantu-European Student Christian Conference organized by Max Yergan, held June 27, 1930. The building was built by funds Yergan secured from Rockefeller, Carnegie, and Phelps Stokes. It still stands on the campus of Fort Hare University. Reprinted with permission, Rockefeller Archive Center.

Top: Max Yergan, Susie Wiseman Yergan, and children Charles, Frederick, and Max Jr., circa 1930. Reprinted with permission, Kautz Family YMCA Archives, University of Minnesota Libraries. *Bottom*: Max Yergan's home on the Fort Hare campus, Alice, Ciskei, Eastern Cape, South Africa, circa 1936. Reprinted with permission, Eslanda Robeson Collection, Moorland-Spingarn Research Center, Howard University.

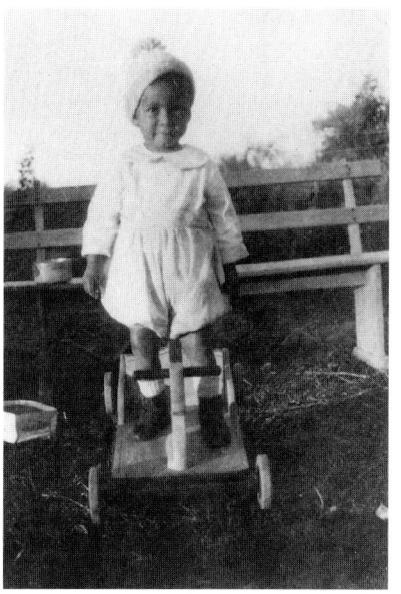

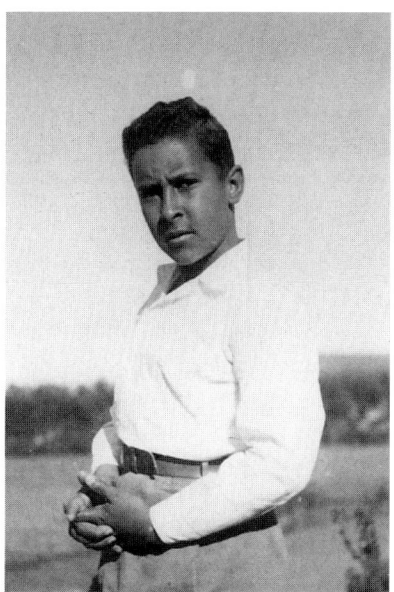

Above left: Yergan's son, Max Yergan Jr. (born July 12, 1923), South Africa. *Above right*: Yergan's daughter, Mary "Bunny" Yergan at age six (born November 9, 1930), South Africa, circa 1936. *Left*: Yergan's son Charles Yergan at age twelve (born September 14, 1924), South Africa, circa 1936. All reprinted with permission, Eslanda Goode Robeson Collection, Moorland-Spingarn Research Center, Howard University.

Above left: All African Convention at Bloemfontein, Orange Free State, South Africa, 1936. Left to right: Max Yergan, Fort Hare Professor Z. K. Mathews, African National Congress President Alfred Bitini Xuma. Reprinted with permission, Eslanda Goode Robeson Collection, Moorland-Spingarn Research Center, Howard University. *Above right*: September 28, 1946. Max Yergan, president, National Negro Congress, speaking at Metropolitan AME Church, as 100-day lynch rally opened in nation capital. Speakers urged federal legislation against mob atrocities. Paul Robeson seated at right. Reprinted with permission, Copyright, Afro-American Newspapers Archives and Research Center, Inc. 1991. *Left*: Max Yergan, circa 1940. Reprinted with permission, The George Meany Memorial Archives.

Commission on Human Rights of the UN EcoSoc Council. Representatives of the National Negro Congress present a petition for elimination of political, economic, and social discrimination against Negroes in the United States to P. J. Schmidt, third from left, secretary of the Commission on Human Rights of the UN EcoSoc Council. From left to right: Dr. Herbert Aptheker, Executive Board of the National Negro Congress; Revels Cayton, executive secretary of the National Negro Congress; Mr. Schmidt; Dr. Max Yergan, president of the National Negro Congress; Lyman White, UN Secretariat, and Charles Collins, Executive Board of the National Negro Congress. Hunter College, 6 June 1946. Reprinted with permission, United Nations.

Associated Press photo from New York: appeal for Katanga. Dr. Max Yergan, right, chairman of pro-Katanga secessionists battling United Nations forces, holds press conference at Overseas Press Club in New York, December 14, 1961. James Burnham, left, is a member of the group's executive committee, known as the "American Committee for Aid to Katanga Freedom Fighters." Reprinted with permission, Copyright, Afro-American Newspapers Archives and Research Center, Inc., 1991.

We here in America must now raise our voices more loudly against this one outstanding failure at San Francisco. We must demand of our own government, the Truman administration, that it reverse the denial of freedom for colonial people of which the American delegation at San Francisco was guilty. The action of the British people in their recent elections should inspire us in this task.[156]

Yergan followed this editorial with a six-point program that he sent to Secretary of State James F. Byrnes and to Edward R. Stettinius, the U.S. representative to the United Nations (both southern-born). A copy of this document was printed in full in the September issue of the CAA organ, *New Africa*. Among its principal aims were that Eritrea be restored to Ethiopia and that Libya and Italian Somaliland be placed under the administration of an international commission representing the major powers, including the USSR or the UN. Moreover, the Council opposed annexation of existing mandatories in Africa, urging that these be brought immediately under the UN Trusteeship Council's jurisdiction. The CAA proposed similar sanctions for Portuguese and Spanish overseas possessions in Africa on the grounds that as fascist regimes these nations had no more right to hold colonies than Germany or Japan. The CAA also pushed for the UN to promote the economic and political rights of colonial Africans and to draw up five- to ten-year programs leading to self-government and independence within a specified period.[157] The Council sought to interest others within its orbit, such as noted sociologist and radical Democrat E. Franklin Frazier, in supporting these proposals.[158] At year's end, Max remained highly visible in the CAA, aiding Johannesburg psychiatrist Wulf Sachs, author and editor of an antifascist periodical, *The Democrat,* in his U.S. tour in the late fall. The Council lauded Sachs's work as an advocate for the extension of democracy and equal rights to the African and other non-European populations of South Africa.[159] Yergan stayed on as NNC president, piloting a December Detroit banquet.[160] But all was not well.

Through the course of 1945, Yergan clung cautiously to the boundaries of left-liberal thought, in both domestic and international issues. Among the latter, his arena of expertise remained African affairs. In the same way that the National Negro Congress contemplated the complexion of the post–World War Two Black American situation, Max, Du Bois, Robeson, Hunton, and his other CAA colleagues considered the future of Africa in the postwar epoch. Prominent in this connection was the disposition of colonialism itself, specifically, how racism might affect democratic rights, or, as Du Bois put it in the title of one of his books, articulation among "Color and Democracy, Colonies and Peace."

Tie-ins between these national and international racial matters were logical for that set of persons of African descent who had come to maturity in an era of racialized thinking. These "race men (and women)" had become the leadership stratum of the early twentieth century. Privileging race gained further impetus by colonial expansion, as reflected in the Garvey movement of the World War One period and thereafter. It was rejuvenated by fascism in Italy, Nazism in Germany, and Japanese imperialism. To counter these associations, leftists posited explicit links between race and antifascism, as Jim Crow and anti-Semitism became hot-button issues on both sides of the Atlantic during the Second World War. Politicized African-Americans, alive to the contradiction inherent in risking their lives overseas for rights denied them at home, pledged to fight a two-front war.

Yet it could also be argued that the leadership stratum was fighting for itself as well. Both domestically and in the colonies, educated African-Americans and continental Africans held common aspirations. This was the cohort with which Yergan identified, the so-called school people within South Africa, West Africa's "been-to" stratum, for example, Nigeria's Nnamdi Azikiwe, the Gold Coast's Kwame Nkrumah, and the Afro-Antillean agitator George Padmore. The question for many of these people was, how far would they continue struggling if and when they were able as individuals or as members of a rising class to secure social power? As long as this power was denied them by structural and customary racism, the issue was moot. This was clearly the case in racist South Africa, where long-standing patterns of legislative and customary exclusion steadily rendered majority representation a virtual impossibility. Yet, things were far more fluid in places like the Gold Coast, whose Nkrumah studied the example of India as well as of the USSR.

On the surface, therefore, for many internationally minded Blacks, there did not appear to be a great deal of difference between Du Bois's theory of the "Talented Tenth" that he and his allies sought to apply in the United States and a colonial variation that then-subject populaces in Africa envisioned themselves implementing in a postimperial world. Internationalism was evident in the Pan-African movement, to which Du Bois, Padmore, and other like-minded globalist New World Black thinkers, including Yergan, were deeply committed. All saw their plight in diasporic terms, and their aspirations were revolutionary. However, granted personal success, how far would these revolutionists go? In fairness to them, and to their time, the answer to this question may not have been possible for them to foresee. If there was to be a "freedom train," would all of its passengers get off at the same station?

This question was critical to understanding the fate of the international working-class movement of the interwar era, the fight for world socialism, and the personal and professional trajectory of the visible, vocal Max Yergan. It was what separated Karl Kautsky from V. I. Lenin in 1914 and Trotsky from Stalin a decade later, splitting off followers and putative partisans of the former from those of the latter, with Stalinists using democratic centralist state orthodoxy as a politburo proprietary preserve. If Yergan or others within his circle harbored doubts about the potential of a people's democracy inside the Soviet Union and its fraternal parties, they kept them to themselves. Citizen Max was disciplined from 1936 to 1945; by 1945 the pose became hard to sustain.

The year 1945 saw Yergan preoccupied with domestic and international challenges. On the home front, jubilation over the outcome of the Second World War in Europe was marred by the sudden death of Franklin Roosevelt, which affected him deeply. Overseas, apart from the impending defeat of the Axis powers, his gaze fixed on the disposition of the colonial territories still under European hegemony. This explains his intense interest in the San Francisco United Nations Conference. South Africa remained high on his list of concerns. Though no longer formally a colony, it nursed subimperial ambitions toward Southwest Africa, the former League of Nations mandate taken from Germany at the close of World War One. South Africans were also struck hard by the Second World War. Its peoples, of every description, contributed courageously to the war effort in each one of its theaters.

Now the state had to confront unmet aspirations of African veterans, as well as postwar food shortages. One very hard-hit site was Middledrift in the Eastern Cape. As Wulf Sachs lectured on the prospects for postwar South Africa, the council mounted a relief campaign during the first two months of 1946. Using Rev. Adam Clayton Powell's Abyssinian Baptist Church as a base, the CAA sponsored a star-studded rally on January 7, where an estimated four thousand audience members heard Marian Anderson, Paul Robeson, Hubert Delaney, and many others appearing for famine relief.[161] By February the Council food drive reportedly sent one thousand dollars cash and fifty-two cases of food aboard the steamship *Clan Mellwraith*.[162] CAA members and friends were incensed at the double standard allowing Africans to face starvation as food needed locally was diverted to European refugees.[163]

Amidst the Council's Middledrift food drive, Winston Churchill visited the United States. On March 5, 1946, he delivered his famous "iron curtain" speech in Fulton, Missouri. In the short run, Yergan's response was to note Churchill's omission of the subject of the African famine.[164] A week later he and Paul Robeson published a more formal response in a joint letter that included the following passage:

> Mr Churchill proposed an alliance which is aimed at preserving the British imperialist system with the help of American troops. He castigated an ally, which only yesterday played a leading role in saving both Great Britain and our country from defeat by the forces of fascism. He deliberately omitted any reference to the widespread suppression by Great Britain of the struggle for freedom among the colonial and semi-colonial peoples of Africa, India, Indonesia and elsewhere. In these respects we regard Mr. Churchill's speech as a call to war upon the USSR, and continued oppression of colonial peoples. We do not believe the American people will stand for it.[165]

Meanwhile, council officers continued speaking and organizing for the food drive. CAA educational director W. A. Hunton appeared at an "Africa Speaks" forum at Forest Neighborhood House in the Bronx, where he lectured on "Food in Africa."[166] CAA chair Paul Robeson, on a West Coast tour, addressed a Los Angeles mass meeting on the South African famine toward the end of March. By that time the CAA drive had forwarded eighteen hundred dollars and seventy-seven cases of cans to the African Food Fund in Cape Town for disbursement.[167] As the food drive continued, Yergan also played a leading part in a "Help Organize the South!" rally sponsored by the *People's Voice*,[168] also managing to cable Acting Secretary of State Dean Acheson and the British, French, and Soviet ambassadors, denouncing UN trusteeship.[169] Meanwhile, doubts about the composition and intentions of Yergan's links intensified. Though he still maintained access to the mainstream media, Yergan's efforts were increasingly being tarred with a red brush. In June, for example, Yergan, Robeson, and other CAA members held a rally at Madison Square Garden attracting some fifteen thousand people. In its coverage of the event, the *New York Times* used the word "communist" three times, in each instance either directly or very soon afterward followed by the verb "controlled."[170]

That same week, Max's keynote at the tenth annual convention of the National Negro Congress drew fire from iconoclastic *Pittsburgh Courier* columnist George S. Schuyler, who, calling him a "noted Kremlin apologist," went on to quote Yergan as saying, "from this point on we will drive for unity within the ranks of the Negro people." Schuyler retorted,

> Whenever Communists talk about unity they mean getting everybody else to follow the Stalinist line. Although the name of the organization implies that it consists of Negroes, Dr. Max emphasized that the Congress must no longer view itself as "merely a group of Negroes, since the advance of the trade union movement lies in the single organization of white and black labor."

Holding that Yergan added that Black-White worker unity would not sacrifice Negro unity, the *Courier* editor caviled:

> Translated from the Moscowese this means that with the war over and Russia saved, the NNC is going to drive for "capture" of all the Negroes and will use the support of white Reds to that end. Moreover, it means that a drive will be launched to wean the Negroes away from such organizations as the NAACP or to "capture" it and hitch it to the Kremlin chariot. This was the real purpose for which the NNC was organized, and its return to the old policy was anticipated by all those who are hep to the Communist jive.[171]

A fuller extract of Max's speech came from another observer, Doxey Wilkerson. Noting the NNC's foundation a decade earlier on the anniversary of Frederick Douglass's birth, Yergan hailed the new force that had arisen among Black people. Of it he said, "We saw the potentialities of this development, and sought to hasten the integration of Negro workers into the trade union movement." Assessing its overall impact Max went on to say of the NNC,

> For several years our main emphasis was helping the CIO and other unions to organize, especially in steel and auto. We are proud to take some credit for the growth of Negro-labor unity which makes possible

this convention at which there are more outstanding Negro trade union leaders assembled than ever before in the history of our country.[172]

With the NNC's help, labor stood in the vanguard of progressive action.

This thrust coincided with preparation of a petition on Negro American oppression to be delivered to the UN, and the continuation of the African food drive.[173] The latter was met with a resolution from the African National Congress expressing "sincerest gratitude for assistance given by the Council on African Affairs in the recent distress in Ciskei." The ANC cable also thanked CAA Chairman Robeson and Executive Director Yergan "for the great stand your council is taking on behalf of Africans who have implicit trust in your representation of their case in world councils which they themselves are barred from attending."[174] But this formal ANC endorsement of the CAA and its leadership in relieving Middledrift did not fully reflect the sentiments of all Black South Africans.

In the late summer of 1946, after a hiatus forced by the grave illness of his spouse, Dr. Du Bois resumed a vigorous, multivalent correspondence with Afro-Caribbean Pan-African intellectual and activist George Padmore. Assessing prospects for reinvigorating interest in Africa-related issues, Du Bois mentioned in passing the efforts of Yergan and the Council on African Affairs, especially its widely publicized effort to provide relief for the devastating famine in the Middledrift region of South Africa's Eastern Cape province.

Writing from Paris, the United Kingdom–based Padmore responded to Du Bois by portraying Max in a novel way, as the noted Pan-African theorist baldly stated,

> In regard to Yergan, I do not know the man personally, but there are now quite a number of South African Negro doctors here in England, most of whom are in Manchester and Birmingham; and as they are connected with the Federation, I have had the opportunity of getting their opinion on Yergan. To say the least, it is very low. It would appear from what they assert that Yergan identified himself as much as possible with the white church community in South Africa (the YMCA) and treated the Africans, even the intellectuals at Fort Hare, the students and Professor (D. D.) Jabavu, with the greatest contempt. He was so disliked that it affected his work among the Africans and contributed to his having to leave South Africa. Whatever the truth of these assertions, his

name undoubtedly stinks among the South Africans in Britain. No doubt his present efforts constitute an attempt to redress his lost status, but he seemed to have had a warm welcome when he originally went out. No doubt, too, he has contacts with the Communist Party in South Africa and that gives a link with the communists in this African Council, but I am afraid that it will take more than a few food boxes to make this man Max Yergan persona grata with the African intellectuals. However, that should not prevent us from collaborating with them as far as possible.[175]

Padmore is somewhat disingenuous here; although never a familiar, he did know Yergan, having met him in 1937 at the London flat of Ralph and Ruth Bunche during a European trip undertaken while what was then the International Committee on African Affairs was in its formative stages.[176] Much more damaging was the credence Padmore gave to the low esteem in which Max was now allegedly held by expatriate Black South African doctors practicing and studying in the United Kingdom. The supercilious air Padmore attributed to Yergan is corroborated by other acquaintances. One, Phyllis Ntantala, an ex-student at Fort Hare, where the Yergans lived and labored for fifteen taxing years, shared this pointed recollection: "Why did America send Yergan there? He was distant. America had sent Yergan out to show white South Africans how well a black man could live; to show that he could live as well as a white South African."[177] Whether or not Max was aware of them, such musings were auguries of things to come. Taken together, they suggest an alarming discrepancy between the way Yergan saw himself in relation to the South African freedom struggle and the way its vanguard forces viewed him. They also cast light upon his efforts to seek reconciliation with former benefactors. This reflects a level of cognitive dissonance that became even more evident during the course of 1947.

Max's domestic profile in 1946 pivoted around the NNC June 6 UN petition and various campaigns to increase voter participation in the Jim Crow South. In July he had sought to enlist aid from Black leaders in the prior effort, including mainstream notables like Mary McLeod Bethune, whose petition response was judicious. Acknowledging receipt and promising board consideration of the petition,[178] she later wrote,

I am not fully certain about the call for investigation by the UN into the plight of the 13 million Negro citizens here in America. Certainly, from all our discussions we are thoroughly in accord with the necessity for the removal of segregation and injustice of all kinds; but there is a question in our minds as to whether the approach to the existing conditions here in our own US should come through the UN, whose problems for consideration are international rather than national. I have wanted very much to have a full discussion with you on this point in order to have my own thinking straightened.[179]

In the late fall, the CAA sponsored a visit by ANC leader Alfred Bitini Xuma, an old Yergan acquaintance and sometime correspondent. Yergan, previously ANC external affairs secretary, had through the CAA maintained a close watch on South Africa's plans to annex former German-ruled Southwest Africa, formerly a League of Nations mandate and now one of the proposed Trust Territories. The outspoken Xuma voice his opinion:

> When I was asked by authorities to keep quiet on South African affairs prior to coming to the US I answered them that I would keep quiet if I were dead! I do not think that South Africa should be allowed to annex South West Africa, or any other territory. She does not know how to treat the subjects over which she has control. I will do everything in my power to let the UN committee know the feelings of the people of South West Africa. They do not want South Africa to annex them. The UN should take over the territory as a trusteeship.[180]

Looking to India for inspiration, the Council kept close counsel with Nehru, along with his U.S.-based representatives and roving ambassadors, such as his sister Vijaya Lakshmi Pandit, who was in regular contact with Robeson and Yergan in 1946. She appeared at a fall CAA rally protesting South Africa irredentism in Southwest Africa along with Xuma, his countrymen H. A. Naidoo and Senator H. M. Basner, the fiery V. K. Krishna Menon, and Frank Anthony, UN delegate and leader of India's Anglo-India community.[181]

Matters came to a head between 1947 and 1948. In late January 1947, Yergan mysteriously failed to show up at an important NNC gathering in Detroit, ostensibly because of inclement weather.[182] On Monday, January 26, 1947, Trinidad-born Claudia Jones,[183] a high-profile Communist was arrested by the Immigration and Naturalization Service on a deportation warrant and later released on one thousand dollars' bail. Communist Harlem Councilman Ben J. Davis called a press conference charging the Justice Department together with the INS with seeking to "make newspaper headlines by intimidating people who hold certain beliefs."[184] The arrest had far-reaching implications, not least for Yergan, who knew Jones well, but also for foreign-born Communists and sympathizers, especially other West Indians.[185] It also spurred defections from the National Negro Congress and other organizations that the Justice Department characterized as Communist controlled. A high-level example was that of National Negro Congress legislative secretary Dorothy Kelso Funn, who abruptly resigned from the NNC staff in February 12, ostensibly to return to work as a New York City school teacher the next day. On its face Funn's exit seemed a straightforward matter:

> It is with deep regret that I leave the staff of the Congress. This resignation affects in no way my conviction that the Congress has a very important role to play in the struggle for Negro liberation; that the Congress must be built on the basis of its very correct program. I am not resigning from the National Board nor giving up the important task of reconstituting the Brooklyn Council of the Congress. In fact the invaluable experience received in my three years' association with the organization and its devoted officers will help immeasurably in the tasks that present themselves to the Brooklyn Council.[186]

But this was by no means Dorothy Funn's last word about the National Negro Congress.

By March, Labor Secretary Lewis B. Schwellenbach proposed outlawing the Communist Party. Again this prompted swift reaction from communist councilman Vito Marcantonio and left activists Charles A. Petioni, Adam Powell, Gene Connolly, NNC official Revels Cayton, and Yergan.[187] The following month the full NNC directorate called "a special meeting of all Eastern seaboard members of the National Board of the National Negro Congress together with local leaders," to be held inside Max's office on Saturday, April 26, 1947, at 2:00 A.M. In detailing the need for a summit, President Yergan reflected how deeply tests of patriotism had struck at America's core as he reported,

> At a recent emergency meeting of the Executive Committee of the Congress it was agreed that we should launch an intensive campaign against

Executive Order 9835 on Loyalty Dismissals. This latest move on the part of the President is another step in the campaign to further limit the civil rights of government employees, and strikes at the very heart of all progressive activity in the country. Nearly 2/3 of our entire Washington Council membership will be directly affected by this Order if it is carried out in its present form, and ultimately our organization and all true fighters for democracy will be affected adversely. We must act quickly and effectively. We are aware that our Board has many persons in it, but we are asking you to make a very special effort to let nothing interfere with your attendance at this important meeting.[188]

On July 21, 1947, Walter S. Steele, addressing the House Un-American Activities Committee, named scores of Communists and communist sympathizers, calling Yergan a "Negro Communist from New York," citing him fully seventy-eight times in communist and front affiliations.[189] That month its board, with Max's assent, fired *People's Voice* editor Doxey Wilkerson. Wilkerson had never concealed his Party membership. He had been active in both the NNC and the CAA, and his dismissal had both immediate and long-range implications for Yergan in the U.S. Left. He seemed to be scrambling to placate both progressives and government, an impossible stretch yet one not wholly out of keeping with previous precedent for Max.

By autumn word came that A. A. Zhdanov had established a Communist Information Bureau (Cominform) in Poland. On November 7, Oetje John Rogge, ex–U.S. assistant attorney general, "leaked" Justice Department plans to round up dozens of communist leaders and alleged fellow travelers on or about November 17. Two days prior to the deadline, the *People's Voice* revealed that Yergan had followed Dorothy K. Funn's lead, having resigned from the National Negro Congress. Citing a need to devote more time and energy to CAA work, he claimed,

The increasing volume and importance of the work of the Council on African Affairs requires all of the time that I can give to it. This, I am sure you will understand in the light of the new level of the struggle for African freedom as reflected, for example, in the UNO—a struggle in which we Negroes have a real stake.[190]

By November 22, the *People's Voice* printed a statement of nonpartisanship. A fortnight later, in a letter released to Loyalty Review Boards,

Attorney General Tom Clark cited several alleged "front" organizations, including the National Negro Congress and the Council on African Affairs, as "subversive and communist." Late in December, the *Daily Worker* published an attack on the *People's Voice,* written by ex-editor Doxey Wilkerson. Wilkerson criticized his dismissal by the *People's Voice* board of directors and the recent nonpartisan statement. By January 1948, the *People's Voice* heralded a "new" directorial board, with Yergan as president, Deton J. Brooks Jr. as general manager, Leonard Lowe as advertising manager, and Mac C. Davies as circulation manager.[191] Later that month, Max marshaled troops in the CAA, aiming at a policy change there. Yergan sought a neutrality statement for the Council like that now in force at the *People's Voice.*

Leftist members of the organization like Robeson and Hunton refused to be drawn in by what they saw as red-baiting efforts at thought control by the Truman administration. Tactically, they felt they had to fight these unjust attempts to limit freedom of expression by systematic noncooperation—not unlike M. K. Gandhi's policy in India. In their eyes Yergan's retreat, as evinced by the actions of the *People's Voice* board, played into the hands of enemies of the First and Fifth Amendments. Soon, Max would have to choose between the *politesse* of expediency and the principle of independence of thought, action, and association. Robeson and Hunton had fought the deportation of Claudia Jones. They had also resisted the threats to outlaw the Communist Party, and reflexive anti-Sovietism. Yergan had stood with them on those issues but had suffered a change of heart. For him it may just have seemed a progression; for them it was breaking ranks or, worse, betrayal.

In the January *People's Voice* Paul Robeson, reviewing his relationship to *PV,* wrote,

> When I first joined the staff of *People's Voice,* my convictions and those of the management were in general agreement. This situation no longer obtains, although there has been no change in my convictions. The continuance of my column in *People's Voice* under the circumstances can only lead to confusion. I regret therefore that I must discontinue my column as of this date.[192]

For all practical purposes we can date the end of the broader perception of Yergan as a progressive leader from this point in 1948. Few could have predicted what 1948 would bring, but some insisted they knew what was in the offing. Since 1947, Max had been backpedaling on his formerly hard-line, uncompromisingly militant political stance. Until the loyalty oaths and then the advent of listings of subversive organizations such as the National Negro Congress, the Council on African Affairs, and a score more on whose letterhead Max's name had been prominent, he had been one of the stalwarts, his identity inseparable from that of peoples' struggles. Since hindsight is always twenty-twenty, it is difficult to take some claims at face value, and yet it did seem that there may have been murmurings about Max among the legions of the Left, and he was not alone in retreating.

6

About Face, 1948–1975

The retreat from a prominent position within the Left that had characterized Yergan's behavior during 1947 intensified during 1948, becoming increasingly public as his attempt to offer a less critical face to the fierce Cold Warriors now ruling postwar Washington met opposition inside the Council on African Affairs. In the *People's Voice* Max's solution was to eject left-wing elements while issuing a series of statements establishing the tabloid's "non-partisan" credentials.[1] Between February and August this sparked an outright schism between pro- and anti-Yergan factions. The media combat turned ugly, eventually involving police, lawsuits, and extreme embarrassment for the organization Max and Robeson had started.[2] In a protracted battle mirroring the world situation, Yergan was separated from the executive directorship, divested of the platform that had anchored his publicist persona since 1937.

The Council, like the National Negro Congress and Max's former CUNY post, had fallen hostage to a severe intolerance for left-wing ideas, now approaching incendiary levels. An equivalent paranoia within the Soviet Union and its allies during this of atomic diplomacy claimed hundreds of victims in purges, disappearances, trials, and assassinations. In the shadow of Smith Act deportations and prosecutions, Yergan contemplated the future. In part seeking relief, in part to remake himself, during October 1948 Max took a European trip to codify his opposition to communism. Traveling to Belgium, France, Switzerland, and the United Kingdom, he renewed old acquaintances in missionary and governmental circles of Europe's colonial capitals while working the press coverage of his exculpatory initiative.[3]

On December 23, 1948, and January 4, 1949, Yergan testified before the grand jury in the Alger Hiss case.[4] Although he was only tangentially involved with contributing evidence concerning Hiss, his very private appearance was paradoxically closed to the majority of the

American populace yet reported extensively by the local and national press. The substance of Max's Hiss testimony revolved around his own personal history in the Council and the NNC, told from the perspective of his present stance as he sought to further distance himself from the individuals and organizations with which he had been closely identified for the prior decade. His testimony had less to do with Hiss as such than with Yergan's own endeavor to reposition himself. Now widely available to the general public, the transcript was restricted for half a century.

Within the Hiss hearing Max revisited his transition from South African missionary to American activist, maintaining that he had been sought after and cultivated by the Left. Questioned by a surprisingly gentle prosecutor, Max underwent a cross-examination that seems to have been intended to authenticate his version of events in case such a legal record might later become necessary. Since federal government personnel, especially those involved in investigations or attorneys who petitioned for the right to do so, were the only persons potentially eligible to view this text, this seems the most credible explanation for the court having issued him a subpoena. Nothing said hurt or helped Hiss; taking the stand made Yergan a witness in his own behalf.[5]

On March 30, 1949, Yergan conveyed a memorandum to the South African embassy reviewing (somewhat inaccurately) his prior residence in the country and his Council on African Affairs activities (revised with a rightist slant), alleging communist manipulation, and red-baiting Hunton, Robeson, and Wilkerson. The text recalled the Middledrift drought-relief campaign of 1945–1947, citing what at present he contended was the "grave menace" communism posed and the urgency of Christian state action. This language, laying emphasis upon Christianity and state-based anticommunist policies, played into the hands of the framers of apartheid.[6]

A month later, on April 23, he had a letter printed in the *Herald Tribune*. A week after it appeared Phelps Stokes wrote Max about the *Herald Tribune* letter. "Negroes overstate the Soviet lack of racism; in a recent talk with the Liberian ambassador he stated not more than 5000 Negroes in all of Russia." Phelps Stokes argued that in the USSR there was "nothing corresponding to interracial problem in this country." He concluded by saying, "People are beginning to realize that with all the defects our achievements in behalf of interracial understanding and Negro progress in this country are very substantial, and that the situation is encouraging."[7] Phelps Stokes also articulated a fear that "our old friend Du Bois is apparently being misled by Soviet propaganda."[8] Neither the demographic argument Phelps Stokes made nor the question of whether an octogenarian Du Bois had been "taken in" was as significant as the fact that Yergan had managed to reenlist him as a powerful ally.

Four days later Max replied to Phelps Stokes, thanking him for providing "sympathetic encouragement" when his "inner resources have been considerably drawn upon to do what" his "better self and" his "convictions have led" him to do:

> In leaving the CAA I realized that it was an organization which I had brought into existence. I had also to take some of the responsibility for the fact that communists had found their way into the organization and had rendered it useless in the service of the African people. I may state, however, that I had no hesitancy whatever in severing my connection completely because I came to realize the evil character of communism and its effect upon all who submitted themselves to its control, its discipline and purposes. I can rejoice in the fact that I am again led by that light which I saw so clearly during the early years of my work in Africa. I derive great satisfaction also from my deep conviction that it is that light and its reflection of great spiritual and civic principles that is today in Africa, as elsewhere, the one factor that will meet man's needs.[9]

In mid-May 1949 Max wrote Phelps Stokes stressing the necessity of strengthening and augmenting "good relations between Western Europe and America on one hand and the African people on the other." Improving these contacts "and the consequent blocking of communist advances in Africa must be based on a genuine and expanding program of democratic development in Africa." European travels and the talks in which he participated then and afterwards convinced Yergan that he needed a new organization that he described to Phelps Stokes as an "American Committee for Cooperation with Africa." The group's aim should be "keeping before governments and the large industrial concerns that do business with Africa, the ever important need for a policy of progress—economic, political and spiritual,—in their official and business relations with that continent."[10]

By June Yergan had tried to gain a five-month visa to travel to South Africa.[11] Later that month, the Robeson-Yergan split in the CAA reached *Ilanga Lase Natal*.[12] In early August Dean Acheson wrote the American Embassy in Pretoria that while Yergan had appeared, on the basis of his own utterances and the fact that he had been attacked in the *Daily Worker*, to have changed his mind about communism, said in fact a confidential informant said "that no information had been received to indicate that subject has in any way changed his anti-communist attitude." Secretary of State Acheson urged extreme discretion in divulging this belief to the South African government.[13]

International Confederation of Free Trade Unions

In the spring of 1950, Yergan began an intimate association with the International Confederation of Free Trade Unions (ICFTU), the overseas arm of the American Federation of Labor (AFL). In May an article of his ran in its printed organ, *ICFTU News*. Entitled "ICFTU's Opportunity in Africa," the piece allowed Max to reach a new audience, mainstream trade unionists, as he aimed at building bridges with African labor.[14] Not since his presidency of the National Negro Congress ended in 1947 had he made such direct appeals to labor; then his focus had been on the AFL's leftist rival, the Congress of Industrial Organizations. Becoming involved with the Confederation was also a tactical move to regain access to an internationalist constituency. This one was supervised by the AFL's Free Trade Union Committee, led by Irving Brown and Richard Deverall, architects of the AFL overseas strategy of containment of communism. Yergan thus connected himself to the AFL-CIO leadership's anticommunist crusade and the CIA.

Before Yergan joined the Confederation it was concerned primarily with Europe and Asia, where it concentrated on checking communist influence in the workers' movements of those continents. Africa was beyond their gaze. Seizing upon this oversight, Yergan used an approach first mooted earlier with Phelps Stokes:

> One of the urgent tasks confronting the forces of democratic progress in European countries related to Africa is that of applying to Africa the lessons which Europe was not wise enough to use in her experience with the colonial areas of the East. Can Europe recognize, with regard to Africa, that the era of the old imperialism has ended and that an altogether new approach must be made to the problems which cry

out for redress and which will not be denied? The answer to this question will determine the effectiveness with which this newly organized force in world labor will utilize its truly unprecedented opportunities in Africa.[15]

Yergan highlighted the rapidly altered pace of development evident across Africa, from north to south and west to east. This movement needed ICFTU recognition:

Africans, too, want an improved standard of living and they are demanding the wages necessary to provide it. They want adequate educational, social and health facilities and they want—and are strongly demanding—an effective voice in their political life. These demands are reasonable. They reflect age-old irrepressible human aspirations. They would exist even if the character of Africa's past relations with the rest of the world had been different. However, it becomes at once a more complex and a more urgent task to realize the present reasonable demands of Africans because of the character of past European rule in Africa.[16]

For Yergan world labor needed to know about European rule within Africa whereby foreign powers had "produced a colonial system with which Africans are not satisfied and against which they are struggling." Materially, to Max Africa was potentially wealthy, and its "rich deposits of gold, copper and other minerals as well as extensive agricultural developments in cocoa, rubber, vegetable oils, and far greater agricultural, industrial and commercial possibilities are the foundations for the new life which must be built." The Soviet-directed World Federation of Trade Unions could not be entrusted with this responsibility, Yergan argued, because it was "divisive" and "totalitarian." But the ICFTU, coinciding with UN trusteeship (which he now vigorously backed) and Truman's "Point Four" program and built on the foundation of the Marshall Plan, could provide such aid for Africa. "This," he foresaw, "may well prove to be one of the greatest services by the ICFTU for Africa and Europe, as well as for world peace and prosperity."[17]

By 1950 Max had befriended *Pittsburgh Courier* columnist, essayist, and sometime novelist George Schuyler. Earlier, Schuyler had unsparingly pilloried Yergan as a communist dupe. Now, however, he accepted him as a fellow anticommunist crusader. For two decades the two would appear almost inseparable, black beacons on an otherwise white beach, addressing international conferences, sharing space on mast-heads of right-wing organizations, and occasionally traveling together on "fact-finding missions" for this or that conservative cause. Together the two integrated the Congress of Cultural Freedom, an attempt to forge an intellectual phalanx to counter the influence exerted by left-leaning *littérateurs* in the Cold War. A transatlantic movement, this had two components, one European, one American.

Congress of Cultural Freedom

Started in 1938 as a Committee on Cultural Freedom, by the late forties the Congress on Cultural Freedom had attracted an impressive array of high-profile ex-communists and repentant socialists on both sides of the Atlantic. Capitalizing on the successes of well-marketed memoirs by Sidney Hook, Ignazio Silone, Richard Crossman, and Arthur Koestler, who disavowed radical pasts, and given further impetus by heightened Cold War tensions from 1948 onward, the CCF seemed made to order for professional publicist Yergan and a newfound friend, his former foe, the iconoclastic career anticommunist and seasoned scrapper George Schuyler.

Schuyler's autobiography relates his recruitment into the CCF, which he was invited to join in 1950 by *Der Monat* editor Mel Lasky, on Sidney Hook's insistence.[18] Though Schuyler and Yergan shared CCF stages, Max's relation to the trend was subtle and complex. The Congress might help rekindle his flagging career. CCF plenaries in Paris, Brussels, Rome, and Berlin held appeal, letting him push both African and African-American agendas, thereby infusing racial and colonial issues into its debates.

Sharing similar emphases with Schuyler, Max's pronouncements could complement or differ from those of his colleague. In their first CCF meeting, the June 26–30, 1950, Berlin round, Schuyler spoke on "The Negro Question without Propaganda" at *Amerika Haus* on June 29. Addressing the assembly on the issues facing Black America, Yergan spoke in a timely and triumphalist tone. Using as his point of departure the Supreme Court decisions of June 5, 1950, which linked the Henderson, Sweatt, and McLaurin cases challenging the principle of equal but separate accommodations and educational facilities, Yergan cited the ongoing struggle of minorities for democratic rights while staking out a hard line against communism. His arguments were quasi-legalistic, intended to drive a wedge between Black aspirations and the aims of left-wing intellectuals and activists. Conceding that fighting for civil rights had been an uphill battle for Blacks, Max vehemently contradicted a stance he had resolutely defended only a few years before:

> We may therefore explode once and for all the ridiculous thesis of the communists that Negroes are so pathetic, bedeviled and oppressed that they must be considered as a *special case*—indeed as a *special people*. It is this communist nonsense which has sought to establish the idea of a "Negro nation" in America and has tried to give special meaning to the term the "Negro people."
>
> Negroes in America have regarded this effort to separate them from the body of the American people as the insidious Communist device that it is. They have completely rejected it, for they know that it is the poison which Communists have sought to spread everywhere. Negroes in America know, accept and wish to be a part of but one nation—the American nation.[19]

In November Schuyler and Yergan were again together at a CCF Brussels meeting of its international committee, where Max stressed the importance of Africa.[20] Asking the audience to note those in Eastern countries seeking the bounties of Western "liberty and who are also struggling for these," he said it would be a "grave error to consider Africa differently from other areas of the world," adding that "Africans believe in cultural freedom no less than the peoples of the West."[21]

Yergan closely linked his ICFTU work with that of the CCF, and his Berlin CCF address was printed in *ICFTU News*. Though the two constituencies differed, one consisting of working-class American unionists and the other of European intellectuals, they were connected by their anticommunism, though this varied considerably between Yankee hardliners and more pliable continentals. Max also kept close contact with Anson Phelps Stokes, sending him a copy of his Berlin CCF address,[22] and Dr. Ralph J. Bunche, lauding him on winning the Nobel Peace Prize and telling him about the CCF.[23]

By year's end, Max and his spouse Lena Halpern were among the subjects of an *Ebony* feature on interracial couples. The article pictured him in a nonthreatening setting, smiling and quietly sitting in his garden, one of his private passions.[24] The next year would not seem so idyllic as Cold War storm clouds continued to gather.

In mid-January 1951 Yergan attended a testimonial dinner honoring Ralph Bunche.[25] By March he was en route to India for a Congress of Cultural Freedom conference.[26] Joining such foreign guests as Stephen Spender, Norman Thomas, W. H. Auden, and James Burnham, he shared the stage with local luminary and CCF chair Jaya Prakash Narayan. In two appearances, Yergan opened and closed the conference. His contributions, like his much earlier CCF presentations at Berlin and Brussels, revolved around familiar themes: America, while a slightly flawed republic hampered by a "lawless element" that persisted in using discriminatory measures and lynch terror, had made great strides in democratization, particularly where persons of African descent were concerned. Whatever its shortcomings, for Yergan there was no comparison between life in the United States and conditions behind the iron curtain. During his closing remarks, Max presented "American Racial Policy and the Situation of American Negroes," arguing that "culture and freedom involve people, the forces affecting their lives and their ability to create."[27] His address stressed that the highest expression of American cultural, economic, and social power lay in recent juridical decisions affecting the lives of Negroes: the prohibition of racial segregation in higher education and railway dining cars and a presidential executive order eliminating structural segregation in the U.S. armed forces.[28]

His concluding point was that in the final analysis the rule of law would prevail for Blacks. By contrast, the Cold War opposition would appear to have little to offer and few takers:

> It is this reasonable certainty of the realisation of full democracy that has played an important part in the ideological choice of American Negro[e]s. It is important to point out that amongst these fifteen millions of American citizens, the communist appeal has met with little success, for the communists can count not more than one thousand Negro[e]s amongst the forty or fifty thousand members whom they claim in the United States. This is striking evidence of the power of democracy as a means towards the solution of present problems and is further evidence of the rejection of the totalitarian concept and practice.[29]

While India's CCF got scant U.S. coverage,[30] Yergan sent Eleanor Roosevelt an offprint and other material.[31]

Home from India, with AFL official Jay Lovestone interceding, Max met Internal Security Committee counsel Bob Morris and Benjamin Mandel on Friday, June 1. Morris wrote that while twelve months earlier Yergan had pledged to cooperate anonymously and privately, he would now go public, adding, "However, like all communists, he is still not as direct as you or I would be."[32] By Monday, June 4, Morris, more confident that Yergan would testify as desired, opined after a second chat, "It should be noted that he is characteristic of a breaking Communist. It takes them a long time and the process calls for a great deal of patience."[33]

Yergan went on the offensive in 1952. On May 4 he was one of several African-Americans named by ex-NNC staffer Dorothy K. Funn as a Communist. On May 13 he testified before a Senate Internal Security subcommittee, claiming to have been duped and "used" by Communists for a decade.[34] A partial script written by Yergan in advance of his later appearance before HUAC vigorously denied this willing association with communism. Referring HUAC members to his Senate Internal Security committee testimony, Yergan claimed that he "stated under oath that [he] was not and never had been a member of the Communist Party." He then further pointed out that "I am now and have always been unalterably opposed to the Communist conspiracy."[35]

On June 5, a year to the day after Bob Morris's lengthy interview memo, Max wrote Jay Lovestone concerning a Ford Foundation proposal jointly prepared with "mutual friend" Albert E. ("Bert") Jolis preceding an imminent "fact-finding mission" to Europe and Africa.[36] They planned a four-month trip across Africa "to warn and advise against communist activities" there. Jolis, a diamond financier and one-time OSS operative had been deeply involved in African mining for decades.[37]

By June Yergan was in England, planning to visit Paris, Brussels, and Geneva to meet with government "officials and African leaders." Later in June Max would fly "from Lisbon down West coast of Africa," for "Dakar, Monrovia, Accra, Lagos, Brazzaville and Leopoldville," with "motor trips to the interior." From Congo he would go to South Africa for a month, then Salisbury and Bulawayo in Southern Rhodesia, Northern Rhodesia, and Nairobi (Kenya), then spend another month in Eastern Africa (Uganda, Dar es Salaam in Tanganyika, Mombasa in

Kenya, then Ethiopia and Cairo) and then return to the United States.[38] A few days after writing Lovestone, he tried contacting Richard Wright in Paris.[39] By June 9 he heard from Jay Lovestone, who expressed interest in three subjects: "the specific imperialist conduct of Britain, France or any other colonial power; Communist penetration and influence and exploitation of imperialist policy"; and any help that he could provide. If his synopsis proved interesting, Lovestone would recommend compensation.[40]

With Lovestone, whose brief was the AFL's international arm, which was tethered to the CIA, as well as ex-agent Bert Jolis and Internal Security Committee counsel Bob Morris, Max had entered a new milieu. From now on there would be no turning back. Late in 1951 Jolis had conferred with Allen Dulles prior to the latter's nomination as CIA director, when he was still prominent in the intelligence community. Jolis, asked by Dulles for his views, wrote a memorandum on Black Africa, to which Yergan added a statement and proposal of his own. Jolis later excerpted part of Max's section in his autobiography, repeating this observation:

> The most important recent victory for Communism in Africa has been its capture of the African National Congress, the organization now leading the passive resistance campaign against the Malan government in South Africa. The known Communist leaders of the African National Congress are John Marks of Capetown, David Bopape of Johannesburg and Moses Kotane, also of Johannesburg. These men have all been to Europe, and in the case of Bopape and Kotane, also to Russia. From knowing them personally, I can report they are highly capable, ruthless and hardworking leaders, who are largely responsible for organizing and carrying out the campaign against Apartheid in South Africa.[41]

Yergan's contribution identified "an anti-Communist secondary leadership in the ANC" that he felt "is gradually being pushed aside and will soon be eliminated." Among the anti-Communists Max mentioned were A. B. Xuma and L. D. Ncwana. Jolis maintained that Yergan's report was presented to Allen Dulles for review.[42] Yergan's itinerary for his 1952 Africa tour named Dr. Xuma as his contact person. Ncwana and Yergan went back to the latter's Student Christian Association days. By 1952 these veterans, firebrands in their day, would have become the old guard. There was bitterness in the fact that they had been displaced by the "young lions." But there was also the question of how Yergan knew Bopape,[43] Marks, and Kotane. On May 13, 1952, in the appearance before the Senate Internal Security Committee referred to above, Yergan asserted that Communists were "interested in exploiting undesirable conditions and in preventing a solution of racial problems."[44] News of his testimony was picked up by both the establishment and Negro press.[45] The testimony itself focused on the Institute of Pacific Relations, whose director, Edward Clark Carter, had been a Yergan YMCA mentor. Ned Carter had taken him to India in 1916 and had remained in contact with him for at least two decades thereafter, occasionally helping to facilitate contacts between Yergan and critical foundation representatives. Now Carter and the Institute personnel, including Fred Field, a Council on African Affairs member with whom Yergan had been on very good terms prior to the 1948 split, were seen by Max as implacable foes. Questioning was done by subcommittee counsel Morris.

Responding to the queries of Morris, Yergan outlined his background, his YMCA work in India and Eastern and Southern Africa, and his involvement with the National Negro Congress. Morris asked if the NNC was a communist organization; Max replied negatively, at the beginning. Pressed on what Communists he had known and when, Yergan indicated,

> I came back from Africa in 1937. I left the work of the YMCA because I felt that a new committee at that time was needed which could deal much more directly with the issues then developing in Africa. They were political and economic. I thought that the American public needed to be informed in a way which I could not do too well under the YMCA. Now, the Communists made a strong plea for me when I came back. I knew James Ford. I had known him as a student. I think he may have been one of the Communist leaders who was told to make a strong plea for me. I was invited to speak at meetings which ostensibly had the interests of Africa as their purpose.[46]

At this point Yergan said Communists had no interest in changing conditions. From then onward he named names, told of his new anticommunist philosophy, and proffered extensive testimony on the subject of the Committee for a Democratic Far Eastern Policy, a group of keen interest to the China Lobby for its opposition to Chiang Kai-shek. Then

Max spoke of 1937 and a nascent International Committee on African Affairs, reconstructing this history as follows:

> The only individual that I now recall who was definitely associated with a communist outfit who was on the committee is Paul Robeson, as I recall. However, Communists were brought into the organization. They were proposed by Robeson. I think I must have proposed some. Certainly I didn't object to those who were brought in, so that I take some responsibility for their presence. This organization had one or two main purposes: One, to inform American opinion about the changes that were taking place in a more or less unknown great colonial area of the world. During the war we sought to involve Africans as fighters on the allied side through correspondence with governments in Europe and the South African governments. We didn't succeed too much in that. We were interested also in developing a helpful interest, not only from a humanitarian point of view, but in terms of developing the democratic idea and winning Africans who would be coming into positions of leadership to the side of the democratic cause. Now, the Communists saw that and they saw that here was an organization that appealed to Negroes and to non-Negroes in this country, because Africa was then becoming of great interest. By 1945, by the end of the war, the Communists' strength in the organization was considerable. They didn't have a majority of the people, but it was considerable. Robeson was chairman and I was executive head. By the end of the war, actually in 1946, in the organizations to which I belonged, the National Negro Congress, the Civil Rights Congress, I began to see clearly the issues on which and the procedure on which I could not agree with the Communists.[47]

The fuller story was far more complicated, and less clear cut in terms of culpability; this version, however, suited the purposes of both a repentant Yergan and the McCarran Act.

It is also significant that the Yergan statement submitted to Allen Dulles by Albert Jolis contained a proposal that he would tout before a number of foundations for an Institute of International African Affairs. In his memoir Jolis argued that "the proposed organization would do for the West in Africa, what . . . the Institute of Pacific Relations did for the Soviet Union in Asia."[48] Yergan had in mind a vehicle through which to garner aid for anticommunist African leaders, by means of conferences, publications, and grants. In other words, it would be a combination of the institutional approaches with which he had previously been involved: the global conference movement of the YMCA and its allies, the think tank approach mastered by the IPR, the plan laid out in his Fort Hare training scheme, and the contacts and methods of publicity painstakingly nurtured in the NNC and CAA.

Soon after testifying, Yergan left on a "fact-finding mission" designed to dissuade Africans from being led astray by close cooperation with Communists. His June itinerary placed him in London, Brussels, Paris, and Lisbon for a few weeks, prior to journeys to Dakar, Monrovia, Accra, Lagos, Brazzaville, Leopoldville, Bulawayo, Salisbury, Nairobi, Kampala, Dar es Salaam, Addis Ababa, and Cairo. On the eve of the European leg of his whirlwind transcontinental tour, Yergan paused to tell the media that the trip was being made largely at his own expense. His press briefing characterized his chief aim this way:

> One of my purposes will be to warn Africans against the snare and delusion of Communist propaganda and to point out specifically that among Negroes in America as well as among so-called underprivileged peoples elsewhere, particularly the Colonial peoples of Africa, Communists mean no good but to hypocritically and irresponsibly exploit the conditions of the people altogether in the interest of the Communist overlords in the Kremlin and their stooges elsewhere.[49]

The pace of his trip was dizzying. He reached Paris on June 9. Spending the next few weeks in Europe, he arrived in Monrovia later that month. Yet from June 26 to 28, South Africa was experiencing a momentous upsurge of opposition to apartheid. This "Defiance Campaign" was a nationwide series of acts of civil disobedience protesting its unjust laws. One of the landmarks of the modern anti-apartheid struggle, the Defiance Campaign had depended upon the mass mobilization of all of the major organizations fighting against the pass laws and other restrictive legislative acts and promoting broader democratic rights.

While the African National Congress, the Indian National Congress, and their allies were strategizing to apply popular pressure to the apartheid government, Yergan appeared, organizing meetings of his own with carefully chosen colleagues from long ago. Led by R. V. Selope Thema, they formed a cabal of disaffected "nationalists" critical of Congress leaders Dr. J. S. Moroka, R. T. Bokwe, W. M. Sisulu, Z. K.

Matthews, and J. B. Marks.[50] Early in August he and his spouse were guests of Ray Phillips, American Board of Foreign Commissioners missionary, who had continued Max's Y work, in his Johannesburg home.[51]

From August 14 to 21 he was in Nairobi. A year earlier he had been a guest of Indian commissioner Apa B. Pant; now, however, he suggested that he had been "high pressured" into the meeting, and feared he had been "used" by Pant, at which point he was advised not to associate too closely with him this time. The next day, Yergan was the subject of queries directed at the U.S. consulate general by representatives of Kenya's Criminal Investigation Division, who were seeking to determine the purposes of his visit. This interest in Max's activities also dated from Max's prior visit in 1951 and hints at the sensitive climate at the time he returned during the Mau Mau Emergency—the Kikuyu resistance to British rule in Kenya:

> In the course of the conversation it was ascertained that the interest of the police in his activities was due to an incident which had occurred on his previous visit. At that time he had gone on a motor trip with Mr. Pant and their car had broken down near the residence of Jomo Kenyatta, the Kenya African Union leader. They then spent some time in Kenyatta's home and remarks which Yergan made were translated to Africans present by Kenyatta. According to the CID informant, the mistranslation of Kenyatta was such that the statements of Dr. Yergan, when rendered into Kikuyu, were subversive. Dr. Yergan's statements as to the purpose of his visit to Kenya were passed to the CID representative, who indicated that they were not concerned over the good intentions of Dr Yergan and expressed the hope that he would not allow himself to be misquoted on this visit. The interest of the CID in his activities was not reported to Dr. Yergan.[52]

The commentator added ironically, "In view of all this, it came as somewhat of a surprise to learn through the press that Dr. Yergan was to speak on August 20 on the subject of 'Developments in Africa Today' for the Kenya League, presided over by Mr. Pant."[53]

Returning from Europe and Africa late in December 1953, Yergan was not under attack in the opposition press in South Africa for his stance on the Defiance Campaign. Volunteer-in-chief and ANC Youth League president Nelson Mandela then said of him:

I was struck by the fact that Mr Yergan made no attempt to meet the Non-European leaders and discuss the Defiance campaign with them direct. He came to this country to study the campaign, yet all his impressions were second hand or gleaned from newspapers which cannot speak for the campaign.

His visit to South Africa seemed to me to be very suspicious and Africans are asking if he didn't come here on a mission for the US government. He said not a word of condemnation of the racial policies of the Malan Government which, from a man professing to be active in his people's struggles in his country, seemed to us very strange. His warning to us in our activities sounded far more like the warnings of a US government spokesman than from a Negro participating in any movement for Negro rights.[54]

But this was only a prelude to the response Yergan received when an interview he did for *U.S. News and World Report* reached the news-stands on May 1, 1953. Entitled "Africa: Next Goal of Communists," the piece was a sweeping reprise of his most recent tour. But no part of the interview attracted attention like the sections dealing with South Africa. Although critical of apartheid, Yergan emphasized the dangers communism posed to Africa. In a survey of several regions of the continent, Yergan showed himself generally well informed regarding currents of opinion and processes of democratic struggle underway in Northern, Western, Eastern, and Southern Africa. But his take on South Africa drew fire. Readers replied to it almost immediately, from the United States and from South Africa itself. Within days of its appearance, long-time anticommunist NAACP leader Walter White wrote India's prime minister, Jawaharlal Pandit Nehru, and Central Intelligence Agency director Allen Dulles about it; a *Baltimore Afro-American* editorial denounced it; Paul Robeson's *Freedom* scored it, and the Communist Party's *Daily Worker* savaged it.[55] Even Max's old acquaintance and sometime correspondent Z. K. Matthews refuted him.[56] Indeed, few local or international Black leaders now countenanced Yergan's perspective. Matthews was quoted in a New York Negro weekly as having rebutted, "Yergan is very much mistaken," adding,

This is a moral and not an arithmetical problem. There have been terrific struggles in America for instance, despite the Negro's minority status. And in the last 20 years, the Negro's position has improved—but not because of a decline in numbers.[57]

Matthews went even further in a later interview done for Paul Robeson's *Freedom*, saying,

> During his long stay in the Union of South Africa, [Yergan] had little or no first hand contact with African political organizations such as the African National Congress. To my knowledge he first made contact with an African political organization in 1936 when he attended some meetings of the AAC. This was shortly before he returned to the US, where as the world knows, he was one of the foundation members and the executive secretary of the Council on African Affairs. Through that organization he maintained contact with the Union of South Africa until he broke with that organization.[58]

Slightly more than a fortnight after the *U.S. News* piece, a far more obscure quotation from Yergan appeared in a place that was nevertheless of considerable significance. On the heels of a stopover in the Belgian Congo, Yergan was cited in the prosettler Katanga mining periodical, *Bulletin de l'Association des Intérêts Coloniaux Belges*, as having said, "the Belgians have focused in the Congo, on economic development and seek to satisfy the basic needs of the indigenous workers." Yet, by disregarding African rights, "they might have committed an error."[59] As in his criticism of apartheid while Max admonished his hosts, more evident was his overall acquiescence in the Belgian Colonial Association's view of the situation and the fact that his voice was used to add credence to their position.

The two articles showed a willingness to be critical but an overwhelming acceptance of the authority of colonial and minority rule in Africa as something that still remained legitimate. While this view might have appeared defensible before 1945, by 1953 it had become passé. Increasingly, those accepting the status quo were only those able to earn something from it. Yergan's views continued to bring responses from both African-Americans and Africans who had known him at earlier stages in his life. A Yergan defense of segregationist James F. Byrnes added fuel to the fire.[60] While conservative columnist George Sokolsky found much to admire in the new Yergan,[61] NAACP leader Walter F. White felt otherwise:

A final word about Dr. Yergan. I have known him well and personally during many years. I knew him when he first went out to Africa as a YMCA missionary. I knew him when he worked intimately with the Communists and deplored his decision to cast his lot with them. I knew him when at last he broke with them and welcomed his return to the democratic fold. Although I have by no means always agreed with him I had refrained from any public attack upon him until last May when his indefensible article of Malanism in SA was published in *US News and World Report.* This was too much for me. I may add that practically the entire Negro press and other Negro spokesmen condemned that article, many of them in much harsher language than I used. I am sorry to see that you were inveigled into a total distortion of both the basis and the facts of my criticism of him.[62]

By late August, Yergan had written another *New York Times* letter a week after South African prime minister and apartheid theoretician D. F. Malan had used its pages to make the case for "separate development." Yergan responded to Malan by writing that his suggestions for "an African charter" were "significant in their implications." In his view,

Everything depends upon the spirit and the imagination with which consultation is undertaken and the willingness to apply the lessons of contemporary history. The more serious issues in Africa have come into existence w/in a comparatively short space of time. W/ the possible exception of SA, nowhere are the roots of the difficulties extraordinarily deep. Change and adjustment are still possible to make new history in that continent in which all may rejoice. In Tanganyika, Belgian Congo, Uganda, Gold Coast and Nigeria and the Transkeian area of South Africa, to mention but a few areas, there is solid achievement to impart confidence for the future.[63]

Yergan's new stance brought criticism not only from the Communist Party[64] but also from a range of mainstream African-American leaders and spurred a detailed retort from Walter Sisulu:

In so far as South Africa is concerned, Dr Yergan apart from justifying the suppressive policy of the Nationalist government towards the non-Europeans, has either deliberately distorted the true position to suit his special mission or he has accepted in toto a statement from Government officials. He alleges that the Government among other things is faced with the task of suppressing Communism. The suppression of Communism includes this in South Africa: "any scheme which aims at bringing about any political, industrial, social or economic change within the Union by the promotion of disturbance or disorder, by unlawful acts or omissions or threats." (See Section 1(b) Suppression of Communism Act, 1950).[65]

Sisulu and ANC colleague Nelson Mandela had been in attendance at a Yergan public address in Johannesburg during the Defiance Campaign in 1952. Each had found the address brilliant until Yergan reached the subject of communism. In an interview Sisulu also recalled that Yergan had attempted to talk the Congress Alliance out of undertaking the endeavor.[66]

In November Yergan embarked upon a five-month round-the-world tour lasting through March as he and spouse Lena Halpern visited Hawaii, Japan, Hong Kong, Siam, Burma, India, Ceylon, Pakistan, Turkey, Afghanistan, Yugoslavia, France, and the United Kingdom.

By spring of 1954, James Burnham, George Schuyler, and Yergan resigned from the Congress of Cultural Freedom. In June Schuyler ran the first of three installments of Max's travels, entitled "Finds World Curious about American Negroes," in the *Pittsburgh Courier*.[67] In early November Yergan's early mentor and guide through India and into the offices of the Rockefeller, Carnegie, and Phelps Stokes funds, Edward Clark Carter, died.[68]

Bandung, April 18–24, 1955

Between April 18 and 24, 1955, with both Justice Department and Central Intelligence Agency officials still looking over his shoulder, having retained his passport, Yergan attended the landmark Bandung Asian-African Conference in Indonesia. Bandung was one of the defining moments of the nascent "Nonaligned" movement then taking shape in the former and late colonial world. Led by India's magnetic prime minister, Jawaharlal Pandit Nehru, this alliance of non-Western territories and newly independent nations struggled to assert an identity separate and distinct from that imposed upon them by the greater powers of the capitalist West and socialist East. But how was this to be done? Those intermediate territories lying between East and West wanted to carve out a niche capacious enough to permit them to find a feasible arrangement with the more ardent Cold Warriors upon whom they had to rely politically and economically. Those who strove toward this goal risked the West's rancor, among them Nehru, Egypt's revolutionary coup d'état leader, General Gamal Abdel Nasser, and Indonesia's own president, Ahmed Sukarno.

It was thus a shrewd move on Nehru's part to frame Bandung as an opportunity for the "Coloured Peoples of the World" to assemble as a bloc, without direct interference from White Europe, whose imperial and colonial past and present practice were tainted by race-driven policies—the nonaligned nations decrying the Western powers—along with their Warsaw Pact rivals. Western responses to Nehru's lockout, which they saw as a cynical ploy, were almost universally negative and typically condescending. John Foster Dulles, for example, referred to it as a "so-called Asian-African Conference." The principal beneficiary of Nehru's race-conscious remedy was the People's Republic of China, embodied by Vice Premier Chou en-Lai. Chou exhibited superior diplomatic skills, surprising many with his charm, restraint, and humility. This unexpectedly flexible performance reassured fearful disciples of the liberal democratic West, who saw communism as a wolf in sheep's clothing and were eager to voice these anxieties. Within this context Bandung had unprecedented meaning for the Nonaligned.

Among those in attendance were not only Third World leaders and delegations but African-American observers as well, including Richard Wright, Adam Clayton Powell Jr.—and Max Yergan. Wright discussed his reactions in *The Color Curtain*. Though this work did not mention Yergan by name, it alluded to positions taken by both of the former *People's Voice* associates.[69] Powell was interviewed in the April 29, 1955, issue of *U.S. News and World Report*. Yergan's analysis appeared in the same periodical, in its June 3, 1955, edition. Yergan distinguished his position from that of one-time colleague Congressman Powell in a discourse sometimes subtle in its criticism of those with different views. Max's interviewer began by asking if he, as an American Negro, felt that color was "enough" at Bandung "to bind the nonwhite nations together in a bloc." He then replied,

I certainly do not think so; quite the contrary. I think the Conference proved the accidental and superficial importance of color. President Sukarno of Indonesia and some of the other speakers suggested that Asia and Africa could be united on the basis of color. But Asia and Africa did not unite at the Conference. When it came down to fundamental issues, each delegation looked at the problem from the viewpoint of national interest, and this was a conference very largely of colored peoples.[70]

Two weeks after the newsstand appearance of Yergan's June 3 *U.S. News* interview, on June 17, 1955, the Council on African Affairs announced its forced dissolution, due to the cumulative effects of unrelenting U.S. government harassment. If there was a payoff for Max's cooperation in helping achieve that outcome, it was not immediately apparent in the internal security traffic that continued to circulate within the Justice Department about him. A scant fortnight after the CAA's demise, this Yergan-inspired memo passed between J. Edgar Hoover and Assistant Attorney General William F. Tompkins:

Director, Federal Bureau of Investigation   July 1 1955
William F. Tompkins, Assistant Attorney General   WFT:BA:dbm
Internal Security Division   146-7-51-1119
Typed: 6/28/55

MAX YERGAN
SECURITY MATTER — C
PERJURY

This is with reference to your memorandum of June 21, 1955 in which you stated that the Central Intelligence Agency has contacted the subject regarding foreign intelligence matters and has requested that you furnish them any information which may bear on their relationship with him.

Under these circumstances this Division has no objection to the Central Intelligence Agency being informed that prosecution of Yergan for a violation of Title 18, U.S.C., Section 1621 is under consideration.

cc: Records
    Alvey (2 copies to FBI)

A few months later, this memo was placed in Yergan's file:

CONFIDENTIAL

>Declassified-Date 1/3/83
>Pursuant to 28 C.F.R. 17.26
>George W. Calhoun

Office Memorandum • UNITED STATES GOVERNMENT

TO: File DATE: January 16, 1956
FROM: Francis E. Jordan FEJ:ali
SUBJECT: Max Yergan 146-7-51-1119

CONFIDENTIAL

On December 20, 1955 Mr. Robert D. Johnson of the Passport Office, Department of State, telephoned the writer to inquire whether the Department of Justice wanted the restriction retained concerning subject's passport. The writer advised Mr. Johnson he would consult with his superiors, and would then notify him of the Department's recommendation.

Since the writer had knowledge that the Yergan matter was being reviewed by the Subversive Activities Section for a possible perjury indictment, he telephoned, later the same day, Brandon Alvey, Head of the Perjury and Fraud Unit. This was done to enable the writer to fully apprise his superiors of the status of the perjury review.

Mr. Alvey advised that the review had not been completed and would not be for another two weeks. He stated that in his opinion, the case against Yergan was "weak," and that he, personally, did not want to at this time go on record as recommending such a prosecution. He elaborated by saying that after one of his subordinates had completed the review he, personally, was going to recommend further investigation by the Bureau.

The writer explained to him Mr. Johnson's request, and asked if, in his opinion, we could advise Mr. Johnson by Thursday, December 29, 1955. Mr. Alvey replied he would attempt to have a recommendation by that date, but he did not believe it possible.

On Thursday, December 28, 1955, Mr. Alvey advised it would not be possible to have his recommendation for several weeks. On December 28, 1955, the writer telephoned William E. Foley, Executive Assistant to William F. Tompkins, Assistant Attorney General, Internal

Security Division, to acquaint him with the facts and ask his recommendation. He advised the writer to notify Mr. Johnson that the Department was not recommending that the restriction be removed nor that it be retained, but any action taken by them would be solely within their discretion.

On Thursday, December 29, 1955 the writer telephoned Mr. Johnson's office and left a message for Mr. Johnson to call him, since at that time Mr. Johnson was out of his office. Mr. Johnson telephoned the writer on Tuesday, January 3, 1956, and the writer advised him according to Mr. Foley's instructions.

Declassified Date 6/3/83
Pursuant to C.F.R. 17 .26
George W. Calhoun

During the first three weeks of December 1957, Yergan and his spouse, Lena Halpern, visited the Federation of the Rhodesias and Nyasaland. Then Yergan spent several days in the Republic of South Africa after leaving Halpern at the Rhodesian border in the Victoria Falls Hotel, citing "obvious reasons" for taking this course. While the visit was ostensibly undertaken under private auspices, Max's presence attracted consular attention, on several fronts. The most evident stimulus for this interest was the increasingly sensitive racial climate of the Federation, where the pressure of rising nationalist sentiment was beginning to rock the three constituents of the alliance, the Rhodesias (Northern and Southern) and Nyasaland. Each had vigorous nationalist movements, and Yergan's arrival brought in its train questions about his views on these militant movements, their leaders and followers.

While in Rhodesia Yergan and Halpern paid a courtesy call on the acting consul general in the American Embassy. Staying at the Meikles Hotel, they held talks with two members of the African petit-bourgeoisie, Lawrence Vambe, editor-in-chief of African Newspapers, Ltd., and a recent returnee from a U.S. study tour, and Herbert Chitepo, the pioneer Black lawyer in the Federation and later a pivotal figure in the nationalist movement. Yergan had already met with Kenneth Kaunda, then general secretary of the Northern Rhodesia branch of the African National Congress, and the six African members of Parliament in the Federation. He had also spoken with Federation prime minister, Sir Roy Welensky and Southern Rhodesian prime minister Garfield Todd. But it was within the context of the encounter with Vambe and Chitepo that the essence of the Rhodesian struggle could be glimpsed. Synopses of their exchanges were captured by a U.S. embassy official. Quoted at length, they give texture to Yergan's presence and its larger historical significance:

Two conversations of the Yergans with Africans, in which the reporting officer participated, are of some interest. One was with Mr Herbert Chitepo, the Federation's only African lawyer, in his offices in the Advocate Chambers in a downtown Salisbury office building. (They could not, of course, meet at the Yergans' hotel or any of the public places in Salisbury.) The other was with Lawrence Vambe. The conversations represented contrasting strains in African thinking with Mr Chitepo sounding bitter, disillusioned, and offering no constructive suggestions; and Mr Vambe, while expressing concern over increasing tensions, indicating that he still has faith in the basic good sense and decency of most Europeans in the Federation and in the possibility of making "partnership" a reality through persistent rational negotiation and compromise.

Mr Chitepo appeared to feel that from the African viewpoint things were getting worse not better. He was particularly bitter over the British Government's approval of the Constitution Amendment Bill (enlarging the Fed Assembly) over the objections of the African Affairs Board. This action, he said, eliminated any remaining faith the Africans may have had in the effectiveness of constitutional safeguards of African interests. It had, he said, made thinking Africans realize that from now on they must depend wholly on their own efforts to achieve equality. He could see nothing ahead but a long "struggle," with the Africans seeking to wrest their rights from Europeans. He refused to say what form he thought the struggle might take, although there was no doubt in his mind that the Africans would win it.

After the interview Mrs. Yergan commented, "What an angry young man!" Dr Yergan wondered if he were not expressing somewhat more extreme views than he actually felt, evidencing the impatience and frustration of youth rather than his considered opinions. While Mr Chitepo is not a member of Congress (at least so far as is known) and while he does work hard on constructive activities, e.g. serving as a member of the Urban Areas Board, he does appear to the reporting officer to have developed an increasingly pessimistic outlook during the past 2 and 1/2 years since he established himself in Salisbury.

Mr Vambe, who is considered a "moderate" by Europeans and a stooge by extreme African nationalists, is nevertheless respected by many in both groups as a man of independence and principle. He and his wife were the Acting Consul General's dinner guests, with the Yergans. Mr Vambe said he had returned from America "inspired" by the accomplishment of the American negro and progress made in integrating him into American life. What he saw in America made him more determined than ever to continue to press for the raising of African standards on a wide front before demanding full political rights. He was particularly impressed that negroes had accomplished so much through their own efforts and recognizes that the basis for their successful efforts has been the increasingly high standard of education that they have achieved. Increasing the number of educated Africans here is, he feels, the only way to provide a solid basis for the political claims now being advanced by African nationalists. He was also impressed by the fact that negro accomplishments in such fields as sports, entertainment, education, business and science has frequently been responsible for breaking down the color bar—rather than direct political action. He would advise African nationalists not to concentrate so exclusively on political agitation but to encourage and work for African advancement in all fields.

He was pleased to hear Dr Yergan express hopefulness about the possibilities of racial cooperation in the Federation, as well as agreement with his (Vambe's) views on the sterility of pure political agitation unrelated to accomplishments, and the dangers of nationalist intolerance of other opinions. He said he hoped Dr Yergan was expressing such views to African nationalist leaders. Dr Yergan said he had done so in conversations with Mr Kenneth Kaunda, General Secretary of the Northern Rhodesian African National Congress, and the 6 African Federation MPs, whom he met twice as a group.[71]

In fact, these discourses may also be read as a long soliloquy, with the militant Chitepo standing for the younger Yergan and the moderate Vambe representing his older alter ego. Both sides of the coin represent stages in Yergan's thinking about Africa, about political change and social progress, and about democracy, and even if the elder eschewed Chitepo's approach, it was in no sense entirely foreign to him even then, in this rigidly segregated polity.

During the final years of the 1950s Yergan seems to have withdrawn for a time from public view, for reasons that are not altogether certain, though they may have been influenced by a suicide attempt of a close relative in 1958 that received considerable news coverage. It may also be that his plans for a new career did not find favor in the quarters where they were directed, leaving him uncertain where and how to proceed. He was by now approaching seventy, and retirement would not have been an unrealistic possibility. Yet retirement would not afford him access to the limelight, which he sought once again when Africa was back in the news. By 1960, when British prime minister Harold MacMillan proclaimed that "the winds of change" were sweeping Africa, Yergan responded like a phoenix from the ashes, resurfacing a year later, in another conspicuous and seemingly stagnant locality, Angola.

Full Circle: The American African Affairs Association

The final fifteen years of Max Yergan's life were taken up with a new organization superficially resembling the International Committee on African Affairs and its successor, the now defunct Council on African Affairs. Like them it bore "African Affairs" in its title, under a masthead of readily recognizable personalities; unlike its left-liberal predecessor, however, this group was inclined to the far Right. It represented ultraconservative ideologues, key members of whom coalesced around the *National Review* and the Conservative Book Club, and was libertarian, Republican, heavily Christian (especially Catholic), and committed to contesting and combating procommunist influence domestically and internationally. Beyond these common features, it is not always easy to determine, much less state, what the men in this organization had in common. They tended to be members of the financial and educational elite and were frequently Anglo-, Franco-, or more generically Europhile in orientation. Outsiders, they were disdainful of government intervention in private affairs, including income taxes used to finance excessive social spending, as well as what they typically saw as an effete, flaccid, permissive society, lacking order and morals. A cross-section was foreign born, more apt to be Germanic than Slavic, Gentiles than Jews. Beyond Yergan and George S. Schuyler, few were nonwhites, and there were few nonsecretarial females. How then would Max Yergan have gained access to this cohort, and how would it approach Africa?

The answer to this question lies in Yergan's geopolitical perspective vis-à-vis "the Communist conspiracy." By the late fifties, Yergan's major

South African support would have come from the pro-apartheid, government-funded South Africa Foundation, closely allied to the ultra-Right inside North America. American conservatives by and large looked at South Africa as a flawed NATO ally in the furious mortal combat against communism, but one nonetheless worthy of steadfast U.S. support, since it was doing a dirty job that no one else could, would, or should do for them by rooting out leftist and pro-Soviet agitators and domestic dupes unwilling or unable to see that the agitators' ostensible support for African and "non-European" rights was merely a cynical cover to cloak their real imperial designs. This attitude was the logical extension of the positions taken by Max in his return trips to South Africa, and would have made him a sought-after public figure in South African and conservative U.S. circles, since not many American Negro "leaders" would dare sit on the same side of the fence as South Africa, even ancient anti-Communists like the now late Walter White or his successor, Roy Wilkins, who each supported majoritarian Southern African liberation.

By contrast, Yergan, having lost credibility with the Left, left-liberals, and the center, could only cultivate a conservative constituency, closing himself off to domestic "colored" colleagues, particularly those within the civil rights community, who saw their struggles as linked to those of the opponents of White minority rule in the same way as had the radical-left Yergan in the thirties and forties. Now, Max Yergan, like Marx's Louis Napoleon, stood in his Eighteenth Brumaire. He had rededicated himself to religion and had rejoined Africa's battle for democracy; but the way he did so, and the particular soldiers and weapons he chose, were out of phase with the tenor of the times in which he used them. Thus, several saw him as a shadow of his former self and sadly shook their heads at his present publicism.

The American African Affairs Association owed its existence to the decisions of four unpopular African White minority regimes to undergo systematic propaganda facelifts by successively engaging a retinue of seasoned overseas public relations specialists in the twilight of European-settler rule, starting around the year 1960. Although this PR campaign was undertaken separately by four different regimes, the political economy of Southern Africa, with its interlocking companies and labor boards, made cross-border communications a practical necessity for capital. Once one concession knew where to find a capable image polisher, it tended to pass the word along to others.

The year 1960, popularly called "Africa year" to honor the dizzying pace at which former colonial territories were outwardly throwing off the trappings of alien rule, was a watershed, moving Britain's prime minister Harold MacMillan to proclaim that "winds of change" were sweeping the continent. This turn of events not only empowered the colonized; it was also a spur to the business allies of possibly soon-to-be-former colonizers to seek methods of derailing or delaying a seemingly inevitable march toward flag independence that could mean an end to a profitable and luxurious existence they could never replicate in Europe.

In August 1960, Moise Tshombe, a well-fed, Belgian-backed, rightist Congolese, pushing a program of ethnically and regionally rooted subnationalism, led a secessionist movement of the minerally rich Katanga province, claiming to champion democracy in its battle against the allegedly "pro-Soviet" rule of the charismatic nationalist prime minister Patrice Emery Lumumba. Nothing about the Congo crisis of that year had been simple, because of the hasty circumstances leading to the downfall of eighty-odd years of outwardly benevolent "platonist" despotism in a corporatist state whose ruling paternalism neglected to prepare more than a handful of its African subjects for the inevitable day of freedom.

While most of the beneficiaries of Congo's status quo ante had been Belgian, by the fifties the exigencies of the Cold War had brought the strategically vital mineral endowment of the Congo to the attention of gregarious American speculators and their allies. When the Republican Eisenhower administration was succeeded by that of liberal Democrat John Fitzgerald Kennedy, a politician never favored by conservatives, his fellow party man, the Connecticut conservative Thomas Dodd, caught their attention and consequently came to the aid of Katanga's anticommunist contra clique. Corporate sponsorship behind that effort had come from Marvin Liebman, a China Lobby member, and Max Yergan, who joined Liebman in forming an American Committee to Aid Katanga Freedom Fighters.[72]

The rise of party politics in the Congo had been extremely recent, dating only from the premiere elections in 1957. Preceding this poll, Congolese nationalist expression had been deeply fragmented, wracked by ethnic, regional, linguistic, and class strife. Prior to the 1950s, the mass response to earthly oppression typically took the form of syncretic Afro-Christian millennialism, exemplified most explosively in chiliastic outbursts like the one identified with catechist Simon Kimbangu in 1921, close to Thysville. Soon followed the Southern Rhodesia–based Mwana Lesa ("Song of God") trend that entered Katanga around 1935, and the Kitawala movement, first appearing around 1930. Secular politics, while regionally and ethnically rooted, tended to be more urban, beginning with World War Two, typically motivated by laborite responses to the conditions in mining compounds, such as those of the extractive behemoth Union Miniére. It was within such a context that ABAKO (an ethnic association centering around the powerful Bakongo group, who had led the great Kongo kingdom in the sixteenth–nineteenth centuries) became the pioneer nationalist party between 1954–1960, under the guidance of Joseph Kasavubu, victor in the 1957 Leopoldville elections. In short order, ABAKO was joined by the centrally based Lulua Frères, piloted by Chief Kalamba. But by 1960, Congolese were swept up in Lumumba's meteoric rise. A modest, brilliant mission product with untapped skills, Lumumba had painstakingly built a national base from 1953 on, sparking the Mouvement Nationale Congolaise (MNC/L).[73]

Lumumba emerged as a territory-wide figure in the late fifties, and his popularity peaked when he appeared in 1958 at an Accra meeting of the Afro-Asian People's Solidarity Organization, from which he emerged as a protégé of Pan-Africanist prophet and first prime minister of Ghana, Kwame Nkrumah. At this point Lumumba became a favorite among nationalists both within and beyond the Congo. He gained a reputation as an indefatigable worker, an incomparable debater, and an all-around magnetic personality. While ABAKO and then Lulua Frères (later to run in alliance with Lumumba under the title of Union Congolaise) broadened their ethnic bases, Lumumba galvanized the electorate. By July 1960, the Belgian colony had been granted independence. As soon as this became evident to the overseas-based mining interests controlling Katanga, however, they engineered several schemes to ensure that they would not be a party to independence, the most significant idea being a provincial, ethnically based secession, which first had been attempted in December 1959 and would recur on July 11, 1960. This plan was designed to counter Lumumba, who had fought for national independence.

In six months, Lumumba's star had risen and fallen, as he had become ensnared in Cold War rivalries among the USSR, the United

States, and the UN that led to foreign intervention, with a charismatic Lumumba and countless other Congolese being compelled to pay the ultimate price. Witnesses put Tshombe and cohort, Katanga interior minister Godefroid Munongo, on the scene when Lumumba was dispatched. These men handed Lumumba over on January 17 to Colonel Joseph Desiré Mobutu in Elizabethville, where he was tortured and killed; his demise was revealed February 13, 1961.[74]

Also by the beginning of 1961, Max Yergan would become identified with a campaign engineered by the colonial government of Portugal, which was ruled by the iron fist of the long-lived fascist dictator Antonio Salazar. Salazar urged a consortium of sixty enterprises, known as the Overseas Companies of Portugal, to retain the services of a North American public relations firm, Selvage and Lee (later Manning, Selvage, and Lee) in order to help sanitize the notorious image of this colonial government.[75]

At the time gruesome and graphic tales of Portuguese atrocities in Angola had been given ample space in the Washington *Post* and *Harpers,* among other periodicals, and had even received attention at the United Nations, where they sparked vigorous protests. As Russell Warren Howe and Sarah Hays Trott later revealed in their muckraking exposé of Washington lobbyists, *The Power Peddlers,* one of the participants in this process to refurbish Lusitania's tarnished finish was *Pittsburgh Courier* publisher, columnist, and Yergan crony, George Schuyler. He sent his like-minded daughter, piano prodigy and author, Philippa, to the scene as a stringer, courtesy of Selvage and Lee, where she yielded pro-Portuguese stories for the *New York Daily Mirror* that did not reveal the sources financing her trip. A conspicuous feature of this state campaign was its use of high-profile American Negro publicists to buttress strongman Salazar's increasingly infamous fascistic regime.[76]

Midway through February, American officials in Dakar, Senegal, sent this cable:

Embassy received brief visit February 6 from a Dr. MAX YERGAN (and his wife) whose card describes him as an "Africa Consultant" residing at Pinesbridge Road, Ossining, N.Y. (Tel. Wilson 1-1030). Dr. Yergan was referred to the Embassy by M. Le Mire, Diplomatic Counselor of the French High Representation, who stated Yergans were recommended by French Information Service, New York.[77]

Dr. Yergan was not particularly communicative regarding purpose or aegis his present trip to West Africa other than to state he planned visit Abidjan, Cotonou, Brazzaville, and Luanda, Angola, returning to U.S. about mid-March. Said he had called at ConGen Dakar in 1958, but Embassy Files show no record this visit. Expressed interest in Embassy getting him an appointment with Mamadou DIA (in Senghor's absence), but did not press point when told this would be difficult.

Then the embassy official, H. S. V. Villard, with whom Yergan had met in a highly publicized delegation concerned with U.S. policy toward Africa during 1944, commented,

Ambassador recalls that Max Yergan enjoyed somewhat questionable reputation around 1940–45 as Commie-line anti-colonialist. Embassy does not know what evolution of Yergan's political outlook in intervening years may have been but presumes Dept. may have more information. [line deleted] Dept. may wish notify Luanda.[78]

It was a small world indeed. And many of its inhabitants had painfully long memories.

In early March 1961, at much the same time that President John Kennedy had directed UN ambassador Adlai Stevenson to cast a vote favoring a resolution to censure Salazar, Yergan and Lena Halpern flew into Luanda, Angola, from Lisbon. An American consular official wired the secretary of state that Yergan was "described by airline representative as UN official," adding that Yergan denied this, "claiming to be 'consultant' on Africa." The American functionary further informed the secretary that "his remarks [were] guarded as to his employers."[79]

Yergan's Angolan trip lasted some six days from touchdown to departure. Yet there was a further twist to this sojourn. Following his exit flight on March 8, he made a follow-up visit to Luanda on April 29, this time accompanied by *Pittsburgh Courier* associate editor and ex-Congress of Cultural Freedom collaborator, George Schuyler. Together Yergan and Schuyler undertook an oddly timed scenic tour. Consular officers in the American Embassy revealingly reported its highlights:

Visited mixed race homes Sunday, local industries Monday, Cambambe Dam Tuesday. Apparently being hospitably treated Portuguese, whose policies he seems in main to uphold. In conversation yesterday he seemed reasonable, knowledgeable and tolerant. Believe Portuguese kindness to American Negro at this moment highly significant and encouraging.[80]

The fact that Yergan and Schuyler, two Black Americans, were touring Portuguese-ruled Angola in March 1961 was no idle matter.[81] Nor was it insignificant that they chose that precise moment to put a pleasant face on an increasingly unpopular colonial apparatus, noted for its systematic suppression of human rights and reliance upon torture. Many now knew of the infamous *palmatoria,* a perforated paddle, specially designed to maximize pain and scarring during interrogation. This was used to intimidate and extract confessions from suspect detainees, particularly among targeted trade unionists and/or nationalist activists.

By mid-December, Yergan and conservative ideologue James Burnham (whom Max had known since 1950) held a news conference at New York's Overseas Press Club to announce the formation of an American Committee to Aid Katanga Freedom Fighters,[82] a rightist venture aiding the Belgian-backed enclave of Congo copper baron Moise Tshombe. The "freedom fighters" would soon be revealed as mostly White foreign mercenary recruits. Nonetheless Yergan firmly identified himself with this effort to resist "communist" control.

Yergan and his allies supported the "anti-Communist" antics of the settler-backed pseudosecession of the mineral rich Katanga province of the Congo. Long a sore spot in the heart of Africa, the Congo had endured nearly eight decades of fierce foreign rule, nowhere more exploitative than in the copper-rich region now known by the mineral's Kiswahili name, Shaba. Katanga, as it was then, was a paradise for the European "experts" engaged with the mining and ancillary industries who extracted considerable profits while their African wards, the primary producers, writhed in abject penury. Tales of the abuses heaped upon the hapless helpers of the Congo's Belgian invaders had hurt the hearts of many over the years since King Leopold's tragic condominium, whose excesses reached the eyes of Mark Twain, George Washington Williams, Roger Casement, and other muckrakers. Max's allies in defending this regime included would-be ex-Communist Frank S. Meyer, then a born-again rightist zealot, and hosts of like-minded conservative celebrities who, calling for individual rights, actually were bolstering settler-controlled private property over African democracy.

Some time in the early sixties, Herbert Aptheker, who had met Yergan at the time of the first National Negro Congress in 1936 and had worked with him in the Council on African Affairs until the 1948 split, had a chance encounter with Yergan in Manhattan. As Aptheker recalled it,

> I was on Fifth Avenue and he got off the Fifth Avenue bus. He was dressed in his high fashion, as he always was. I think he had a cane. I believe he wore spats, and a hat; he looked like some sort of English barrister. He came off the bus . . . and he saw me and he turned away, I thought with embarrassment. I may be mistaken; he may have turned away with disgust, I don't know. But he saw me and he obviously didn't want to say anything to me or have me confront him or do anything with him. And I thought to myself at the time, and I said to myself, what a pity. That's what I said to myself. What a pity.[83]

Yergan again briefly captured headlines the following year. In 1964, South Africa was in the throes of a terrifying treason trial whose roots lay in a July 11, 1963, raid on Lilliesleaf farm. The raid resulted in the arrest of several prominent prodemocracy activists, including Nelson Mandela, then in hiding from state authorities while they planned the next stage in an underground strategy to force the apartheid government to grant them their citizenship rights. This event precipitated what would be known as the Rivonia Treason Trial. By the first of January 1964, the government had promulgated a Suppression of Communism Act, aimed at identifying and detaining those suspected of either belonging to the banned Communist Party or working in common purpose with it. These two related stories dominated domestic and international headlines all during that year. In November Yergan, supported by the progovernment South Africa Foundation, returned, arriving around November 3. Ten days later, Max's visit brought this reflection from an American consular officer:

> Dr. Max Yergan, an American Negro, is currently visiting South Africa under auspices of South Africa Foundation. He is described by the Foundation as a distinguished American sociologist, a specialist in African affairs, and Vice-Chairman of the American Afro-Asian Educational Exchange Program.

Mr L. B. Gerber, Director of the South Africa Foundation, informed the Embassy by letter on October 22, 1964 that Dr Yergan would visit South Africa as a guest of Foundation from November 3–30. The itinerary arranged for him by the Foundation includes visits to Johannesburg, the Northern Transvaal, Pretoria (interviews with Government officials), Daveyton area (meet with members of Urban Bantu Council), Kruger Park, Basutoland, Cape Town, East London, Transkei and Durban. A press conference is scheduled for November 29 in Johannesburg. He will leave November 30 for Lourenço Marques. Pursuant to the request of Mr Gerber, the Embassy advised the Consulates at Johannesburg, Port Elizabeth, Cape Times, and Durban of Dr Yergan's visits to those consular districts.

In an interview in the *Sunday Express,* November 8, Dr. Yergan is reported as saying that he sensed a great sincerity among Afrikaans and English-speaking South Africans and non-Whites, to come to grips with pressing issues, and that "There appears to be strong evidence of a genuine effort to deal with these issues with justice." According to the *Express,* Dr Yergan was formerly a lecturer at Fort Hare University and he first came to South Africa more than 30 years ago.[84]

On November 25, Yergan was the subject of an article in the Johannesburg *Star* in which he was quoted as having stated publicly,

"I do not hesitate to say that the responsibility rests with the rest of the world to understand separate development more fully than they do now and to give South Africa a more honest, objective, and fair judgment." Yergan also reportedly said that South Africa was "in every sense a bright spot on the continent of Africa—a spot which can grow even brighter when the rest of the world understands separate development better."[85]

The same day he got sterner treatment from East London's *Daily Dispatch*. Noting the curious concatenation of circumstances whereby Max stayed at a "whites-only" hotel in Umtata, Transkei, the *Dispatch,* following the lead of the locally published *Umthunywa* of November 24, asked why it was that even Transkeian cabinet ministers, not to mention opposition leader Kaiser Matanzima, could not do likewise. Taking the point further, indicating that Chief Minister Matanzima had arranged a "state dinner" for his American guest in the Transkei Legislative Assembly's restaurant, it reiterated *Umthunywa*'s query: "What would happen if Dr. Yergan reciprocated this gesture by inviting his hosts to dinner at the all-white hotel?" The press felt this farcical.[86]

In a matter of days, the scandal had reached *New York Times* reporter Anthony Lukas, who devoted considerable space of his own to this anachronistic performance.[87]

By early December, American Embassy staff in South Africa discussed Yergan.[88]

> Dr. Max YERGAN, the American Negro who is visiting the Republic as a guest of the South Africa Foundation (refair), stated in Umtata, Transkei, that separate development was a "realistic policy" marked by qualities of sincerity and honest commitment, according to *The Star* (Johannesburg) of November 25. These remarks were made at a dinner in the Transkei Legislative Assembly attended by 30 Africans, including Chief Minister Kaiser Matanzima and members of the Transkei Cabinet, the press stated, adding that in Umtata he was staying at a leading White hotel.[89]

William L. Swing, American vice consul in Port Elizabeth (later U.S. Ambassador to Haiti) filed a similar report, recapping the *Daily Dispatch* article and then offering this observation:

> The reporting officer's visit to the Transkei happened to coincide with that of Dr. Yergan. Although I stayed in the same hotel as he and although I saw him on several occasions in Umtata and in remote areas of the Transkei, I did not have an opportunity to speak with him since his time was very tightly scheduled. In conversations with representatives of the civic, Transkeian and South African governments, I emphasized that Dr. Yergan was traveling under the auspices of the South African Foundation, and that the opinions he expressed did not reflect official USG[overnment] policy toward South Africa.
>
> The Mayor of Umtata, Councilor D. F. THOMPSON, told the reporting officer in Umtata on November 26 that neither the Umtata City Council nor any other civic group, on which "Europeans" are represented, was invited to participate in any way in Dr. Yergan's visit to Umtata and the Transkei. At the TLA dinner arranged by Chief Minis-

ter Matanzima, a former student of Dr. Yergan at Fort Hare, "European" press and radio correspondents were admitted only during Dr. Yergan's speech. It is significant to note, with regard to the segregation so strictly adhered to, that neither Paramount Chief Victor POTO, leader of the Opposition in the TLA, nor Mr. Knowledge GUZANA, Opposition Chief Whip, attended the "state" dinner for Dr. Yergan, although both had been invited.[90]

Given that Yergan had served as an apologist for apartheid, a backer of Portuguese colonialism in Angola, and a bankroller of provincial neocolonialism in secessionist Katanga, it was not out of character for a born-again Yergan to join another minority-rule bandwagon, this time hitching his horse to the atavistic Ian Smith's breakaway Southern Rhodesian rebellion. In 1965, when most Africans, and scores of their erstwhile overlords in Europe's metropoles, read majority rule as the handwriting on the wall, some die-hards still stubbornly refused to see it, and did all in their power to resist the inevitable, aping kindred spirits in Lisbon and Brussels. Defying Great Britain, the colonial authority, the United Nations, and the world community, Smith's Rhodesian Front–dominated White minority government delivered an astonishing soi-disant "Unilateral Declaration of Independence," cutting its UK ties. Rebel Rhodesia quickly realized that it needed Western friends. There to answer Smith's call was publicist Yergan. Yergan was still currying favor in lofty places, and his latest foray into right-wing public relations again seized the eye of some occupants of the leeward side of the Capitol.

On January 21, 1966, G. Mennen "Soapy" Williams, the assistant secretary of the State Department's Bureau of African Affairs (later Democratic governor of Michigan), met Ohio congressman John H. Ashbrook, a Yergan confidant, regarding the representative's plan to visit Southern Rhodesia on a fact-finding mission. The day before, Williams had tried unsuccessfully to contact Ashbrook in both Washington and his district office. Williams, who had a rare knowledge of Africa, reprised the crux of their talks this way:

Since he was contemplating a trip to Southern Rhodesia, I pointed out to him the fact that the United States Government had officially sought to discourage US citizens traveling there and that British visas were necessary.

My next move was to indicate to him that if he went, I thought he would find himself faced with one or two alternatives. One, he might be attacked, not necessarily as the three British MP's, but possibly verbally. The other alternative could be that the government would endeavor to use him. He said he certainly didn't want to be used.

He then indicated that he was traveling with Max Yergan, Mr William A Rusher and a third journalist. I thereupon pointed out to him that Max Yergan was undoubtedly a white supremist and was going to Southern Rhodesia for that purpose. I pointed out to the Congressman that he had recently formed an organization called American-African Affairs Association, Inc., and I showed him the letterhead. This letter included sentences like the following : "And much of our government's and people's knowledge of Africa is colored by racist dogma (white Africans are always wrong; colored Africans are always right), etc."

The Congressman expressed appreciation for the way I had put the matter; I had insisted obviously he was free to make any decision that he wanted to, but that I felt obligated to present him with the facts as we saw them as well as the Government's position.

The Congressman indicated that he wanted to think the whole matter over and that he might not make the trip. He expressed interest in seeing certain materials showing the basis for our action in Southern Rhodesia etc, which I promised him for that afternoon.

On Saturday, January 22, Representative Ashbrook departed New York for London, arriving in London at 9:35 A.M. the next day. While the congressman was en route, Secretary of State Dean Rusk contacted the American Embassy in London, and consular officers in Johannesburg and Salisbury provided information to U.S. Embassy personnel in Pretoria and Cape Town of the flight plans of the party, as well as the substance of the exchange between Assistant Secretary Williams and Representative Ashbrook.

Ashbrook then departed London on Sunday, January 23, by South African Airways Flight 221 bound for Salisbury, expecting to visit South Africa. Ashbrook, the ranking Republican on the House Un-American Activities Committee did not provide the State Department with data allowing it to "ascertain specific purpose of visit."[91] Reportedly traveling with him were Max Yergan and perhaps others from London. Rusher did not accompany them.[92]

On January 25, this official message was sent to Secretary of State Dean Rusk:

1. CONGRESSMAN JOHN M. ASHBROOK, DR. MAX YERGAN AND RALPH DE TOLEDANO MET ON ARRIVAL SALISBURY AIRPORT 1030 JANUARY 24 BY RHODESIAN INFORMATION MINISTRY OFFICIAL; ASHBROOK DEPARTING JANUARY 26, DE TOLEDANO JANUARY 28. AND YERGAN JANUARY 30. I ARRANGED TO BE AT AIRPORT INFORMALLY INFORM ASHBROOK OUR PRESENCE IN EVENT HE NEEDED ANY ASSISTANCE. TRIO WAS RECEIVED AT 1530 BY MINJUSTICE LAW AND ORDER LARDNER-BURKE AND, AS NOTHING SCHEDULED EARLIER BY RHODESIANS, ALL THREE HAD LUNCH WITH ME AT OFFICIAL RESIDENCE.

2. IN COURSE LUNCHEON CONVERSATION, I STRESSED PROBLEMS CONFRONTING REGIME AND NEED TO VIEW PRESENT SITUATION REALISTICALLY IN TERMS OF SANCTIONS EFFECTS ALREADY REGISTERED ON RHODESIAN ECONOMY AND PROBABLE ADDITIONAL IMPACT IN WEEKS AND MONTHS TO COME. ALTHOUGH THEIR PERSONAL BIAS OBVIOUS AND THEY MAY HAVE BEEN MORE CIRCUMSPECT IN MY PRESENCE THAN THEY WILL BE WITH REGIME OFFICIALS, ALL THREE GAVE IMPRESSION THAT REGRETFULLY THEY WOULD NOT REPEAT NOT BUILD UP REGIME HOPES OF ANY CHANGE IN US SUPPORT FOR HMG OR HOLD OUT PROSPECT FOR EASING OF SANCTIONS. ASHBROOK TOLD ME SEPARATELY HE CONSIDERED USG POLICY BROADLY SUPPORTED AT HOME AND WOULD SO STATE IF ASKED BY REGIME LEADERS.

3. TRIO SCHEDULED MEET SMITH JANUARY 26 AND APPOINT-MENTS ARE BEING ARRANGED WITH BUSINESS AND OPPOSITION LEADERS BY INFORMATION MINISTRY. IT WAS MADE CLEAR THROUGH INFORMAL UNOFFICIAL CONTACTS AT WORKING LEVEL THAT VISIT COMPLETELY PRIVATE AND ALL THREE SEEM SENSITIVE TO DELICATE SITUATION OF CONGEN.

4. SO FAR, NEWS MEDIA HAVE NOT REPEAT NOT GIVEN VISIT ANY PLAY. ASHBROOK STRESSED THAT WE DID NOT REPEAT NOT INTEND TO MAKE PRESS STATEMENTS OR TRY TO ATTRACT PUBLICITY DURING VISIT; IT PERHAPS LESS CERTAIN THAT HIS PARTNERS WILL SHOW SAME RESTRAINT.[93]

On January 27 Yergan visited the American Consulate at Salisbury, Rhodesia. The following day a consular official filed this report from that location:

1. ASHBROOK-DE TOLEDANO — YERGAN SPENT JANUARY 26 VISIT-
   ING KARIBA DAM AND NEITHER ASHBROOK NOR DE TOLEDANO
   MADE ANY EFFORT TO SEE ANYONE AT CONSULATE. YERGAN,
   HOWEVER, PAID VISIT MORNING JANUARY 27.
2. YERGAN SINGULARLY UNCOMMUNICATIVE RE PROSPECTS SMITH
   REGIME BUT GAVE EVER EVIDENCE OF DISCOURAGEMENT AND
   SAID HE PROPOSED CUT SHORT PLANNED VACATION STAY
   ATHENS, GREECE IN ORDER RETURN NEW YORK, "GET IN TOUCH
   WITH FRIENDS URGENTLY AND SEE IF ANYTHING CAN BE
   DONE."
3. YERGAN DISCOURSED AT LENGTH ON DANGERS POSSIBLE
   CHAOS IN RHODESIA WHICH COULD SPREAD RAPIDLY
   THROUGHOUT SOUTHERN AFRICA, EXPRESSED DISAGREEMENT
   WITH UK–US POLICY WHICH "CREATING VACUUM IN VITAL
   AREA" YERGAN IMPRESSED BY DETERMINATION RESIST ON PART
   WHITE RHODESIANS ALTHOUGH MOST UNWILLING MAKE ANY
   PREDICTION RE: REGIME'S STAYING POWER, AND SHOCK AT
   INTRANSIGENCE AFRICANS WITH WHOM HE MET, INCLUDING
   UPP MEMBERS; HE ASSERTED THEY UNANIMOUS IN SAYING
   "WE MUST RULE NOW AND BRITISH REALIZE THIS."
4. COMMENT: YERGAN GAVE IMPRESSION HE WOULD FIGHT GOOD
   FIGHT FOR SMITH REGIME, BUT THAT SITUATION APPEARED
   MORE CRITICAL THAN HE HAD ANTICIPATED.

While in the short run it proved possible to keep a lid on these proceedings, by spring news of them had reached other reporters. Among those in the know was noted Negro journalist Carl Rowan, who had many government sources. Once again, Yergan's name appeared on Oval Office stationery, this time in a memorandum from Rick Haynes:

Columnist Carl Rowan phoned me today to ask if I could give him any leads on public sources of information on the Communist background of Max Yergan, Co-Chairman of the right-wing American-African Affairs Association. Recalling that Yergan had been a prime mover in Tshombe's secessionist Katanga Lobby, I suggested that he check the

Reader's Guide on the Katanga Lobby as several newspaper and magazine articles were written about it in the early 60s. Rowan said that he already had the record of Yergan's admissions to the House Un-American Activities Committee in 1952 of Communist Associations.[94]

During the next five years Yergan continued traveling. He went somewhere via Air France in autumn 1967, perhaps to Francophone Africa or maybe just the French "motherland." But there were few notices of these trips in either Black or establishment newspapers, as Max faded into obscurity. His name still showed prominently on the masthead of the American-African Affairs Association, and his colleagues there continued turning out defenses of White rule in Rhodesia and South Africa and issuing attacks on "Communist-inspired" terrorism, which most Africans preferred to call the armed struggle. By 1970 Max's health had deteriorated, causing complaints of "unsteadiness" in his legs, as well as speech difficulties.[95] This continued into the next year.[96] Then, in March 1971, Susie Wiseman Yergan died.[97] That same year, the AAAA sent a three-man study team to Southern Africa, led by Alvin J. Cottrell, director of research for the Center for Strategic and International Studies (CSIS) of Georgetown University, whose report exposed "communist activity in the Indian ocean area and the value of South Africa as an ally in dealing with it."[98] CSIS is frequently understood to be an institution with close CIA links, and thus it is likely that at least some AAAA members had connections with the CIA. While the CIA characteristically would not comment upon whether or not it knew of Yergan's activities, the circumstances of his foreign public-relations contracts make that a legitimate question.

The following year, on April 16, Dr. Lena Halpern Yergan died at home in Ossining at the age of sixty-four.[99] Yergan clearly felt her loss deeply. His own medical state continued to cause problems.[100] Then, nearing the end of his own life, Max sent a poignant letter of apology to Paul Robeson, lamenting the loss of what had once been a valued and vibrant friendship.[101] Robeson apparently did not reply. In a year both men would be dead.

On Friday, April 11, 1975, after a long illness, Max Yergan died in Mount Kisco, New York, at the age of eighty-two. Two days later his long life was recalled in the *New York Times,* and a month thereafter in the *National Review.* At his death he was convinced that no one could comprehend why his life went in the direction that it did, and he routinely resisted requests to discuss the matter—with one exception: acquaintance Ruby Pagano, with whom he spoke about the past and to whom he gave access to his papers, among them letters to and from Susie Wiseman, Mary White Ovington, and countless other confidantes, but that might not be seen by anyone else until perhaps some time in the twenty-first century. How is Yergan to be remembered? What did he leave for posterity? These are difficult questions. For decades, without access to his papers, they could not be answered; now they can.

Epilogue

In 2002, after pursuing leads on this biography for a quarter of a century, this writer was able to examine the Max Yergan papers at Howard University. Though they contained no "smoking gun" of any kind, as they had been vetted prior to their donation, they did confirm a number of the suspicions that arose from close study of Yergan's letters, essays, speeches, sermons, and other documentary source material written about or by him. While space limitations have forced a drastic reduction of the work that this investigation had initially yielded, the contours of Yergan's public life and its intersection with his private mind can now be reconstructed.

Max Yergan left far more paper behind than anyone outside of his family may have known. An incessant writer, he seems to have put pen to paper on a daily basis. In addition to scores of articles in newspapers, journals, and pamphlets printed in the United States and South Africa, his papers contain several unpublished manuscripts, including at least one full-length book. Yergan was both more prolific and more intellectually accomplished than has thus far been acknowledged. This might be one of the reasons why he clung so tenaciously to his honorary doctorate, using it as if it had been earned in graduate study. In fact it had. Max's postgraduate "school" was the YMCA and SCA mission field of South Africa, his thesis was "Africa, the West, and Christianity," his dissertation, *Christian Students and Modern South Africa*. Though the last was an edited volume, it fully represented his thought.

Embedded within his work and life story are several other sagas. There is, first, the tale of the Black YMCA, which Nina Mjagkij has addressed in such rich and nuanced ways. Equally arresting, however, is the legend of Nonwhite involvement in the South African YMCA and Student Christian Association, neither of which has yet found its historian(s). Yergan's contribution is essential to any such reconstruction. Next is the body of work that Yergan produced, none of it anthologized

271

—a fact that led this writer to create an edited volume bearing the working title "African Affairs: A Max Yergan Reader." A second narrative, "Abundant Life: The South African Odysseys of Max Yergan," is also in progress.

Among the more challenging aspects of a Yergan biography is the fact that each of his associations yielded an intricate paper trail. My initial reaction to this reality was to produce a work that reflected the breadth of every one of these thematic and bibliographical pathways. I also quickly recognized that some of these stories could in turn lead to other examinations. For example, I thought about doing books on the National Negro Congress, the Council on African Affairs, and Blacks on the Left—again using Yergan's experience as normative. Over time, however, rejecting these temptations, I settled down to do the best Yergan book I could.

Because my time in the Yergan papers was limited, I cannot say I "know" them, but I am aware that accessing them was a privilege very few other scholars have had. In a very focused day and a half, I examined the entire list of items, examined every photograph, and copied all relevant manuscripts. I have tried to balance what I have seen against what I think about these events and the characters who took part in them, though space limitations have made it impossible to include everything I found, as I learned from the very first drafts of this work. In fact, this iteration is a fraction of the size of the original. Perhaps some day that version may make its way into print so that everyone will be able to benefit from the archive that I have accumulated of "Yergania," as my colleague Bob Edgar has so aptly christened it. At the moment I am striving to find a home for this documentation, as it has outgrown each of my living and working spaces. The chronology alone approaches two hundred pages. None of this effort would have been necessary had the papers been available in 1975, when my work on this project started. But then I would not have learned that which has caused me to write what follows:

In an earlier version of this book I ventured to offer that Yergan was a man out of time, either ahead of or behind many of his peers. At first he was very far advanced, meeting Gandhi and becoming exposed to Indian nationalism in World War One, a full generation before Howard Thurman and other African-Americans encountered India and Gandhi. In South Africa he made the transition from the social gospel to historical materialism that so distinguished Black South African ex-Christian communist radicals Moses Kotane, Edwin Mofutsanyana, Alfred Nzula, Walter Sisulu, and Yergan's youthful protégé, Govan Mbeki. A race leader in the thirties and forties, by the fifties he had fallen far afoul of the freedom movement, fading into obscurity. Yet popular parts of his work outlived him.

Until I gained access to the materials still available only in South African archives and repositories, I had no idea of the scale of his influence in that setting. This South African material has led me to conclude that the larger significance of the life and work of Max Yergan extends beyond the limits of this volume. He was a true diasporic figure. His contributions to the worldwide YMCA movement alone were formidable, and his dedication to broadening the base of the South African youth volunteer movement to embrace Africans was extremely momentous. I have begun to explore this in other publications and have sketched out a second biography that centers upon Yergan within and beyond South Africa. While clearly an extension of the work that began here, it has a distinct trajectory of interest to Pan-Africanists, South Africa, South Africans, and Southern Africanists. It will establish the fact that, irrespective of political changes, there was a surprising degree of consistency to Yergan's commitment to Africa and Africans, in the terms of his place and time, a commitment to achieving their "redemption."

Because Max Yergan has many living descendants, I have tried to be even-handed in my discussions of his life. I do not regard this as a simple intellectual endeavor. It is not just something that one can sit at a café to discuss because this is not a work of fiction. Nor do we have the luxury of a century or more separating us from the action and great controversies described here. Yergan did not live to see the Berlin Wall fall or the collapse of the Soviet Union, or the bombings of the World Trade Center, for that matter. He did stop to express regret at the loss of his friendship with Paul Robeson. We do not know if he had second thoughts about the role he played in the final decades of his life. We do know that irony abounds in our consideration of his fate. Perhaps there is no greater irony than that the key to understanding Max Yergan's life came from the land that both radicalized and then conservatized him, South Africa. I believe that it was there that he did his greatest work, between 1922 and 1936. That was also his laboratory for publicism and teaching. It was in interwar-era South Africa that Yergan was able to hone his talents as a lecturer, sermonizer, writer, impresario, manager, politician, and public relations specialist. For the remainder of his life he applied the lessons learned during that period, making himself a leader among African-Americans, Africans, church people, liberals, leftists, and, ultimately, ultraconservatives. At each stage of his life he occupied the space of the race pioneer, always modeling the profile of the "exceptional" Negro. In time his circle of familiars contracted to one in which race seemed to be of diminishing significance. In fact, at the end of his life, he may not have had more than a handful of fellow "race" men and women as friends; most of his acquaintances were White, in America, Europe, and Africa.

In many ways, this turn of events was the logical conclusion of a life of standing apart from the stereotyped behavior expected of the mass of persons of African descent. Yergan made certain to distinguish himself from the downtrodden, the unlettered, the "sporting" underworld, and those damned to do menial tasks. He saw himself as a leader and did everything in his power to live out his destiny as one whose public posture would attract attention, even if this involved controversy. He "made it" in every sense of the world he inhabited, reproducing his social position among his progeny and theirs, so that now one encounters Yergans in prominent positions in many leading American cities. However they consider the various phases of his personal and political life, they readily recognize and acknowledge a debt to him. This is part of the story of how that patriarch organized his mental and material universe. He was a person of his place and time, but the space within which he operated was expansive indeed. While not a first-tier leader of the rank of Dr. Du Bois or the other elite trained members of the African-American professional stratum, he nevertheless made his mark. His major challenge was doing well by doing good. Over time the particulars regarding how this could be achieved altered profoundly in Yergan's mind and work. Beyond his individual eccentricities, he also faced the contradictions of his class.

From his early life as a campaigner against discrimination in the Jim Crow South, Yergan came from a milieu richly fusing spiritual and political combat against oppression. At the inception of his public career, that background led him into progressive politics. Depression and fascism sharpened the edge of the spiritual dimension, taking him into the secular realm. As the global struggle between good and evil seemed to him to require the anti-Axis alliance forged during the Popular Front and United Front eras, he felt able to straddle his old and new worlds as a secular humanist whose social gospel moralist sense had been christened, as it were, in the Christian church. However he strove to separate himself from that fact in his public utterances and writings, he was never able to sever his spiritual ties. In the end, when his confidence in communism and socialism was called into question by Cold War conflict and he increasingly questioned of the price of principle, on one hand, and the relentless, still largely secret pressures to which he and his family were subjected by the intelligence community, on the other, he cracked, breaking ranks and seeking the path of least resistance.

It is almost certain that this happened because of some information that fell into the hands of the FBI that forced his hand, compelling him to assume an impossible position. Only Yergan himself and the small group of people who convinced him to "turn" knew precisely what this was. It is not to be found in the Yergan papers. It is hinted at in his FBI file, however, where among bowdlerized and redacted documents lie the traces of betrayal or vengeance or other emotionally laden acts by which sensitive material was leaked to the Bureau. Whatever the contents of these files, they must have deeply wounded Yergan, for they brought an end to his career as a progressive leader. That this did not immediately lead to an about-face appears to have reflected the fact that despite his defection from the Left, it took Yergan a full two years to completely capitulate to conservatism. In the interval he was still trying to negotiate a middle ground, to establish an increasingly critical position on communism while not completely breaking with the Left, as long as he could avoid doing so.

By 1950, however, the CIA, the FBI, and the weight of McCarthy and McCarran had all but obliterated this narrow political space, which, while greatly diminished, feebly persisted beyond the demise of FDR and into the Truman era. It is likely that by then Yergan feared not only for himself but also for his children, and for them he was willing to sacrifice anything and everything, even if it meant denouncing and being denounced by progressive Africa. His junkets from then on, on behalf of the AFL-CIO, the South Africa Foundation, the Belgian Congo, and later the Portuguese, Rhodesian, and again South African governments, were all related to this campaign to protect by drawing fire as a "point man" for counterrevolution. If one compares the writing done during this period to that which immediately preceded it, one can see that neither has the force of the work he did during the twenties and thirties when he was at the height of his powers. This seems not only to have been a matter of ability; it also seems to have been reflective of the

passion animating the work, passion that was at its highest and most flu-
ent when his political ardor was married to his spiritual force.

This confluence of political and spiritual energies was precisely what
Gandhi manifested in *satyagraha*, "soul force," which he transmitted
to African-American theologian Howard Thurman and which the next
generation of nascent civil rights leaders, among them James Farmer
and ultimately Martin Luther King, integrated into their practice in the
forties and fifties. While this should not be overstated, Yergan was way
ahead of them. Because of the covert nature of the federal campaign
against him, however, it is difficult to determine just what made Yergan
leave the struggle to which he had dedicated his life. He sacrificed himself in that process, leaving himself open to all manner of charges of
selling out, and causing friends and acquaintances alike to scratch their
scalps in chagrin. Yet Max Yergan did not turn his back on Africa. In
spite of serving as an apologist for the most odious systems on earth, he
went to conferences to argue, sometimes single-handedly, for an appreciation of the "African Personality," an idea progressive Africans had
been touting for a century. Moreover, he was discussing the now popular South African notion of "Ubuntu" (personhood) in the fifties, a full
three decades before it was popularized by historian Leonard Thompson. All of this adds up to a need for a reappraisal of Yergan, the man
and his times. This book should serve as one contribution in that direction as we seek to unravel the lives of Max Yergan.

Notes

NOTES TO CHAPTER I

1. Ruby Pagano, "Max Yergan, A Biography." Unpublished manuscript. Copy in author's possession, 1, 4. Pagano indicated that Yergan's mother hung a portrait of this emperor. It is not easy to verify whether this is accurate, for two reasons. First, there seems not to have been a Roman Emperor named "Maximilian," although, to be sure, there were other rulers with names that seemed to bear a superficial resemblance to this, e.g., Aulus Maximian, r. 286–305 and 307–10; Maximinus, r. 235–38; or A. Maximus, r. 383–87. My thanks to Gary Miles for this insight. Secondly, an emperor who did go by the name "Maximilian" was the Austrian ruler of Mexico, not a contemporary of Yergan but a figure well known during the lifetime of his grandfather, Frederick. I am grateful to David Sweet for bringing this to my attention. In fact, unless the enumerator erred in copying Yergan's name, it appears that he might well have altered it himself, as he evidently did for his surname, which he seems to have simplified, while his mother Lizzie continued to spell it "Yeargan." L. B. Yeargan to J. E. Moorland, 6 February 1917, courtesy Moorland Collection, Manuscripts and Archives, Moorland-Spingarn Research Center, Howard University (MSRC/HU).

2. Yergan told Ralph Johnson Bunche during 1937 that his father had been "a prize s.o.b." Bunche, Diary (unpublished), entry, 21 April 1937, Ralph Johnson Bunche Papers, UCLA. I owe this choice reference to Robert Edgar. For fuller descriptions of the Bunche-Yergan relationship, consult Robert R. Edgar, ed., *An African-American in South Africa: The Travel Notes of Ralph J. Bunche, 28 September 1937–1 January 1938* (Athens: Ohio University Press, and Johannesburg: Witwatersrand University Press, 1992), and Brian Urquhart, *Ralph Bunche: An American Life* (1st ed., New York: Norton, 1993). Their interaction shall be examined in depth in succeeding pages.

3. Jonathan Daniels, *A Southerner Discovers the South* (New York: Macmillan, 1938), 3.

4. Daniels, *A Southerner*, 3–4.

5. *Raleigh News and Observer*, 20 July 1892, 1.

6. "He Got His Dues: A Camden County Fiend Hanged and Riddled: A

Negro Brute Who Makes a Horrible Assault Is Visited with Retribution," *Raleigh News and Observer,* 4 October 1892.

7. Pagano, "Max Yergan," 4. Attempts to contact the centenarian Delany sisters, who almost certainly knew Yergan, as they grew up in Black Raleigh during the same decade, proved unavailing. Through their publicity agent they communicated the sad news that they either would not or could not help in "any way, shape, form, or fashion." Personal communication, 11 April 1994.

8. Of course, this may be a deceptively simple characterization of a far more complex reality, especially in view of how little is known about Yergan's absentee father. Perhaps grandfather Fred sought to provide his grandson with a more acceptable father figure than the man who actually sired him, for reasons that only a family could know. On the Raleigh upbringing of the Delany sisters, see Sarah and A. Elizabeth Delany, with Amy Hill Hearth, *Having Our Say: The Delany Sisters' First Hundred Years* (Thorndike, Me.: G. K. Hall, and Kodansha International Publishing, 1993), 63–67, 70–77. Hubert Delany, younger brother of Sadie and Bessie and noted legal figure, became an associate of Yergan during their Harlem years.

9. Ralph W. Bullock, *In Spite of Handicaps* (New York: Association Press, 1927), 111.

10. Booker T. Washington, "Atlanta Exposition Address," in William L. Andrews, ed., *Up from Slavery* (New York: Norton, 1996), 101–2.

11. John Hope Franklin, *The Free Negro in North Carolina, 1790–1860* (Chapel Hill: University of North Carolina Press, 1943), 205–6.

12. Frenise A. Logan, *The Negro in North Carolina, 1876–1894* (Chapel Hill: University of North Carolina Press, 1964), 121.

13. A crucial element of this ideology, "Ethiopianism," is discussed in Wilson J. Moses, *The Golden Age of Black Nationalism, 1850–1925* (New York: Oxford University Press, 1978), 23–24. Moses defines the term thus: "Ethiopianism involved a cyclical view of history—the idea that the ascendancy of the White race was only temporary, and that the divine providence of history was working to elevate the African peoples." For an earlier view from a White evangelical supporter of the idea of using Black missionaries to "uplift" Africa, see Rev. F. Freeman, *Africa's Redemption: The Salvation of Our Country* (Fanshaw, N.Y.: 1852; reprinted Westport, Conn.: Negro Universities Press, 1970). The literature on this topic is too extensive to adequately summarize. A helpful introduction is provided by Sylvia M. Jacobs in her detailed literature survey, "Black Americans and the Missionary Movement to Africa: A Bibliography," in Jacobs, ed., *Black Americans and the Missionary Movement to Africa* (Westport, Conn.: Greenwood Press, 1982).

14. On Shaw University see Rev. J. A. Whitted, "Shaw University," in *A History of the Negro Baptists of North Carolina* (Raleigh, N.C.: Edwards and Broughton, 1908), 146–65; Clara Barnes Jenkins, "An Historical Study of

Shaw University, 1865–1963," Ed.D. dissertation, University of Pittsburgh, 1965; and Wilmoth A. Carter, *Shaw's Universe: A Monument to Educational Innovation* (Rockville, Md.: D.C. National Publishing [for Shaw University], 1973).

15. Benjamin E. Mays, *Born to Rebel* (New York: Scribner, 1971), 126–27.

16. *The New Voice in Race Adjustments: Addresses and Reports Presented at the Negro Christian Student Conference, Atlanta, Georgia, May 14–18, 1914,* A. M. Trawick, ed. (New York: Student Volunteer Movement, 1914). The YMCA sessions that Yergan most likely attended were those of Channing H. Tobias and Addie W. Hunton.

17. Sarah A. Allen, "A New Profession: The First Colored Graduate of the Y.M.C.A. Training School, Springfield, Mass.," *Colored American Magazine,* September 1903, 661–63. Allen revealed that as of September 1, Wilder took charge of the "Colored" Y in New Haven.

18. Personal communication, Gerald F. Davis (Director, Babson Library, Springfield College) to Anthony, 18 February 1985.

19. Max Yergan File, YMCA Headquarters Library.

20. "Max Yergan, National Secretary for Africa," *The Intercollegian* (devoted to work of YMCAs in universities, colleges, and schools) 39:5 (February 1922): 4.

21. Yergan to Moorland, Box 126-64 File 1231, "YMCA—M Y—Correspondence—1916," Moorland Papers, Manuscript Division, MSRC/HU.

22. J. E. Moorland, "The Young Men's Christian Association and the War," *Crisis,* December 1917, 65.

23. Benjamin Elijah Mays, *Born to Rebel: An Autobiography* (New York: Scribner, 1971), 126–27.

24. Robert E. Jones, "Breaking over Race Lines," *Southwest Christian Advocate,* 27 July 1916, 1.

25. Kirby Page, Second Day Out—July 12th, On Board—"New Amsterdam"—June 11th–20th, 1916, Kirby L. Page Papers, File Cabinet 1, Drawer 1, Claremont School of Theology, Claremont, California. Document generously made available by Joseph "Kip" Kosek, Ph.D. candidate, Yale University, 24 August 2002.

26. Page, Fifth Day Out—July 15th, Page Papers. Reference courtesy Joseph "Kip" Kosek, Yale University.

27. Gray, a YMCA worker in Europe, subsequently became a well-known conscientious objector. Gray's references to Yergan appear in Kenneth Irving Brown, ed., *Character "Bad": The Story of a Conscientious Objector, as Told in the Letters of Harold Studley Gray* (New York: Harper and Brothers, 1934), 10, 12. I am grateful to Joseph "Kip" Kosek for sharing these citations. Kosek to Anthony, 17 April 2002.

28. Yergan to Moorland, 7 October 1916, Moorland Papers, MSRC/HU. By

20 =

this time Max was by his own estimation "within days of leaving for East Africa."

29. Robert E. Jones, "Breaking over Race Lines," *Southwestern Christian Advocate,* 27 July 1916.

30. Sherwood Eddy, *A Century with Youth: A History of the Y.M.C.A. from 1844 to 1944* (New York: Association Press, 1944), 67.

31. Pagano, "Max Yergan," 16–17. *Paan,* as this is often written, is widely associated with overseas Indian diaspora communities in Eastern, Central, or Southern Africa, as well as in the Caribbean, notably Guyana and Trinidad. *Biri* resembles *biriyani,* a rice medley, and *metai* may be *methi,* fenugreek leaves, which, like *paan,* could easily have been sold to train riders.

32. For comprehensive compendia on the civilization of Mysore in all its complexity, consult Hebbalalu Velpanuru Nanjudayya, diwan Bahadur, *The Ethnographic Survey of Mysore* (Bangalore: Government Press, 1906–15); *Mysore Gazetteer, Compiled for Government,* C. Hayavadana Rao, ed. (Bangalore: Government Press, 1930), 2–242. Bangalore district is dealt with in volume 5. On Bangalore's Christian tribes see H. V. Nanjundayya and Rao Bahadur L. K. Ananthakrishna Iyer, *The Mysore Tribes and Castes,* vol. 3 (Bangalore: Mysore University Press, 1930), chapter 1, "Indian Christian" (Roman Catholic), 1–60, and chapter 2, "Indian Christian" (Protestant), 61–76.

33. Yergan to Moorland, 30 August 1916, Box 126-64, File 1231, "YMCA —Max Yergan—Correspondence—1916," Moorland Papers, Manuscript Division, MSRC/HU.

34. Mark Naison, *Communists in Harlem during the Depression* (New York: Grove Press, 1984), 293.

35. Mary White Ovington, *Portraits in Color* (New York, 1927), 34.

36. A. J. (Aiyadurai Jesudasen) Appasamy, "A Challenge to India's Educators," *The Young Men of India* 29:11 (November 1918): 653–62; and 29:12 (December 1918): 708–16.

37. Pagano, "Max Yergan, a Biography," chapter 7, 57. For barrister Gandhi's South African apprenticeship, see his *Satyagraha in South Africa* (1928; reprinted Ahmedabad: Navajivan Trust, 1970); *An Autobiography: The Story of My Experiments with Truth* (Boston: Beacon, 1957), passim; John Haynes Holmes et al., *Mahatma Gandhi, The World Significance: Appended with Mahatma Gandhi's Jail Experiences, Both South African and Indian, and All about His Fast* (Calcutta: C. C. Basak, [1925?]); and Maureen Swan, *Gandhi: The South African Experience* (Johannesburg: Ravan Press, 1985).

NOTES TO CHAPTER 2

1. Yergan to Moorland, 12 October 1916, Moorland Papers, Moorland-Spingarn Research Center, Howard University (MSRC/HU).

26 -

2. Yergan to Moorland, 7 November 1916, Mombasa, Moorland Papers, MSRC/HU.

3. Every recruit received a copy of the Field Manual.

4. Yergan to Moorland, 26 November 1916, Dar-es-Salaam, Moorland Papers, MSRC/HU. He mentioned military censorship.

5. Yergan to Moorland, "Somewhere in German East Africa," 19 December 1916, Moorland Papers, MSRC/HU.

6. Yergan to Moorland, "Somewhere in German East Africa," 23 December 1916, Moorland Papers, MSRC/HU.

7. Yergan to Moorland, 23 February 1917, Moorland Papers, MSRC/HU. Yergan erred in inscribing Lloyd's middle initial as "A."

8. Moorland to Yergan, 14 March 1917, Moorland Papers, MSRC/HU. The saga of American Negro missionaries in East Africa during World War One is treated in Rodney Hugh Orr's "African American Missionaries to East Africa, 1900–1926: A Study of the Ethnic Reconnection of the Gospel," Ph.D. dissertation (History), Edinburgh University, 1998.

9. Yergan to Dr. Sanders, Dar es Salaam, British East Africa, 17 March 1917.

10. Caption beneath photo titled, "Our Army Secretaries in Africa," *Association Men* 43:3 (November 1917): 213A.

11. Yergan to Moorland, 18 September 1917, Moorland Papers, MSRC/HU.

12. Herbert Stuart, "Colonel Newcome in Dar es Salaam, *The Young Men of India* 29:1 (January 1918): 29. A *banda* is a tent.

13. "The Men of Me," n.d., YMCA pamphlet, YMCA Bowne Historical Library, now in YMCA Archives.

14. Stuart, "Colonel Newcome," 29.

15. Vernon Nash, "The Y.M.C.A. in East Africa in 1917," *The Young Men of India* 29:6 (June 1918): 355.

16. Yergan to Moorland, 8 March 1917, Moorland Papers, MSRC/HU.

17. J. E. Moorland, "The Y.M.C.A. and the War," *Crisis* 40:2 (December 1917): 68.

18. Max Yergan, "A Y.M.C.A. Secretary in Africa," *Southern Workman* 48 (August 1918): 401–3.

19. Kenneth James King, *Pan Africanism and Education* (New York and London: Oxford University Press, 1971), 59, footnote 3. Thanks to David Carmichael, YMCA of the USA Archives, for providing copies of the World War One card files of Ballou and Lloyd. Ballou, Lloyd, and Yergan are pictured with Webster in *Association Men* 43:3 (November 1917): 213A. A copy of this photo was provided by the YMCA of the USA archives. Reprinted with permission, Kautz Family YMCA Archives, University of Minnesota Libraries. A separate image of Ballou (misidentified as "Hallon") appeared in *Young Men of India* 29 (November 1918) sans Pritchett. A death notice was run in *Young Men of India* 29 (November 1918). Memorials also appeared in *Summary of World*

33‒

War Work of the YMCA (N.p.: Young Men's Christian Association, National War Work Council, ca. 1920). See "Honor Roll," Frederick D. Ballou, 229, and Robert S. Pritchett, 232.

20. Report of the International Committee, YMCA, to the 40th Annual International Convention, Detroit, 19‒23 November 1919, Part 2, Work of National War Work Councils, 132, Moorland File, Box 126-66, folder 1272, Manuscript Division, MSRC/HU.

21. Moorland, "The YMCA and the War," *Crisis* 15:2 (1917): 68.

22. From Torrey B. Stearns, "Max Yergan: Missionary to His Own People," *Christian Herald* (n.d.), courtesy of Ruth Hartson, YMCA International Division. The line, "Dar es Salaam had become one of the world's most cosmopolitan cities," appears to have been lifted from Webster. See his "Wide Open Africa," *Association Men* 43:6 (February 1918): 432.

23. K. J. Saunders to A. K. Yapp (cc Edward Clark Carter, Yergan, and Mott), 1 August 1919, YMCA of the USA Archives.

24. D. H. Anthony, "Oswin Boys Bull and the Emergence of Southern African 'Nonwhite' YMCA Work." Unpublished manuscript.

25. Bull to Mott, 23 July 1919, Max Yergan File, YMCA of the USA Archives.

26. Saunders to Yapp, 1 August 1919, Yergan File, YMCA of the USA Archives.

27. Kenneth J. Saunders, London, to Edward Clark Carter, Paris, 1 August 1919.

28. Carter to Jenkins, 8 August 1919.

29. Carter to C. V. Hibbard, 8 August 1919.

30. Statement of Returning Secretary for Registration. YMCA of the USA Archives.

31. E. C. Jenkins to Yergan, 16 September 1919.

32. J. E. K. Aggrey to Oswin B. Bull, 19 June 1921. Secretary's Record, YMCA Archives.

33. Aggrey to Bull, 19 June 1921.

34. Yergan to John W. Davis, 16 and 29 November 1920, John W. Davis Papers, West Virginia State College Archives, Institute, West Virginia.

35. Davis to Yergan, 3 December; Yergan to Davis, 8 December; Davis to Yergan, 13 December; Yergan to Davis, 21 December; Davis to Yergan, 23 December; Davis to Yergan, 28 December; Davis to Yergan, 31 December 1920, John W. Davis Papers, West Virginia State College Archives (JWDP/WVSCA).

36. Yergan to Davis, 10 January and 5 February 1921 (JWDP/WVSCA).

37. Bull to Mott, 18 February 1921, Yergan file, YMCA. A copy later reached Dr. Du Bois. W. E. B. Du Bois Papers, reel 9.

38. Bull to Mott, 18 February 1921.

39. On Jones the best source remains Kenneth James King, *Pan-Africanism and Education: Africa and the Southern States of America* (Oxford: Clarendon

Press, 1971). King held that Jones, Loram, and J. H. Oldham of the International Missionary Council became triumvirs on the subject of interwar-era African education.

40. *Education in Africa: A Study of West, South, and Equatorial Africa by the African Education Commission, under the Auspices of the Phelps-Stokes Fund and Foreign Mission Societies of North America and Europe: Report Prepared by Thomas Jesse Jones, Chairman of the Commission* (New York: Phelps-Stokes Fund, ca. 1922).

41. Bull to Mott, 18 February, Yergan file, YMCA.

42. Aggrey to Bull, 30 June 1921, Yergan file, YMCA.

43. Edwin W. Smith, *Aggrey of Africa: A Study in Black and White* (London: Student Christian Movement, 1929), chapter 11, "South Africa," 166.

44. Yergan to Moton, Yergan to M. W. Johnson, Yergan to J. W. Dillard, 29 March 1921; M. W. Johnson to Du Bois, 23 May 1921; J. W. D. to Yergan, 31 March 1921, Du Bois Papers, reel 9.

45. Yergan to Davis, 29 March 1921, JWDP/WVSCA.

46. Yergan to Davis, 29 March 1921, JWDP/WVSCA. This was the subsequent written communication of the same date.

47. Davis to Yergan, 31 March 1921, JWDP/WVSCA.

48. Davis to Yergan, 31 March 1921, JWDP/WVSCA. A copy of this letter also made its way to Du Bois.

49. L. G. Jordan to Yergan, 4 April (replying to Yergan to Jordan, 2 April); A. A. Graham (Lott Carey Baptist Foreign Mission Convention) to Yergan, 5 April; M. W. Johnson to Yergan, 20 April; Yergan to F. de Frantz, 21 April 1921; copies in Du Bois Papers, reel 9. Yergan to J. J. Rho[a]des, 22 April 1921, Tuskegee University Archives, General Correspondence, Box 71, File 477.

50. Du Bois to Yergan, 18 May; Du Bois to J. W. Dillard, 19 May; Yergan to Du Bois (handwritten), 23 May; Mordecai W. Johnson to Du Bois, 23 May; Du Bois to Rev L. Fenninger, Hampton Institute, 26 May 1921, Du Bois Papers, reel 9. A rare dissenting voice on Jones was John Hope. Hope to Du Bois, 1 June 1921.

51. Yergan to Moton, 2 September; Moton to Yergan, 15 September, Yergan to Moton, 21 September 1921, Tuskegee University Archives and Max Yergan file, YMCA.

52. N. B. Young, Florida A & M, to Du Bois, and Lyman Ward, principal, Southern Industrial Institute, to Du Bois, 30 September; James E. Shepard, National Training School, to Du Bois, 1 November 1921, Du Bois Papers, reel 9.

NOTES TO CHAPTER 3

1. Xhosa, "people with a hole" or "pierced people." Noni Jabavu, *Drawn in Colour* (New York: St. Martin's Press, 1960), 130.

-52

2. Zulu, "believers," used of converts. Albert Luthuli, *Let My People Go* (New York: McGraw Hill, 1962).

3. Gilbert Anthony Williams, *The Christian Recorder, Newspaper of the African Methodist Episcopal Church: History of a Forum for Ideas, 1854–1902* (Jefferson, N.C., and London: McFarland, 1996), 81–102; James T. Campbell, *Songs of Zion: The African Methodist Episcopal Church in the United States and South Africa* (New York and Oxford: Oxford University Press, 1995); J. Mutero Chirenje, *Ethiopianism and Afro-Americans in Southern Africa, 1883–1916* (Baton Rouge and London: Louisiana State University Press, 1987), passim; Bengt Sundkler, *Bantu Prophets in South Africa* (Oxford, 1948); Josephus R. Coan, "The Expansion of the Missions of the African Methodist Episcopal Church in South Africa, 1896–1908," Ph.D. dissertation, Hartford Seminary, 1961.

4. Campbell, *Songs of Zion*; Chirenje, *Ethiopianism and Afro-Americans*, 75–76; Carol Ann Page, "Black Americans in White South Africa: Church and State Reaction to the AME Church in Cape Colony and Transvaal, 1896–1910," Ph.D. dissertation, History, Edinburgh University, 1978.

5. Sundkler, *Bantu Prophets in South Africa,* chapter 2, "The Rise of the Independent Church Movement"; Edwin S. Redkey, *Black Exodus: Nationalist and Back-to-Africa Movements, 1890–1910* (New Haven, Conn.: Yale University Press, 1969) and *Respect Black: The Writings and Speeches of Henry M. Turner* (New York: Arno, 1971); Chirenje, *Ethiopianism and Afro-Americans*, 62–64.

6. Report, Charles Loram Papers, Yale.

7. A Congregationalist, Yergan had ties to both denominations. Black YMCA pioneer W. A. Hunton was converted by AME cleric J. Albert Johnson, posted to South Africa in 1910. Yergan's grandfather Frederick had been a Baptist elder and trustee. Shaw University emerged out of First Baptist Church (Colored) and was funded by the American Baptist Home Mission Society. In April 1921 he had met with National Baptist Convention Foreign Mission corresponding secretary L. G. Jordan on discrimination against American Negroes. The same year Yergan had been in touch with AME Bishop W. T. Vernon, who was posted to South Africa from 1920 to 1924 and would become a Yergan familiar. Black Y staff were part of each church.

8. Julia C. Wells, *We Now Demand! The History of Women's Resistance to Pass Laws in South Africa* (Johannesburg: Witwatersrand University Press, 1993), 53–54. For the 1913 antecedent of this threat see chapter 1, "The Bloemfontein Milieu," 15–31.

9. F. G. Bridgman to E. W. Riggs, 9 January 1922, American Board of Commissioners for Foreign Missions (ABCFM) Papers, Box 805, Houghton Library, Harvard University.

10. Bridgman to Riggs, 14 March 1922. ABCFM Collection, Box 805, Houghton Library, Harvard.

11. "Confidential Memorandum on the Attitude of South African Political Parties towards the Native Population," appended to Report Letter for year ending 31 December 1922, Max Yergan, Cape Town, S. A. Moorland Papers, Moorland-Spingarn Research Center, Howard University (MSRC/HU). Yergan closed: "I hand you this full statement of what I believe to be the beliefs desires and practices characterizing European life in South Africa in the midst of which millions of Natives have got to make their future. You cannot think of the Native apart from the entire life of the country. What touches one touches all." This presages the slogan of the later Congress of South African Trade Unions (COSATU), founded 1955: "An injury to one is an injury to all."

12. Fraser to Mott, 18 February 1897, 3–4. World Student Christian Federation (WSCF) Collection, MS 46, John R. Mott Papers, Box 254, Folder 2129, Mott Room, Divinity School Library, Manuscripts and Archives, Yale University (DSLMA/YU).

13. Fraser to Mott, 1 February 1897, WSCF Collection, MS 46, John R. Mott Papers, Box 254, Folder 2129, Mott Room, DSLMA/YU.

14. "Mr John R. Mott to Visit South Africa," *Rand Young Men's Journal (RYMJ)* 3:1 (March 1906): 9; "Mr. John R. Mott, M.A. Work in South Africa Conference This Month," *RYMJ* 3:3 (May 1906): 15.

15. Mott, Amanzimtoti, Natal, 6 June 1906, John R. Mott Papers, MS Collection #45, Box 117, Folder 1940, "Reports, Letters, Diaries, Visit to South Africa, 1906," Mott Room, DSLMA/YU.

16. Mott, letter written on *S.S. Highland Mary,* crossing the South Atlantic, 4 July 1906, Mott Papers, Manuscript Collection 45, Box 117, Folder 1940, Mott Room, DSLMA/YU.

17. Mott, 4 July 1906.

18. Yergan to Mott, 18 August 1922, cited in Basil Mathews, *John R. Mott, World Citizen* (New York and London: Harper and Brothers, 1934), 1775.

19. Bull to Mott, Stellenbosch, C[ape].C[olony]., 6.2.08 (6 February 1908), WSCF Collection, MS #46, Box 253, Folder 2119, "Correspondence Bull to Mott, 1906–1909," Mott Room, DSLMA/YU.

20. "Max Yergan, National Secretary for Africa," *Intercollegian* 39:5 (February 1922): 4.

21. "News from Max Yergan," Number 1, February 1922, filed 1 June 1929, Box C, YMCA Historical Library.

22. *A.M.E. Church Review* 39:1 (April 1922).

23. "The Negro in Africa: No Answer but God," *Association Men* 47:12 (August 1922): 561.

24. Max Yergan, "On the YMCA in North America," *Manhood* 3:7 (November 1922): 151–57.

25. "A Letter from Max Yergan, Alice, Cape Province, South Africa, 7 April, 1924," *Howard University Record* 18 (1923–24): 537.

26. Yergan to Henriod, 30 August 1923, File Max Yergan 1922–24, Box 43-45, WSCF Archives, Geneva.

27. "Visit of Max Yergan to Natal University College," *Universitas* 3:4 (December 1923).

28. "Some Impressions of a Conference Held at Rustoord, Somerset Strand," *Universitas* 3:4 (December 1923): 24–26.

29. Founded in 1868 as the Normal School, Morija, as it is now known, was also called Thabeng School (Sesotho: "on the mountain") during the times when Yergan visited. After 1948 it became Basutoland Training College. Long the preeminent publisher of Sesotho literature, Morija is the site of a museum, archive, and annual festival. Stephen Gill, Curator, Morija Museum and Archives to Anthony, 23 April 2003.

30. "Our Visitors," *Leselinyana la Lesotho*, 30 November 1923, 1–2. Original in Sesotho. Translated by Thabo M. Leanya. Typed by Mrs. Tiisetso Pitso and Mrs. 'Mamatong Massa. Provided by Stephen J. Gill, Morija Museum and Archives. I appreciate the hours that went into this. Contact made through Bob Edgar.

31. L. M. Moletsane, "To the Members of the Progressive Association of Lesotho" (Morija Branch), *Leselinyana*, 30 November 1923, 2. Sesotho original translated by T. M. Leanya; sent by Stephen Gill, Curator, Morija Museum and Archives.

32. L. M. Moletsane, "Baeti ba Rona (Our Visitors) Part III)," *Leselinyana*, 7 December 1923, 2. Sesotho original. T. M. Leanya, translator. Text provided by Stephen Gill, Morija Museum and Archives, Lesotho.

33. During the early twentieth century, an African-American sojourner named Conrad Rideout lived in Basutoland. He spent at least part of 1903 there. See J. Mutero Chirenje, *Ethiopianism and Afro-Americans in Southern Africa, 1883–1916* (Baton Rouge and London: Louisiana State University Press, 1982), chapter 4, "Growth of the AME Church, the Witch Hunt, and Its Aftermath," 99.

34. Sotho-Tswana speakers would have been familiar with servile cultural institutions resembling slavery. See Thomas Tlou, "Servility and Political Control: Botlhanka among the BaTawana of Northwestern Botswana, ca. 1750–1906," in Suzanne Miers and Igor Kopytoff, eds., *Slavery in Africa: Historical and Anthropological Perspectives* (Madison: University of Wisconsin Press, 1977), 367–414.

35. On this see Daniel P. Kunene, *Heroic Poetry of the Basotho* (Oxford: Clarendon Press, 1971), and M. Damane and Peter Sanders, *Lithoko: Sotho Praise Poems* (Oxford: Clarendon Press, 1974).

36. Yergan to Henriod, 10 January 1924, WSCF Collection, Geneva.

37. Bull to E. C. Jenkins, 20 February 1924, YMCA Archives.

38. Yergan, "The Native Students of South Africa and Their Problems," *Student World* 62 (April 1923): 62–67.

39. The High Leigh Conference on African Education held 8–13 September 1924, called by Dr J. H. Oldham, laid the foundation for the 1926 Le Zoute Conference and the establishment of the International Institute of African Languages and Cultures. Edwin William Smith, *Aggrey of Africa: A Study in Black and White* (London: Student Christian Movement, 1929), 231.

40. Bull to Jenkins, 20 February 1924, WSCF MS Collection #46, Box 253, Folder 2120, Correspondence Mott-Bull, 1910–1925, Mott Room, DSLMA/YU.

41. *Imvo Zabantzundu,* 25 March, 8 April, and 15 April 1924.

42. Bull to Mott, 29 April 1924, WSCF MS Collection #46, Box 253 Folder 2120, Mott Room, DSLMA/YU.

43. Yergan to Kerr, 6 September 1924, PR4090/3, Alexander Kerr Papers, Cory Library for Historical Research, Rhodes University, Grahamstown.

44. Smith, *Aggrey of Africa,* 231.

45. E. W. Smith, *The Christian Mission in Africa: A Study Based on the Work of the International Conference at Le Zoute, Belgium, September 14th to 21st, 1926* (London: 1926).

46. Yergan to Moorland, 1 June 1925, MSRC/HU.

47. Yergan to Moorland, 1 June 1925, MSRC/HU.

48. Yergan to Moorland, 1 June 1925, MSRC/HU.

49. News Letter, Student Christian Association (Native Department), No. 32, March 1926, Moorland Papers, MSRC/HU. In this newsletter, compiled by Yergan, the teachers referred to by their surnames were Zachariah Keodirelang Matthews, Albert (later Chief) John Lut[h]uli, Roseberry Tandwefika Bokwe, R. Guma, and a Mr. Mbamba.

50. Smith, *The Christian Mission in Africa,* 26, 28. Also attending were J. H. Oldham, Anson Phelps Stokes, Thomas Jesse Jones, John Dube, ANC leader Z. R. Mahabane, and John Hope. Author Smith praised Yergan for the "sincerity and restraint of his contributions." Phelps Stokes made an appraisal of his own. It appears in the Max Yergan file, n.d., filed 5 January 1927, YMCA Historical Library.

51. "Race Relations in South Africa," *Tuskegee Messenger,* 30 October 1926, 8.

52. Yergan received a Phelps Stokes grant on November 10, was interviewed at Rockefeller on October 21 and November 11, and was the subject of news reports about the aid by year's end. Anson Phelps Stokes to George Edmund Haynes, 10 November 1927, Anson Phelps Stokes Papers, Group 299, Series I, Box 24, folder 382, Sterling Memorial Library, Yale. *Imvo Zabantsundu,* 6 December 1927; "Rockefeller Gives $25,000 for Africans," *New York Times,* 7 December 1927, 20:5; "*Ama £5000 ku Nokoleji!*" (Translated as "General

Notes: Another Fort Hare Gift.") *Imvo Zabantsundu,* 13 December 1927; "Max Yergan Returns to African Veldt with Rockefeller Gift," *Tuskegee Messenger,* 14–29 January 1928; "What Others Say: The YMCA in Africa," *Southern Workman,* March 1928.

53. "Race Issue Is Subject of Northfield Talk," *New York Times,* 14 July 1927.

54. Ovington to William Jay Schieffelin, 7 December 1927, NAACP Papers, Container 8, Library of Congress.

55. "Max Yergan," in Ralph W. Bullock, *In Spite of Handicaps* (New York: Associated Press, 1927); "Max Yergan," in Mary White Ovington, *Portraits in Color* (New York: Viking, 1927).

56. To Yergan, 14 December 1927, WSCF Archives, Geneva, Switzerland.

57. "The Strength and Weakness of the Missionary Movement in Africa," in Gordon Poteat, ed., *Students and the Future of Christian Missions: Report of the Tenth Quadrennial Convention of the Student Volunteer Movement for Foreign Missions, Detroit, Michigan, December 28, 1927 to January 1, 1928* (New York: Student Volunteer Movement for Foreign Missions, 1928), 38.

58. "Strength and Weakness," 38.

59. "Talks with Boys about Our Attitude toward the Boys of Other Races," *World's Youth* 4:1 (January 1928): 9.

60. "Talks with Boys," 9.

61. "Talks with Boys," 9.

62. "Talks with Boys," 11.

63. Mordecai Johnson to Yergan, 10 February 1927; Yergan to Moorland, 14 February 1927; J. E. Moorland Papers, MSRC/HU, Box 126-65, file 1243— YMCA Max Yergan Correspondence—1928-29. "Northeastern at Work in Africa," *Northeastern News* (Northeastern University), Yergan File, YMCA Historical Library.

64. Thamae to Yergan, 15 March 1928, Max Yergan Papers, MSRC/HU.

65. Stephen Gish, *Alfred B. Xuma: African, American, South African* (New York: New York University Press, 2000), 13.

66. Xuma to Yergan, 4 June 1928, Max Yergan Papers, MSRC/HU.

67. Xuma to Yergan, 7 June 1928. Arthur later authored the influential text *Life on the Negro Frontier* (New York: Association Press, 1944).

68. Xuma to Yergan, 27 July 1928, A. B. Yuma Papers, Hoover Institution.

69. Yergan to Ovington, 26 June 1928, NAACP Papers, I, container 88, Library of Congress.

70. Thomas Jesse Jones to Anson Phelps Stokes, 26 June 1927, Phelps Stokes Papers, Yale.

71. Yergan, "Impressions of the Port Elizabeth Conference," *Universitas* 8:8 (August 1928).

72. Ovington to Yergan, 24 October 1928, NAACP Papers, Library of Congress.

NOTES TO CHAPTER 4

1. "Max Yergan of Africa Is Guest of the Cedar Y," *Cleveland Red Triangle,* 9 January 1928.

2. *Cleveland Red Triangle.*

3. "Northeastern at Work in South Africa: Entire University Sponsors Max Yergan's Educational Project," *Northeastern News,* n.d. (ca. March–April 1928). Copy courtesy of Ruth Hartson, International Division, YMCA.

4. "Max Yergan Spoke on 'The New Africa' at N.U. Mass Meeting," *Northeastern News,* n.d.

5. "Recent Cablegram Emphasizes Needs," *Northeastern News,* n.d.

6. "American Institutions Support Work in Far Distant Lands," *Northeastern News,* n.d.

7. John N. Thomas, *The Institute of Pacific Relations: Asian Scholars and American Politics* (Seattle and London, University of Washington Press, 1974), 3.

8. Yergan, "Report for the Year 1928."

9. Yergan to Ovington, 26 June 1928, NAACP Papers, Container 88, Library of Congress. The conference yielded a book, *The Realignment of Native Life on a Christian Basis: The Seventh General Missionary Conference of South Africa Held at Lovedale, June 26–29, 1928.* In addition to Yergan and Kadalie, Charlotte Maxeke made a noteworthy contribution on African women.

10. On Jimmy la Guma see Alex la Guma, *Jimmy la Guma: A Biography,* ed. Mohamed Adhikari (Cape Town: Friends of the South African Library, 1997).

11. *The Communist International, 1919–1943: Documents,* vol. 2, *1923–1928,* selected and edited by Jane Degras (London, New York, and Toronto: Oxford University Press, 1960), 97.

12. Degras, ed., *Communist International,* 2:164.

13. See Hyman Kublin, *Asian Revolutionary: The Life of Katayama Sen* (Princeton, N.J.: Princeton University Press, 1964).

14. "Extracts from the Theses on the Revolutionary Movement in Colonial and Semi-Colonial Countries Adopted by the Sixth Comintern Congress, IV: The Immediate Tasks of the Communists," in Degras, ed., *The Communist International,* 2:546–47.

15. "Extracts From the Theses on the Revolutionary Movement," in Degras, ed., *The Communist International,* 2:546–47.

16. Henri-Louis Henriod to Yergan, 7 May 1928, Box 84, WSCF Archives, Geneva.

17. Alexander Kerr, "Visit of Max Yergan, M.A., to India," n.d. (ca. 1928). Typescript, copy courtesy of Ruth Hartson, YMCA International Division.

18. It was thoroughly up to date, citing Parker Moon's 1926 *Imperialism and World Politics,* Leonard Woolf's 1919 *Empire and Commerce in Africa,* J. A. I. Agar-Hamilton's 1928 *Native Policy of the Voortrekkers,* Lord Frederick

Lugard's 1922 *Dual Mandate,* Raymond Buell's 1927 *Native Problem in Africa,* W. M. MacMillan's 1927 *Cape Colour Question* and E. H. Brookes's 1924 *Native Policy in South Africa.*

19. 22–23.

20. 31–32.

21. 50.

22. William J. Schieffelin to F. P. Keppel, 7 March 1929, notes courtesy R. Hunt Davis Jr.

23. Yergan to "Dear Francis" (Miller), 26 March 1929, YMCA Student Division Papers, Correspondence, Box 13, Folder 191, D. R. Porter to Max Yergan, WSCF Collection, Mott Room, Divinity School Library, Yale University.

24. Yergan to Porter, 5 April 1929, YMCA Student Division Papers, Correspondence, Box 13, Folder 191, D. R. Porter to Max Yergan. WSCF Collection, John Mott Room, Divinity School Library, Yale.

25. Yergan to Porter, 5 April 1929.

26. Porter to "Dear Max," 24 May 1929, Yergan file, YMCA

27. "News from Max Yergan, No. 2," 15 April 1929, YMCA Archives, courtesy Ruth Hartson.

28. 1/ALC, volume 10/4, file 18/10/2, Cape Archives Depot, Republic of South Africa (RSA), 3 pages (correspondence between the principal of Fort Hare and the magistrate of Alice and a letter from D. H. Ecker to the South African government trade commissioner regarding work carried out in South Africa.

29. Yergan to Henriod, 25 June 1929, Box 123, Max Yergan File, 1928–1929, WSCF Archives, Geneva.

30. Yergan to Porter, 23 July 1920, Box 123, Yergan file, 1928–1929, WSCF Archives, Geneva.

31. Yergan to Ovington, 2 August 1929, Mary White Ovington Collection, Box 2, folder 2-1, Wayne State University Archives of Labor and Urban Affairs, Walter P. Reuther Library, Courtesy of Raymond Boryczka, Research Archivist, Reuther Library, Wayne State University (WSU), Detroit.

32. On this see D. Anthony, "Max Yergan and South Africa: Theological Perspectives on Race," *Journal of Religion in Africa* 34:3 (September 2004): 235–65.

33. "Whites Pay Africans Liquor Wages," *Afro-American,* 12 October 1929.

34. Jan Christian Smuts, "African Settlement," in *Africa and Some World Problems* (Oxford: 1930), 47–48.

35. "African Settlement," 74–75.

36. "African Settlement," 76–77.

37. "African Settlement," 77–78.

38. "African Settlement," 91–93.

39. Yergan to Henriod, 11 November 1929, Box 123, File Max Yergan, 1928–1929, WSCF Archives, Geneva.

40. Born in Ladysmith, Natal, in 1910, but raised in Cape Town, the son of a

Methodist minister, M'Timkulu had attended Lovedale in Alice and Adams College in Natal, where he was taught and mentored by Albert Luthuli. M'Timkulu earned two degrees at Fort Hare, a 1927 A.B., and an M.A. that he would complete slightly later, in the 1930s.

41. Don M'Timkulu telephone interview, 29 March 1994.

42. Don M'Timkulu telephone interview.

43. This group came to include pioneer leader T. William Thibedi—the chief CPSA African functionary from 1921 to 1926—and was later joined by Albert Nzula, John B. Marks, Edwin Mofutsanyana, J. Sepeng, P. G. Moloinjane, S. M. Kotu, Gana Makabeni, B. Molobi, O. Motuba, W. Nchie, J. Ngedlane, Johannes Nkosi, W. Tayi, and Moses Kotane. Among African women the most well-known organizers were Josie Mpama (Palmer) and Hilda Msichane.

44. Teachers in these schools included such activists as Edward and Winifred Roux, E. S. "Solly" Sachs, Charles Baker, Bennie Sachs, Wilhelmina Taylor, Eva Green, and other volunteers, both Black and White.

45. E. Roux, *Sidney Bunting: A Political Biography* (Cape Town: African Bookman, 1944), 71–72.

46. B. Bunting, *Moses Kotane, South African Revolutionary: A Political Biography* (London: Inkululeko Publications, 1975).

47. Helmut Gruber, *Soviet Russia Masters the Comintern: International Communism in the Era of Stalin's Ascendancy* (New York: Doubleday Anchor Books, 1974), 244–46. On Roy see his *Memoirs* (Bombay: Allied Publishers, 1964) and John Patrick Haithcox, *Communism and Nationalism in India: M. N. Roy and Comintern Policy, 1920–1939* (Princeton, N.J.: Princeton University Press, 1971), as well as Roy's *Selected Works*. Roy's *Memoirs* include a terse but tantalizing tidbit about meeting "Negro" Comintern delegates from North America and South Africa in Moscow during the summer of 1920, attending the Second World Congress (345). Fisk-educated Katayama Sen is profiled in Hyman Kublin, *Asian Revolutionary: The Life of Katayama Sen* (Princeton, N.J.: Princeton University Press, 1964). In his autobiography former Comintern rep Claude McKay credits Katayama with contributing to the formulation of the "Negro Question." See McKay, *A Long Way from Home* (New York, 1937; reprinted Arno and the New York Times, 1969), 164–66. Though still not fully apparent, it is evident that Yergan knew such Black South African Comintern functionaries as Edwin Mofutsanyana, and probably Jimmy La Guma and John Gomas as well. His relationship with Edward Roux is uncertain, yet likely in view of Roux's activity in Fort Hare's environs. Finally, he may have also learned a lot through his relationship with James W. Ford, who was intimately involved in both the Negro and Native questions amid the pivotal 1928 Moscow debates and thereafter. Brief reference to the Negro Question appears in the *Report of the Fourth Congress of the R.I.L.U.* (Red International of Labor Unions) (London: Minority Movement, July 1928), 187. The Fourth

Congress instructs the Executive Bureau to call together the representatives of the Negro workers for carrying into effect the policy laid down in regard to the question of organizing Negro workers in the United States and in Africa.

48. George E. Haynes, "Record of Interview with: 10 Ministers and Capetown YMCA Sec. in Conference 3–5 p.m. May 6, 1930," George Edmund Haynes Papers, Sterling Library, Yale University. Yergan arranged this.

49. Haynes, "Record of Interview."

50. Haynes, "Record of Interview."

51. Haynes, "Record of Interview."

52. East London *Daily Dispatch*, 28 June 1930.

53. The best single source on this is the published proceedings, *Christian Students and Modern South Africa: A Report of the Bantu-European Student Christian Conference, Fort Hare, June 27th–July 3rd, 1930* (Fort Hare: Student Christian Association, 1930). For a descriptive day-to-day survey, see the *South African Outlook*, 1 August 1930, 146–63.

54. Howard Pim, *Introduction to Bantu Economics: Paper Prepared for Conference of European and Bantu Christian Associations Held at Fort Hare, 27th June to 3rd July, 1930* (Lovedale: 1930), 12.

55. Pim, *Introduction to Bantu Economics*, 15.

56. This fact was not ignored by *Die Burger*.

57. E. H. Brookes, "The Fort Hare Conference and Its Meaning," *Student World*, 1930, 390.

58. Telephone interview, Professor Donald G. S. M'Timkulu, Tuesday, 29 March 1994.

59. Helen R. Bryan, "Max Yergan, Uplifter of South Africa," *Crisis* (December 1932): 375.

60. *Die Burger*, 21 July 1930.

61. M'Timkulu interview, 29 March 1994.

62. M'Timkulu interview, 29 March 1994.

63. Alexander Kerr, *Fort Hare, 1915–48: The Evolution of an African College* (London: C. Hurst, 1968), 162.

64. Thomas Jesse Jones to Anson Phelps Stokes, 29 August 1930, copy provided by H. Davis.

65. Appleget to Yergan, 26 September 1930, Rockefeller Foundation Collection, RG2 1930 Series 487: South Africa, Box 45, Folder 37, Rockefeller Archive Center (RAC).

66. Ridgely Torrence, *The Story of John Hope* (New York: Macmillan, 1948), 329.

67. Yergan to "My dear dear Friends" (Mr. and Mrs. J. E. Moorland), 27 October 1931, Moorland Papers, Moorland-Spingarn Research Center, Howard University.

68. Yergan to "My dear dear Friends."

69. Ruth Rouse, *The World's Student Christian Federation* (London: SCM Press, 1947), 116.

70. Francis Pickens Miller, *Man from the Valley: Memoirs of a Twentieth-Century Virginian* (Chapel Hill: University of North Carolina Press, l969), 67.

71. On S. K. Datta's relationship to the Indian YMCA see H. A. Popley, *K. T. Paul, Christian Leader* (Calcutta: YMCA Publishing House, 1938), passim. Datta edited the Indian YMCA periodical *Young Men of India* and was the author of such books as *The Desire of India* (London: 1908) and *Asiatic Asia* (London: 1932). Paul himself requested that Yergan spend five to six weeks visiting the main YMCA centers in Madras, Calcutta, Delhi, Lahore, and Bombay. Henri-Louis Henriod to Yergan, 7 May 1928, Box 84, WSCF Archives. Yergan first mentions Rena Datta in Yergan to F. P. Miller, WSCF Archives, Geneva.

72. Yergan, *Secretary's Record,* YMCA, YMCA Bowne Historical Library; Yergan to Phelps Stokes, 25 April 1931, Anson Phelps Stokes Papers, Box 98, Folder 1592, Correspondence, Manuscripts and Archives, Sterling Memorial Library, Yale.

73. Cable, Miller to Martin and 'T Hooft, 28 April 1931, Miller Collection, Alderman Library.

74. Phelps Stokes to Yergan, 29 April 1931, Phelps Stokes Papers, Box 98, Folder 1592, Sterling Library, Yale University.

75. Phelps Stokes to Yergan, 29 April 1931, Phelps Stokes Papers, Box 98, Folder 1592, Sterling Library, Yale University.

76. Appleget to Yergan, 20 April 1931, Rockefeller Foundation Collection, RGS, 1931, Series 487, Yergan, Subseries, "South Africa: Yergan, Max," Box 60, Folder 495, Rockefeller Archive Center (RAC).

77. Appleget to Dr. Anson Phelps Stokes, 8 May 1931, Rockefeller Foundation Archives, RG2, General Correspondence 1931, Series 487, Yergan, Subseries, "South Africa: Yergan, Max." Box 60, Folder 495, RAC.

78. A. Lyon, J. M. Speer, and F. W. Ramsey to Phelps Stokes, 8 May 1931, Phelps Stokes Papers, Box 98, Folder 1592, Sterling Memorial Library, Yale University.

79. Phelps Stokes to Appleget, 11 May 1931, Rockefeller Foundation Archives, RG2, General Correspondence, 1931, Series 487, Yergan, Subseries, "South Africa: Yergan, Max," Box 60, Folder 495, RAC.

80. A. W. Packard, "Memorandum: Y.M.C.A. Luncheon in Honor of Mr. Colton and Mr Yergan," 20 May 1931, Rockefeller Family Archives, RG2 (OMR) Series; Welfare-Youth Box 35 Folder, YMCA-National Committee, Max Yergan Work in Africa, RAC.

81. Yergan to Saunders, April 1932, WSCF Papers, Geneva.

82. Yergan, Alice, to Hon. Patrick Duncan, Trustee, Carnegie Corporation, S.A., 14 June 1932. I thank Prof. R. Hunt Davis Jr. for sharing his notes from Carnegie Corporation Archives.

83. C. T. Loram to F. P. Keppel, 1 August 1932, from C.C. notes provided by R. Hunt Davis Jr.

84. Phelps Stokes to Yergan, Phelps Stokes Papers, Sterling Library, Yale University.

85. Stokes, Durban, to Jesse Jones, 6 September 1932, Phelps Stokes Papers, I, Box 70, Folder 1170, Sterling Library, Yale University.

86. Yergan to Henson, 1 November 1932, Box 67, File South Africa Reports, YMCA Historical Library; Yergan to Porter, 1 November, 1932, YMCA Student Division Papers, Correspondence, Box 13, Folder 191, WSCF Collection, John R. Mott Room, Divinity School Library, Yale University.

87. Porter to Yergan, 6 September 1932. YMCA Student Division Papers, Correspondence, Box 13, Folder 191, D. R. Porter to Max Yergan, WSCF Collection, Divinity School Library, Yale University.

88. Yergan to Porter, 15 November 1932, YMCA Student Division Papers, Box 13, Folder 191, Correspondence, D. R. Porter to Max Yergan, WSCF Collection, John R. Mott Room, Divinity School Library, Yale University.

89. Yergan to Porter, 15 November 1932.

90. Derricotte to Yergan, 24 July 1929, WSCF Student Division Papers, Correspondence, Box 13, Folder 191, D. R. Porter to Max Yergan, Divinity School Library, Yale University.

91. Derricotte to Yergan, 24 July 1929.

92. In Marion Cuthbert, *Juliette Derricotte* (New York: Woman's Press, 1936).

93. Du Bois to the Members of the Spingarn Medal Committee, 27 January 1933, NAACP Administrative File, Subject File Awards, Spingarn Medal, 1933 NAACP Papers, Box C-212, MS Division, Library of Congress.

94. "Max Yergan, Y.M.C.A. Worker in Africa, Gets Spingarn Medal," Press Release, NAACP Administrative File, Subject File, Awards, Spingarn Medal, 1933, NAACP Papers, Box C-212, Library of Congress.

95. "Max Yergan," *Pittsburgh Courier,* 1 April, 1933; "Sees Hope for South Africa," *Boston Chronicle,* 15 April 1933; "Max Yergan Speaks at Harlem YMCA," *New York Age,* 22 April 1933; "Max Yergan Tells Crowd of Work Among Africans," *Chicago Defender,* 23 April 1933; E. T. Rouzeau, "Teaching of Christianity Only Part of Job Says Yergan, 'Y' Missionary," *New York Amsterdam News,* 3 May 1933.

96. "Race Problems Acute in South Africa, Say Max Yergan and O. B. Bull, Interracial Leaders There," FCC News Release, New York City, 26 May 1933, AD 843/B97.9.2. South African Institute of Race Relations (SAIRR).

97. Tobias to Claude Barnett, 17 July 1933, Claude Barnett Papers/Associated Negro Press Papers, Chicago Historical Society.

98. C. T. Loram to F. P. Keppel, 6 September 1933, from notes provided by R. Hunt Davis Jr.

99. Yergan to Robert M. Lester, Carnegie Corporation, 12 December 1933, from notes provided by R. Hunt Davis Jr.

100. Loram to R. M. Lester, Carnegie Corporation, 26 January 1934, courtesy of R. Hunt Davis Jr.

101. Telegram, Yergan to Keppel, 22 February 1934, extract from notes of R. Hunt Davis Jr.

102. Patrick Duncan, to F. P. Keppel, 30 April 1934, from notes provided by R. Hunt Davis Jr.

103. C. C. Beasley, "A Negro Leader in South Africa," *Boston Evening Transcript,* 19 May 1934. Copy courtesy Ruth Hartson, YMCA International Division.

104. Keppel to Yergan, New York, 29 May 1934, from notes provided by R. Hunt Davis Jr.

105. Yergan to Keppel, 22 June 1934, from notes provided by R. Hunt Davis Jr.

106. Personal communication, Professor John Hope Franklin to author, 19 January 1987.

107. C. Bundy, *Learning from Robben Island: The Prison Writings of Govan Mbeki* (Athens: Ohio University Press, 1991).

108. Thami Mkhwanazi, "How a Schoolboy's Rage Turned Mbeki toward Marxism," *Weekly Mail* (Johannesburg), 13–19 November 1987.

109. Robert Edgar, interview with Govan Mbeki, August 1990.

110. Edgar interview, 1990.

111. Edgar interview, 1990.

112. Edgar interview, 1990.

113. Russell B. Porter, "Charge Exploiting of African Natives," *New York Times,* 28 August 1928, 25:1. Though Johnson retreated slightly in the face of criticisms by procolonial apologists, one of whom, Belgian M.P. Louis Pierard, was quoted as saying that nobody "except childish Bolsheviki" would advocate withdrawal from the colonies, by and large he stood his ground. Further evidence is his elegiac "Lincoln's Views on Equality Praised: Dr. Johnson Says Leader Assumed All People Deserved Equal Consideration," *New York Times,* 4 February 1929, 26:6. Here Johnson brings to mind Bishop Montgomery Brown's *Communism and Christianism.*

114. Mark Naison, *Communists in Harlem during the Depression* (New York: Grove Press, 1984), passim. For an illuminating profile of Ford see *New York Amsterdam News,* 28 February 1934.

115. See "Communists Name Foster and Ford: 1,200 in Chicago Convention Cheer Old Leader and Negro Running Mate," *New York Times,* 29 May 1932, 2:1; and "Reds Hail Candidate for Vice Presidency: 200 at Coney Island Give

10-Minute Ovation to Negro Nominee of Communists," *New York Times,* 10 July 1932, 11:1.

116. "Bonus Stragglers 'Mopped Up' by Troops: 36 Reds Seized; Grand Jury Inquiry On; Hoover Denounces Attempt at Mob Rule," *New York Times,* 30 July 1932, 1:8.

117. Naison, *Communists in Harlem,* 293. The progression from YMCA to radicalism was not at all unusual. For midthirties examples of YMCA ideological resistance to pro-Sovietism, see, e.g., E. T. Colton, *The XYZ of Communism* (New York: Macmillan, 1931) and his *Four Patterns of Revolution* (New York: Association Press, 1935). B. Russell, J. Dewey, M. Cohen, S. Hook, and S. Eddy, *The Meaning of Marx: A Symposium* (New York: Farrar and Rinehart, 1934).

118. *Ras Makonnen: Pan Africanism from Within, as Recorded and Edited by Kenneth King* (Nairobi, Oxford, and New York: Oxford University Press, 1973), 50.

119. Xuma to Yergan, 4 June 1928; Yergan to Xuma; Xuma to Yergan, 7 June 1928. The letter broaching the marriage question is Xuma to Yergan, 27 July 1928, Max Yergan Papers, Moorland-Spingarn Research Center, Howard University (MSRC/HU).

120. Yergan to Xuma, 10 June 1930, Max Yergan Papers, MSRC/HU.

121. Yergan to Dr. and Mrs. Xuma, 22 February 1932, ABX 32 0222, A. B. Xuma Papers, Box A (1918–1933), University of the Witwatersrand, Johannesburg.

122. Yergan to Xuma, 18 June 1935, ABX 350618 (Race Relations), A. B. Xuma Papers, Box B (1934–1939), University of the Witwatersrand, Johannesburg.

123. Yergan to Xuma, 18 June 1935.

124. Yergan to Xuma, 1 October 1935, ABX 351001a, Box A (1934–1937), A. B. Xuma Papers, Institute of Race Relations Collection, University of the Witwatersrand Library, Johannesburg.

125. Xuma to Yergan, 21 June 1935, Yergan Papers, MSRC/HU.

126. Yergan to Xuma, 22 April 1936, ABX 3604226, A. B. Xuma Papers, Box B (1934–1937), Institute of Race Relations Collection, University of the Witwatersrand Library, Johannesburg.

127. Yergan to Xuma, 7 May 1936, ABX 360507, A. B. Xuma Papers, Box B (1934–1937), Institute of Race Relations Collection, University of the Witwatersrand, Johannesburg.

128. Telephone interview, Phyllis Ntantala Jordan, 20 May 1974. This ethnic attribution may well be apocryphal, as it describes a social type, even a stereotype, symbolizing the perception of a "typical" White female communist sympathizer in interwar-era South Africa (and, to some extent, the United States as well). Neugebauer is actually a Prussian name (often preceded by the courtly *von*); Frieda's sister wed Anglo-Afrikaner G. Lindsay, whose mother claimed

Voortrekker descent. "Three Generations," Rand Daily *Mail,* 29 May 1947, 5. The matriarch gave Du Plessis as her maiden name. Given the deeply rooted anti-Semitism and pervasive stigmatization of interfaith marriages characteristic of this time and place, it is debatable whether such a union would have been tolerated, and, therefore, whether the statement was factually accurate. In fact, Neugebauer was a Gentile.

129. Personal communication, Donald Guy Sidney M'Timkulu, Ph.D., 29 March 1994.

130. Nancy Dick to author, 23 October 1990.

131. Robert Edgar, notes from interview with Mrs. Edgar Thamae, Sea Point, Maseru, Lesotho, 22 May 1985; phone interview, Phyllis Ntantala-Jordan, 20 May 1975, Madison, Wisconsin.

132. It is rather surprising that references to Neugebauer do not appear in Ruby Pagano's unpublished biography of Max Yergan, although Neugebauer's presence may be deduced by reading between the lines. The perception of scandal remained well after Yergan became a noted member of the American Left. Interview, Louise Thompson Patterson, 11 November 1988, Oakland, California.

133. The public awareness that the Yergan marriage was in trouble during their final years at Fort Hare was more or less general. Although this was undoubtedly exacerbated by the political stress placed upon their relationship by life in South Africa, other forces were evident as well. Quarrels were noticed by those with whom they interacted socially.

134. Davis to Yergan, 31 January 1936, National Negro Congress Papers, Correspond., "XYZ," reel 8, Schomburg Library.

135. Yergan to Slack, 6 March 1936, Box 67, File South Africa 1936, YMCA Historical Library.

136. Yergan to Slack, 6 March 1936.

137. Confidential: Bull to Slack, 5 June 1936, YMCA Archives.

138. Yergan, "The Communist Threat in Africa," in Charles Grove Haines, ed., *Africa Today* (Baltimore, Md.: Johns Hopkins University Press, 1955), 263–64.

139. Personal communication, Nancy Dick to Anthony, 23 October 1990.

140. T. Mkhwanazi, "How Mbeki Turned from a Schoolboy's Rage to Marxism," (Johannesburg) *Weekly Mail,* 13–19 November 1987; R. Edgar, Mbeki interview, August 1990; C. Bundy, *Learning from Robben Island* (Athens: Ohio University Press, 1991), introduction, xi–xii.

141. Gilliam, *Paul Robeson, All-American* (Washington, D.C.: New Republic Book Co., 1976), 89.

142. Yergan to Bunche, 29 April 1936. Courtesy of Charles P. Henry.

143. E. Mofutsanyana to Yergan, 1936, Max Yergan Papers, MSRC/HU.

144. Eslanda Goode Robeson, *African Journey* (New York: John Day, 1945),
47.

164

145. "Why Max Yergan Left South Africa," *Imvo Zabantsundu*, 17 April 1937.

146. "Why Max Yergan Left South Africa."

147. *African Heroes and Heroines*, 2d ed. (Washington, D.C.: Associated Publishers, l939, l944), 208.

148. Ralph Bunche, Field Notes in a Visit to South Africa, 1937, Bunche Papers, UCLA Library, Special Collections.

149. Tabata to Anthony, personal communication, Dar es Salaam, Tanzania, 1976.

NOTES TO CHAPTER 5

1. Yergan to Pickett, 1936, American Friends Service Committee Archives, Philadelphia.

2. On the Joint Committee see John P. Davis, "What Price National Recovery," *Crisis* 40 (December 1933): 271–72; reprinted in Herbert Aptheker, ed., *A Documentary History of the Negro People in the United States from the Beginning of the New Deal to the End of the Second World War* (Secaucus, N.J.: Citadel Press, 1974), 49–55. In this era African-Americans often used "National" to mean "Negro." Responding to segregation, examples were National Medical Association and National Tennis Association.

3. "The National Negro Congress, the Call," in *Black Protest*, ed. Joanne Grant (New York: 1968). Aptheker (present at its founding and active in the group throughout its existence) introduces the NNC, Aptheker, *A Documentary History*, 211–35.

4. William Scott, Lecture, "Afro-American Responses to the Italo-Ethiopian War," University of Wisconsin-Madison, 9 October 1972. Mussolini's invasion so incited tensions between African-American and Italian-American communities that 1935 Harlem "had become an armed camp." William Scott, *The Sons of Sheba's Race: African-Americans in the Italo-Ethiopian War, 1935–1941* (Bloomington: Indiana University Press, 1993).

5. James W. Ford, "Political Highlights of the National Negro Congress," *Communist* 15:5 (May 1936): 458. *The Communist* gave major space to the NNC. See its April, May, and June 1936 issues, and that of June 1940.

6. Ford, "Political Highlights," 457.

7. John Davis to Yergan, 31 January 1936, Folder XYZ, National Negro Congress Papers, Box 8, Schomburg Center for Research in Black Culture.

8. Ford, "Political Highlights," 460–61. Yergan began by stating,

I have spent the past 15 years in Africa, traveling and working in all parts of the continent. However, I will speak today mainly of Ethiopia. Through the attack on this small country we are becoming aware of the

169 –

aggressive nature of Fascism, and of the necessity for an intelligent, organized resistance. This thing called Fascism is the outgrowth of a larger force—imperialism. Imperialism has reached such a point that it controls much of finance capitalism.

9. Herbert Newton, "The National Negro Congress, USA," *Negro Worker* (London?), May–June 1936.

10. Mark Naison, *Communists in Harlem during the Depression* (New York: Grove Press, 1984), 293. The phrase was Abner Berry's.

11. He was also noted by historian and former CP leader Herbert Aptheker. Interview, 16 September 1988.

12. "Excerpts from Speech of Max Yergan, Capetown, South Africa, Secretary, South African Work of International Committee of the Young Men's Christian Association, Saturday, February 15, 1936," in *Proceedings of the National Negro Congress, Washington, D.C.* (NNC, 1936).

13. Chatwood Hall, "Why Max Yergan Left South Africa," *Imvo Zabantsundu* (King Williams Town), 17 April 1937; "Dr. Max Yergan on South Africa's Native Policy," *Bantu World* (Johannesburg), 8 May 1937; Smith subsequently penned *Black Man in Red Russia: A Memoir* (Chicago: Johnson, 1964).

14. "Africa in Need of Basic Change, Yergan Says, Returning to Post," New York *Amsterdam News,* 7 March 1936.

15. "Africa in Need of Basic Change."

16. Yergan to Bunche, 29 April 1936. Copy courtesy of Charles Henry.

17. Xuma to Yergan, 27 November 1937, Xuma Papers, ABX 361127c, South African Institute of Race Relations Collection, University of Witwatersrand Library, Johannesburg (SAIRR/UW).

18. Xuma to Yergan, 27 November 1937.

19. Yergan to Xuma, 25 January 1937, ABX 370125, SAIRR/UW.

20. Yergan to "My Dear Friend," 25 February 1937, File "B," Box 68, YMCA Headquarters Library.

21. Yergan to "Dear Friend."

22. Yergan to "Dear Friend."

23. Yergan to "Dear Friend."

24. Yergan to Xuma, 4 February 1937, Xuma Papers.

25. Xuma to Yergan, 5 March 1937, Xuma Papers, ABX 370305e, SAIRR/UW.

26. Xuma to Yergan, 5 March 1937, University of Witwatersrand.

27. Yergan to Xuma, 10 March 1937, Xuma Papers, Hoover Institution.

28. Yergan to Bunche, 9 March 1937, Bunche Papers, Box 180, Folder—Yergan/Additional Data, UCLA.

29. Yergan to Bunche, 17 March 1937, Box 180, Bunche Papers, Folder—Yergan/Additional Data, UCLA.

30. Yergan to "My Dear Friend," 1 May 1937, Box 180, Bunche Papers, Folder—Yergan/Additional Data, UCLA. This was still the era of the Popular Front.

31. Yergan (Brussels) to Bunche, 15 April 1937, Box 180, Bunche Papers, Folder—Yergan/Additional Data, UCLA.

32. For evidence of Frieda as intermediary see S. Neugebauer (Frieda's sister) to Bunche, 14 October 1937, Ralph Johnson Bunche Papers, Box 1B, Schomburg Collection.

33. The FBI compiled an ongoing list of people photographed in the *Daily Worker*. Yergan appeared twice, on 14 April 1937 and 26 July 1938. The list was forwarded to the Navy. "Index of Photographs Which Appeared in the *Daily Worker* from February 2, 1932 to December 31, 1942," appended to Jean S. Conover, Information and Privacy Coordinator, Naval Investigative Service, to author, 26 February 1985.

34. Robert Edgar, ed., *An African-American in South Africa: The Travel Notes of Ralph Bunche* (Athens: Ohio University Press, 1992).

35. Yergan (London) to "My Dear Friend," 1 May 1937, Box 180, Bunche Papers, Folder—Yergan/Additional Data, UCLA.

36. Diary, Ralph Bunche, 1937. See Edgar, *An African-American in South Africa*.

37. Yergan to Bunche, 17 May 1937, Box 180, Folder—Yergan/Additional Data, Bunche Papers, UCLA.

38. *Ras Makonnen: Pan Africanism from Within,* as told to Kenneth James King (London: Oxford University Press, 1973), 158. Makonnen, however, who had read Marx, insisted he was not anticommunist, but like Padmore considered African interests to take priority over those of the Soviet Union.

39. Nkrumah, *Ghana: The Autobiography of Kwame Nkrumah* (New York: International Publishers, 1957; reprinted 1972), 22–23; "A Full and Illustrated Report of the Proceedings of the Restoration of the Ashanti Confederacy, January 31–February 4, 1935" (Accra: West African Sentinel, n.d. [ca. 1935]). On WASU see Gabriel Olakunle Olusanya, *The West African Students' Union and the Politics of Decolonisation, 1925–1958* (Ibadan: Daystar Press, 1982).

40. Essie's assessment is in *African Journey*, 86–129. For a symbolic look at Nyabongo's universe see *The Story of an African Chief* (New York: Scribner, 1935), *Africa Answers Back* (London: Routledge and Sons, 1936), and *Winds and Lights: African Fairy Tales* (New York: Voice of Ethiopia, n.d. [ca. 1939]).

41. Telephone interview, Donald G. S. M'Timkulu (Canada), 29 March 1994. He died at ninety-two in 2000. Among Yale's first African students, during the war years he attended the London School of Economics. M'Timkulu was headmaster at the ABCFM-run Adams College, later becoming a Fort Hare education professor.

182 -

42. Yergan to "My Dear Friend," 1 May 1937, Box 180, Folder—Yergan/ Additional Data, Bunche Papers, UCLA.

43. Yergan to Robeson, 25 May 1937, Paul Robeson Papers, MSRC/HU.

44. Yergan to "My Dear Friend," 1 May 1937.

45. Dorothy Butler Gilliam, *Paul Robeson: All American* (Washington, D.C.: New Republic, 1976), 89.

46. Yergan to Bunche, 26 January 1936, copy courtesy of Charles P. Henry, African-American Studies, University of California–Berkeley.

47. Yergan to Locke, 17 May 1937, Alain Locke Papers, MSRC/HU.

48. Meeting cards "Announcing an Important Meeting at International House," 31 August and 7 September 1937, courtesy Charles P. Henry, University of California–Berkeley.

49. Jones to Tobias, 8 September 1937, Yergan File, UCLA. Ex-Colored Work Department secretary Tobias was a Yergan ally.

50. "Negro for College Post: Max Yergan Recommended for New Course at City Institution," *New York Times,* 15 April 1937; "Negro Appointed to CCNY Teaching Staff: First of Race," *Reporter* (School of Business and Civic Administration), 3 May 1937. Courtesy Ruth Hartson, YMCA International Division.

51. Telephone interview, Morris Urman Schappes, editor, *Jewish Currents,* 5 May 1994.

52. Interview, Herbert Aptheker, San Jose, California, 16 September 1988.

53. Morris Schappes interview, 5 May 1994.

54. Morris Schappes interview, 5 May 1994.

55. "Negro Appointed to CCNY Teaching Staff."

56. Morris Schappes interview, 5 May 1994.

57. Telephone interview, Morris Urman Schappes, editor, *Jewish Currents,* 19 April 1994.

58. Though evidence is scanty, Yergan was associated with the Meröe and Frederick Douglass societies. Prominent in the latter was the young Black Communist Louis Burnham. See Robert (Robbie) Cohen, *When the Old Left Was Young* (New York: Oxford University Press, 1993), chapter 7, part 4.

59. I owe this document to Carol Smith of City College. Copy Tamiment Library. While the texts are not mentioned in full, they may have been as follows: Lucy Mair, *Primitive Government*; Carter G. Woodson, *The African Background Outlined*; Maurice Delafosse, *The Negroes of Africa*; and John Henderson Soga, *The South-Eastern Bantu (Abe-Nguni, Aba-Mbo, Ama-Lala).* That seems more plausible than Soga's later *The Ama-Xosa: Life and Customs* (Lovedale Institution, Alice, South Africa: Lovedale Press, 1932). He also used a text by Franz Boas, with whom he later corresponded.

60. Yergan to Secretary to President, 12 November 1937, President's Per-

187-

sonal File 4266; Telegram, M. H. McIntyre, Secretary to the President, to Yergan, 13 November 1937, FDR Library, Hyde Park.

61. Yergan to Secretary to the President, 12 November 1937, President's Personal File 4266, FDR Library, Hyde Park.

62. Telegram, M. H. McIntyre, Secretary to the President, to Max Yergan, 13
November 1937; Telegram, Yergan to Secretary to the President, 15 November
1937; Telegram, Yergan to M. H. McIntyre, Secretary to the President, 15 November 1937. The final telegram withdrew the request, due to the pressure of
time. President's Personal File 4266, FDR Library, Hyde Park.

63. Wilson to Yergan, 28 October 1937, Frank T. Wilson Papers, Lincoln
University Archives.

64. "Max Yergan Addresses Chapel," *Lincolnian,* 10 December 1937.

65. Max Yergan, National Negro Congress, to Excellency, 9 December 1937,
State Department Central Decimal Files, National Archives, File 738.39/221 LS.

66. Welles to Yergan, 19 December 1937, State Department Central Decimal
Files, National Archives, File 738.39/221 LS. Earlier, Welles had told his aide
that he wondered whether a response to Yergan was "necessary or desirable,"
and he allowed the aide to draft an acknowledgment letter for his signature.
Welles to Duggan, 9 December 1937.

67. John Baxter Streater, "The National Negro Congress, 1936–1947,"
Ph.D. dissertation, University of Cincinnati, 1981, 225.

68. Yergan to J. H. Harmon Jr., 7 January 1938; L. D. Reddick to Yergan, 11
January 1938 and 15 January 1938; Davis to Randolph, 21 January 1938;
H. M. Rollins to Davis, 22 January; William A. Braxton to Yergan, 29 January
1938; Helen R. Bryan, Committee on Race Relations, Society of Friends, to
John P. Davis, 24 January 1938, all in National Negro Congress Papers, Reel
14., Schomburg Center for Research in Black Culture.

69. LeBron Simmons to John P. Davis, 8 February 1938, NNC Papers.

70. Clarence Pickett, *Journal,* 8 February 1938. Courtesy American Friends
Service Committee Archives, Philadelphia, Pennsylvania.

71. The 28 February event was in *Flash* (CCNY Communist Youth League).
FBI Max Yergan file, Confidential: 19 March 1942. FOIA declassified and provided to author.

72. Record of Interview, President's Office, Carnegie Corporation, 11 May
1938, Carnegie Archives.

73. Mary van Kleeck to Yergan, 28 June, 5 July, 13 July; GMW for Associate
Director [Mary van Kleeck] to Yergan, 9 August; Yergan to Miss Meyer, International Industrial Relations Institute, 26 August; GMW to Yergan, 14 September; Yergan to E. C. Morris, Office Secretary to Yergan, 16 September; Yergan
to van Kleeck, 4 October, 1938, Mary van Kleeck Papers, Sophie Smith Collection, Smith College.

74. Mary van Kleeck to Yergan 26 October 1938, Mary van Kleeck Papers,

189.

Sophie Smith Collection, Smith Collection. This was the organ of the Royal Institute of International Affairs.

75. Yergan to Bunche, 23 November 1938, Box 180, Bunche Papers, Folder —Yergan/Additional Data, UCLA.

76. Bunche to Yergan, 13 December 1938, Box 180, Bunche Papers, Folder —Yergan/Additional Data, UCLA.

77. "Book Notes," *International Labour Review* 38:6 (December 1938).

78. Mary van Kleeck to Yergan, 10 January 1938, Mary van Kleeck Papers, Sophie Smith Collection, Smith College.

79. Mary van Kleeck to Yergan, 3 January; Yergan to van Kleeck, 16 May 1939, Mary van Kleeck Papers, Sophie Smith Collection, Smith College.

80. Mary van Kleeck Papers, Box 9, Folder 17, Archives of Labor History and Urban Affairs, Wayne State University, Detroit. Reference provided courtesy of Raymond Boryczka.

81. "Dr. Yergan Enlightens Student Body on Plight of South African Natives," *Lincolnian* (Lincoln University), 4 November 1939.

82. *Lincolnian* (Lincoln University), 4 November 1939.

83. Yergan to Boas, 30 November 1939, Franz Boas Collection, American Philosophical Library, Philadelphia. I thank Robert S. Cox, keeper of manuscripts, for providing me with this copy.

84. Boas to Yergan, 9 December 1939, Boas Papers, American Philosophical Library, Philadelphia.

85. "Woman Journalist's Safari," *Rand Daily Mail,* 26 August 1947, 5; Anthony, "Who Was Frieda Neugebauer?" Unpublished manuscript.

86. Bunche, Davis, to van Kleeck, 25 February 1935; Helen B. Russell to Ralph J. Bunche, 27 February 1945; Bunche to van Kleeck, 1 March, 1935; Ralph Bunche file, Box 10, folder 163, Mary van Kleeck Papers, Sophie Smith Collection, Smith College.

87. "Minutes of the Meeting of the National Committee of the National Joint Action Committee for Genuine Social Insurance Held February 21, 1935 at the City College of New York," National Negro Congress Papers, I.

88. *The Russell Sage Foundation and Social Action in America, 1907–47: A Guide to the Microfilm Collection,* David Hammock, editorial adviser (New York: University Press of America, 1988).

89. New York City *Equity,* December 1935, Russell Sage Foundation Collection, Early Office Files, Box 14, RG IV4B1. Folders 120–126, 158, Department of Industrial Studies—Gen, 1927-1937, Rockefeller Archive Center, Pocantico Hills, N.Y.

90. M. van Kleeck, VI, Important Interviews, Yergan, Max, regarding his paper on "Standards of Living of Native Workers in Africa," also for IIRI Conference. Report for month ended 30 June 1937, dated 1 July 1937, Russell Sage Foundation, Early Office Files 158, Department of Industrial Studies, Monthly

1955

Reports, 1937–1943, IV 4B1.B Box 15 Folder 127, Rockefeller Archive Center, Pocantico Hills, N. Tarrytown, N.Y.

91. Yergan to Bunche, 22 June 1937, Bunche Papers, Box 180, Folder—Yergan/Additional Data, UCLA (hereafter RJBP).

92. "To IRI Members and Others Interested," appended to van Kleeck to Bunche, 2 July 1937, RJBP.

93. Yergan to Bunche, 6 July 1937, RJBP.

94. Yergan to Bunche, 26 July 1937, RJBP.

95. Van Kleeck (The Hague) to Bunche, 6 August 1937, RJBP.

96. Yergan to Bunche, 13 August 1937, RJBP.

97. "Dear Friend," 31 August 1937, RJBP.

98. Yergan to Xuma, 3 September 1937, Xuma Papers, UCLA.

99. *Grondwet* meant "Constitution" in Dutch and Afrikaans. The irony was that this lofty democratic device applied only to Union Whites, a point Yergan wanted Xuma to capture.

100. Jones to Tobias, 8 September 1937, File B, Box 68, YMCA Bowne Historical Library.

101. Max mischievously wrote that Jones's hostile response constituted "the best evidence of the value of the meeting." Yergan to Wilson, 16 September 1937; Wilson to Yergan, 23 September 1937, Frank Wilson Collection, University Archives, Langston Hughes Memorial Library, Lincoln University, Pennsylvania.

102. Yergan to Wilson, 16 September 1937, Wilson Papers, Langston Hughes Library, Lincoln University.

103. Yergan to "Dear Friend," 9 October 1937, File B, Box 68, Bowne YMCA Headquarters Library. Though often eschewing racial nationalism, Max was not above using it. This is consistent with the position of many Black leftists.

104. Yergan, "The Historical Struggle of the Negro People," *Official Proceedings of the Second National Negro Congress, Metropolitan Opera House Philadelphia, Pennsylvania, October 15–17, 1937* (Philadelphia: NNC, 1937).

105. Interview, Louise Thompson Patterson, Oakland, California.

106. Yergan, Foreword, *Fight the Fifth Column,* ed. Martha Millet (1940).

107. Charles V. Hamilton, *Adam Clayton Powell: The Political Biography of an American Dilemma* (New York: Collier-Macmillan, 1991), 105.

108. Yergan to Mr. Paul Robeson, c/o Clarence Mews [*sic*], 18 February 1942, Correspondence—Yergan, Max, Robeson Papers, MSRC/HU. Clarence Muse (1889–1979) was a famous African-American actor.

109. Yergan to Robeson, 18 February 1942, Correspondence, S–Z, Robeson Papers, MSRC/HU.

110. Yergan to Robeson, 18 February 1942.

111. Telegram, Yergan to Early, 18 February 1942, President's Official File, Box 4, Folder OF 93, McIntyre to Yergan with Attachments, 19 February 1942,

FDR Presidential Library, Hyde Park, National Archives and Records Administration (NARA).

112. Yergan to Marvin McIntyre, Secretary to the President, 19 February 1942, President's Official File, box 4, Folder OF 93, FDR Presidential Library, Hyde Park, NARA.

113. President's Official File (OF), Box 4, Folder OF 93, FDR Presidential Library, Hyde Park, NARA.

114. Letter, McIntyre to Yergan with attachments, 19 February 1942.

115. Telegram, Stephen Early, Secretary to President, to Yergan, 19 February 1942.

116. The significance of the southern background of McIntyre and Early is discussed in Charles W. Eagles, *Jonathan Daniels and Race Relations: The Evolution of a Southern Liberal* (Knoxville: University of Tennessee Press, 1982), 88. "Two of [FDR's] personal assistants, Stephen Early and Marvin McIntyre, were white Southerners who disliked the efforts of Mrs. Roosevelt and others in the administration to aid Negroes." Williams seems to have been more pliable, but not where Black left-wingers were concerned.

117. Llewellyn Ransom, "All-Harlem Conference Calls for National Unity," *People's Voice,* 7 March 1942, 24.

118. Telegram, Max Yergan to Richard Wright, 4 March 1942, James W. Johnson Collection, Beinecke Rare Books and MS Library, Yale University.

119. Yergan, Max, Ref: 3RD card, 3-6-42, American Committee to Save Refugees, 100-26011-3, appended to Robert S. Tolle, Captain, U.S. Navy, Director, Naval Investigative Service, to Anthony, 22 May 1985, ref 5262 F85-76 Ser 02-00499. This may also have been spurred or reinforced by the coincidence that Yergan's namesake, Max Jr., allegedly held a Young Communist League card. Yergan, Jr., Max. ONI-FBI-MIS, B-7-CP, 3-5-43, 100-26011-13. Declassified through FOIA and sent to author.

120. Younger to Ladd, 19 March 1942, Max Yergan File. FOIA declassified and sent to author. John Baxter Streater Jr., "The National Negro Congress, 1936–1947," Ph.D. dissertation, University of Cincinnati, 1981, 306–7.

121. Hackworth to Welles, 27 May 1942, 800,20211, "Council for Pan American Democracy," State Department Archives, NARA. For evidence of Hackworth's specialist credentials see *Digest of International Law* (Washington, D.C.: U.S. Government Printing Office, 1940–1944).

122. Yergan, Max, Ref: 3RD card. FOIA declassified and sent to author.

123. *Daily Worker,* 7 November 1942.

124. Edward Strong to Mary McLeod Bethune, 3 January 1943.

125. "South Africa's Aid in War Described," *New York Times,* 26 January 1943, 6:7.

126. Confidential. War Department, Headquarters Second Service Command, Governors Island, New York, 14 April 1943, Subject: Eastern Seaboard

Conference on the Problems of the War and the Negro People. Seven days later this was sent by the Director, Intelligence Division, 2nd S.C. to FBI Headquarters, N.Y. (Regraded Unclassified 18 October 1984).

127. Yergan to FDR, 27 April 1943. Official File (OF) Box 5, Folder OF 4245-G, FDR Presidential Library, NARA.

128. Bunche to Yergan, 29 April 1943, Box 180, Bunche Papers, UCLA.

129. "Yergan Speaks Here Sunday," *Chicago Defender,* 29 April 1943.

130. "A Former Associate of Powell," "Confidential letter to the Members of the City Council," La Guardia Papers, Box 3316 #203 1943, Mayor's Committee on Conditions in Harlem: Race Discrimination—Detroit Investigation, Departmental Correspondence Received and Sent Personal Memos, Folder #1A, New York Municipal Archives and Record Collection.

131. "Harlem Disorders Bring Quick Action by City and Army," *New York Times,* 2 August 1943, 1, 16.

132. J. Edgar Hoover to Major General Edwin M. Watson, Secretary to President, Letters, 2 and 4 August 1943, President's Official File, Box 18, Folder OF 10-B, No 2375, FDR Presidential Library, Hyde Park, NARA.

133. Yergan to Walter F. White, 6 August 1943, NAACP Papers, Library of Congress; "Minutes of Harlem Cultural Committee Meeting," 10 August 1943, NNC Papers, Schomburg Center for Research in Black Culture.

134. Yergan met the mayor on August 27, September 21, and, with Tobias and another local leader, December 20. Fiorello H. La Guardia Appointment book, MARC. Hoover, however, continued disparaging him. Hoover to Watson, 24 September 1943, President's Official File, Box 21, Folder OF 10-B, FDR Library, Hyde Park, NARA.

135. *Congress Vue* 1:10 (March 1944): 6.

136. Yergan to Eleanor Roosevelt, 25 February 1944; Roosevelt to Yergan, 3 March 1944, Eleanor Roosevelt Collection, Box 50, Folder 20.1 (1944–1945), FDR Library, Hyde Park, NARA. E.R. tactically begged off, however.

137. "State Department Hears Yergan on Plans to Help Africa," *Daily Worker,* 28 March 1943.

138. Eichelberger Commission to Study the Organization of Peace to Bunche, 5 April 1944; Bunche to Eichelberger, 11 April 1944; Bunche Papers, UCLA.

139. "Welfare of African People Theme of N.Y. Conference," *People's Voice,* 15 April 1944, 7; "Would Help Colonies: International Agency to Rule in Africa Is Proposed," *New York Times,* 15 April 1944, 5. *Proceedings of the Conference on Africa—New Perspectives: Under Auspices of Council on African Affairs at the Institute of International Democracy—April 14, 1944* (New York: Council on African Affairs, 1944).

140. "The Future of Africa," *New Masses,* 18 April 1944.

141. Yergan to Jackman, 9 May 1943, Cullen-Jackman Ms Collection, Robert W. Woodruff Library, Atlanta University Center, Wilson N. Flemister, Head,

Archives and Special Collections. Yergan to Spingarn, 12 May 1944; Edward Franklin Frazier Papers, MSRC/HU, Box 131-30, Jeanetta Welch Brown, National Council of Negro Women, to Yergan, 19 May and 5 and 19 June 1944; Records of the NCNW, Series 5, Box 38, Folder 542, Bethune Museum and Archives, Washington, D.C.; "There Is a Basis for Solution of Anglo-American Trade Problems," *Daily Worker,* 8 June 1944; "The Colonial Peoples and World Production Possibilities," *Daily Worker,* 22 June 1944; "National Negro Congress Asks Fourth Term for FDR," *People's Voice,* 27 May 1944, 10; Yergan to E. Roosevelt, 30 June 1934; E.R. (Secretary) to Yergan, 7 July, 1944. Max tried meeting with E.R. on Negro reelection strategy; she declined.

142. Edward Lawson, a staff member of the New York CRFE Regional Office told the gathering how many workers would be made redundant at war's end: more than one million from the shipping industry, of whom 125,000 were Black; one million from the ordnance and communications industry, of whom 65,000 were Black; 20,000 Negro metal workers, 100,000 from munitions and 50,000 from various government war agencies. These 500,000 unemployed Negro civilians would be joined by one million African-American vets, all seeking gainful employment. Streater, "National Negro Congress," chapter 6, 214–15; "Negro Congress Acts to Preserve War Gains," *People's Voice,* 20 January 1945, 12.

143. "NNC Adopts Unity Program," *People's Voice,* 3 February 1945, 15.

144. "Negro Red Leader Divorced in Reno," New York *World Telegram,* 28 February 1945.

145. "Max Yergans Split," *People's Voice,* 10 March 1945, 11.

146. "Parley on Colonies Called by NAACP," *People's Voice,* 31 March 1945, 5.

147. Max Yergan, President, National Negro Congress, to Harry S. Truman, 13 April 1945. Harry S. Truman Papers, President's Personal File, Truman Library, Independence, Missouri. Subsequently, Jonathan Daniels, Truman's secretary and Yergan's fellow Raleighan, told a White House staffer that he knew the NNC president well, and that indeed "Yergan *is* the leading Negro Communist in the country today." A[ubrey].W[illiams]. to Mr. Hassett, n.d., President's Personal File, Harry S. Truman Papers.

148. "Franklin D. Roosevelt: His Monument and Lessons," *People's Voice,* 21 April 1945, 16.

149. "Excerpt from Report of FBI, date San Francisco, May 19, 1945," Ralph Johnson Bunche Papers, Box 180, Folder—Yergan/Additional Data, UCLA.

150. Interview, Herbert Aptheker, 16 September 1988, 480 N. First St., San Jose, California.

151. "Here's What the Great Victory Means to the Negro," Victory in Europe Section, *People's Voice,* 12 May 1945, 6.

152. "Yergan Points Out Dangerous Emphasis," *People's Voice,* 19 May 1945.

153. "Real Peace Basis Won, Says Yergan," *People's Voice,* 26 May 1945, 3.

154. "British Plan Opposed as Dangerous," *People's Voice,* 16 June 1945.

155. Proceedings, National Conference of Negro Leaders, 23 June 1945, Records of the National Council of Negro Women, Series 5, Box 24, Folder 359, Bethune Archives, Washington, D.C. In addition to Mrs. Bethune, the call for the conference was issued by Adam Clayton Powell Jr., William Dawson, John Sengstacke, Marshall Shepard, Tobias, Yergan, and White. See "Leaders Call for Conference," *People's Voice,* 23 June 1935, 4.

156. Yergan, Guest Editorial, "British Labor Victory and the Colonies," *People's Voice,* 4 August 1945, 14.

157. "Peace Settlement of Colonies Urged: Program for Africa Sent to State Department," *People's Voice,* 15 September 1945, 5.

158. Council on African Affairs to "Dear Friend," E. Franklin Frazier Papers, MSRC/HU, Box 131-330, Council on African Affairs.

159. Yergan to Wright, 31 October 1945, James Weldon Johnson Collection, Beinecke Library, Yale University.

160. Revels Cayton to Mervin Rathbone, 21 December 1945, NNC Papers, Part II: Records and Correspondence, 1943–45, Reel 36, folder 54, Correspondence, 1946, Box 72, Schomburg Center for Research in Black Culture.

161. "Robeson, Anderson Pack 'Aid to Africa Meeting,'" *People's Voice,* 12 January 1946, 12.

162. "Food on Way," *People's Voice,* 2 February 1945; "Starving Africans Sent Food, Cash by New York Council," *Chicago Defender,* 2 February 1946.

163. "Britain to Get Food from Starving Africa," *People's Voice,* 23 February 1945. Yergan reported that in the previous month Field Marshal J. C. Smuts had launched a campaign to spend $8 million on gifts of food to be sent to Britain while doing nothing for African famine victims. In reply the Council on African Affairs (CAA) considered picketing the British Consulate. "Let's Picket for Africa, Ben Davis Clubs Suggest," *People's Voice,* 2 March 1946, 9; "Seamen to Spearhead Fight for Africans," *People's Voice,* 2 March 1946, 7.

164. "African Food Needs as Urgent as Europe's," *People's Voice,* 9 March 1946, 5.

165. "Churchill Gets 'No!' to Next War Build-up," *People's Voice,* 16 March 1946, 3.

166. "Forum on Africa At Forest House," *People's Voice,* 16 March 1946, 8.

167. "Robeson Asks for Food Aid in South Africa," *People's Voice,* 23 March 1946.

168. "New York CIO Board Greets May 5 Rally," *People's Voice,* 4 May 1946, 3.

169. "British Trusteeship Called Land Grab," *People's Voice,* 11 May 1946, 5.

170. "Colonial Empires Assailed in Rally: Communist-Controlled Council Says U.S. Aids Others in 'Plundering' Africa," *New York Times,* 7 June 1946, 7:1.

171. George Schuyler, "Views and Reviews," *Pittsburgh Courier,* 8 June 1946.

172. Doxey Wilkerson, "Negro-Labor United Hits High in Detroit," *People's Voice,* 8 June 1946.

173. "More Food For Africa! Cry 15,000 at Garden," *People's Voice,* 15 June 1946; Adam Clayton Powell, "Soapbox, in Washington," *People's Voice,* 22 June 1946.

174. "Africans Thank Robeson, Yergan," *People's Voice,* 20 July 1946, 15.

175. Padmore to Du Bois, 9 August 1946, in Herbert Aptheker, ed., *The Correspondence of W. E. B. Du Bois,* vol. 3, *Selections, 1944–1963* (Amherst: University of Massachusetts Press, 1978), 146–47.

176. Robert R. Edgar, ed., *An African-American in South Africa: The Travel Notes of Ralph J. Bunche, 28 September 1937–1 January 1938* (Athens: Ohio University Press, 1992).

177. Telephone interview, Phyllis Jordan Ntantala, Madison, Wisconsin, 20 May 1974. At the time, Ntantala, widow of the South African Xhosa-speaking writer and Wisconsin professor of African Languages and Literature, A. C. Jordan, lived in Middleton, a town adjoining the state capital, Madison. *A Life's Mosaic: The Autobiography of Phyllis Ntantala* (Berkeley: University of California Press, 1992).

178. Yergan to Bethune, 12 July 1946, National Negro Congress Papers, Series II, reel 31, Box 66, Folder, "To Be Filed." Bethune to Yergan, 1 August 1946, Records of the National Council of Negro Women, Series 5, Box 38, Folder 542, Bethune Archives; copy in NNC Papers, Series II, reel 31, Box 66, "To Be Filed." Dorothy K. Funn to Yergan, 8 August 1946, NNC Papers, Ser. II, reel 31, Box 66, "To Be Filed." Schomburg Center for Research in Black Culture.

179. M. M. Bethune to Yergan, 15 November 1946, Records of the National Council of Negro Women, Series 5, Box 38, Folder 542, Bethune Archives, Washington, D.C.

180. "Dr. Xuma Fights Smuts Proposal," *People's Voice,* 9 November 1946, 3, Schomburg Center for Research in Black Culture.

181. "Harlem Rally Hears General Smuts Blasted," *People's Voice,* 23 November 1946, 5; "Smuts Defies UN on African Plan, *People's Voice,* 23 November 1946; "African Plan Assailed," *Chicago Sun,* 23 November 1946.

182. Cayton to Yergan, 23 January 1947, NNC Papers, Part II, Records and Correspondence, 1943–47, folder 55, Correspondence 1947, Box 72.

183. On Claudia Jones see *Notes on the Life and Times of Claudia Jones*; Buzz Johnson, *I Think of My Mother* (London: Karia Press, 1985); Angela Davis, "Communist Women," in *Women, Race, and Class.*

184. "'Hysteria' Is Behind Arrest Says Alien Red," *People's Voice,* 31 January 1947.

185. "West Indians Here Say Deportations May Affect Large Numbers," *People's Voice,* 7 February 1947.

186. Funn to Yergan, 22 February 1947, NNC Papers, Part 2, 1943–47, Reel 36, Folder 59, Funn, Dorothy, 1947, Schomburg Center for Research in Black Culture.

187. "Ban on Communism Step towards Fascism," *People's Voice,* 22 March 1947, 15.

188. Yergan to "Dear Friend," 15 April 1947, NNC Papers, Part II, Folder 55, Correspondence 1947, Box 72, Schomburg Center for Research in Black Culture.

189. U.S. Congress, House, Committee on Un-American Activities, *Testimony of Walter S. Steele regarding Communist Activities in the United States. Hearings before Committee on Un-American Activities, House of Representatives, Eightieth Congress, First Session, on HR 1884 and HR 2122, Bills to Curb or Outlaw the Communist Party,* 21 July 1947 (Washington, D.C.: Government Printing Office, 1947). Robert Carr, *The House Un-American Activities Committee* (New York: 1952), 52–55; Walter Goodman, *The Committee: The Extraordinary Career of the House Committee on Un-American Activities* (New York: 1968), 190–225.

190. "Max Yergan Quits Negro Congress," *People's Voice,* 15 November 1947.

191. *People's Voice,* 3 January 1948.

192. Robeson to "Dear Max," 2 January 1948, in Ruby Pagano, "Max Yergan, a Biography," n.d. (ca. 1975). Copy in author's possession.

NOTES TO CHAPTER 6

1. *People's Voice,* January 3, showcased the management and staff of the New *People's Voice*; "People's Voice Policy Assailed by Former Editor," *California Eagle,* 8 January 1948.

2. Telegram, Yergan to E. Franklin Frazier, 29 January 1948, E. Franklin Frazier Papers, MSRC/HU; telegram, Robeson to Yergan, Omaha, 14 April 1948, Paul Robeson Papers; "Yergan Fights Red Grab," "Yergan Supported in Council Fight," *People's Voice,* 17 April 1948; CAA News Release, 21 April 1948; "Battles Left Wing for Group's Office," *New York Times,* 26 May 1948; "No Cause for Action," *New York Times,* 2 June 1948; "Yergan Accuses Five of Assault," *New York Times,* 20 June 1948; "Court Frees 3 Men Accused by Yergan," *New York Times,* 29 June 1948; Yergan Seeks Court Aid: Asks Invalidation of Ouster from African Affairs Post," *New York Times,* 25 August 1948;

"Two Yergan Suits United: CAA Case to Be Heard September 20," *New York Times,* 26 August 1948.

3. Frederick Woltman, "Yergan Denounces Commies as Wreckers," *New York World-Telegram,* 13 October 1948; "American Negro on Race Relations Mission," *Pittsburgh Courier,* 14 October 1948.

4. *Records of U.S. Attorneys and Marshals: Transcripts of Grand Jury Testimony in Alger Hiss Case,* Record Group 118, Dates 1947–1949, Box 4, Federal Grand Jury Southern District of New York, Harry S. Truman Library, Independence, MO. Russell Porter, "Spy Case Jury Hears Sayre Then Recesses till January 3," *New York Times,* 23 December 1948. Allen Weinstein, *Perjury: The Hiss-Chambers Case* (New York: Knopf, 1978)

5. Testimony of Max Yergan, 4 January 1949, *Records of U.S. Attorneys and Marshals.*

6. Memorandum, Yergan to South African government, 30 March 1949, Yergan File, State Department.

7. Phelps Stokes to Yergan, 30 April 1949, Anson Phelps Stokes Papers, Box 128, Folder 2304, Manuscripts & Archives, Sterling Library, Yale University.

8. Phelps Stokes to Yergan, 30 April 1949, Anson Phelps Stokes Papers, Box 128, Folder 2304, Manuscripts & Archives, Sterling Library, Yale University.

9. Yergan to Phelps Stokes, 4 May 1949, Anson Phelps Stokes Papers, Box 128, Folder 2304, Manuscripts and Archives, Sterling Library, Yale University.

10. Yergan to Anson Phelps Stokes, 16 May 1949, Anson Phelps Stokes Papers, Box 128, 2304, Manuscripts & Archives, Sterling Library, Yale University.

11. D. D. Forsyth to H. E. North Winship, U.S. Ambassador, CT Confidential Enclosure to Despatch No. 74 (Cape Town Series), dated June 7, 1949, from American Embassy, Cape Town, South Africa; Despatch No. 74 American Embassy (Cape Town Series) Cape Town, Union of South Africa, 7 June 1949, Confidential Subject: Request of Dr. Max Yergan for permission to Enter the Union of South Africa, 848A.111/6-749 State Department Decimal File, NARA.

12. "Items about the Negroes (Culled by X): Politics: Yergan versus Robeson," *Ilanga lase Natal Ngongqibelo,* 18 June 1949.

13. Acheson to AMEMBASSY, Pretoria, A-127, 8 August 1949, Reference to American Embassy's Despatch No. 74 dated June 7, 1949, concerning the Communist tendencies of Dr. Max Yergan. Confidential RG 59, State Department Decimal File, Max Yergan, 848A.111/6749, NARA, 18 August, Jack Neal, Chief of Security, State Department to JEH re. Max Yergan.

14. Yergan, "ICFTU's Opportunity in Africa," *International Free Trade Union News* 5:5 (May 1950).

15. "ICFTU's Opportunity in Africa," 8.

16. "ICFTU's Opportunity in Africa."

17. "ICFTU's Opportunity in Africa."

18. George S. Schuyler, *Black and Conservative: The Autobiography of George S. Schuyler* (New Rochelle, N.Y.: Arlington House, 1966), 317.

19. Yergan, "Negroes and Democracy in the U.S.," *International Free Trade Union News* 5:11 (November 1950): 8.

20. Peter Coleman, *The Liberal Conspiracy: The Congress on Cultural Freedom and the Struggle for the Mind of Postwar Europe* (New York: Free Press, 1989), 51; Schuyler, *Black and Conservative*, 324–25.

21. Minutes, Congress for Cultural Freedom, Brussels, November 1950. I am grateful to Peter Coleman for supplying me with an extract of these. The French text ran as follows:

M. MAX YERGAN a souligné que le Congrès devrait indiquer clairement qu'il desire collaborer avec des personnes qui se trouvent dan les pays de l'Est, mais qui croient intensément aux idées de liberte et qui, luttent aussi pour elles.

D'autre part, M. Yergan a exprimé l'idée que ce serait une grave erreur de considérer différemment l'Afrique et les autres parties du monde. Nous devons faire comprendre très clairementaux peuples d'Afrique, a-t-il, que nos croyances en la liberté de la culture ne sont pas limitées aux seuls pays de l'Ouest.

Peter Coleman to Anthony, 18 April 1994.

22. Anson Phelps Stokes to Yergan, 13 November 1950, Anson Phelps Stokes Papers, Box 128, Folder 2304, Manuscripts & Archives, Sterling Library, Yale University.

23. Yergan to "Dear Ralph," 21 November 1950; Bunche to Yergan, 23 November 1950, Ralph J. Bunche Papers, UCLA. Courtesy R. R. Edgar.

24. "Famous Negroes Married to Whites," *Ebony* 2:5 (December 1950).

25. "Ralph Johnson Bunche, Peacemaker," Phelps Stokes Papers, MS Group 299, Series III, Box 180, Folder 158, Dinner in honor Ralph Bunche, Sterling Library, Yale University.

26. Pearl Kluger to Burnham, 8 February 1951; Burnham to Herb Passin, February 16, 1951; Ram Swalup to Burnham, 6 March 1951, Burnham Papers, Box 8, folder 6, Congress for Cultural Freedom, Hoover Institution, Stanford University.

27. "American Racial Policy and the Situation of American Negroes," *International Congress of Free Trade Union News.*

28. "American Racial Policy and the Situation of American Negroes."

29. Address, Max Yergan, *Indian Congress for Cultural Freedom, March 28–31, 1951* (Bombay: Kanada Press, 1951), 32–33.

30. Robert Trumbull, "India Parley Links Food and Freedom" and "Cultural Congress Speakers Say Democracies Lag in Fight on Communism in Asia," *New York Times,* 29 March 1951.

31. Yergan to Eleanor Roosevelt with attachments, 2 May 1951, Eleanor Roosevelt Collection, Box 3956, General Correspondence (1951, Y), FDR Library, Hyde Park. He also included the article, "Totalitarianism Menaces Freedom of Thought," *American Reporter,* 4 April 1951, 11.

32. Confidential Memorandum Dr. Max Yergan (prepared by Robert Morris), 5 June 1951, National Archives.

33. Confidential Memorandum Dr. Max Yergan (prepared by Robert Morris), 5 June 1951, National Archives.

34. "Negroes Should Shun Reds as 'Conspiracy,' Yergan Tells Senators," *Washington Evening Star,* 14 May 1952; "Ruse on Negroes Laid to Conspiracy," *New York Times,* 14 May 1952.

35. Handwritten statement dated 13 May 1952, Max Yergan Papers, MSRC/HU.

36. Yergan to Lovestone, 5 June 1952, Jay Lovestone Papers, RG 18-0033 Box 677, Folder 21, George Meany Memorial Archives, Silver Spring, Md.

37. Albert Jolis, *A Clutch of Reds and Diamonds: A Twentieth-Century Odyssey* (Boulder, Colo.: East European Monographs, 1996). Distributed by Columbia University Press, New York.

38. Yergan to Lovestone, 6 May 1952, Jay Lovestone Papers, RG 18-003 (Lovestone), Box 677, Folder 21, George Meany Memorial Archives, Silver Spring, Md.

39. Yergan to Wright, Paris, 7 June 1952, James Weldon Johnson Collection, Beinecke Rare Books and Manuscripts Library, Yale University.

40. Lovestone to Yergan, 9 June 1952, Jay Lovestone Papers, RG 18-0003 (Lovestone), Box 677, Folder 21; Lovestone to Yergan, 6 September 1952, George Meany Memorial Archives, Silver Spring, Md.

41. Jolis, *A Clutch of Reds and Diamonds,* 315.

42. Jolis, *A Clutch of Reds and Diamonds,* 316.

43. David Bopape, secretary of the East Rand District Committee of the Communist Party and editorial board member of the Communist Party newspaper *Inkululeko,* was at one time a member of the National Executive of the ANC. Unlike stalwarts A. P. Mda, Nelson Mandela, James Njongwe, Walter Sisulu, and Oliver Tambo, a Youth League planner of the action program, Bopape was subsequently revealed as an informant.

44. "Ruse on Negroes Laid to Reds," *New York Times,* 14 May 1952, 12.

45. "'Reds Used Me 10 Years'—Yergan," *Journal and Guide,* 24 May 1952.

46. Institute of Pacific Relations, Hearings Before the Subcommittee to Investigate the Administration of the Internal Security Act and Other Internal Security Laws of the Committee on the Judiciary, United States Senate, 82 Congress, Second Session, Part 13, April 2, 4l, 5, 7, 8, May 15, 18, 19, and 29, 1952, "Testimony of Max Yergan, Ossining, N.Y.," 13 May 1952, 4596–97.

47. Institute of Pacific Relations, "Testimony of Max Yergan," 4606–7.

48. Jolis, *A Clutch of Reds and Diamonds,* 314. Jolis was evidently unaware of the Sino-Soviet dispute.

49. "Yergan Taking Anti-Communist Warning to Africans: Will Warn Natives of Red Poison," *Journal and Guide,* 14 June 1952.

50. Personal communication, Robert Matji to Robert Edgar, April 1989; Edgar to Anthony, 21 April 1989. Matji claimed this may have had something to do with the mixed race backgrounds of these leading figures.

Half a century later Walter Sisulu recalled Yergan's attempt at dissuading the Defiance Campaigners. Sisulu to Anthony, interview at the Walter and Albertina Sisulu home, Johannesburg (Gauteng), 2 July 2000.

51. "Phillips News" (Johannesburg), 10 August 1952, ABCFM Collection, Houghton Library, Harvard University. Phillips, Yergan's senior by three years, also preceded him in South Africa, arriving in 1917 after being appointed to the Zulu Mission and remaining on the Rand for some twenty years beyond Max's departure.

52. Confidential, Richard I. Phillips, Acting American Consulate General, Kenya, "Subject: Visit of Dr. Max Yergan to Kenya, 28 August, 1952," 032-Yergan, Dr Max/8-2852, State Department Archives, NARA.

53. Confidential, Phillips, "Visit of Max Yergan to Kenya."

54. "South African Leaders Blast Yergan," *Freedom* 2:10 (October 1952).

55. White to Nehru, 4 May 1953; White to Dulles, 6 May 1953, NAACP Papers, Library of Congress; Editorial, *Baltimore Afro-American,* 9 May 1953; "Time Running Out," *Freedom* 3:5 (May 1953); Abner Berry, "A Brain Washed Yergan Fills Master's Order," *Daily Worker,* 12 May 1953.

56. Richard Lincoln, "Black South African Forced Back Home," *New York Amsterdam News,* 23 May 1953.

57. Lincoln, "Black South African Forced Back Home."

58. "An African Leader Exposes Max Yergan," *Freedom* 3:6 (June 1953).

59. Cited and translated from the French in D. N. Gibbs, *Political Economy of Third World Intervention: Mines, Money, and U.S. Policy in the Congo Crisis* (Chicago: University of Chicago Press, 1991), 121–22, 257n. 131.

60. Yergan, letter to the editor, *New York Times,* written 28 July, printed 3 August 1953. He later wrote a similar letter to the *New York Herald Tribune* on August 2. NAACP Papers, Library of Congress.

61. George Sokolsky, *New York Journal American,* 29 July 1953.

62. Walter F. White to George Sokolsky, *New York Journal American,* 31 July 1953, NAACP Papers, Library of Congress.

63. Yergan, letter to the editor, *New York Times,* written 18 August, published 19 August 1953.

64. "Yergan Intrigues in South Africa against Fighters of Jim Crow," *Daily Worker,* 11 September 1953.

65. *African Lodestar,* November 1953 (ANC Transvaal Youth League Publication), Issued by W. M. Sisulu (Secretary-General, ANC of South Africa).

66. Interview, Walter M. Sisulu, Johannesburg, 4 July 2000.

67. "Finds World Curious About American Negroes," *Pittsburgh Courier,* 19 June, 26 June, 3 July 1954.

68. *New York Times* obituary, 10 November 1954; *Time* magazine obituary, 22 November 1954.

69. More concerned with the conferees, Wright gave American policy short shrift. A relevant allusion was the following terse dismissal: "The United States, though not present, had its spokesmen for the policy of 'containment of Communism.'" Since Yergan and Powell were among the diminutive number of American mouthpieces at Bandung, with himself and journalist Carl Rowan both being in quest of books, it appears his comment referred to one or perhaps both deft public speakers, Powell and Yergan. By contrast, Wright and Rowan tended to prefer the printed page. Richard Wright, *The Color Curtain: A Report on the Bandung Conference* (Cleveland and New York: World Publishing Company, 1956), 181.

70. "Why There's No Colored Bloc; Interview with Max Yergan, American Negro Authority on Africa," *U.S. News and World Report,* 3 June 1955, 96.

71. 032-Yergan, Max, Dr./12-2057 Despatch no. 236 from Salisbury, State Department Archives, NARA.

72. Russell Warren Howe and Sarah Hays Trott, *The Power Peddlers* (Garden City, N.Y.: Doubleday, 1977), 176. The best introduction to this subject remains Crawford Young, *Politics in the Congo: Decolonization and Independence* (Princeton, N.J.: Princeton University Press, 1965); for a contemporary "Onusian" (UNO) view, see Conor Cruise O'Brien, *To Katanga and Back: A UN Case History* (New York: Grosset and Dunlap, 1966). For an example of the work of the ACAKFF see Anthony Trawick Bouscaren, *Tshombe* (New York: Twin Circle, 1967).

73. Young, *Politics in the Congo,* 284–95.

74. O'Brien, *To Katanga and Back,* 97. For fuller treatments of Lumumba, see Colin Legum, *Congo Disaster* (Baltimore: Penguin, 1961); Thomas Kanza, *Conflict in the Congo: The Rise and Fall of Lumumba* (Baltimore: Penguin, 1972). On American governmental reaction to Lumumba see John Stockwell, *In Search of Enemies: A CIA Story* (New York: Norton, 1978); Henry F. Jackson, *From the Congo to Soweto: U.S. Foreign Policy toward Africa since 1960* (New York: William Morrow, 1982); Madeleine G. Kalb, *The Congo Cables: The Cold War in Africa—From Eisenhower to Kennedy* (New York: Macmillan, 1982); and Richard D. Mahoney, *JFK: Ordeal in Africa* (New York: Oxford University Press, 1983). For two excellent revisitings of these subjects see Ludo de Witte, *The Assassination of Lumumba* (New York and London: Verso,

2001), and Georges Nzongola-Ntalaja, *The Congo from Leopold to Kabila: A People's History* (London and New York: Zed Books, 2002).

75. Russell Warren Howe and Sarah Hays Trott, "Out of Whitest Africa," chapter 4 in *The Power Peddlers: How Lobbyists Mold America's Foreign Policy* (Garden City, N.Y.: Doubleday, 1977), 171.

76. Howe and Trott, *The Power Peddlers,* 172–73.

77. Confidential, H. S. V. Villard, Amembassy Dakar to SecState WASHDC, 10 February 1961, 032-Yergan, Max (Dr and Mrs)/2-136 1LLR, Declassified 13 February 1985, State Department Archives, NARA.

78. Confidential, H. S. V. Villard.

79. 3 March, Luanda to Secretary of State, no 109, Mar 1, 10 A.M. 032-Yergan, Max (Dr.)/3-161, State Department Archives, NARA.

80. Gibson, Luanda, Confidential Telegram, to Secretary of State, 221, 4 May 1961, 3 P.M., State Department Records, File 032-Yergan, Max (Dr.)/5-461, released 13 February 1985, State Department Archives, NARA.

81. 21/61, "Dakar reports American negro Dr Max Yergan may visit Luanda early March," outgoing telegram American Consul Luanda, Rept Info: American Embassy Dakar (Pouch) 032-Yergan, Max (Dr.)/2-2761CS/CS, State Department Archives, NARA.

82. *Afro-American,* December 1961. Article and photo supplied courtesy of *Afro-American* archivist Mary Beth Prior.

83. Herbert Aptheker interview, 16 September 1988, 480 North First Street, San Jose, California.

84. American Embassy, Pretoria, Visit to South Africa of Dr. Max Yergan, 13 November 1964, State Department Archives.

85. Cited in AmEmb Pretoria, 3 December 1964 to Secretary of State, State Department Archives.

86. "All Right for Negro, Why Not Kaiser, Asks Paper," *Daily Dispatch,* 25 November 1964. For further examples see "Transkei Paper Asks: Why Not Matanzima? Negro 'White' Hotel Guest," *Rand Daily Mail,* 27 November 1964; "The Joke of the Year," *Daily Dispatch,* 27 November 1964.

87. J. Anthony Lukas, "Negro Sociologist Praises South Africa's Apartheid Policy," *New York Times,* 30 November 1964.

88. American Embassy Pretoria Airgram A-66 Subject, Dr Max Yergan, American Negro Visitor, Comments on South African Race Policy, 3 December 1964, State Department Decimal File, NARA.

89. William H. Witt, First Secretary of the Embassy, Pretoria, to Secstate Washington, 3 December 1964, Subject: Dr. Max Yergan, American Negro Visitor, Comments on SA Race Policy Ref Embassy's A-207, 13 November 1964, State Department Archives, NARA.

90. William L. Swing, American Vice Consul Airgram A-66, 8 December 1964, AmConsul Port Elizabeth to Department of State, Subject, Transkei Visit

of Dr Max Yergan Causes Stir, Ref Embassy's A-207, 13 November 1964, Yergan, Max, State Department Archives, NARA.

91. Confidential Outgoing Telegram AFE W. C. Kinsey to Department of State, 22 January 1966, Leg 7 Ashbrook Trv—Yergan, Max (Dr) 12248, Declassified 13 February 1985, State Department Archives, NARA.

92. Interview, William A. Rusher, University Club, San Francisco, 9 December 1996.

93. Secret, Incoming Telegram, Department of State, Leg 7 Ashbrook, 25 January 1966, Declassified 13 February 1985, State Department Archives, NARA.

94. For the president's night reading from: Bill Moyers, 8 March 1966, enclosure: Rick Haynes, the White House, Memorandum for Bromley K. Smith, 7 March 1966 (cc. R. W. Komer), White House Central Files, Name File, "American A," Lyndon Baines Johnson Library, Austin, Texas.

95. Yergan to Bill Rusher, 7 January, 19 October 1970, William Rusher Papers, Library of Congress.

96. Rusher to Yergan, Guadalajara, Mexico, 1 March, and Yergan to Rusher, 15 March 1971, Rusher Papers, Library of Congress.

97. Obituary, *New York Times,* 23 March 1971: 23 March Susie Wiseman Yergan lies in repose, George L. Jones Funeral Home, 455 Lenox Avenue, NYC. At 11 A.M. Wednesday, the 24th of March, 1971, she was funeralized, at St. James Presbyterian Church, 141 St. & St. Nicholas Avenue. It is unknown if Max attended.

98. Howe and Trott, *The Power Peddlers,* 202–3.

99. *New York Times* obituary of Lena Halpern Yergan, 17 April 1972.

100. Yergan to Rusher and B. B. Connell to Rusher, 1 May 1972; Yergan to Rusher, 9 May 1972, Rusher Papers, Library of Congress.

101. Martin Bauml Duberman, personal communication. See also *Paul Robeson, a Biography* (New York: Ballantine, 1989).

Bibliography

Note on Sources

Researching the life of Max Yergan resembles reconstructing African history. In spite of a documentary plethora, there is a paucity of prima facie evidence. Though he left a rich record, scores of silences, some deliberate, others mere happenstance, persist, perhaps permanently. Materials available concerning various aspects of the professional life of Max Yergan, if surprisingly abundant, do present special problems. They are extremely widely spread out and are as likely to be encountered in Europe and Africa as in North America. For a long time the greatest question mark was what lay in the uncatalogued files of the indefinitely restricted, fifty-year-rule-ridden Max Yergan papers collection at Howard University. I saw these for a day and a half in April 2002.

Of source materials at the disposal of researchers, a good place to start is at the YMCA of the USA Archives at the University of Minnesota. This archive represents a reorganization of documents previously housed at the former YMCA Bowne Historical Library in Manhattan. Before the latter was reconfigured during the late seventies, the author utilized this hoary collection in its raw form, throughout the summer of 1975. Data was then filed in thousands of folders laid in hundreds of boxes. Since that time, though most original documents have been microfilmed, institutional policy shifts have, on occasion, redirected parts of what I once experienced as a user-friendly sequencing of documents, with most of the documents being retained in St. Paul, many being sent to Chicago, and still others being redeployed back to prior YMCA branch offices, presumably for local use. These now form the YMCA of the USA Archives under the kind custodianship and philanthropic largesse of the generous Kautz family.

Second in importance stand several key manuscript collections filed within the Moorland-Spingarn Research Center of Howard University, especially the papers of Howard luminaries Jesse Edward Moorland

and Edward Franklin Frazier. Yergan correspondence is to be found among the Paul and Eslanda Goode Robeson collections, and it seems likely that "Yergania" may also be found in the Mordecai Johnson files when these are catalogued and opened to the public within the near future.

Next are several letters, reports, and circulars amassed during the course of Yergan's service term in the World's Student Christian Federation, a body organically affiliated with the YMCA. These two symbiotically related institutions were akin to interlocking directorates. The WSCF was also linked to the Student Christian Movement (also Student Christian Association) and the World Alliance of YMCAs. Hence, documents dealing with one will often lead to others. Thus, even when originals are misplaced, copies sometimes surface in sister institution repositories. There are two major WSCF libraries, the WSCF archives in Geneva, Switzerland, affiliated with the World Council of Churches, and the one compiled by John Raleigh Mott, late North American YMCA director, out of his correspondence, housed in the Mott Room of the Divinity School Library of Yale University. Researchers wishing to make maximal use of these facilities, though, are well advised to first familiarize themselves with the extensive official literature on the YMCA, WSCF, and SCM before doing so.

Sporadic, evanescent traces of Yergania are interspersed among the official correspondence of the Rockefeller, Carnegie, and Phelps-Stokes Funds, although these files are not always accessible to the public and occasionally become inaccessible even to bona fide researchers. The writer managed to gain limited access to them after persistent prodding and much collegial aid, particularly in the latter two cases. Fortunately, however, the Rockefeller Archive Center proved much more forthcoming, and for the same reasons as hold true for YMCA and sibling agencies, one foundation's files typically lead to another's.

South Africa is also a logical source for much of the documentary evidence about Yergan's tenure between 1922 and 1936, but documents here seem few and far between. Many of Yergan's closest colleagues and most intimate friends during these decades transacted great parts of their professional and private business with him in person, leaving little in the way of a paper trail. This is both consistent with his style of work and politically prudent. We have no idea if data has been destroyed, either by him or by his correspondents, on one hand, or "lost" by the authorities, on the other.

Microfilmed editions of papers from institutions with which Yergan became closely involved include the National Negro Congress Papers and the *People's Voice,* a tabloid newspaper in which Yergan had a financial interest. Yergan also contributed columns to the *Daily Worker* and often was the subject of articles within both the establishment and Negro press. Particularly intriguing are a series of "live" radio broadcasts, evidently lost, made intermittently in the thirties and forties, locally, nationally, and internationally (at least one aired from Toronto, Ontario, on the Canadian Broadcasting Corporation). All of these are described in written materials but have not resurfaced in aural form.

The final repository is that set of documents generated through domestic surveillance in this country, and made available via FOIA, i.e., Freedom of Information Act, requests. This data is of highly uneven quality, and must, without exception, be treated with caution and extreme circumspection. The data being redolent with innuendo and character assassination, one is hard pressed to assess the veracity of allegations advanced within them by persons unknown, often with questionable motives. Even so, these materials cannot be dismissed out of hand; indeed, the very scale of intelligence gathering directed at Yergan would seem to have been extraordinarily thorough, for, in addition to eliciting information from the Federal Bureau of Investigation, i.e., the Justice Department, FOIA requests have also elicited material from the Departments of State, the Army, the Navy, the Air Force, and Customs and Immigration. True to form, Central Intelligence Agency respondents professed an inability to locate data on Yergan; it is clear from cross-referencing papers of supporting agencies, as well as perusing the work of colleagues, however, that this was not quite the case. However, since contesting the CIA's claim would require litigation, I deemed it unwise to press the matter.

In addition to these documents, another FBI file was loaned me by a colleague, Harvey Klehr, who was researching related questions concerning the National Negro Congress. At one time, Yergan's relationship to this group appeared to have been largely peripheral, since there are indications that the presidency was conceived primarily as a symbolic office, at least initially, responsibility for most NNC decisions lying within the secretariat. From 1936 to 1943, then, the true "power behind the throne" ostensibly was John Davis, the national secretary, rather than President Yergan. Nevertheless, this distinction was not deemed significant enough to disabuse the FBI of the notion that Yergan's activities

were possibly subversive. This collection is at once more voluminou
 and less enlightening than Yergan's personal file, although it does help
in charting the course of the organization. The FBI's NNC and Yergan
files both share Hoover's lurid preoccupation with the public record, as
most intelligence sources used in constructing the NNC file originated
in accounts in newspapers, while Yergan's personal dossier was arranged
via data drawn from scores of shadowy confidential informants, infiltra-
tors, and wiretap logs. In the matter of the paid informants, only rarely
might one identify them from the tenor and context of their remarks. For
the most part, unmasking informants is a virtual impossibility. Hence,
corroboration of their often gross allegations is similarly difficult.

Max Yergan: A Collection of Primary and Secondary Sources

This list constitutes a cumulative bibliography on the life and work of
Max Yergan. It includes almost all of the articles, lectures, public presentations, and correspondence either by or concerning him. Since this
book was written over a long period of time, many of the materials I
had consulted at different stages of the project were moved around
from one archive to another. Consequently, readers who wish to locate these sources should be guided by date rather than file and/or box
number.

Part 1: Primary Data Held in Archives and Repositories

American Philosophical Society, Philadelphia, Pennsylvania:
   Franz Boas Collection. Letters exchanged between Boas and Yergan.

Atlanta University Center, Robert W. Woodruff Library:
   Harold Jackman Correspondence. Cullen-Jackman MS Collection. Three
   mimeographed fliers advertising events of International Committee on African Affairs, and its successor, the Council on African Affairs dated 20 November 1939, 9 May 1944, and 12 November 1945.

William G. Ballinger Papers:
   University of Cape Town Collection, BC 347. Mostly correspondence.
      Yergan to Ballinger, 30 January 1930, BC 347 B4.II.1
      Program, Fort Hare Conference, 1930, BC 347, II, 2
      Yergan to Ballinger, 24 March 1930, BC 347 F3.II.1. 6

Yergan to Ballinger, 9 June 1930, BC 347 F3.II.1.8
Yergan to Ballinger, 11 July 1930, BC 347 F3.II.1.10
Yergan to Ballinger, 22 April 1953, BC 347 B3.IV.4.1
University of the Witwatersrand Collection, c2.7.1. One letter. See infra.

Beinecke Library, Yale University:
James Weldon Johnson Collection. Five brief letters to Richard Wright.
Letters to and from Ralph Johnson Bunche

Mary McLeod Bethune Museum and Archives, Washington, D.C.:
Records of the National Council of Negro Women.
Series 5, Box 10, Folder 171 (Council on African Affairs)
Series 5, Box 24, Folder 359
Series 5, Box 25, Folder 372
Series 5, Box 38, Folder 542 (Yergan correspondence)

Ralph Johnson Bunche Papers:
Schomburg Collection for Afro-American Research. Critical materials concerning the National Negro Congress in Carnegie Commission Files.

James Burnham Papers, Hoover Institution Archives, Stanford University:
Box 9, File Congress for Cultural Freedom.

Killie Campbell Africana Collection, University of Natal, South Africa:
Minutes of the College Council, Fort Hare Native College, 12 Nov. 1924.
Minutes of the Governing Council, Fort Hare Native College.
9 March 1927, Item 421
9 November 1927, Item 441
21 March 1928, Item 466
24 October 1928, Item 479
13 March 1930, Item 495
12/13 March 1930, Item 532
9 March 1932, Item 592
2 November 1932, Item 613
7 March 1935, Item 733

Carnegie Corporation Archives, New York:
Correspondence concerning Yergan's South African activities, mainly those related to funding construction of the YMCA's Christian Union Building on the campus of Fort Hare "Native" College in Alice, E. Cape. Correspondence, press releases related to International Committee on African Africans and successor institution, Council on African Affairs.

F[rederick] PK[eppel], Memorandum of Interview, Max Yergan, 16 November 1927

Yergan to Keppel, 14 December 1927

Keppel to Yergan, 16 December 1927

William Jay Schieffelin to Keppel, 7 March 1929

Keppel to Schieffelin, 14 March 1929

Keppel to Appleget, 23 July 1931

Appleget to Keppel, 27 July 1931

Keppel to Appleget, 28 July 1931

Keppel to Appleget, 1 October 1931

$5,000 Appropriation, 11 October 1931

Keppel to Yergan, 13 October 1931 (incl. notice of $10,000 award)

Yergan to Keppel, 17 November 1931

Keppel to Yergan, 17 December 1931

"A Project for Training Native Social Workers in South Africa: An Institute of Social Research and Service." Memorandum prepared for the Honourable Patrick Duncan, Trustee, Carnegie Corporation, by Max Yergan, Alice, C.P., South Africa, 1 June 1932

Yergan to Hon. Patrick Duncan, 14 June 1932

Yergan to Frederick Keppel, 22 June 1932 (incl. Yergan Memo to Patrick Duncan, 1 June 1932, above)

RML [for Keppel] to Yergan, 21 July 1932

Loram to Keppel, 1 August 1932, incl. Yergan to Loram, 17 June 1932.

Keppel to Yergan, 28 October 1932, incl. Yergan to Keppel, 28 September 1932

Yergan to Lester, 1 November 1932 (incl. Report to Carnegie Corp.)

Yergan to Lester, 12 December 1932

"Memorandum of Interview, FPK and Max Yergan, May 9, 1933"

Yergan to Keppel, 1 September 1933

Loram to Keppel, 6 September 1933

Memo, "Proposal for Institute of Social Research and Service for non-Europeans in South Africa 10/9/33" (stamped "Peffer")

Duncan to Keppel, 30 April 1934

Keppel to Yergan, 29 May 1934

Keppel to Duncan, 29 May 1934

Yergan to Keppel, 22 June 1934

Yergan to Keppel, 3 October 1934

Keppel to Yergan, 4 October 1934

Memorandum of Interview, JMR and Max Yergan, 11 January 1935

Yergan to Keppel, 3 May 1935

Yergan to Keppel, 10 May 1935

Keppel to Yergan, 13 June 1935
Keppel to Duncan, 13 June 1935
Keppel to Yergan, 10 October 1935
Yergan to Keppel, 21 February 1936
Record of Interview, FPK and Max Yergan, 28 February 1936
Yergan to Keppel, 19 January 1938
Yergan to Keppel, 2 May 1938
Record of Interview, JMR and Max Yergan, 11 May 1938
Yergan to John M. Russell, 17 May 1938
Record of Interview, WHS and Max Yergan, 24 September 1949

George Edward Cory Library Collection for Historical Research, Rhodes University Library, Grahamstown, South Africa:
Die Christen-Studentevereniging/The Christian Student Association, 1896–1936. Contains:
H. P. Cruse, "Die C.S.V. En Die Nie-Blanke Rasse van Suid-Afrika" (135–37) and C. P. Dent, "The Bantu S.CA." Ibid., 137–39
D. J. Kritzinger, "Die Konferensie Op Fort Hare" (29–30)
Christianity and the Natives of South Africa: A Year-Book of South African Missions," Bloemfontein (?) n.d., ca. 1927 or 1928
The Realignment of Native Life on a Christian Basis. Being the Seventh General Missionary Conference of South Africa Held at Lovedale June 26–29, 1928 (MS 16 602)

William Edward Burghardt Du Bois Papers. Microfilm edition

Dwight David Eisenhower Presidential Library, Abilene, Kansas

Hampton Institute Archives, Collis P. Huntington Memorial Library:
"News from Max Yergan," No. 1.
Max Yergan, "A Y.M.C.A. Secretary in Africa," *Southern Workman* 47 (August 1918) (Excerpts from an address made at Hampton, 21 April 1918)
"Hampton Incidents." *Southern Workman* 49 (1920) (re. Max Yergan address to Hampton student body Sunday evening, 30 November 1919, en route to France)
Kenneth Saunders, "A Forward Move in Africa." *Southern Workman* 49 (1920)
Max Yergan, "Race Currents and Conditions in South Africa," Part 1. *Southern Workman* 56 (March 1927) and Part 2 (May 1927)
"The Y.M.C.A. in Africa" and "What Others Say." *Southern Workman* 57 (March 1928)

Lyndon Baines Johnson Presidential Library, Austin, Texas:
　White House Central Files, Name File, "American A":
　　White House Central Files, memo, Rick Haynes to Bromley Smith, 3-7-66
　　White House Central Files, letter, Wm. Rusher & Max Yergan to "Friend,"
　　　9-13-65
　　White House Central Files, memo, American- African Affairs Association
　　　To All Concerned, 11-30-67
　National Security Files, Name File, "Haynes Memos" Box 3:
　　National Security File, memo, for the Record, 2-17-66

Mary van Kleeck Papers, Sophia Smith Collection, Smith College:
　Twelve letters written between 1938 and 1940 in folders entitled "Max Yer-
　gan" and correspondence, typed manuscript of "Gold and Poverty in South
　Africa" in "I.R.I. publications—Max Yergan, 1938."

Library of Congress, Manuscript Division:
　National Association for the Advancement of Colored People Papers:
　Group I, Administrative File:
　　Box C212, Awards, Spingarn Medal, 1933
　　Box C298, Federal Council of Churches
　　Box C383, National Negro Congress, 7 April–2 December 1938
　Group II, NAACP, 1940–55, General Office File, 1940–1955:
　　Box A7, Africa, South Africa General, 1950–55
　　Box A444, National Negro Congress, 1945–47
　　Box C365, Leagues—Council on African Affairs
　　Box A373, Leagues—Council on African Affairs, 1948–55
　　Box A675, Max Yergan, 1941–53
　Materials total approximately one hundred pages.

Lincoln University Archives, Lincoln University, Pennsylvania:
　Frank Wilson Collection. Correspondence, fliers from Max Yergan re. Inter-
　national Committee and Its Successor, Council on African Affairs.

Alain Locke Papers, Manuscripts and Archives, Moorland-Spingarn Research
　　Center, Howard University:
　One letter, Yergan to Locke, 17 May 1937, concerning Yergan's recent visit
　to Europe and describing dinner as guest of M. and Mme. René Maran at
　their Paris residence.

Charles Templeman Loram Papers, Sterling Library, Yale University:
　A Yale-educated South African, Loram served on the Native Affairs Com-

mission from l920 to 1930. Correspondence with philanthropist A. P. Stokes. The files contain a few isolated but key references to Yergan.

Francis Pickens Miller Papers, Alderman Library, University of Virginia:
Number 9760, Box 2, 1930–31. "The Affair." Re: Yergan and Rena Carswell Datta, administrative secretary of the World's Student Christian Federation from April 1928 to June 1930. F. P. Miller chaired the World's Student Christian Federation from 1928 to 1938. Approx. fifty pages.

Jesse Edward Moorland Collection, Moorland-Spingarn Research Center, Howard University:
One of the most extensive repositories of data on Yergan's early life and career, covering circa 1915–1930s.

Jesse Edward Moorland Reading Room, Howard University:
Marieta Harper, "Case Study of the Relationship of Max Yergan and Paul Robeson in the Historical Development of the Council on African Affairs," Seminar Paper, History Department, 1974

Robert Russa Moton Papers, Tuskegee University Archives, Tuskegee University:
General Correspondence, Box 71, File 477. Letters written in 1921, principally concerning Yergan's efforts to enter South Africa.

John Raleigh Mott Papers. Mott Room, Divinity School Library, Yale University:
Manuscript Collection #45, Box 117, Folder 1940, Reports, Letters, Diaries, Concerning Mott's Official YMCA Visit to South Africa, 1906.
Box 101, Folder 1779, Correspondence with Max Yergan, 1948–1952.
World Student Christian Federation MS Collection #46, see below.

Municipal Archives, New York City:
Fiorello H. La Guardia Papers:
Harlem—1943 Race Riots. Correspondence on racial unrest.
Mayor La Guardia's Daily Appointment Book, 1943.

National Council of Negro Women, Records of the, Washington, D.C.:
See Mary McLeod Bethune Museum and Archives listing above.

National Negro Congress Papers:
Microfilm. Originals in Schomburg Center for Afro-American Research, New York Public Library.

Anson Phelps Stokes Papers, Sterling Library, Yale University:
Correspondence, 1920–1950. Official and unofficial documentation:
Manuscript Group 299A. P. Stokes Papers, Series I, Box 31, Folder 512—
"General Correspondence, 1922–1930." Includes miscellany by, from, to,
or about C. T. Loram, T. J. Jones, inter alia.
Box 98, Folder 1592
Yergan to APS, 22 October 1930
Yergan to APS, 25 April 1931
APS to Yergan, 29 April 1931
APS to Yergan, 2 May 1931
Yergan to APS, 4 May 1931
Lyon et al. to APS, 8 May 1931
Box 98, Folder 1593
Yergan to APS, 6 July 1931
Yergan to APS, 1 February 1934
APS to Yergan, 2 February 1934
Yergan to APS, 8 February 1934
APS to Yergan, 9 February 1934
Yergan to APS, 13 February 1934
Box 128, Folder 2301
Yergan to APS, 26 August 1941
APS to Yergan, 28 August 1941
Yergan to APS, 2 September 1941
APS to Yergan, 2 November 1943
Box 128, Folder 2302
APS to Yergan, 9 February 1944
Yergan to APS, 22 March 1944
APS to Yergan, 28 March 1944
Box 138, Folder 2304
"The American Negro and Mr Robeson," *New York Herald Tribune*, 23
April 1949
APS to Yergan, 30 April 1949
Yergan to APS, 4 May 1949
Yergan to APS, 16 May 1949
APS to Yergan, 21 May 1949
Yergan to APS, 3 June 1949
APS to Yergan, 13 November 1950

Journal of Clarence Pickett, American Friends Service Committee Archives,
American Friends Service Committee, Philadelphia, Penn.:
Entry dated 2/8/38 treating meeting with Pickett, Mary van Kleeck, M.
Fled[d]erus, Helen Bryan, and Yergan "about plans for a conference on

Negro standards of living and labor conditions throughout the world, which conference is to be conducted next October." The paper Yergan presented was published as *Gold and Poverty in South Africa.*

Paul Robeson Archives, New York:
  Correspondence and Council on African Affairs–related documents. Written and photographic data generated by both Paul and Eslanda Robeson, as well as occasional ephemera by and about Max Yergan. This archive was closed in 1975, at which time the vast majority of its contents were transferred to the Manuscript Division, Moorland-Spingarn Research Center, Howard University, Washington, D.C. (see below).

Paul Robeson Papers, Manuscripts and Archives Division, Moorland-Spingarn Research Center, Howard University, Washington, D.C.:
  These appear to be the same papers as listed immediately above.

Rockefeller Archive Center, Pocantico Hills, N. Tarrytown, New York:
  Rockefeller Family Archives, RG 2 John D. Rockefeller, Jr.:
    Sub-Series Welfare Interests—Youth, folder, "YMCA—National Council Max Yergan—Work in Africa, 1927–1947" (Box 35) (John D. Rockefeller Jr.'s financial assistance to Yergan's bldg. project).
    21 October 1927 to 29 May 1947 (approx. one hundred pages re. So. Africa 1927–1931)
  Rockefeller Foundation Archives, RG General Correspondence, Series 487:
    South Africa: Box 45 (1930) folder 367
    Box 60 (1931) folder 495
    Box 423 (1948) folder 2857
  Laura Spelman Rockefeller Memorial Fund, Series Three, Box 101:
    Folder 1021, "Negro Problems 1927–1929." Two memoranda, dated 21 October and 11 November 1927, specifically single out Yergan.
  Russell Sage Foundation, Early Office Files, 138. The Department of Industrial Studies, Monthly Reports, 1937–1943. IV4B1. Memoranda, notes, and letters concerning activities of Mary van Kleeck, Mary L. Fleddérus, International Industrial Relations Institute, and Yergan.

Franklin Delano Roosevelt Presidential Library, Hyde Park, New York:
  Materials sent to author.

Schomburg Center for Research in Black Culture, New York Public Library:
  Council on African Affairs Vertical File
  National Negro Congress Vertical File
  Max Yergan Vertical File

Ralph Johnson Bunche Papers
Alphaeus Hunton Papers MG 290
National Negro Congress Papers
Paul Robeson Papers

Harry S. Truman Presidential Library, Independence, Missouri:
President's Personal File:
Papers of Harry S. Truman. Official File.
    Telegram, Yergan to Truman, 13 April 1945
    Jonathan Daniels to Yergan, 1 May 1945
    Memo, AW to [W. D.] Hassett [Secretary to the President], n.d.
    Yergan to the President, White House, 27 March 1946
    Hassett to Yergan, 24 May 1946
    Memo, WDH, referred to David K. Niles, 16 May 1946
    Yergan to Harry S. Truman, 15 May 1946
    Handbill Advertising Tenth National Negro Congress, Detroit, 30 May–2
        June, bearing slogan, "Death Blow to Jim Crow"
    Papers of Philleo Nash
    Revels Cayton to President Harry S. Truman, 18 March 1946
    Yergan and Revels Cayton to Harry S. Truman, 1 June 1946
    Petition to the Economic and Social Council of the United Nations . . . on
        Behalf of the Negro People of America by the NNC . . .
Files of Philleo Nash:
Papers of Harry S. Truman.
    David K. Niles to Yergan, 24 May 1949
General File:
Papers of Harry S. Truman.
    Memorandum, W.D.H. referred to Mr Niles, 5 August 1946
    Memorandum, M. C. Latta, referred to Department of State, 14 June
        1946
    Memorandum, William D. Hassett to the President, 6 June 1946
    Yergan, Telegram to President Urging Permanent Fair Employment Prac-
        tices Committee, 6 June 1945
    M. C. Latta, Memo, Department of State, 15 November 1945
    M. C. Latta, Memo, Department of State, 10 November 1945
    W. D. Hassett, Memo, Secretary of War, 31 October 1945
    Yergan, Letter to President, 15 October 1945
Official File:
Papers of Harry S. Truman.
    Telegram, Yergan to Truman, 28 July 1946
    Telegram, Robeson to David K. Niles, White House, 19 September 1946
    Telegram, Robeson to the President, 13 September 1946

Memo, "The Following Delegation will meet with the President 11:30 A.M.," 23 September 1946

Memo, M.J.C. to David K. Niles, 13 September 1946

President's Secretary's Files:

Personal and Confidential. By Special Messenger. J. Edgar Hoover to Major General Harry Hawkins Vaughan, Military Aide to the President, 19 November 1946.

Personal and Confidential. By Special Messenger. J. Edgar Hoover to Major General Harry Hawkins Vaughan, Military Aide to the President, 13 November 1946.

United Nations Archives:

Registry Records (TRI 132/1/04, Future Status and Administration of Mandated Territories, South West Africa Petitions)

Photograph: Yergan presenting petition on the status of South West Africa to P. T. Schmidt, shown with Herbert Aptheker, Revels Cayton, Lyman White, and Charles Collins, June 13, 1946. (*People's Voice* photo, A. Hansen. Courtesy United Nations Library)

University of the Witwatersrand Library, Johannesburg, So. Africa:

William G. Ballinger Collection:

A 410/C2.7.1 (File 1), Yergan to Ballinger, 11 May 1930

Joint Council Collection:

AD 1433/Cj2.1.6c. Yergan to J. D. Rheinallt Jones, 28 August 1928

AD 1433/Cj2.1.7. Yergan to F. P. Keppel, Carnegie Corporation, 23 November 1927 and "General Statement in Support of the Request for the Building in Connection with the Work of Max Yergan in South Africa . . ."

Howard Pim Collection:

A 881/Bl1, Correspondence. Letters to Pim. Political (General) S–Z. Yergan to Pim, 21 December 1932

South African Institute of Race Relations Collection:

AD 843/B3.11.1, Notes by J. D. R. Jones on a Memo by M. Yergan, 1934

AD 843/B97.9.2, "Race Problems Acute in South Africa," by Max Yergan and Oswin Bull, undated [ca. 1930]

The People's Voice, newspaper:

"On Africa," 13 February 1943

"Max Yergan on Africa and the War: The Stake of Colonial Peoples in the War," 13 March 1943, 10

"Max Yergan on Africa and the War," 20 March 1943, 10

"Max Yergan on Africa and the War," 27 March 1943, 11

"Max Yergan on Africa and the War," 3 April 1943, 11

Guest editorial, "Franklin D. Roosevelt: His Monument and Lessons," 21 April 1945, 16

Guest editorial, "British Labor Victory and the Colonies," 4 August 1945

"Murder Was in Their Hearts: Eyewitness Account of a City Banning Paul Robeson" 26 April 1947

Walter P. Reuther Library, Wayne State University, Detroit, Michigan. Archives of Labor History, Urban Affairs, and University Archives:

Mary van Kleeck Papers:

Max Yergan Typescript, "Standards of Living in Colonial Areas, As Influenced by Governments," address given at Annual Summer Conference of the International Industrial Relations Institute, The Hague, The Netherlands, 31 August 1939

Mary White Ovington Papers:

Letter, Yergan to Ovington, 2 August 1929, Box 2, Folder 2-1

World Alliance of YMCAs Library, Geneva, Switzerland:

"I Would Not Be Able to Rest, If I Did Not Go Back to Africa." *All One*, Vol. 1, No. 3 (30 November 1921) [New York: YMCA International Committee]

"News from Max Yergan," No. 1 [1928?] X314.12 (68)

Yergan to W. Gethman, 30 October 1929

Yergan to Miss Una Saunders, 25 April 1932. X 314.12 (67)

George Edmund Haynes, *Report of The Young Men's Christian Association in South Africa* (1930)

C. Howard Hopkins, *History of the Y.M.C.A. in North America,* 1951

Kenneth Scott Latourette, *World Service: A History of the Foreign Work and World Service of the Young Men's Christian Associations of the United States and Canada* (New York: Association Press)

Clarence Prouty Shedd, *History of the World Alliance of Young Men's Christian Associations.* London: Published for the World's Committee of Young Men's Christian Associations by S.P.C.K., 1955

World Council of Churches Library, Geneva, Switzerland:

Correspondence between Max Yergan and staff members of World's Student Christian Federation, 1928–1932 (approx. one hundred letters). See below.

World Student Christian Federation Archives, Geneva, Switzerland:

Box 27, File Sud Afrique, 1922–1924

Box 43–45, File Max Yergan, 1922–1924

Box 69, SCYM, File Questions re race noire
Box 84, File Max Yergan, 1926–1928
Box 98A, File Afrique du Sud, 1926–1928
Box 123, File Max Yergan, 1928–1929
Box 140, File Afrique du Sud, 1928–1929
Box 154, File Max Yergan, 1930
Box 167, File Afrique du Sud, 1930
Box 181, File Max Yergan, 1931

World Student Christian Federation Collection, John R. Mott Papers, John R.
    Mott Room, Divinity School Library, Yale University:
Manuscript Collection #46:
    Box 253, Folder 2119, Correspondence, Mott-Bull, 1906–1909
    Box 253, Folder 2120, Correspondence, Mott-Bull, 1910–1925
    Box 254, Folder 2129, "Important Letters," Report of Donald Fraser to
    Mott concerning 1897 South Africa Tour

Filed in former YMCA Bowne Historical Library, 291 Broadway, N.Y.:
Now held in YMCA of the USA Archives, Minneapolis, Minnesota.

Alfred Bitini Xuma Papers:
    Hoover Institution, Stanford University, and the University of the Witwater-
    srand, Johannesburg, Tvl., So. Africa
    Twenty-seven letters exchanged between Xuma and Yergan, 1928–1942.
    AD843.

Part 2: Formerly Classified U.S. Government Documents
Released through Freedom of Information Act

Department of the Navy. 100.3633:
    "Index of Photographs Which Appeared in the Daily Worker from February
    2, 1932–December 31, 1942."
    p 34, Yergan, Max. 7/26/38 p. 7.4/14/37 p. 2.

United States Justice Department, Federal Bureau of Investigation:
    Of particular interest is the manner in which Yergan's life was complicated
    by radical acquaintances—the way the FBI has historically pursued a policy
    of guilt by association, especially in cases where Communists, real or imag-
    ined, may have been involved. This policy has had a particularly chilling
    effect in cases involving people of color. This is clear from documentation
    released to me via the FOIA, even though most of it was highly expurgated.

These documents need to be indexed in some way that will render them more decipherable. This guide has been prepared in an effort to address that need. A select listing of the documents is as follows:

Dr. Max Yergan, File No. 100-210026, Vol. 1, Serials X–48
Dr. Max Yergan, File No. 100-210026, Vol. 2, Serials 49–73
Dr. Max Yergan, File No. 100-210026, Vol. 3, Serials 74–111
Dr. Max Yergan, File No. 100-210026, Vol. 4, Serials 112–117
Dr. Max Yergan, File No. 100-210026, Vol. 5, Serial 118 only
Dr. Max Yergan, File No. 100-210026, Vol. 6, Serials 119–145
Dr. Max Yergan, File No. 100-210026, Vol. 7, Serials 146–158
Dr. Max Yergan, File No. 100-210026, Vol. 8, Serials 159–181
Dr. Max Yergan, File No. 100-210026, Vol. 9, Serial 182
Dr. Max Yergan, File No. 100-210026, Vol. 10, Serial 183–205
Dr. Max Yergan, File No. 100-210026, Vol. 11, Serial 206–224
Dr. Max Yergan, File No. 100-210026, Vol. 12, Serials 225–270
Dr. Max Yergan, File No. 100-210026, Vol. 13, Serials 271–306

U.S. Department of Justice. Federal Bureau of Investigation:
Criminal Investigation Division, CRM 6197F
Internal Security Division, 146-7-51-1119
Subversive Organizations Section, 146-28-376, CAA
Subversive Activities Section

Responses to FOIA Requests from FBI Regional Offices:
File 146-200-3652 New York Grand Jury Testimony
Council of African Affairs, 146-28-376

State Department Archives, National Archives Trust Fund Board, National Archives State Department Decimal Files. 811.00B/12-644.

Part 3: Inventory: Writings and Speeches by Max Yergan

"A Y.M.C.A. Secretary in Africa." *Southern Workman* 47:8 (August 1918): 401–3.
"The Negro in Africa: No Answer but God." *Association Men* 47:12 (August 1922): 561.
"On the Y.M.C.A. in North America." *Manhood: Organ of the Cape Town Y.M.C.A.* 3:7 (November 1922): 151–57.
"The Native Students of South Africa and Their Problems." *The Student World* 62 (April 1923): 62–67.
Devotional Service, conducted by Max Yergan, of South Africa. Thursday, August 8, 1926. In *Youth Faces Life: Being the Report of the Nineteenth World*

Conference of Y.M.C.A.'s at Helsingfors, August 1–6, 1926. Geneva: World's Committee of YMCAs, 1926.

"Youth's Challenge to Youth." In *Thinking with Africa: Chapters by a Group of Nationals Interpreting the Christian Movement.* Assembled and edited by Milton Stauffer. Published for the Student Volunteer Movement for Foreign Missions by the Missionary Education Movement of the United States and Canada. New York: 1927.

"Race Currents and Conditions in South Africa." *Southern Workman.* In two separate installments. Part 1, 56:3 (March 1927): 109–12. Part 2, 56:5 (May 1927): 209–12.

"The Message of the Jerusalem Meeting of the International Missionary Council: Its Significance to South Africa." In *The Realignment of Native Life on a Christian Basis: A Report of the Proceedings of the Seventh General Missionary Conference of South Africa, Held at Lovedale, June 26–29, 1928.* 131–52.

Africa, the West, and Christianity. [Speech Presented] for Distribution to the General Committee of the World's Student Christian Federation [Meeting,] Mysore, India, 5–16 December 1928.

"The Student Christian Association of South Africa (Native Department) from Material Supplied by Rev. Max Yergan, Secretary." In *Christianity and the Natives of South Africa: A Yearbook of South African Missions.* n.d. [l928?] Cory Library for Historical Research, Rhodes University Library, Grahamstown, Eastern Cape, South Africa.

"African Youth of Tomorrow." *Missionary Review of the World* (March 1929): 187–95. *Student World* (April 1929).

Christian Students and Modern South Africa: A Report of the Bantu-European Student Christian Conference, Fort Hare, June 27th–July 3rd, 1930. Fort Hare: Student Christian Association of South Africa [Bantu Section] Christian Union, 1930.

"New Ventures in Race Relations in South Africa." Unpublished typescript, WSCF Archives, World Council of Churches, Geneva.

"Aspects of the Present Interracial Situation in Africa." *Student World* 23:4 (October 1930): 366–75.

"Human Possibility: Bantu-European Student Conference in South Africa." *Presbyterian Magazine,* November 1930, 653–55.

National Negro Congress. Official Proceedings, Feb. 14–16, 1936.

"The Significance of Race in Human Relations." *Friends Intelligencer,* 26 February 1938, 135–37.

Gold and Poverty in South Africa: A Study of Economic Organization and Standards of Living. New York and The Hague: International Industrial Relations Institute with the Cooperation of the International Committee on African Affairs, 1938.

"The Status of the Natives in South Africa." *Journal of Negro History* 24 (January 1939).

"An Answer to Japanese Propaganda among American Negroes." *China Today* 5:8 (May 1939): 9–10, 19.

Democracy and the Negro People Today. An address given at a meeting sponsored by the Church League for Industrial Democracy. October 16, 1940. New York: National Negro Congress, 1940.

"Forgotten Ideas, Forgotten People." *New Masses*, 16 February 1941.

Africa in the War. New York: Council on African Affairs, 1942.

Negro America and the War for Survival. People's World, 1942. An address delivered at the Philharmonic Auditorium, Los Angeles, 17 September 1942. 16 pp.

"Negro Congress Head to Speak Here." *Montreal Daily Star,* 27 January 1944.

"Authority on Africa Our Special Speaker." Canadian Broadcasting Corporation *Program Schedule,* Week of 6 February 1944.

"Dr. Yergan Speaks in Canada." *Congress Vue,* March 1944.

"Africa: New Perspectives." Main Conference Address, 14 April 1944. In *For a New Africa: Proceedings of the Conference on Africa—New Perspectives.* Institute for International Democracy, 14 April 1944. New York: Council on African Affairs, 1944.

"The Future of Africa." *New Masses,* 18 April 1944.

"An Insult to American Negroes That Did Not Go Unchallenged." *Daily Worker,* 4 May 1944.

"There Is a Basis for Solution of Anglo-American Trade Problems." *Daily Worker,* 8 June 1944.

"Three Proposals to Make Teheran a Postwar Reality for Colonials." *Daily Worker,* 1 July 1944.

"South Africa Has Its Rankins and Bilbos." *Daily Worker,* 15 July 1944.

"The Colonial Peoples and World Production Possibilities." *Daily Worker,* 22 July 1944.

"Franklin D. Roosevelt: His Monument and Lessons." Guest Editorial. *People's Voice,* 21 April 1945, 16.

"British Labor Victory and the Colonies," Guest Editorial. *People's Voice,* 4 August 1945, 14.

"America's Stake in Colonial Freedom." In *Trust and the Non Self-Governing Territories.* Edited by Merze Tate. Volume 6, number 1 of the Howard University Studies in the Social Sciences. Proceedings of the Conference on Africa held 8–9 April 1947. Speech delivered Wednesday afternoon 9 April 1947. Washington, D.C.: 1947. 48–55.

"I.C.F.T.U.'s Opportunity in Africa." *International Free Trade Union News* 5:5 (May 1950): 8.

"Negroes and Democracy in the U.S." *International Free Trade Union News* 5:11 (November 1950): 8.

"Negroes and Democracy in the U.S." *International Free Trade Union News* 5:12 (December 1950): 12.

"American Racial Policy and the Situation of American Negroes." Presented to the Indian Congress for Cultural Freedom, Bombay, 28–31 March 1951 (appended to Yergan to Roosevelt, 2 May 1951).

Address, Proceedings of the Open Session (28 March [1951]), and "American Racial Policy and the Situation of American Negroes." In *Indian Congress for Cultural Freedom, March 28 to 31, 1951.* Bombay: Kanada Press, 1951. 30–33, 271–81, resp.

"Developments in Africa Today." Desai Memorial Hall, sponsored by Kenya League, Nairobi, 20 August 1952. Nairobi, Foreign Service Dispatch No. 34, 28 August 1952. (Visit from 14–21 August 1952.)

"Africa: Next Goal of Communists: Interview with Dr. Max Yergan, America's Foremost Authority on Africa." *U.S. News and World Report*, 1 May 1953, 52–63.

Letter to the Editor. *New York Times*, 10 August 1953.

"The Communist Threat in Africa." In *Africa Today*. Edited by Charles Grove Haines. New York: Collingwood Press, 1955; reprinted l968. 262–79.

"Why There's No Colored Bloc: Interview with Dr. Max Yergan, American Negro Authority on Africa." *U.S. News and World Report*, 3 June 1955, 96–97.

Part 4: Articles Written about Max and/or Susie Yergan

"Breaking over Race Lines." *Southwestern Christian Advocate*, 27 July 1916. (Profile of Yergan and his mission work in India.)

Stuart, Herbert. "Colonel Newcome in Dar-es-Salaam." *Young Men of India* (Calcutta) 29:1 (January 1918): 27–31.

Webster, C. R. "Wide Open Africa." *Association Men* 43:6 (New York) (February 1918): 432–33.

Nash, Vernon. "The Y.M.C.A. in East Africa in 1917." *Young Men of India* (Calcutta) 29:6 (June 1918): 351–56.

Saunders, Kenneth. "A Forward Move in Africa." *Southern Workman* 49 (1920).

"I Would Not Be Able to Rest, If I Did Not Go Back to Africa." *All One*, 30 November 1921.

Tobias, Channing H. "A Decade of Student Y.M.C.A. Work." *Crisis* 24:6 (October 1922): 265–66.

"Foreign Flashes." *Association Men* 18:4 (December 1922): 185. ("Day and night work is necessary, Max Yergan finds in his Cape Province Program. He has already organized 9 Student Christian Associations in 14 educational institutions.")

"Membership." *Association Men* 48:8 (April 1923): 390. (Re: "Dr J. M. Gregory, a black dentist who raised money for support of Max Yergan in South Africa.")

Article, *New York Evening World,* 7 February 1927.

"Seeking Greater Justice." *Men of New York,* April 1927.

"Race Issue Subject in Northfield Talk: Max Yergan, Negro Y.M.C.A. Secretary in Africa, Speaks at Women's Conference," *New York Times,* 14 July 1927, 9:1.

Bullock, Ralph W. "Max Yergan." In *In Spite of Handicaps.* New York: Association Press, 1927.

Ovington, Mary White. "Max Yergan." In *Portraits in Color.* New York: Viking, 1927. 31–42.

"Youth's Challenge to Youth." In *Thinking with Africa: Chapters by a Group of Nationals Interpreting the Christian Movement, Assembled and Edited by Milton Stauffer.* New York: Published for the Student Volunteer Movement for Foreign Missions by Missionary Education Movement for United States and Canada, 1927.

"Rockefeller Jr. Gives $25,000 for Africans." *New York Times,* 7 December 1927, 20:5.

"Max Yergan of Africa Is Guest of the Cedar Y," *Cleveland Red Triangle* (local YMCA publication), 9 January 1928.

Bryan, Helen R. "Max Yergan, Uplifter of South Africa." *Crisis* 39:12 (December 1932): 375–76. (Reprinted in *Bantu World,* 14 January 1933, 9; and idem, 21 January 1933, 9.)

"Eighteenth Spingarn Medal Goes to Max Yergan." *Afro-American,* 25 March 1933.

"Max Yergan." *Pittsburgh Courier,* 1 April 1933.

"Sees Hope for South Africa." *Boston Chronicle,* 15 April 1933.

"Max Yergan Tells Crowd of Work among Africans." *Chicago Defender,* 29 April 1933.

"Degrees Awarded 130 at Exercises of Local College." *Springfield (Massachusetts) Daily Republican,* 12 June 1933.

"Dr. Max Yergan Is Coming!" 6 December 1933, at the Founders' Day Celebration, Gammon Theological Seminary. (Handbill, YMCA Headquarters Library.)

Beasley, C. C. "A Negro Leader in South Africa." *Boston Evening Transcript,* 19 May 1934.

"Negro for College Post: Max Yergan Recommended for New Course at City Institution." *New York Times,* 15 April 1937, 13:3.

Lawrence, Will. "Max Yergan, Progressive Leader." *Daily Worker,* 30 September 1938.

"Assails Race Prejudice: Head of African Affairs Group Scores Anti-Negro Feeling." *New York Times,* 7 April 1940, 40:6.

"Negro Congress Adjourns in Spirit of Unity." *Daily Worker,* 30 April 1940.

"Negroes Are Called to Form '2D' Party: National Congress Head Says Only One Major Group Is Left." *New York Times,* 18 November 1940, 7:6.

"City College Removes Yergan, Negro Educator." *Daily Worker,* 28 April 1941.

"Start Campaign to Reinstate Dr. Max Yergan." *Daily Worker,* 24 May 1941.

"Dr. Yergan Challenges 60 on Civil Rights Sincerity." *Daily Worker,* 24 May 1941.

"Boston Negro Paper Assails Yergan Firing." *Daily Worker,* 28 May 1941.

"Teachers Union Protests Yergan Firing." *Daily Worker,* 30 May 1941.

"Left Wing of Labor for Hitler Defeat." *New York Times,* 11 July 1941.

"ALP Expected to Name Dr. Yergan, Eugene Connolly." *Daily Worker,* 30 September 1941.

"Connolly Scores O'Dwyer on Reds." *New York Times,* 3 October 1941.

"Mayor Is Assured of Labor Backing. " *New York Times,* 9 October 1941, 46.

"Group Friction Here Held Undemocratic: Pearl Buck Speaks at Rally of Council on African Affairs." *New York Times,* 9 April 1942, 7:4.

"South Africa's Aid in War Described." *New York Times,* 26 January 1943, 6:7.

"'Act Together Now for Unity, Protection, Victory'—Yergan." *People's Voice,* 3 July 1943.

"Council Hails USSR-Ethiopia Agreement." *People's Voice,* 10 July 1943.

"Cleveland NNC Sponsors Unity Victory Meeting" and "National Organizations Unite on New Program." *People's Voice,* 17 July 1943.

"Yergan Sees South Africa Poll Vital to War." *Daily Worker,* 21 July 1943.

"Harlem Disorders Bring Quick Action by City and Army." *New York Times,* 2 August 1943, 1:1, 16.

"NNC Launches Program to Democratize Arts" and Ransom, Llewellyn, "Racial Element Not Present in New York Riot: Leaders Act Quickly to Restore Law and Order." *People's Voice,* 7 August 1943.

"Alphaeus Hunton Joins African Affairs Council," "Yergan Asks Mayors to Act against Riots," and "South African Elections Viewed as Pro-War Victory." *People's Voice,* 14 August 1943.

"City-Wide Council of Races Formed to Probe, Wipe Out Riot Causes." *People's Voice,* 28 August 1943.

"Future of Africa Is Future of World." *People's Voice,* 25 September 1943.

"Hunter College Meeting Hears about Harlem." *People's Voice,* 2 October 1943.

"National Negro Congress Greets UAW Convention" and "NNC Announces Lobby to End Jimcro in Army." *People's Voice,* 16 October 1943.

"Carver School in Harlem Has Democratic Curriculum" and "Dr. Max Yergan Pleads for Unity," *People's Voice*, 23 October 1943.

"Post-War Africa Theme of Series." *People's Voice*, 13 November 1943.

"National Negro Congress Opens Office in D.C." *People's Voice*, 20 November 1943.

"Cultural Group Stresses Negro Art Contribution." *People's Voice*, 4 December 1943.

"Teacher-Unionist Joins Negro Congress Staff." *People's Voice*, 18 December 1943.

"Harlem Set for Action Conference." *People's Voice*, 11 March 1944, 13.

"Would Help Colonies: International Agency to Rule in Africa Is Proposed." *New York Times*, 15 April 1944, 5.

Streator, George. "Negro Praised in Fascism Defeat." *New York Times*, 31 May 1945, 38:1.

"Colonial Empires Assailed in Rally." *New York Times*, 7 June 1946, 7:1.

"Action on Bilbo Asked by Yergan." *People's Voice*, 29 June 1946.

Letter to the Editor. *New York Times*, 6 July 1946, 14:7.

"Negro Answer to Bilbo Gets Nationwide Hookup." *People's Voice*, 7 September 1946.

"Bids Labor, Negroes Join to Fight Bias." *New York Times*, 29 September 1946, 4:1.

"Anti-Lynching Pledges Asked." *New York Times*, 19 October 1946, 34:1.

Streator, George. "Negro Youth Told Future Is in South." *New York Times*, 21 October 1946, 31:1.

"Smuts Pulls a Bilbo on Africa." *People's Voice*, 26 October 1946.

Wood, Lewis. "90 Groups, Schools Named on U.S. List as Being Disloyal." *New York Times*, 5 December 1947, 1, 18.

"Yergan African Council Plot Flops." *Daily Worker*, 28 May 1948.

"Battles Left Wing for Group's Office: Dr. Yergan, Leader of Council on African Affairs, Asks Aid of the Police, Courts." *New York Times*, 29 May 1948.

"No Cause for Action: Hogan Takes Stand after Study of Dr. Yergan's Complaint." *New York Times*, 2 June 1948.

"Yergan Accuses Five of Assault." *New York Times*, 20 June 1948, 24.

"Court Frees 3 Men Accused by Yergan." *New York Times*, 29 June 1948.

"Yergan Seeks Court Aid: Asks Invalidation of Ouster from Council on African Affairs Post." *New York Times*, 25 August 1948.

"Two Yergan Suits United: Council on African Affairs Case to Be Heard Sept. 20." *New York Times*, 26 August 1948.

Porter, Russell. "Spy Case Jury Hears Sayre, Then Recesses Until Jan. 3." *New York Times*, 23 December 1948, 1, 8.

"An American Negro's View of Africa: Dr. Max Yergan Utters a Warning." *East*

African Standard (Nairobi), 7 April 1951. (Re: March 15–19 visit en route to New Delhi Congress of Cultural Freedom.)

Narain, K. V. "Totalitarianism Menaces Freedom of Thought, Indian Cultural Congress Warns." *American Reporter* (New Delhi), 4 April 1951, 11 (enclosure, Yergan to E. Roosevelt, 2 May 1951).

"Negroes Should Shun Reds as 'Conspiracy,' Yergan Tells Senators." *Evening Star* (Washington, D.C.), 14 May 1952.

"Ruse on Negroes Laid to Reds." *New York Times*, 14 May 1952, 12.

Lautier, Louis. "Yeargan Forsakes Communists, Finds They Mislead Negroes." *Norfolk Journal and Guide*, 24 May 1952.

"South African Leaders Blast Yergan." *Freedom* 2:10 (October 1952).

Kihss, Peter. "Artie Shaw Says He Was Red 'Dupe.'" *New York Times*, 5 May 1953.

"List of Persons Named as Reds." *New York Times*, 5 May 1953.

Matthews, Z. K. "An African Leader Exposes Max Yergan." *Freedom* 3:6 (May 1953).

White, Walter. Letter to the Editor. *New York Times*, 10 August 1953.

Sisulu, Walter. "What Was Dr. Max Yergan's Mission to South Africa?" *African Lodestar* (Transvaal ANC Youth League), November 1953. Carter-Karis Collection of Documents on South Africa, reel 2:DA 16/3:85/1.

"Dr. Max Yergan Is Dead at 82: Black Leader and an Educator." Obituary. *New York Times*, 13 April 1975.

"Max Yergan, Educator and Civil Rights Leader, Dies." *Jet*, 8 May 1975, 30.

Rusher, William A. "Max Yergan, RIP." *National Review*, 9 May 1975, 496–97.

Part 5: References to Max and/or Susie Yergan Appearing in Periodicals Published in Africa

Alice Times, Seymour and Peddie Gazette (Alice, Ciskei, Eastern Cape, South Africa)
"Who Is Max Yergan? Vindication of Local Missionary." 23 May 1929.

The Bantu World (Johannesburg)
Bryan, Helen R. "Max Yergan, Uplifter of South Africa" (in 2 parts). Part 1: 14 January 1933, 9. Part 2: 21 January 1933, 9. (Reprinted from *Crisis* 39:12 [December 1932].)
"Fort Hare News." 5 September 1936.
"Social and Personal News: Who's Who in the News This Week." 21 September 1935, 4.
"More News from Different Centres: Fort Hare News." 5 September 1936. (Re: July 30 departure of the Yergans from SA.)

[Smith, Homer.] "Dr Max Yergan on South Africa's Native Policy." 8 May 1937.

Cape Argus (Cape Town, South Africa)
"Spreading the Light." 15 May 1929.
"Bantustan Policy Is Praised by Visiting Negro." 26 November 1964.
"Matanzima on Negro's Stay in Transkei." 27 November 1964.

Daily Chronicle (Nairobi, Kenya)
19–25 March 1951

East African Standard (Nairobi, Kenya)
"An American Negro's View of Africa: Dr. Max Yergan Utters a Warning." 7 April 1951. Reporting Yergan visit and Nairobi Press Conference.

Ilange Lase Natal Ngongqibelo
"Items about the Negroes (Culled by X), Politics: Yergan vs. Robeson." 18 June 1949.

Imvo Zabantsundu (African Opinion) (King William's Town)
"Native Social Life." 20 March 1922.
"Student's Christian Association (Report for 1923 by the Travelling Secretary, Mr. Max Yergan, B. A.)." 25 March 1924.
"Max Yergan." 4 April 1922 (Xhosa).
"Max Yergan." 27 April 1926.
"*Abantu*" (People). 25 May 1926 (Xhosa).
[Note concerning establishment of £30 bursaries by Transkei Bunga.] 2 December 1927.
"*Ama £5,000 ku Nokoleji!*" 13 December 1927 (Xhosa). (Announcing Rockefeller award for construction of Public Hall on Fort Hare campus.)
"General Notes: Another Fort Hare Gift." (English translation.) Op. cit.

Other South African Newspapers:
"American Negro on Race Relations Mission." *Friend,* 14 October 1948.
Sunday Express, 8 November 1964.
"Negro in a White Hotel." *Cape Times,* 20 November 1964.
"All Right for Negro, Why Not Kaiser, Asks Paper." *Daily Dispatch* (East London, South Africa), 25 November 1964. *Johannesburg Star,* 25 November 1964.
"Transkei Paper Asks: Why Not Matanzima? Negro 'White' Hotel Guest." *Rand Daily Mail,* 27 November 1964.

"The Joke of the Year." (East London) *Daily Dispatch,* 27 November 1964. *Rand Daily Mail* (Johannesburg), 27 November 1964.

Editorial, *Umthunywa* (Umtata, Transkei, Cape), 27 November 1964.

Part 6: Written References to Radio Broadcasts Aired in Which Max Yergan Was an Interviewee, Speaker, or Subject

Yergan talks on "The Darker Races and the War" and FEPC, WINS, 7 April 1942, 12:45–1:00 P.M. Joe Bostic, "Dial Time." *People's Voice,* 11 April 1942, 29.

Frieda Neugebauer, Publications Editor, Council on African Affairs, discusses "Africa's Strategic Role in the War," Lisa Sergio Program, WQXR, 1 May 1942, 10:00 A.M. Joe Bostic, "Dial Time." *People's Voice,* 2 May 1942, 29.

Frieda Neugebauer guest, "Those Who Have Made Good," with Clifford Burdette, WNYC, 24 May 1942, 4 P.M. Joe Bostic, "Dial Time." *People's Voice,* 23 May 1942, 29.

Mayor Fiorello La Guardia, Yergan, Ferdinand Smith, and Hope Stevens speak to quell Harlem residents, WABC, 1 August 1943. "Harlem Disorders Bring Quick Action by City and Army." *New York Times,* 2 August 1943, 1, 16.

"Authority on Africa Our Special Speaker." *Special Speaker,* 6 February 1944, 8:45 P.M. EDT, 9.45 P.M. ADT, Trans-Canada Network, *CBC Program Schedule* (issued by Press and Information Service, Canadian Broadcasting Corporation), Eastern Regional, Davenport Road, Toronto, Canada, Week of 6 February 1944, 1.

Yergan speaks on "The Atlantic Charter and Colonial People in Africa." CBC, Toronto, Trans-Canada Network. *Congress Vue* 1:10 (March 1944): 6.

Yergan participates as one of a group of Negro leaders in Roundtable Discussion heard over Mutual Network in rebuttal to Mississippi's Senator Thomas G. Bilbo. "Negro Answer to Bilbo Gets Nationwide Hookup." *People's Voice,* 7 September 1946, 5.

USIA Broadcast for Africa, Nairobi, Kenya, 27 March 1951 (ref. State Dept. Dispatch).

Part 7: Yergan-Related Testimony Offered at Legislative Hearings

Carter, Edward Clark. Hearings, Institute of Pacific Relations. 27 March 1952.

Field, Frederick V. Testimony. U.S. Senate. Subcommittee to Investigate the Administration of the Internal Security Act and Other Internal Security Laws of the Committee on the Judiciary. Hearings on the Institute of Pacific Relations. 28 March 1952.

Funn, Dorothy Kelso. Testimony. U.S. House of Representatives. Subcommittee of the Committee on Un-American Activities. Investigation of Communist Activities in the Philadelphia Area—Part 2. 17 November 1953.

Steele, Walter S. Testimony. House Un-American Affairs Committee. 21 July 1947.

Tobias, Channing Heggie. U.S. Congress. Senate. Hearing before a Subcommittee of the Committee on Foreign Relations. U.S. Senate, 82nd Congress, First Session on Nomination of Channing Tobias to Be Alternate Representative of the United States at Sixth General Assembly of the United Nations. 18 October 1951.

Yergan, Max. Testimony. U.S. Senate. Subcommittee to Investigate the Administration of the Internal Security Act and Other Internal Security Laws of the Committee on the Judiciary. Hearings on the Institute of Pacific Relations. 13 May 1952.

Part 8: Other Unpublished Materials Bearing on Max Yergan's Life

DOCTORAL DISSERTATIONS

Berman, Edward Henry. "Education in Africa and America: A History of the Phelps-Stokes Fund, 1911–45." Columbia University, Ed.D. 1970.

Coan, Josephus R. "The Expansion of Missions of the A.M.E. Church in South Africa, 1896–1908." Hartford Seminary Foundation, Ph.D. 1961.

Campbell, James. "Our Father, Our Children: The African Methodist Church in the United States and South Africa." Stanford University, Ph.D. 1990.

Gilmore, Glenda Elizabeth. "Gender and Jim Crow: Women and the Politics of White Supremacy in North Carolina, 1896–1920." University of North Carolina at Chapel Hill, Ph.D. 1992.

Harr, Wilbur C. "The Negro as an American Protestant Missionary in Africa." University of Chicago Divinity School, Ph.D. 1945.

Heyman, Richard David. "The Role of Carnegie Corporation in African Education, 1925–1960." Teachers College, Columbia University, Ed.D. 1969.

Hughes, Cicero Alvin. "Toward a Black United Front: The National Negro Congress Movement." Ohio University, Ph.D. 1982.

Hunter, Gary Jerome. "Don't Buy Where You Can't Work: Black Urban Boycott Movements during the Depression, 1929–1941." University of Michigan, Ph.D. 1977.

Jenkins, Clara Barnes. "An Historical View of Shaw University, 1865–1963." University of Pittsburgh, Ed.D. 1965.

Johns, Sheridan Waite, III. "Marxism-Leninism in a Multi-Racial Environment:

The Origins and Early History of the Communist Party of South Africa, 1914–1932." Harvard University, Ph.D. 1965.

Keto, Clement Tsehloane. "American Involvement in South Africa, 1870–1915: The Role of Americans in the Creation of Modern South Africa." Georgetown University, Ph.D. 1972.

Kifer, Allen. "The Negro under the New Deal, 1933–1941." University of Wisconsin, Ph.D. 1961.

Lawrence, Charles R. "Negro Organizations in Crisis: Depression, New Deal, World War Two." Columbia University, Ph.D. 1953.

Marable, William Manning. "African Nationalist: The Life of John Langalibalele Dube." University of Maryland, Ph.D. 1976.

Morsell, John Albert. "The Political Behavior of Negroes in New York City." Columbia University, Ph.D. 1950.

Naison, Mark D. "The Communist Party in Harlem: 1928–1936." Columbia University, Ph.D. 1975.

Orr, Rodney Hugh. "African American Missionaries to East Africa, 1900–1926: A Study of the Ethnic Reconnection of the Gospel." University of Edinburgh, Ph.D. 1998.

Page, Carol M. "Black America in White South Africa: Church and State Reaction to the African Methodist Episcopal Church in Cape Colony and the Transvaal, 1896–1910." University of Edinburgh, Ph.D. 1978.

Perlman, Daniel J. "Stirring the White Conscience: The Life of George Edmund Haynes." New York University, Ph.D. 1972.

Solomon, Mark D. "Red and Black: Negroes and Communism, 1929–1932." Harvard University, Ph.D. 1972.

Streater, John Baxter. "The National Negro Congress, 1936–1947." University of Cincinnati, Ph.D. 1981.

Tillman, Nathaniel Patrick, Jr. "Walter Francis White: A Study in Interest Group Leadership." University of Wisconsin, Ph.D. 1961.

THESES AND SEMINAR PAPERS

Anthony, David H., III. "Max Yergan: A Pan African Enigma." M.A. Thesis (History), University of Wisconsin–Madison, 1975.

Faison, Marvin L. "Max Yergan: The South Africa Years, 1921–1936." Columbia University.

Harper, Marieta. "Case Study of the Relationship of Max Yergan and Paul Robeson in the Historical Development of the Council on African Affairs." Seminar Paper (History), Howard University, 1974.

Herndon, Jane Walter. "Henry McNeal Turner: Exponent of American Negritude." M.A. Thesis (History), Georgia State College, 1967.

Weiss, Melville. "Don't Buy Where You Can't Work." M.A. Thesis (History), Columbia University, 1941.

MANUSCRIPTS

Kerr, Alexander. "Visit of Max Yergan, M.A., to India (n.d., ca. 1928)." Copy courtesy of Ms. Ruth Hartson, formerly of International Division, Young Men's Christian Association, New York City, 1975.

INTERVIEWS

Aptheker, Herbert. San Jose, Calif., 16 September 1988.
Bam, Villiers G. Maseru. Telephone interview, Lesotho.
Beichman, Arnold. Hoover Institution, Stanford University, 13 December 1993.
Daniels-Halisi, Clyde. Dar es Salaam, Tanzania, 1976–1977.
Duberman, Martin Bauml. Telephone interview, 27 January 1985.
Edgar, Robert Russell. Audiotape extract of interview with Govan A. M. Mbeki, South Africa, August 1990.
———. Transcript from an interview with Edwin Mofutsanyana, Lesotho, n.d.
———. Notes from interview with Mrs. Edgar Thamae, Lesotho, 22 May 1985.
———. Notes from interview with W. M. Tsotsi, Lesotho, 11 March 1985.
Fobo, Fanana "Roch." Roma, Lesotho, 8 February 1988.
Hill, Robert A. Madison, Wisconsin, 1980.
Honono, N. "Chucha." University of Dar es Salaam, Tanzania, 5 March 1977.
Jordan, Phyllis (Ntantala). Telephone interview, 20 May 1974.
Khabele, Joan. Maseru and Roma, Lesotho, l987–1988.
Mafeje, Archie. University of Dar es Salaam, 5 March 1977; and Hotel Victoria, Maseru, Lesotho, 24 December 1987.
Mahomo, Nana. Madison, Wisconsin, May 1976.
———. London, England, June 1976.
Mbeki, Govan Archibald M. Port Elizabeth, South Africa, 2000.
Mesnick, Ed. Telephone interview, 19 April 1994.
Mohapeloa, J. M., Maseru, Lesotho, 16 May 1988.
M'Timkulu, Donald Guy Sydney. Telephone interview, 29 March 1994.
Patterson, Louise Thompson. Oakland, Calif., 11 November 1988.
Robeson, Paul, Jr. Telephone interviews.
Schappes, Morris Urman. Telephone interview, 5 May 1994.
Sisulu, Walter M. Johannesburg, South Africa, 2000.
Tabata, I. B. University of Dar es Salaam, Tanzania, 5 March 1977.
Tsotsi, Wycliffe Mlungisi. Maseru, Lesotho. 19 October 1987; 9, 17, and 24 November 1987; and 21 January 1988, 3.30–5.15 p. (last interview taped).

Part 9: Other Published Materials Bearing on Max Yergan's Life

BOOKS

Anderson, Eric. *Race and Politics in North Carolina, 1872–1901: The Black Second.* Baton Rouge and London: Louisiana State University Press, 1981.

Anderson, Jervis. *A. Philip Randolph: A Biographical Portrait.* New York: Harbrace, 1973.

————. *This Was Harlem: A Cultural Portrait, 1900–1950.* New York: Farrar, Straus, Giroux, 1982.

Aptheker, Herbert, ed. *The Correspondence of W. E. B. Du Bois.* Vol. 3, *Selections, 1944–1963.* Amherst: University of Massachusetts Press.

Arthur, George A. *Life on the Negro Frontier.* New York: Association Press, 1935.

Atwood, Jesse H. *The Racial Factor in Y.M.C.A.'s: A Report on Negro-White Relationships in Twenty-Four Cities.* New York: Association Press, 1946.

Barbeau, Arthur T., and Florette Henri. *The Unknown Soldiers: Black Americans and World War One.* New York: Oxford University Press.

Bassett, J. S. *Slavery and Servitude in the Colony of North Carolina.* Johns Hopkins University Studies, 14, nos. 4 and 5. Baltimore, Md.: Johns Hopkins University Press.

Borstelmann, Thomas. *Apartheid's Reluctant Uncle: The United States and Southern Africa in the Early Cold War.* New York: Oxford University Press, 1993.

Brownell, Herbert, with John P. Burke. *Advising Ike: The Memoirs of Attorney General Herbert Brownell.* Lawrence: University Press of Kansas, 1993.

Bullock, Ralph W. *In Spite of Handicaps.* New York: Association Press, 1927.

Burt, Olive Wooley. *Black Women of Valor.* New York: J. Messner, 1974.

Butler, R., R. Elphick, and D. Welsh, eds. *Democratic Liberalism in South Africa: Its History and Prospect.* Middletown, Conn.: Wesleyan University Press, 1987.

Butterfield, Kenyon L. *Report of Dr. Kenyon L. Butterfield on Rural Conditions and Sociological Problems in South Africa.* New York: Carnegie Corporation, 1929.

Campbell, James T. *Songs of Zion: The African Methodist Episcopal Church.* New York: Oxford University Press, 1995.

Carr, Robert K. *The House Un-American Activities Committee.* New York, 1952.

Carter, Dan T. *Scottsboro: A Tragedy of the American South.* Baton Rouge: Louisiana State University Press, 1969; reprinted New York: Oxford University Press, 1976.

Carter, Edward Clark. *Preliminary Draft: Discussion Outlines to Help Prepare for the World's YMCA Conference to Be Held at Helsingfors, Finland, August, 1926.* New York: The Inquiry, 1925.

Carter, Gwendolen, and Thomas Karis, eds. *From Protest to Challenge: A Documentary History of African Politics in South Africa, 1884–1964,* vol. 4. Stanford: Hoover Institution Press, 1977.

Carter, Wilmoth D. *The Urban Negro in the South.* New York: Vantage Press, 1961.

———. *Shaw's Universe: A Monument to Educational Innovation.* Rockville, Md.: D.C. National Publishing, 1973.

Cell, John W. *The Highest Stage of White Supremacy: The Origins of Segregation in South Africa and the American South.* New York and Cambridge: Cambridge University Press, 1982.

Chamberlain, Lawrence H. *Loyalty and Legislative Action: A Survey of Activity by the New York State Legislature, 1919–1949.* Ithaca, N.Y.: Cornell University Press, 1951.

Chirenje, J. Mutero. *Ethiopianism and Afro-Americans in Southern Africa, 1883–1916.* Baton Rouge and London: Louisiana State University Press, 1987.

Coffman, Edward M. *The War to End All Wars: The American Military Experience in World War I.* New York: Oxford University Press, 1968.

Cohen, Robert. *When the Old Left Was Young: Student Radicals and America's First Mass Student Movement, 1929–1941.* New York: Oxford University Press, 1993.

Convention of the Freedmen of North Carolina. Official Proceedings. Raleigh, N.C.: 1865.

Crossman, Richard H., ed. *The God That Failed.* New York: Harpers, 1949.

Cuthbert, Marion. *Juliette Derricotte.* New York: Women's Press, 1933.

David, M. D. *The YMCA and the Making of Modern India: A Centenary History.* New Delhi: National Council of YMCAs of India, 1992.

Davis, Benjamin Jefferson. *Communist Councilman from Harlem: Autobiographical Notes Written in a Federal Penitentiary.* New York: International Publishers, 1969.

Davis, John P. *Let Us Build a National Negro Congress.* Washington, D.C.: National Sponsoring Committee for a National Negro Congress, 1935.

Dean, Harry. *The Pedro Gorino: The Adventures of a Negro Sea-Captain in Africa and on the Seven Seas in His Attempts to Found an Ethiopian Empire. An Autobiographical Narrative . . . written with the Assistance of Sterling North.* Boston and New York: Houghton Mifflin, 1929.

Dennis, Peggy. *The Autobiography of an American Communist: A Personal View of a Political Life, 1925–1975.* Westport, Conn., and Berkeley, Calif.: Lawrence Hill and Company and Creative Arts, 1975.

Douglas, W. M. *Andrew Murray and His Message.* London and Edinburgh: Oliphants, 1927.

Draper, Theodore. *American Communism and Soviet Russia: The Formative Period.* New York: Viking, 1961.

Duberman, Martin Bauml. *Paul Robeson.* New York: Ballantine, 1989.

Du Bois, William Edward Burghardt. *The Souls of Black Folk.* 1903. Repr., Greenwich, Conn.: Fawcett, 1961.

———. *Dusk of Dawn: An Essay toward an Autobiography of a Race Concept.* 1940. Repr., New York: Schocken, 1968.

———. *Color and Democracy: Colonies and Peace.* New York: 1945.

———. *The World and Africa.* New York: International Publishers, 1965.

Du Plessis, Johannes. *The Life of Andrew Murray of South Africa.* London: Marshall Brothers, 1920.

Dykeman, Wilma, and James Stokely. *Seeds of Southern Change: The Life of Will Alexander.* New York: Norton, 1962.

Eagles, Charles W. *Jonathan Daniels and Race Relations: The Evolution of a Southern Liberal.* Knoxville: University of Tennessee Press, 1982.

Edgar, Robert R., ed. *An African-American in South Africa: The Travel Notes of Ralph J. Bunche, 28 September 1937–1 January 1938.* Athens: Ohio University Press, 1992.

Edwards, Brent Hayes. *The Practice of Diaspora: Literature, Translation, and the Rise of Black Internationalism.* Cambridge and London: Harvard University Press, 2003.

Foner, Philip Sheridan, and Herbert Shapiro, eds. *American Communism and Black Americans: A Documentary History, 1930–1934.* Philadelphia: Temple University Press, 1991.

Franklin, John Hope. *The Free Negro in North Carolina, 1790–1860.* Chapel Hill: University of North Carolina Press, 1943.

Frederickson, George M. *White Supremacy: A Comparative Study in American and South African History.* Oxford and New York: Oxford University Press, 1981.

Freeman, Edward A. *The Epoch of Negro Baptists and the Foreign Mission Board.* Kansas City, Mo.: Central Seminary Press, 1953; reprinted New York: Arno, 1980.

Freeman, F. *Africa's Redemption: The Salvation of Our Country.* Fanshaw, N.Y.: 1852. Repr., Westport, Conn.: Negro Universities Press, 1970.

Gandhi, Mohandas Karamchand. *An Autobiography: The Story of My Experiments with Truth.* Boston: Beacon Press, 1957.

———. *Satyagraha in South Africa.* 1928. Repr., Ahmedabad: Navajivan Publishing House, 1972.

Garfinkel, Herbert. *When Negroes March.* Glencoe, Ill.: Atheneum, 1959.

Garrow, David. *The FBI and Dr. Martin Luther King, Jr.* New York: Penguin, 1984.

General Staff, Defence Headquarters, Pretoria. *The Union of South Africa and the Great War, 1914–1918: Official History*. Pretoria: Government Printing and Stationery Office, 1924.

Goldstein, Robert Justin. *Political Repression in Modern America from 1870 to the Present*. Cambridge: Schenkman, 1978.

Goodman, Walter. *The Committee: The Extraordinary Career of the House Committee on Un-American Activities*. New York: 1968.

Gornick, Vivian. *The Romance of American Communism*. New York: Basic Books, 1977.

Graham, Shirley. *Paul Robeson, Citizen of the World*. New York: Messner, 1946.

Groves, C. P. *The Planting of Christianity in Africa*. Vol. 4, 1914–1954. London: Butterworth, 1964.

Hall, Jacquelyn Dowd. *Revolt against Chivalry: Jessie Daniel Ames and the Women's Campaign against Lynching*. New York: Columbia University Press, 1979.

Hamilton, Charles V. *Adam Clayton Powell, Jr.: The Political Biography of an American Dilemma*. New York: Collier, 1991.

Harmon Foundation Yearbook, 1924–1926. New York: 1926.

Haywood, Harry. *Black Bolshevik: The Autobiography of an Afro-American Communist*. Chicago: Liberator Press, 1978.

Hearth, Amy Hill, ed. *Having Our Say: The Delany Sisters' First Hundred Years*. Thorndike, Me.: G. K. Hall, 1993.

Hellman, Lillian. *Scoundrel Time*. New York.

Herndon, Angelo. *Let Me Live*. New York: Arno and the New York Times.

Hill, Patricia R. *The World Their Household: The American Woman's Foreign Mission Movement and Cultural Transformation, 1870–1920*. Ann Arbor: University of Michigan Press, 1985.

Hill, Robert A., ed. *The Marcus Garvey Papers*. Berkeley: University of California Press.

Hooker, James R. *Black Revolutionary: George Padmore's Path from Communism to Pan-Africanism*. London and New York: Praeger, 1967.

———. *Henry Sylvester Williams: Imperial Pan-Africanist*. London: Rex Collings, 1975.

Hopkins, C. Howard. *History of The Y.M.C.A. in North America*. New York: Association Press, 1951.

Houser, George M. *No One Can Stop the Rain: Glimpses of Africa's Liberation Struggle*. New York: Pilgrim Press, 1989.

Howe, Irving, and Lewis Coser. *The American Communist Party: A Critical History, 1919–1957*. Boston: Beacon Press, 1957.

Howe, Russell Warren, and Sarah Hays Trott. *The Power Peddlers*. Garden City, N.Y.: Doubleday, 1977.

Hunton, Addie W. *William Alphaeus Hunton: A Pioneer Prophet of Young Men*. New York: Association Press, 1938.

Hunton, Addie W., and Kathryn M. Johnson. *Two Colored Women with the American Expeditionary Forces.* New York: Brooklyn Eagle Press, 1920.

Hunton, Dorothy K. *Alphaeus Hunton: The Unsung Valiant.* New York: published by the author, 1986.

Hurmence, Belinda, ed. *My Folks Don't Want Me to Talk about Slavery: 21 Oral Histories of Former North Carolina Slaves.* Winston-Salem, N.C.: Blair, 1984.

International Committee of Young Men's Christian Associations. *Summary of War Work of the American YMCA.* New York: 1920.

Jacobs, Sylvia M., ed. *Black Americans and the Missionary Movement to Africa.* Westport, Conn.: Greenwood Press, 1982.

Kadalie, Clements. *My Life and the ICU: The Autobiography of a Black Trade Unionist in South Africa.* Atlantic Highlands, N.J.: Humanities Press, 1970.

Kalb, Madeline G. *The Congo Cables: The Cold War in Africa from Eisenhower to Kennedy.* New York: Macmillan, 1982.

Kallaway, Peter, ed. *Apartheid and Education,* vol. 1. Johannesburg: Ravan Press.

Kapur, Sudarshan. *Raising Up a Prophet: The African-American Encounter with Gandhi.* Boston: Beacon Press, 1992.

Kelley, Robin D. G. *Hammer and Hoe: Alabama Communists during the Great Depression.* Chapel Hill: University of North Carolina Press, 1990.

Kerr, Alexander. *Fort Hare, 1915–48: The Evolution of an African College.* London: Hurst, 1968.

King, Kenneth J. *Pan-Africanism and Education: A Study of Race Philanthropy and Education in the Southern States of America and East Africa.* London: Oxford University Press, 1971.

———, ed. *Ras Makonnen: Pan-Africanism from Within.* Nairobi: Oxford University Press, 1973.

Kuper, Leo. *Passive Resistance in South Africa.* New Haven, Conn.: Yale University Press, 1957.

Lester, Julius, ed. *The Seventh Son: The Thought and Writings of W. E. B. Du Bois.* New York: Random House, 1975.

Lewis, David Levering. *When Harlem Was in Vogue.* New York: Knopf, 1984.

———. *W. E. B. Du Bois: Biography of a Race, 1868–1919.* New York: Holt, 1993.

Lodge, Tom. *Black Politics in South Africa since 1945.* London and New York: Longman Group, 1983.

Logan, Frenise A. *The Negro in North Carolina, 1876–1894.* Chapel Hill: University of North Carolina Press, 1964.

Lynch, Hollis R. *Black American Radicals and the Liberation of Africa: The Council on African Affairs, 1937–1955.* Ithaca, N.Y.: Cornell University Africana Studies Center, 1978.

McDowell, John Patrick. *The Social Gospel in the South: The Women's Home*

Mission Movement in the Methodist Episcopal Church, South, 1886–1939.
Baton Rouge: Louisiana State University Press, 1982.

MacFarland, Charles S., ed. *The Churches of the Federal Council: Their History, Organization, and Distinctive Characteristics and a Statement of the Development of the Federal Council.* London and Edinburgh: Revell, 1916.

———. *The Progress of Church Federation to 1922.* New York, Chicago, Toronto, and London: Revell, 1921.

McKay, Claude. *A Long Way from Home.* New York: Arno and the New York Times, 1969.

———. *The Negroes in America.* Translated from the Russian by Robert J. Winter. Edited by Alan L. McLeod. Port Washington, New York, and London: Kennikat Press, 1979.

Mahoney, Richard D. *JFK: Ordeal in Africa.* New York: Oxford University Press, 1983.

Martin, Charles. *The Angelo Herndon Case and Southern Justice.* Baton Rouge: Louisiana State University Press, 1976.

Mathews, Basil. *John R. Mott, World Citizen.* New York and London: Harper Brothers, 1934.

Matthews, Zachariah Keodirelang. *Freedom for My People: The Autobiography of Z. K. Matthews; Southern Africa 1901 to 1968. Memoir by Monica Wilson.* Capetown and Johannesburg: David Philip, 1981.

Mays, Benjamin E. *Born to Rebel.* New York: Scribner, 1971.

Miller, Francis Pickens. *Man from the Valley: Memoirs of a Twentieth-Century Virginian.* Chapel Hill: University of North Carolina Press, 1971.

Mjagkij, Nina. *Light in the Darkness: African-Americans and the YMCA, 1852–1946.* Lexington: University Press of Kentucky, 1993.

Mulzac, Hugh. *A Star to Steer By.* New York: International Publishers, 1958.

Naison, Mark. *Communists in Harlem during the Depression.* New York: Grove Press, 1984.

National Negro Congress. *Official Proceedings, Second National Negro Congress, October 15, 16, and 17, 1937, Metropolitan Opera House, Philadelphia, Pennsylvania.* Washington, D.C.: National Negro Congress, n.d. [ca. 1937].

Navasky, Victor. *Naming Names.* New York: Viking Press, 1980.

Nkrumah, Kwame. *Ghana: The Autobiography of Kwame Nkrumah.* New York: International Publishers, 1972.

Noer, Thomas. *Cold War and Black Liberation: The United States and White Rule in Africa, 1948–1968.* Columbia: University of Missouri Press, 1985.

Ober, C. K. *Luther D. Wishard, Projector of World Movements.* New York: Association Press, 1927.

Oldham, J. H. *Christianity and the Race Problem.* London: Student Christian Movement, 1925.

Ottley, Roi. *No Green Pastures.* New York: Scribner, 1951.

Ovington, Mary White. *Portraits in Color.* New York: Viking, 1927.

Padmore, George. *Pan-Africanism or Communism.* Garden City, N.Y.: Double-day Anchor, 1971.

Page, Melvin E., ed. *Africa and the First World War.* London: Macmillan, 1987.

Patton, Cornelius H. *The Lure of Africa.* New York: Board of Foreign Missions of the Presbyterian Church in the U.S.A., 1917.

Paul Robeson: The Great Forerunner. By the editors of *Freedomways.* New York: Dodd, Mead, 1978.

Powell, Adam Clayton, Jr. *Marching Blacks.* New York: Dial Press, 1945; revised edition, Dial Press, 1973.

Powers, Richard Gid. *Secrecy and Power: The Life of J. Edgar Hoover.* New York: Free Press, 1987.

Rabinowitz, Howard. *Race Relations in the Urban South, 1865–1890.* Champaign and Urbana: University of Illinois Press, 1980.

Ray, Ellen, William Schaap, Karl van Meter, and Louis Wolf, eds. *Dirty Work 2: The C.I.A. in Africa.* Secaucus, N.J.: Lyle Stuart, 1979.

Redkey, Edwin S. *Black Exodus: Black Nationalist and Back-to-Africa Movements, 1890–1910.* New Haven, Conn.: Yale University Press, 1970.

———, ed. *Respect Black: The Writings and Speeches of Henry McNeal Turner.* New York: Ayer, 1971.

Rich, Paul B. *White Power and the Liberal Conscience: Racial Segregation and South African Liberalism, 1921–60.* Manchester: Manchester University Press, and Johannesburg: Ravan, 1984.

Richards, Yevette. *Maida Springer: Pan-Africanist and International Labor Leader.* Pittsburgh: University of Pittsburgh Press, 2000.

Robeson, Eslanda Goode. *African Journey.* New York: John Day, 1945.

Robinson, Robert, with Jonathan Slevin. *Black on Red: My 44 Years inside the Soviet Union: An Autobiography by a Black American.* Washington, D.C.: Acropolis Books, 1988.

Romulo, Carlos. *The Meaning of Bandung.* Chapel Hill: University of North Carolina Press, 1956.

Rosengarten, Theodore. *All God's Dangers: The Life of Nate Shaw.* New York: Knopf, 1975.

Rouse, Ruth M. *The World's Student Christian Federation: A History of the First Thirty Years.* London: S.C.M. Press, 1948.

Roux, Edward. *Time Longer Than Rope.* Madison: University of Wisconsin Press, 1966.

Scott, William Randolph. *The Sons of Sheba's Race: African-Americans and the Italo-Ethiopian War, 1935–1941.* Bloomington: Indiana University Press, 1993.

Scruggs, L. A. *Women of Distinction: Remarkable in Works and Invincible in Character.* Raleigh, N.C.: L. A. Scruggs, 1893.

Shepherd, R. H. W. *Lovedale, South Africa: The Story of a Century, 1841–1941.* Lovedale, Cape: Lovedale Press, 1940.

Simons, H. E., and R. A. Simons. *Class and Colour in South Africa, 1850–1950.* Baltimore, Md.: Penguin, 1969.

Skota, T. D. Mweli. *The African Yearly Register: Being an Illustrated National Biographical Dictionary (Who's Who) of Black Folks in Africa.* Johannesburg: R. L. Esson, 1932.

———. *The African Who's Who.* Johannesburg: Central News Agency, 1965.

Smith, Edwin W. *The Christian Mission in Africa: A Study Based on the Work of the International Missionary Conference at Le Zoute, Belgium, September 14th to 21st, 1926.* London: 1926.

Smith, Homer. *Black Man in Red Russia.* Chicago: Johnson, 1964.

Stauffer, Milton, ed. *Thinking with Africa: Chapters by a Group of Nationals Interpreting the Christian Movement.* New York: Missionary Education Movement, 1927.

Stockwell, John. *In Search of Enemies: A CIA Story.* New York: Norton, 1978.

Taylor, Rosser Howard. *Slaveholding in North Carolina: An Economic View.* Chapel Hill: University of North Carolina Press, 1926. Repr., New York: Negro Universities Press, 1969.

Torrence, Ridgely. *The Story of John Hope.* New York: Macmillan, 1948.

Turner, Joyce Moore, and W. Burghardt, eds. *Richard B. Moore: Caribbean Militant in Harlem: Collected Writings, 1920–1972.* Bloomington: Indiana University Press, 1988.

Urquhart, Brian. *Ralph Bunche: An American Life.* New York: Norton, 1993.

Walshe, Peter. *The Rise of African Nationalism in South Africa: The African National Congress, 1912–1971.* Berkeley: University of California Press, 1971.

Walters, Alexander. *My Life and Work.* New York: 1917.

Washburn, Patrick S. *A Question of Sedition: The Federal Government's Investigation of the Black Press during World War II.* New York: Oxford University Press, 1986.

White, Ronald C., Jr., and C. Howard Hopkins. *The Social Gospel in America: Religion and Reform in Changing America.* Philadelphia: Temple University Press, 1976.

White, Walter. *A Rising Wind.* Garden City, N.Y.: Doubleday, Doran, 1945.

Whitted, J. A. *A History of Negro Baptists in North Carolina.* Raleigh: Edwards and Broughton, 1908.

Wickins, Peter. *The Industrial and Commercial Union of Africa.* London: Oxford University Press, 1978.

Willan, Brian. *Sol Plaatje, South African Nationalist, 1876–1932.* Berkeley and Los Angeles: University of California Press, 1984.

Williams, Charles H. *Sidelights on Negro Soldiers.* Boston: B. J. Brimmer, 1923.

Gilbert Wins, The Christian Recorder 1852-1902, Jefferson NC + Lou McFarland 1996

Williams, Walter L. *Black Americans and the Evangelization of Africa, 1877–1900*. Madison: University of Wisconsin Press, 1982.

World's Committee of Y.M.C.A.'s. *Youth Faces Life: Being the Report of the Nineteenth World Conference of Y.M.C.A.'s at Helsingfors, August 1–6, 1926*. Geneva: World's Committee of YMCAs, 1926.

Wright, Richard. *The Color Curtain: A Report on the Bandung Conference*. Cleveland and New York: World, 1956.

Wright, Richard R. *Encyclopedia of African Methodism*. Philadelphia: A.M.E. Book Concern, 1942.

Xuma, Alfred Bitini. *Charlotte Manye (Mrs. Maxeke): "What an Educated African Girl Can Do."* Johannesburg: Women's Parent Mite Missionary Society of the A.M.E. Church, 1930.

———. *Reconstituting the Union of South Africa; or, A More Rational Union Policy: Address Delivered Before a Public Meeting of the Bantu Studies Club of the University of the Witwatersrand, May 30th, 1932*. Alice: Lovedale Press, 1932.

———. *Africans' Claims in South Africa*. Johannesburg: n.d. [ca. December 1943].

NEWSPAPERS AND OTHER PERIODICALS

The African Interpreter (New York), February 1943–Spring 1944.
Afro-American (Washington and Baltimore)
Amsterdam News (New York)
Association Men (New York)
Cape Times (Cape Town, South Africa)
Coming Back (New York: International Committee of the YMCA)
Guardian (Cape Town, South Africa)
L'Illustration Exposition Colonial (Paris), 23 May 1931.
Imvo Zabantsundu (King William's Town, South Africa)
New Masses (New York), 1935–1948
People's Voice (New York)
Umteteli wa Bantu
The Young Men of India

ARTICLES

"Alabama Sharecroppers." "Three Lynch Affidavits." *New Masses*, 22 October 1935, 16–18.

Asante, S. K. B. "The Afro-American and the Italo-Ethiopian Crisis, 1934–1936." *Race* (London) 15:2 (October 1973): 163–84.

Briggs, Leonard M. "My 35 Years of Y.M.C.A. Work." *Outspan* (Johannesburg), 11 October 1945, 17, 109.

Bull, Oswin. "John R. Mott: Servant of Christ and Leader of Men." *South African Outlook,* 1 April 1955.

Burnshaw, Stanley. "The Theatre: Toward a Genuine Negro Drama." *New Masses,* 9 July 1935, 29.

"Case of Paul Robeson—Why Some Americans Can't Get Passports." *U.S. News and World Report,* 26 August 1955, 79–81.

Contee, Clarence G. "Black American 'Reds' and African Liberation: A Case Study of the Council on African Affairs, 1937–1955." In *Proceedings: The Conference on Afro-Americans and Africans: Historical and Political Linkages.* Edited by Lorraine A. Williams. Sponsored by the Department of History, Howard University, June 13–14, 1974. Washington, D.C.: Graduate School, Howard University, 1974. 117–33.

Davis, Benjamin J. "The Communists, the Negro People, and the War." *Communist* 21:7 (August 1942).

Davis, John P. "The National Negro Congress Reports to the People." [Unpublished] mimeo, n.d. (1940), National Negro Congress Papers, Box 21, Schomburg Center for Research in Black Culture.

Deutscher, Isaac. "The Ex-Communist's Conscience: A Review of *The God That Failed.*" In *Heretics and Renegades.* London: H. Hamilton, 1955.

Dodson, Owen. "Negro History: A Sonnet Sequence." *New Masses,* 14 April 1936, 21.

Drake, J. G. St. Clair. "The International Implications of Race and Race Relations." *Social Forces* 20:3 (Summer 1951): 261–78.

"Dr. Xuma Buried." *Rand Daily Mail* (Johannesburg), 2 February 1962.

"Dr. Xuma Dead: Bishop Gow Will Conduct Funeral." *World* (Witwatersrand-Pretoria-Vereeniging), 29 January 1962.

Du Bois, W. E. B. "Thomas Jesse Jones." *Crisis* 22 (October 1921): 252–56.

———. "Thomas Jesse Jones, *Education in Africa*: A Review." *Crisis* 32:2 (June 1926): 86–89.

———. "The Realities in Africa: European Profit or Negro Development?" *Foreign Affairs* 21:4 (July 1943): 721–32.

———. "The Pan-African Movement." In *History of the Pan African Congress: Colonial and Coloured Unity.* Edited by George Padmore. London: Hammersmith, 1945.

Elkin, W. T. "Unrest among the Negroes: A British Document of 1919." *Science and Society* 37:1 (Winter 1968).

Ellison, Ralph. "A Congress Jim Crow Didn't Attend." *New Masses,* 14 May 1940, 5, 7–8.

"The Flight in Harlem." Editorial. *New Masses,* 29 October 1935, 5.

Flandrau, Grace. "Macaroni for Africa." *New Masses,* 31 December 1935, 15–16.

Ford, James W. "Political Highlights of the National Negro Congress." *Communist* 15:5 (May 1936).

Freeman, Joseph. "Ethiopia and World War." *New Masses,* 12 May 1936, 6, 8.

Gold, Michael. "At Last, a Negro Theater?" *New Masses,* 10 March 1936, 18.

Hirsch, Alfred. "Way Down South, 2: On Behalf of Angelo Herndon." *New Masses,* 20 August 1935, 13–14.

Hope, John. "The Colored YMCA." *Crisis* 31:1 (November 1925): 14–17.

"Housing in Harlem." Editorial. *New Masses,* 24 September 1935, 7.

Kelley, Robin D. G. "Organizing the Natives." Unpublished manuscript.

———. "The Religious Odyssey of African Radicals: Notes on the Communist Party of South Africa, 1921–34." *Radical History Review* 51 (Fall 1991): 5–24.

Keto, Clement T. "Black Americans and South Africa, 1890–1910." *Current Bibliography on African Affairs* 5:4 (New Series) (July 1972): 383–406.

King, Kenneth J. "Africa and the Southern States of the U.S.A." *Journal of African History* 10:4 (1969): 59–77.

———. "The American Negro as Missionary to East Africa: A Critical Aspect of Evangelism." *African Historical Studies* 3:1 (1970): 5–22.

Kleeck, Mary van. "United Action for Social Security." *New Masses,* 7 April 1936, 1213.

Kuper, Leo. "The Control of Social Change: A South African Experiment." *Social Forces* 33:1 (October 1954): 19–29.

———. "African Nationalism, 1910–1964." *Oxford History of South Africa,* vol. 2. Edited by Monica Wilson and Leonard Thompson. New York and Oxford: Oxford University Press, 1971. 424–76.

Leberstein, Stephen. "Purging the Profs: The Rapp Coudert Committee in New York, 1940–1942." In *New Studies in the Politics and Culture of U.S. Communism.* Edited by Michael E. Brown, Randy Martin, Frank Rosengarten, and George Snedeker. New York: Monthly Review Press, 1993.

Lenz, Frank B. "An American Negro in South Africa." *World Tomorrow,* August 1931.

"Lincoln and the Negro Youth." Editorial. *New Masses,* 16 February 1937, 22.

McKenzie, Marjorie. "Pursuit of Democracy: Differences of Robeson and Yergan Present Puzzling Question." *Pittsburgh Courier,* 14 February 1948.

Marcantonio, Vito. "Why I Broke with La Guardia." *New Masses,* 3 March 1936, 13–14.

Martin, Tony. "Some Reflexions on Evangelical Pan-Africanism." *Ufahamu* 1:3 (Winter 1971).

Miller, Loren. "Harlem without Makeup." *New Masses,* 13 August 1935.

Miller, Loren. "Last in Peace, Last in War." *New Masses,* 24 September 1935, 16–18.

———. "Labor Trouble in Harlem." *New Masses,* 22 October 1935, 20.

———. "The Theater: 'Porgy and Bess' and 'Mulatto.'" *New Masses,* 5 November 1935, 29–30.

———. "The Negro Middle Class: The Failure of Emancipation." *New Masses,* 7 April 1936, 20–21.

Minton, Bruce. "That Man Marcantonio." *New Masses,* 3 November 1936, 3–5.

Nash, Vernon. "The YMCA in East Africa in 1917." *Young Men of India* 29:6 (June 1918): 351–56.

Nehru, Jawaharlal. "India and a People's Front." *New Masses,* 3 February 1937, 11–14.

Newton, Herbert. "The National Negro Congress, USA." *Negro Worker* (May–June 1936): 24–25.

North, Joseph. "Herndon Is Back in Atlanta." *New Masses,* 5 November 1935, 15–16.

———. "United Front Opens Herndon's Jail. ('I'm Dead Sure You'll Get Me Out Soon')." *New Masses,* 17 December 1935, 15–16.

———. "Herndon Is Free!" *New Masses,* 11 May 1937, 13–14.

"O.B.B." [Oswin Boys Bull]. *South African Outlook* 102:1211 (April 1972).

O'Brien, Frank. "Harlem Shows the Way." *New Masses,* 18 August 1936, 17–18.

Pawa, J. M. "The Search for Black Radicals." *Labor History* 16:2 (Spring 1975).

"Police Terror in Harlem: From the Text of the Suppressed Official Report." *New Masses,* 14 July 1936, 15–16.

Ponsford, T. R. "The Influence of the Y.M.C.A. Is Felt in 66 Countries." *Outspan,* 15 November 1946, 21, 91.

Rabinowitz, Howard. "A Comparative Perspective on Race Relations in Southern and Northern Cities, 1860–1900, with Special Emphasis on Raleigh." In *Black Americans in North Carolina and the South.* Edited by Jeffrey J. Crow and Flora Hatley. Chapel Hill: University of North Carolina Press, 1984.

Record, Wilson. "The Negro Intellectual and Negro Nationalism." *Social Forces* 33:1 (October 1954): 10–18.

"Red China Exposed—Not Dominant in Asia (Interview with Adam Clayton Powell Jr., Negro Leader and Congressman from New York)." *U.S. News and World Report,* 29 April 1955, 42–44.

Redkey, Edwin S. "The Meaning of Africa to Afro-Americans, 1890–1914." Special Studies, Council on International Studies, State University of New York at Buffalo. Buffalo: 1971.

Richardson, Ben. "Can It Happen in Harlem Again?" *New Masses,* 17 August 1943, 14–16.

Roark, James L. "American Black Leaders: The Response to Colonialism and the Cold War, 1943–1953." *African Historical Studies* 4:2 (1971): 253–70.

Saunders, Kenneth. "A Forward Move in Africa." *Southern Workman* 49 (February 1920).

Savage, Donald C., and J. Forbes Munro. "Carrier Corps Recruitment in the British East Africa Protectorate." *Journal of African History* 7:2 (1966).

Seldes, George. "Faking Ethiopian News." *New Masses,* 19 May 1936, 13–14.

Shepperson, George. "Notes on American Negro Influences on the Emergence of African Nationalism." *Journal of African History* 1:2 (1960).

Sisulu, W[alter]. M. "The Development of African Nationalism." *India Quarterly* 10:3 (July/September 1954): 206.

"6,000 Mourn Dr. Xuma." *Post* (Johannesburg), 4 February 1962.

Small, Sasha. "Way Down South, 1: Georgia Is Misunderstood." *New Masses,* 20 August 1935, 11–13.

Solomon, Mark. "Black Critics of Colonialism and the Cold War." In *Cold War Critics: Alternatives to American Foreign Policy in the Truman Years.* Edited by Thomas G. Paterson. Chicago: Quadrangle Press, 1971.

Spivak, John L. "Mussolini's Soldiers Are Deserting." *New Masses,* 21 January 1936, 11–13.

Strachey, John. "Blackmailing Ethiopia." *New Masses,* 17 December 1935.

Stuart, Herbert. "Colonel Newcome in Dar es Salaam." *Young Men of India* 29:1 (January 1918): 27–31.

Sykes, E. W. "Wherever There Is a Y.M.C.A. Hut." *Outspan,* 2 June 1944, 27, 50.

Taylor, Alexander. "The Negro and the Parties." *New Masses,* 14 July 1936, 7.

Tobias, Channing H. "The Colored YMCA." *Crisis* 9:1 (November 1919): 33–36.

Webster, C. R. "Wide Open Africa." *Association Men* (New York) 43:6 (February 1918): 432–33.

"What South Africa Is Doing to Keep White Supremacy (Interview with South Africa's Foreign Minister Eric H. Louw)." *U.S. News and World Report,* 22 July 1955, 58–63.

"While I Think of It: East and Central Africa Social Survey." *Rand Daily Mail* (Johannesburg), 5 August 1947. (Re: F. Neugebauer.)

Wickins, Peter L. "The One Big Union Movement among Black Workers in South Africa." *International Journal of African Historical Studies* 7:3 (1975).

Wittner, Lawrence S. "The National Negro Congress: A Reassessment." *American Quarterly* 12:4 (Winter 1970): 883–901.

Wright, Richard. "Joe Louis Uncovers Dynamite." *New Masses,* 8 October 1935, 18–19.

———. "Two Million Black Voices." *New Masses,* 25 February 1936, 15.

———. "High Tide in Harlem: Joe Louis as a Symbol of Freedom." *New Masses,* 5 July 1938, 18–20.

Index

About the Author

David Henry Anthony III is Associate Professor of History and Provost of Oakes College at the University of California at Santa Cruz.